THE LOGIC OF POETRY

THE LOGIC OF POETRY

Richard Monaco & John Briggs

With Notes on Prosody by Christopher Collins

*McGraw-Hill
Book Company*

*New York
St. Louis
San Francisco
Düsseldorf
Johannesburg
Kuala Lumpur
London
Mexico
Montreal
New Delhi
Panama
Paris
São Paulo
Singapore
Sydney
Tokyo
Toronto*

This book was set in Palatino by Black Dot, Inc.
The editors were David Edwards and James R. Belser;
the designer was J. E. O'Connor;
the production supervisor was Leroy A. Young.
The Murray Printing Company was printer and binder.

THE LOGIC OF POETRY

1 2 3 4 5 6 7 8 9 0   D O D O   7 9 8 7

Library of Congress Cataloging in Publication Data

Monaco, Richard.
The logic of poetry.

1. Metaphor. 2. Poetics. I. Briggs, John D.,
joint author. II. Title.
PN1059.M4M6   808.81   73-21507
ISBN 0-07-042682-1

ACKNOWLEDGMENTS

Petronius Arbiter, "Dreams," translated by Robert Bongiorno and used with his permission.

Guillaume Apollinaire, "The Mirabeau Bridge," translated by Christopher Collins and used with his permission.

John Ashbery, "Last Month," from *Rivers and Mountains* by John Ashbery. Copyright © 1963 by John Ashbery. Reprinted by permission of Holt, Rinehart and Winston, Inc.

Attar of Nishapur, "Light," from *The Way of Sufi*, edited by Idries Shah. Copyright © 1968 by Idries Shah. First published by E. P. Dutton & Company, Inc., 1970 and reprinted by their permission.

W. H. Auden, "Law Like Love," "Lullaby," and "Musée des Beaux Arts," from *Collected Shorter Poems 1927–1957* by W. H. Auden. Copyright 1940 and renewed 1968 by W. H. Auden. Reprinted by permission of Random House, Inc., and Faber and Faber, Ltd.

Sri Aurobindo, "The Blue Bird," from *Poems Past and Present* by Sri Aurobindo. Reprinted by permission of Sri Aurobindo Ashram Press.

Charles Baudelaire, "Correspondences," translated by Christopher Collins and used with his permission.

John Berryman, "The Ball Poem," from *Short Poems* by John Berryman. Copyright 1948 by John Berryman. "Dream Song #176," from *The Dream Songs* by John Berryman. Copyright © 1959, 1962, 1963, 1964, 1965, 1966, 1967, 1968, 1969 by John Berryman. Reprinted by permission of Farrar, Straus & Giroux, Inc.

Gavin Bone, "The Seafarer," translation from *Anglo-Saxon Poetry* by Gavin Bone. Reprinted by permission of The Clarendon Press, Oxford.

Jorge Luis Borges, "Chess," from *A Personal Anthology* by Jorge Luis Borges. Copyright © 1967 by Grove Press, Inc. Reprinted by permission of Grove Press, Inc.

Bertold Brecht, "The Plum Tree," Copyright © 1974 by Stefan Brecht. Reprinted by permission of Stefan Brecht and Insel Verlag.

Robert Bridges, "London Snow," from *The Poetical Works of Robert Bridges.* Reprinted by permission of The Clarendon Press, Oxford.

Gwendolyn Brooks, "my dreams, my works, must wait till after hell," from *The World of Gwendolyn Brooks* by Gwendolyn Brooks. Copyright 1945 by Gwendolyn Brooks Blakely. Reprinted by permission of Harper & Row, Publishers, Inc.

William Cassagrain, "Of Mere Being" and "Lucid Prodigy in Snow." Copyright by William Cassagrain. Included by permission.

Catullus, "Now Spring Brings Back," translated by Robert Bongiorno and used with his permission.

Chuang Tzu, from *The Complete Works of Chuang Tzu,* translated by Burton Watson. Reprinted by permission of Columbia University Press.

Helen Chasin, "Thinking about Paradise." Copyright by Helen Chasin. Included by permission.

Christopher Collins, "Seepage on a January Night." Copyright by Christopher Collins. Included by permission.

Hart Crane, "Legend" and "Moment Fugue," from *The Collected Poems and Selected Letters and Prose of Hart Crane.* Copyright 1933, © 1958, 1966 by Liveright Publishing Corporation. Reprinted by permission.

Robert Creeley, "The Rain," from *For Love* by Robert Creeley. Copyright © 1962 by Robert Creeley. Reprinted by permission of Charles Scribner's Sons and Calder and Boyars, Ltd.

E. E. Cummings, "Buffalo Bill's," from *Complete Poems, 1913–1962* by E. E. Cummings. Copyright 1923, 1951 by e. e. cummings. Reprinted by permission of Harcourt Brace Jovanovich.

Dai-Kwan, "Re-Birth, a Prayer to the New Moon," related by Dai-Kwan and adapted from the translation of W. H. I. Bleek by Jack Cope from *The Penguin Book of South African Verse,* edited by Jack Cope and Uys Krige. Copyright © 1968 by Uys Krige and Jack Cope. Reprinted by permission of Penguin Books, Ltd.

James Dickey, "Cherrylog Road," from *Helmets* by James Dickey. Copyright © 1963 by James Dickey. Reprinted by permission of Wesleyan University Press. This poem was first published in *The New Yorker.*

Alfred Dorn, "The Knowledge of Silence" and "Program for the Computerized," from *New Orlando Poetry Anthology,* Vol. 3, 1968. Copyright by Alfred Dorn. Reprinted by permission of New Orlando Publications.

Richard Eberhart, "On a Squirrel Crossing the Road in Autumn in New England," from *Collected Poems 1930–1960* by Richard Eberhart. © 1960 by Richard Eberhart. Reprinted by permission of Oxford University Press and Chatto & Windus, Ltd.

T. S. Eliot, "Journey of the Magi," from *Collected Poems 1909–1962* by T. S. Eliot. Copyright 1936 by Harcourt Brace Jovanovich, Inc. Copyright © 1963, 1964 by T. S. Eliot. Reprinted by permission of Harcourt Brace Jovanovich, Inc., and Faber and Faber, Ltd.

Robert Frost, "Reluctance," "The Oven Bird," "The Road Not Taken," "A Patch of Snow," and "The Silken Tent," from *The Poetry of Robert Frost* edited by Edward Connery Lathem. Copyright 1916, 1934, © 1969 by Holt, Rinehart and Winston, Inc. Copyright 1944, © 1962 by Robert Frost. Reprinted by permission of Holt, Rinehart and Winston, Inc.

David Galler, "Words from a Cell" and "A Dream." Copyright by David Galler. Included by permission.

Frédérico García Lorca, "The Song Wants to Be Light," from *Obras Conpleatas.* Copyright © Aguilar, S.A. de Edicióes. All Rights Reserved. Reprinted by permission of New Directions Publishing Corporation.

Allen Ginsberg, "Death on All Fronts," from *The Fall of America* by Allen Ginsberg. Copyright © 1972 by Allen Ginsberg. Reprinted by permission of City Lights Books.

Thomas Hardy, "The Walk," from *Collected Poems* by Thomas Hardy. Copyright 1925 by Macmillan Publishing Co., Inc. Reprinted by permission of Macmillan Publishing Co., Inc., the Trustees of the Hardy Estate; Macmillan London & Basingstoke; and The Macmillan Company of Canada, Ltd.

Anthony Hecht, "The End of the Weekend," from *The Hard Hours* by Anthony Hecht. Copyright © 1959 by Anthony E. Hecht. Reprinted by permission of Atheneum Publishers. Originally appeared in *Hudson Review.*

Heinrich Heine, "My Life Is Neither Full Nor Neat," translated by Christopher Collins and used with his permission.

Horace, "To the Lawyer," translated by Christopher Collins and used with his permission.

A. E. Housman, "This Time of Year," from "A Shropshire Lad"—Authorized Edition—from *The Collected Poems of A. E. Housman.* Copyright 1939, 1940, © 1965 by Holt, Rinehart and Winston, Inc. Copyright © 1967, 1968 by Robert E. Symons. Reprinted by permission of Holt, Rinehart and Winston, the Society of Authors as literary representatives of the Estate of A. E. Housman, and Jonathan Cape, Ltd., publishers.

Robert Huff, "Traditional Red," from *Colonel Johnson's Ride* by Robert Huff. Copyright 1959 by Wayne State University Press. Reprinted by permission of Wayne State University Press and Robert Huff.

Langston Hughes, "As I Grew Older," from *Selected Poems* by Langston Hughes. Copyright 1926 by Alfred A. Knopf, Inc., renewed 1954 by Langston Hughes. Reprinted by permission of Alfred A. Knopf, Inc.

Ted Hughes, "The Jaguar" and "The Thought Fox," from *The Hawk in the Rain* by Ted Hughes. Copyright © 1957 by Ted Hughes. Reprinted by permission of Harper & Row, Publishers, Inc.

Richard Hugo, "Blond Road," "In Stafford Country," and "Ocean on Monday." Copyright by Richard Hugo. Included by permission.

J. C. Jacobs, "The Recluse" and "What Exists." Copyright by J. C. Jacobs. Included by permission.

Donald Justice, "On a Painting by Patient B of the Independence State Hospital for the Insane," from *The Summer Anniversaries* by Donald Justice. Copyright © 1954 by Donald Justice. Reprinted by permission of Wesleyan University Press. This poem was first published in *Poetry*.

Galway Kinnell, "To Christ Our Lord," from *What a Kingdom It Was* by Galway Kinnell. Copyright © 1960 by Galway Kinnell. Reprinted by permission of Houghton Mifflin Company.

Stanley Kunitz, "The Science of Night," from *Selected Poems 1928–1938* by Stanley Kunitz. Copyright 1953 by Stanley Kunitz. Reprinted by permission of Little, Brown and Company in association with the Atlantic Monthly Press.

Philip Larkin, "An Arundel Tomb," from *The Whitsun Weddings* by Philip Larkin. Reprinted by permission of Faber and Faber, Ltd.

Giacomo Leopardi, "To the Moon," translated by Robert Bongiorno and used with his permission.

Denise Levertov, "Merritt Parkway," from *The Jacob's Ladder* by Denise Levertov. Copyright © 1958 by Denise Levertov Goodman. Reprinted by permission of New Directions Publishing Corporation.

Philip Levine, "Robert" and "How Much Can It Hurt," from *They Feed the Lion* by Philip Levine. Copyright © 1971, 1972 by Philip Levine. Reprinted by permission of Atheneum Publishers. "Robert" originally appeared in *New American Review;* "How Much Can It Hurt" originally appeared in *Kayak*.

Robert Lowell, "Myopia," from *For the Union Dead* by Robert Lowell. Copyright © 1964 by Robert Lowell. Reprinted by permission of Farrar, Straus & Giroux, Inc. "Noli Me Tangere" from *Lord Weary's Castle* by Robert Lowell. Copyright 1946 by Robert Lowell. Reprinted by permission of Harcourt Brace Jovanovich, Inc.

Archibald MacLeish, "Ars Poetica," from *Collected Poems 1917–1952* by Archibald MacLeish. Copyright © 1962 by Archibald MacLeish. Reprinted by permission of Houghton Mifflin Company.

James Merrill, "Laboratory Poem," from *The Country of a Thousand Years of Peace* by James Merrill. Copyright © 1958 by James Merrill. Reprinted by permission of Atheneum Publishers. Appeared originally in *Poetry*.

W. S. Merwin, "For the Anniversary of My Death," from *The Lice* by W. S. Merwin. Copyright © 1967 by W. S. Merwin. Reprinted by permission of Atheneum Publishers. Appeared originally in *The Southern Review*. "Toro," from *Green with Beasts* Rupert Hart-Davis, England, 1956.

Marianne Moore, "The Mind Is an Enchanting Thing," from *Collected Poems* by Marianne Moore. Copyright 1944 and renewed 1972 by Marianne Moore. Reprinted by permission of Macmillan Publishing Co., Inc.

Christian Morgenstern, "The Local Authorities," translated by Christopher Collins and used with his permission.

Howard Nemerov, "I Only Am Escaped Alone to Tell Thee," from *New and Selected Poems* by Howard Nemerov. Copyright 1960 by University of Chicago. Reprinted by permission of the Margot Johnson Agency.

Pablo Neruda, "Nothing But Death," from *Neruda and Vallejo: Selected Poems*. Copyright © 1968 by Robert Bly, reprinted with his permission.

William Packard, "These Voices," from *Voices/I Hear/Voices* by William Packard. Copyright © 1972 by William Packard. Reprinted by permission of Barlenmir House, Publishers.

Louis Phillips, "Rus in Urbe" and "A Metaphor Carried Almost to Excess." Copyright by Louis Phillips. Included by permission.

Sylvia Plath, "Mirror," from *Crossing the Water* by Sylvia Plath. Copyright © 1963 by Ted Hughes. Copyright 1971 by Ted Hughes. Reprinted by permission of Harper & Row, Publishers, Inc., Faber and Faber, Ltd., and Olwyn Hughes. Originally appeared in *The New Yorker*.

David Posner, "After the Revolution," "The Science of Building," and "In David Hockney's Studio." Copyright David Posner. Included by permission.

Ezra Pound, "The White Stag" and "Portrait d'une Femme," from *Personae* by Ezra Pound. Copyright 1926 by Ezra Pound. Reprinted by permission of New Directions Publishing Corporation.

Rainer Maria Rilke, "The Panther," from *Translations from the Poetry of Rainer Maria Rilke* by M. D. Herter Norton. Copyright 1938 by W. W. Norton & Company, Inc. Copyright renewed 1966 by M. D. Herter Norton. Reprinted by permission of W. W. Norton & Company, Inc. and Insel Verlag. "Sonnet" from *Sonnets to Orpheus* by Rainer Maria Rilke from *The Penguin Book of German Verse*, edited and

ILLUSTRATION CREDITS

Sandro Botticelli (detail from painting, Uffizi Gallery, Florence) p. 372.

Pieter Brughel (Musée Royaux des Beaux Arts, Brussels) p. 254.

C. Chan pp. 42, 366.

Christopher Collins pp. 174, 175, 222, 224, 229, 233, 237, 238, 240, 395.

Gustave Doré (detail from etching) p. 285.

Philip Friedman pp. 128, 184, 271, 273, 279.

Laurence Gelder pp. 16, 61, 149.

Furman Gibson pp. 318, 320, 331, 392.

Doreen Gray pp. 8, 123, 150, 210, 256, 296, 344.

Irving Grouppe (detail from painting) p. 262.

Richard Hunt (detail from lithograph) p. 133.

Sid Kaplan pp. 65, 302.

Gloria Philips pp. (intro. to Ch. 1) 14, 15, 19, 30, 58, 70, 80, 84, 107, 142, 154, 156, 162, 212, 248, 266, 282, 288, 291, 300, 309, 326, 332, 338, 378, 388.

Gordon Price pp. 38, 114, 123, 134, 159, 173, 178, 179, 180, 198, 359.

Layle Silbert pp. 153, 370.

John Williams pp. 22, 23, 26, 34, 43, 78, (The Metropolitan Museum of Art) 88, 90, 92, 96, (The Metropolitan Museum of Art) 103, 144, 152, 167, 169, 171, 183, 193, 257, 258, 347, 354, 374.

CONTENTS

* Asterisks denote poems discussed in text.

CHAPTER 2   METAPHORIC LANGUAGE IN POETRY   50

* Asterisks denote poems discussed in text.

* Asterisks denote poems discussed in text.

CHAPTER 4   THE POEM AS A METAPHOR: *X/Ys*   163

* Asterisks denote poems discussed in text.

CHAPTER 5 THE POEM AS A METAPHOR: *X/?* 196

* Asterisks denote poems discussed in text.

CHAPTER 6 PROPAGANDA, ARGUMENT, AND DESCRIPTION IN POETRY 241

* Asterisks denote poems discussed in text.

CHAPTER 7   DENSE, SUBTLE, AND COMPLEX POETRY   289

CHAPTER 8   THE POEM ITSELF   333

* Asterisks denote poems discussed in text.

CHAPTER 9   METAPHOR AT LARGE   379

APPENDIX   393

CHRONOLOGICAL CONTENTS

The purpose of this second table of contents is to provide a chronological listing of the poets and poems presented in this volume for those who wish to approach the study of poetry in historical sequence. In addition, the original language in which a poem was written as well as the nationality of the poet have been indicated when appropriate. Poems preceded by an asterisk are discussed in the text.

INTRODUCTION

Poetry is special and has special power. The supernatural "force of the word" (called *Logos* in the West and *Vāc* in the East) is said to be inherent in poetry. Ages ago poetry was used for religious ceremonies because it was considered magical. And poetry *is* magical—it is outside our everyday consciousness of life; it excites an absolutely unique awareness and experience.

When someone says, "I don't understand poetry," usually this means he has found that poems don't present "facts," don't serve up information the way a magazine article does, for instance. He has tried to read poetry as if it were like conversation or expository writing. The problem is that poetry isn't trying to explain events, ideas, feelings, or perceptions in a form or logic we're used to. Poetry isn't explaining experience—it is a state of experiencing. Somehow great poetry has the force to go *beyond* our feelings or ideas, and even if we disagree with the content or find the sentiments alien, we can still discover a "sense of rightness, of truth" in a poem. We might find someone offensive personally or politically, but if he writes a poem that works, we forget the man and are moved by the experience. This is poetry's magic. It takes us beyond ourselves, beyond our everyday limitations—or perhaps, in another sense, *into* ourselves.

But poetry baffles the "reasonable" mind. We wonder, "How can I tell when it simply means what it says?" or "Why do these poets say one thing and mean something else? Why don't they just say it directly?"

Reading poetry requires a trained attention, a special state of mind that our daily experiences with thought and language don't demand. Poetic language cannot be understood in the same way that ordinary language is understood. To try to understand it in those terms would be frustrating. The words are ordinary words, but something happens to them in a poem, transforms them, and that is what we want to understand.

We could try to do it by looking separately at all the techniques that generations of scholars and critics have painstakingly identified as "poetic" (rhyme, personification, image, symbol, figure, meter, verse forms, etc.) and then observing how some poems have *this*, but don't have *that*, have more of *this* than *that*, and so on. To some extent, we may have to do this, but if we break poetry up too much in order to see it, we may intensify our difficulty because the poem's magic lies in its wholeness, its complete effect on us. Is there some way to *unify* our perception of the poem, rather than fragment it, to learn to think in poetry the way we can learn to think in music or in a foreign language? In this we're asking a fundamental question: Why read poetry at all? And perhaps we'll discover that when we experience poetry that the question answers itself.

This text focuses on the terms "metaphor" and "metaphoric language." We believe that understanding how these terms can be extended to cover all the major aspects of poetry will bring about a deeper experience of the whole. Aristotle wrote in his *Poetics* and in the *Rhetoric*: "The greatest thing by far is to be a master of metaphor. . . . From metaphor we can best get hold of something fresh." And Robert Frost wrote: "There are many other things I have found myself saying about poetry, but the chiefest of these is that it is metaphor, saying one thing in terms of another."

We consider metaphor in such detail here specifically because:

1. The operations of the simple metaphor (e.g., "A mighty fortress is our God") provide, when extended as *structural* metaphor, an unusual insight into how poetic language evokes its levels of meaning. Perhaps because of this, scholars and critics have expressed a growing interest in metaphor, as the *Princeton Encyclopedia of Poetry and Poetics* indicates: "In recent years the view has gathered weight that metaphor is the radical process by which the internal relationships peculiar to poetry are achieved; some critics maintaining that metaphor marks off the poetic mode of vision and utterance from the logical or discursive modes." So, many feel that metaphor, in this broader sense, is the essence of poetry. They observed that no particular technique is common to all poetry, while metaphoric perception appears to be universal. It is consciously or unconsciously involved in all the techniques poets utilize.

2. Many critics often use the terms "image," "symbol," "metaphor," and "figure" interchangeably and endlessly debate fine distinctions. This sort of discussion is of little use to anyone interested in making contact with a poem. Focusing on metaphor

simplifies things and leaves us free to concentrate fully on each poem itself. The alternatives involve locating limited examples of each characteristic, breaking poetry up into categories (period, style, philosophy, etc.), and constantly distinguishing between critical terms.

3. Seeing poetry as "metaphoric language" instead of "figurative language," as it is often called, keeps us from confusing "rhetorical" figures with "poetic" figures and has the advantage of allowing us to see, as metaphor, the dynamics.

4. Seeing poetics through metaphor can enable us to encounter *any* kind of poetry as part of one process, poetry from any historical period, school, or national or cultural tradition.

Although critical terms are introduced and used from time to time, our primary purpose is not learning definitions but dealing directly with poems, seeing them without preconceptions, theories, or anxieties about what it all "means," about philosophic or cultural value, and so on. In this way, we can become familiar with the major critical concepts (tone, irony, symbol, etc.) as they apply to our experience of each piece. The technical aspects of poetic criticism are dealt with in the Appendix at the back of the book.

It is important to understand that this technique is not a "method." There are no rules to be learned, no checklists to be followed. It is a gradual process of becoming familiar with how metaphoric language works, of developing your "metaphoric eye." While the principle is simple, every poem is a new case of it, and the only way to really understand is through participation. Let's compare it metaphorically with learning to play basketball. A coach can demonstrate the jump shot—can explain, even diagram it so that you understand the reason for all the moves, how to cock your hand, when to release the ball, the principle of spin, etc.—but you have to actually participate if you want to make the basket. To do it, you have to work at it, and one day you go up in the air and it happens. Suddenly it seems natural and makes perfect sense. Reading poetry is not passive watching from the sidelines. So even if you eventually forget all the "rules," the essential understanding will remain a part of you. Learn to read metaphorically, sharpen your metaphoric eye, and though you may forget just what the definition of metaphor is, you'll always be able to get into poetry, any kind of poetry.

As for traditional techniques—rhyme, meter, verse types, and the like—you will see (as we go through the book) that in all the poetic variety, there are no fixed forms or rules. At any point in history a poet is influenced by the tradition of those who wrote before him. More often than not he will stick with that tradition, write in its forms, and tend to deviate according to his personality, interests, and contemporary influences. Since each new generation of poets alters this tradition, we cannot consider any of these techniques the permanent, essential elements of poetry. Consequently, they are dealt with briefly in the discussions and more completely in the Notes on Prosody and glossary.

The questions that follow and precede many of the poems are not meant to have definite answers. What we are after here is learning to perceive and consider the "unanswerable" aspects of a poem. The questions are intended as a vital part of the discussions of the pieces themselves. *In order to participate in a poem, considering the questions is actually more important than trying to answer them.*

The illustrations are to help us understand what the imagination "sees" or cannot "see" in poetry.

Angles of interpretation, poetic theories, detailed concentration on historical factors, philosophy, psychology, are left for the classroom and the contextual preferences of teacher and student.

We might think of it this way: A good poem is like a lens through which you can look at the universe, but the vision is yours. So we want to learn how to focus our minds through a poem and look with our own "sight." How *far* we learn to see depends on us.

A Word on Using this Book

We have tried here to take what amounts to the poet's point of view about poetry, to grasp it as an unfragmented perception and expression. Interpretation is left largely to the reader.

Although the text is designed to present a linear development of the metaphoric concept, the book has been kept flexible. Consequently, it is possible to be selective in choosing poems for study since the text in no way binds the teacher and student to read it from beginning to end. The following are some possible alternative teaching strategies the book will accommodate.

Chapter 1 can be considered the key chapter for understanding the principles of metaphoric reading. Chapter 2 provides a comprehensive look at critical terminology (tone, image, symbol, etc.) in terms of metaphor. Taken together, these two chapters could constitute the basis for a short introductory course or unit in poetry. Other chapters are variations on the theme, providing a comprehensive look at numerous metaphoric tactics poets employ. These chapters can be followed sequentially as time permits.

Chapters 1 and 2 can be supplemented with poems from other chapters taken in whatever sequence, since textual discussions past Chapter 3 are all based on the principles developed in the first two chapters.

In a particularly short course it would also be possible to cover Chapter 1 and the introductions to Chapters 2 to 8, selecting poems from the book in accordance with preference. Another of many possible approaches to the short unit might be to cover the introduction to Chapter 1 plus discussions of key poems throughout the text.

For advanced courses in contemporary poetry, Chapter 7 is recommended, plus discussions of contemporary poems elsewhere in the book.

Several central figures and major poems, both traditional and contemporary, are represented here, permitting some study of individual poets in depth.

In addition, the book can serve a relatively complete survey of English and American poetry.

Though, no one is expected to become a poet simply by doing various exercises, one of the best ways to get a feel for poetry is to write it. The appendix provides several writing suggestions, drawn from the text's investigations into poetic technique. Since mastering technique does not guarantee poetic insights and since poets do not necessarily decide on techniques precompositionally, the essential purpose of the suggestions is to increase the reader's familiarity with basic poetic methods.

Since the focus of the book is on developing the student's ability to recognize levels of meaning and familiarize him with poetic techniques, it should be stressed that for purposes of interpretation—whichever approach or variant is adopted—specific reference to the text isn't necessary. The reader is encouraged to develop his own lines of inquiry.

A Note on Translations

Most of the translations in this book are new. Robert Lowell, among others, has insisted that in translating, the essential thing to capture is "tone." We agree. Accordingly, in this text, although many of the foreign-language poems rhyme in the original, frequently no attempt to rhyme them has been made in the translations. In many languages, particularly inflected ones, rhyming is relatively easy to do and does not impose much of a constraint on the poet, while in English it may pose needless problems for the translator, who, in order to maintain sense and keep up a rhyme scheme, may be forced to wrench and distort the poem's original tone and consequently its meaning. Hoping to avoid this traditional fault of translations, most of the translators here take the position that rhyme is important only insofar as it is an essential part of the original. Thus some poems, usually those with a satiric bent, have been maintained in rhyme; others, more lyrical or philosophic, have been rendered in loose blank verse, accentual verse, or free verse in the manner most consonant with sense. English affords us a subtle control over meter and pace, and those are the elements most stressed here.

The tone's the thing and the translators, where possible, have kept closely to the original: If the original language is spare, the translator has been spare; if the original language is ornate, the translator has been ornate, and so on. A few poems so rely on the peculiarities of their own language that the translators have had to depart significantly from the original wording and imagery in order to maintain the tone and thrust of the piece. Such translations have been labeled "renditions," meaning that some greater degree of liberty has been taken in rendering the spirit of the original into English.

Some Middle English poems have been translated or modernized.

Acknowledgments

The authors wish to thank several people who have aided them materially in preparing this text.

For their astute editoral judgment: Christopher Collins, Associate Professor, New York University; Albert G. Craz, Coordinator of Language Arts, William Floyd Schools; and Richard M. Ludwig, Professor of English, Princeton University.

We also wish to thank Philip Friedman for his photographic advice; Sid Kaplan, of the Custom Work Darkroom, for his master printing of many of the photographs here; David Friedman for his help on translations; Judy Monaco for her editoral eye; Philip Friedman for his ability to find the subtle flow; the students of the Logic of Poetry classes at The New School for their insight and enthusiasm; and New School Dean of Humanities, Dr. Ruben Abel.

Our special thanks go to our editor, David Edwards, and to Alice Felbinger, Mary Moran, James Belser, and Joan O'Connor for their continual encouragement and assistance with this project.

THE LOGIC OF POETRY

CHAPTER 1
THE METAPHORIC
EYE: POETIC VISION

Although we do not usually speak in poetry, when a thing is particularly beautiful, moving, or tragic, even unlikely people become poets for awhile. Ask a doctor, lawyer, businessman, or almost anyone, and he may admit that at some time or other he has "tried to write poetry."

In everyday conversations we hope to be clear and simple whenever possible, but we often fail. We know that communicating clearly with one another through a fog of emotion, uncertainty, or opinion is very difficult. In a way, poetry tries to cut through that fog, expressing not opinion or belief but awareness, a "sense of truth."

The essential difference between everyday language (that used in speech, in newspaper writing, on television, and in most fiction and movie scripts, for example) and poetic language is that you can't just sit back with a poem and be entertained or excited by it or imagine you have understood it just because you happen to know what all the words mean; you have to work a little, work with the poet. It is not a matter of opinion. You don't really agree or disagree with a poem; you *experience* it: not just the sound of the words or their obvious meanings, but something beyond the words, something they are *pointing* at. This is important to understand. Put yourself in the poet's position for a moment. You may have an awareness of some kind and want to express it, to pass it along to others, but you find that there is no word or expression for what you want to say. It isn't something you already know; it's new, unique, the very unfolding of a discovery. Expressing your awareness in logical, expository terms doesn't work; you can't really say it that way. A successful poem, however, becomes in effect a new word for that new awareness and stays new each time it's read. A familiar understanding would not demand a poem.

Poetic language relies primarily on metaphor. All language becomes metaphoric at times to make points clear or add color and life to ideas. We use metaphors consciously or unconsciously: "the ship of state," "I'm hungry as a wolf," "the mouth of a jar," "one's path through life," and so on. But most of the metaphors we hear in everyday speech have been overused and are now clichés, or "dead" metaphors (which is a metaphor too, of course); they have lost their steam.

In everyday language metaphors generally work either: (1) to clarify ideas, feelings, and so on or (2) to convince us of the value, danger, beauty, ugliness, etc., of one thing by comparing it to another which is accepted as valuable, dangerous, beautiful, ugly—for example, "My political enemies are like wolves," "She is like a pig," "Mother is good as gold."

In poetry it's another matter. Put simply, a poetic metaphor is the *union of unlike things (pictures to ideas, ideas to feelings, feelings to objects, objects to pictures, and so on) such that the mind discovers unexpected relationships and comes upon new insight.* While ordinary language sometimes uses metaphor for effect, poetic language is nearly always metaphoric on some level or other. Once you become familiar with this, poetry no longer seems difficult, ambiguous, and recondite.

"Oh my luve is like a red, red rose." Can we look at this well-worn statement as if for the first time? We have probably heard it much too often; it is always turning up in poetry textbooks or being sung and quoted. But instead of letting it get lost in the background, let's concentrate on it, on the way it functions. First, notice that it is really equivalent to: "my luve *is* a red, red rose." Unless you imagine that the speaker is another flower himself or is in love with one, the "like" is understood. What makes metaphor work is what might be called the *unlike factor* between the two things being compared. Without the unlike factor there is no metaphoric action at all, just a simple (if sometimes odd) statement of fact, the kind you would have if a man said of his mistress, "My love is like a girl," words lacking impact and real meaning unless the mistress were rather old. Second, notice some of the ways "luve" connects with "rose." For instance, the girl the poet is writing about might be soft, sweet, fresh, and pure, smell nice, bloom, blush, and have a certain intensity (the intensity of "red, red") as well as sharp thorns (so be careful how you handle her); and so on. Obviously, if you just say "my love" or "a red rose," none of these meanings appear. Not all these meanings necessarily apply; the *focus* is always provided by the poem as a whole. So the metaphor's dynamics operate as follows: "my luve" (*X*) plus "a red, red rose" (*Y*) equals a set of *new* meanings that are not specifically spelled out, a relationship to be discovered by the reader. Even in the simplest case, metaphoric language makes demands on your alertness and requires you to participate in a special way.

In "Oh my luve is like a red, red rose" the *X* and *Y* terms are *compared*: *X* is *like Y*. But metaphoric terms can relate in other ways: They can be *identified, contrasted,* or *associated* with one another. The following are some examples of these other simple *X/Y* metaphoric relationships:

1. From the eighteenth-century poet Alexander Pope: "In Folly's cup still laughs the bubble, joy." Here there are actually two metaphors: (*a*) Folly (*X*) is identified with a cup (*Y*), or you could consider Folly a character who uses the cup, in which case Folly (*X*) is identified as a person (*Y*), and (b) a bubble (*X*) is identified with joy (*Y*).

2. From the twentieth-century poet Wallace Stevens: "The pears are not viols,/Nudes or bottles!" The pears (*X*) are contrasted to each of three *Y*'s: viols, nudes, and bottles. This contrast causes us somehow to relate or try to relate pears to the other terms; that is, why does the poet have to say "Pears are *not* viols . . . "?

3. From Shakespeare: "Ah, but those tears are pearl which thy love sheds/And they're rich and ransom all ill deeds." This metaphor associates tears (X) with pearls (Y) and then extends the association, seeing the pearls as "ransom."
4. From T. S. Eliot: "The eyes that fix you in a formulated phrase,/ And when I am formulated, sprawling on a pin,/When I am pinned and wriggling on the wall." This is a more elaborate metaphor where eyes (X) are associated with formulating a phrase (Y), and then a new X/Y relationship is established as eyes + formulated phrase (X) are identified with a pin (Y). At the same time there is another covert metaphor in which the speaker is identified as some kind of insect.

In all the above instances X and Y are juxtaposed (laid side by side) in some fashion so that a spark of meaning jumps between them. Though they can be helpful, the categories above lack clearly defined boundaries. The point is to be aware of the union of terms in order to experience the poetic effect, the surprising view or insight. *Metaphor reduced to essentials is always a kind of contrast because of the unlike factor*; for example, the eyes and a formulated phrase, the bubble and joy, etc. But since a poet may choose to present it one way or another, it is useful to be alert to these various forms of metaphoric statement. In all the above we are given both terms of the metaphor, the X and the Y, though in the last case the poet does not actually say "insect."

But the metaphor is not always so obvious as X/Y. Often a single word (an X alone) can create a complete metaphor:

Then Jesus said unto them, Take heed and beware of the leaven of the Pharisees and of the Sadducees. And they reasoned among themselves, saying, It is because we have taken no bread. Which when Jesus perceived, he said unto them, O ye of little faith, why reason ye among yourselves, because ye have brought no bread? . . . How is it that ye do not understand that I spake it not to you concerning bread, that ye should beware of the leaven of the Pharisees? . . . Then they understood that he bade them not beware of the leaven of bread, but of the doctrine of the Pharisees and Sadducees.

Christ points to many rich meanings that do not exist when you substitute the word "doctrine." For instance, leaven makes bread rise and puff up; bread is a source of life for mankind; and Christ said (elsewhere) that his teachings were "bread" to sustain men spiritually and give true life, and so it follows that bad "bread" will induce spiritual malnutrition. So the whole concept of nourishing and sustaining is here compressed (as metaphor) into a single word. This intensity is what makes poetry live.

A whole poem, like the single word "leaven," can also be a kind of metaphor itself. Sometimes we seem to have a simple statement such as in Robert Frost's poem "The Road Not Taken": "Two roads diverged in a yellow wood,/And sorry I could not travel both/And be one traveler, long I stood/And looked down one as far as I could/To where it bent in the undergrowth." The poet tells us how the roads looked and how he had to choose between them. On the surface it seems to be simple description, but the moment you realize that the roads are not just roads but are pointing to something more (ways of life, experience, events, past hopes and wishes, the pattern of the future, etc.), you know that the situation is an X being referred to some Y or Y's. You complete the metaphor: The poet choosing between two roads is (like) _____. Obviously there is no one "correct" concept for what the situation represents. It wouldn't be very effective that way—a guessing game rather than a poem. You have to feel your way into this because while there may not be any absolute answers, straining to read anything we wanted into the poem or forcing our opinions on it would be pointless.

Notice the unlike factor in Frost's metaphor: roads are just roads, as roses are roses, but when we add them (in our literary equation) to ideas or feelings about life, events, or people, suddenly there is a tension between the terms and a sense of deeper meaning. In the everyday use of metaphors for clarification or persuasion, the emphasis is nearly always on the similarity between terms; in poetic metaphor, *it is on the tension between them.* Consider the "mouth" of a jar. Somebody noticed the resemblance, and the term stuck. Scholars and philosophers claim that language often extends itself into new areas and includes new objects and experiences by comparing them to old ones. So metaphors of clarification are meant to provide a better picture of something in terms of what we already know. Metaphors used for persuasion also stress the similarity between their terms. If an insurance company compares itself to the Rock of Gibraltar or a cigarette brand is associated with cool water and springtime, the intensions are clear: The qualities of one term (strength/solidarity; freshness/coolness) are meant to be *transferred* to the other. An image is substituted for a word: the Rock of Gibraltar for "solid." In poetic metaphors similarities are played off against differences. Is there a word "rose" is substituted for? Obviously not. The two following sentences are similar: "My company is (like) the Rock of Gibraltar" and "My luve is (like) a red, red rose." But context—that is, where you *find* the statement, whether in a poem, an advertisement, or political speech—makes the crucial difference. The poem that surrounds the metaphor focuses on intensity, discovering meaning, and so on, rather than simply asking you to accept the asserted similarity. Discovering, in this sense, means that you have to keep reacting to the vast difference between the terms. While metaphors of clarification and persuasion are one-leveled, poetic metaphors have many levels and aim at indefinable things rather than obvious fact, belief, or opinion. And because of a multiplicity of connections, many experienced simultaneously in the poetic context, metaphors do not lose their force. In this respect they are never seen the same way twice. To see this for yourself, take some well-worn speech from Shakespeare—say, Hamlet's "to be or not to be" soliloquy—and read it in the context of the whole play. If you really do this, you will find it alive and meaningful. In a strong poem even a thoroughly dead metaphor like the "mouth of a jar" or the "ship of state" might revive itself as other levels and possibilities emerged.

Bear in mind that when we think about these levels or talk about them in the classroom, we have to do it linearly, make a list, as in the rose metaphor: "My love is soft, sweet, fresh, smells nice, blooms, blushes, etc." But when we experience the metaphor in its frame of reference (the poem), we have all these things at once, as something immediate. It is as if our X and Y were joined with a clap, a snap of the fingers: poetic magic.

Poetic language frees the reader to "see" in a unique way. We may ask: What is this "seeing"? Is it really *seeing* at all? What happens when your mind makes these poetic relationships, relates or associates roads and life, tears and pearls, roses and girls, and all that? Let's deal with images for a moment. IMAGE is a literary term referring to words that suggest or describe sights, sounds, tastes, smells, or the act of touching something—words that relate to the function of the five senses. Obviously, if you say "rose," then perhaps from memory you imagine a rose (though hearing a word is not like actual experience—it recalls it). But can a metaphor be pictured or imagined? When we *see* what X/Y adds up to, are we really seeing? What happens when we read William Blake's line, "Bring me my Arrows of desire"? It means something; we can relate to it, but can we *see* it? A little reflection shows that we cannot. Desires are sharp, piercing, swift; we get all that. But what is actually happening in the mind? Something not at all like seeing, tasting, touching, or remembering these experiences; we cannot define it as an idea, but we grasp it all the same. Poetic (metaphoric) language creates these mental effects which seem to be seen, but it is another kind of sight; we might call it *insight*. You can't store this in your brain the way you store facts or the words of a poem because the words simply provide the means to approach this sense of truth, to rediscover it in some way each time you read. The very act of finding out something new obviously cannot belong to the past. It happens only *now*. Looked at this way, the depth of a poem is actually the depth of the reader. And only he can sound it.

What is this insight? It is not remembering, not seeing, not imagining, so what is it? Our poetic sense of rightness, truth, reality—even of cosmic proportions—does not come to us logically, that is, through analysis. Essentially, logic is a process of sorting and comparing things we know with other things we know, therefore measuring the present in terms of the past. As has often been said, a logical conclusion depends entirely on its premises and cannot meaningfully go beyond them. When a man says thus and so is logical, he usually means it seems to agree with what he already believes or thinks or knows. There is no guarantee that such a process leads to truth; it certainly does not lead to something new. For example, a conservative might assert: "It's logical that we should support big business because that's what makes capitalism work, and capitalism is the backbone of a free society." And a liberal: "Logically, big business must be controlled because since it is only out for profit, it can't help but be unresponsive to the rights of the individual." Both arguments are based on what the person already believes, and any deductions he makes prove nothing at all. Let's set logic aside, then—the logic that is really a form of presenting opinions—and deal with the "logic" of poetry, which has to do with order and harmony and a sense of truth which is not something to agree or disagree about, but simply to perceive or not perceive. In doing this we will become involved with poetic statements which the rational mind might consider self-contradictory or impossible. We will see that understanding poetic statements often demands that we set aside our intellectual prejudices, memories, and old habits, and move toward the unknown, experiencing the poem (and the mind itself) on a deeper level. Going beyond what the mind already knows, becoming aware and receptive, isn't limited to certain exceptional people. On some level we all can experience this in poetry.

Bear in mind as you go through the text that none of the discussions or questions are meant to be exhaustive. A strong poem cannot be worn out by talking about it. We are simply looking for effective ways to begin to make contact with given pieces. When we analyze, we are not providing insight—we are just trying to remove impediments to a *direct experience* of poetry. We must understand technique thoroughly before we can confidently put it behind us.

Read this poem through and then go back and look at individual metaphors. Can you observe how your mind is affected by them? What can you say about the meanings you see?

Archibald MacLeish

ARS POETICA

A poem should be palpable and mute
As a globed fruit

Dumb
As old medallions to the thumb

Silent as the sleeve-worn stone
Of casement ledges where the moss has grown—

A poem should be wordless
As the flight of birds

A poem should be motionless in time
As the moon climbs

Leaving, as the moon releases
Twig by twig the night-entangled trees,

Leaving, as the moon behind the winter leaves,
Memory by memory the mind—

A poem should be motionless in time
As the moon climbs

A poem should be equal to:
Not true

For all the history of grief
An empty doorway and a maple leaf

For love
The leaning grasses and two lights above the sea—

A poem should not mean
But be.

Considerations

1. Consider each of this poem's metaphors in turn, locating the *X* and *Y* terms. In several cases there are metaphors within metaphors, something like the T. S. Eliot metaphor (eyes–formulated phrase–pin) discussed earlier in the chapter. Can you work these out? What is being compared to what here?

2. What are some of the levels of meaning you see in each of these metaphors? What do they suggest a poem *is*? Do you see any paradoxical (self-contradictory) statements, that is, statements that are contrary to reality or are impossible to observe in the world? Are these effective as poetic statements? Why? What do they tell you about a "poem"?

3. Consider how the poet has compressed various senses into images (i.e., sound, touch, taste, sight).

4. How are the last two lines justified by the preceding lines?

5. Consider the illustration accompanying this poem. What aspects of the poem's metaphors does the illustration capture? How are they different from the things you see in your imagination when you read the poem? What things has the illustrator omitted? Does his vision restrict or enhance your own, or is it unconnected to your own experience of the piece?

Technical Notes

The poem is written in COUPLETS. Some of them are given EXACT RHYMES, while others are formed by SLANT RHYMES. The meter and rhyme scheme are irregular.

This poem is based on language rich in direct and indirect metaphor. The poet uses these to explore the subject of melancholy and to make the ABSTRACT (vague or general) word CONCRETE, as if it were an object of the senses, something vivid, not just a distant idea. This is one of the major effects of poetic (metaphoric) language.

John Keats

ODE ON MELANCHOLY

No, no, go not to Lethe, neither twist
   Wolfs-bane, tight-rooted, for its poisonous wine;
Nor suffer thy pale forehead to be kiss'd
   By nightshade, ruby grape of Proserpine;
Make not your rosary of yew-berries,
   Nor let the beetle, nor the death-moth be
      Your mournful Psyche,° nor the downy owl
A partner in your sorrow's mysteries;
   For shade to shade will come too drowsily,
      And drown the wakeful anguish of the soul.
°Soul.

But when the melancholy fit shall fall
  Sudden from heaven like a weeping cloud,
That fosters the droop-headed flowers all,
  And hides the green hill in an April shroud;
Then glut thy sorrow on a morning rose,
  Or on the rainbow of the salt sand-wave,
    Or on the wealth of globèd peonies;
Or if thy mistress some rich anger shows,
  Emprison her soft hand, and let her rave,
    And feed deep, deep upon her peerless eyes.

She dwells with Beauty—Beauty that must die;
  And Joy, whose hand is ever at his lips
Bidding adieu; and aching Pleasure nigh,
  Turning to poison while the bee-mouth sips:
Ay, in the very temple of Delight
  Veil'd Melancholy has her sovran shrine,
    Though seen of none save him whose strenuous
      tongue
  Can burst Joy's grape against his palate fine;
His soul shall taste the sadness of her might,
    And be among her cloudy trophies hung.

Considerations

In the first STANZA (poetic paragraph) of the poem, the reader's imagination is stimulated by a list of images: Lethe (the mythical river of forgetfulness, oblivion); wolfs-bane, nightshade, and yew-berries (poisons); and the beetle, the death-moth, the owl, and shades (the shadowy souls of the dead). All these are classically associated with night, darkness, and death. Each term adds distinct qualities which illuminate the abstraction "death" from various angles. This effect adds richness and depth. For example, Lethe suggests a forgetful, almost pleasant oblivion; wolfs-bane and nightshade make it sinister; and the beetle, death-moth, and owl add an ominous atmosphere.

Notice how these evocative terms combine into metaphoric relationships:

Wolfs-bane is (like) wine grapes (association).
Nightshade is (like) the ruby grape (comparison).
Yew-berries are (like) rosary beads (comparison).
Beetle and death-moth are (like) mournful Psyche
  (identification).
Downy owl is (like) a partner (identification).

Shades are (like) water—since they drown the soul
  (association).

"Lethe" is similar to "leaven" in the Christ parable, where we are given only the X term and have to supply the Y ourselves.

Observe how the words interact; for example, rosary/yew-berries suggests religious overtones. How many other such interactions can you see?

Notice that we are concerned not with the DENOTATIONS, the dictionary definitions or literal meanings of the words in the metaphors—with the fact that the beetle is an insect, for instance—but with their CONNOTATIONS, their overtones, their reverberations in our experience. In fact, poetic language is concerned mainly with these connotative levels. Here, the connotations of the images produce a mood and a sense of death that cannot be summed up by saying: "No, no, don't commit suicide." In effect, suicide (X) is (like) (Y) going to Lethe, twisting wolfs-bane, and so on. And since the subject here is *melancholy*, we have death as an overall metaphor (X) and melancholy (Y) being implicitly associated with each other. This sets the stage for a more intense juxtaposition of melancholy + death (*X*) to life (*Y*) in the second stanza. Stanza one ends enjoining against letting death drown the "wakeful anguish of the soul." Why does the poet call anguish "wakeful"? Is some beneficent, positive aspect of melancholy implied?

The second stanza opens with an extended metaphor identifying the "melancholy fit" (*X*) with a rain shower (*Y*). Notice that inside this metaphor is another (like those we looked at in "Ars Poetica"): Instead of "rain cloud," Keats writes "weeping cloud." So we have a compressed identification: rain is (like) weeping. In the third line of the second stanza the rain from the "melancholy fit" falls on a landscape—flowers, a green hill—making a transition to a fresh series of metaphors with a whole new slant on the subject.

In the lines beginning "Then glut thy sorrow," sorrow (*X*) is associated with three *Y*'s: (1) a "morning rose," (2) a "rainbow on a wave," and (3) "globèd peonies." Melancholy is now somehow involved with *joy*. Notice that there is a metaphor within a metaphor here too: wealth (*X*) is identified with "globèd peonies" (*Y*). Since we usually think of wealth in terms of money and material possessions, what effect does applying these associations to natural objects have on your mental "seeing"?

In the final lines of this stanza two descriptive words (images) act as forceful covert metaphors (one-word metaphors like "leaven" or "Lethe"). In the phrase "emprison her soft hand," the word "emprison" is implicitly contrasted with a lover holding the beloved's hand. This might suggest restrictions on freedom, love as a restriction, the binding effect of melancholy, etc. So a common action has a new meaning and quality. Next consider the word "feed" in the last line of the stanza. There is desperation and hunger here. Why? The following line and stanza provide a partial answer: "She dwells with Beauty—Beauty that must die."

In stanza three we read: "And Joy, whose hand is ever at his lips/Bidding adieu. . . ." The technical word critics use for a metaphor comparing or identifying a thing or concept (like joy) with human attributes or actions is PERSONIFICATION. Here joy (*X*) is personified as a lover (*Y*). Joy is (like) this lover. (The rain cloud in the second

stanza was also personified by its identification with "weeping.") This metaphor explores the melancholy of love and its connection with the pleasure of love. Joy and melancholy, life and death, are now seen as part of one process. Next, "and aching Pleasure nigh,/Turning to poison where the bee-mouth sips" would be absurd if we tried to vizualize it. It is certainly not true to nature: Nectar does not become deadly as the bee ingests it. Does this weaken the metaphor in any way? Notice that the line vividly echoes the poison and death theme in stanza one, as well as giving new vigor to the cliché sentiment: "Your sweetness will turn bitter in your mouth, your pleasures will be pain," and so on.

The following two lines identify "Delight" as a temple and "Melancholy" as a shrine in it, suggesting religious connotations, as the rosary did in stanza one. Is it implied that delight is something we worship? Is it a pagan worship? If we worship delight, then don't we have to worship "Veil'd Melancholy" as well?

The dramatic intensity reaches a peak in the next comparison. Joy is now sensual and sensuous, identified with a grape. The tongue bursting it focuses the whole subtle, complex entanglement of joy and melancholy that the poem has been manifesting. The single image unites them: We have to know melancholy to know joy, and vice versa. Why do you think Keats says, "Though seen of none save him. . . "? Why is he asserting that the union of the two can be grasped only by someone with a "palate fine"? Can you see how "palate" might suggest a necessary sensitivity to poetic metaphor, for instance? Logic might demonstrate that this union is a contradiction, but is it? Compressed into this same dense little metaphor is the sense of transience that the whole poem has been suggesting ("Beauty that must die") and the pain of life ("wakeful anguish").

So we have seen how metaphoric language (sometimes called FIGURATIVE LANGUAGE) spins an intricate web of connotation and association and gives a kind of form to difficult abstractions. If you follow this, experience this as you go through the poem, you will discover how metaphors always go beyond the literal and outdistance "logic."

1. An ODE is a poem of praise. Why is this poem called "Ode on Melancholy"?

2. Consider the metaphor in the phrase "night-shade, ruby grape of Proserpine." Proserpine (Persephone) was the goddess associated with spring and rebirth, but she also served as Queen of Hades or Hell, Pluto's wife in his domain. What are the implications of comparing nightshade to a grape of Proserpine? How does this connection relate to others in the poem?

3. Consider the comparison "Nor let the beetle, nor the death-moth be/Your mournful Psyche." What are the implications of this comparison (beetle/death-moth is (like) mournful Psyche) for the rest of the poem?

4. In the last line of the first stanza, "And drown the wakeful anguish of the soul," how is the sense of "wakeful anguish" illustrated by what follows?

5. Consider the phrase "on a morning rose" in the second stanza. A PUN is a play on words with the same or similar sound but with sharply different meanings. What is the pun in this line, and how does it add meaning to the poem?

6. What kinds of meanings does the word "feed" in the last line of the second stanza suggest about melancholy? Are there any other words in this stanza that relate to "feed"?

7. Consider Keats's use of the expression "palate fine." Aside from the question of rhyme, why is the word "fine" so appropriate to this line?

8. How are joy, melancholy, and transience embodied throughout the poem?

9. In the last two lines, why does the poet say "*sadness* of her might"? Why are the trophies "cloudy"?

10. Consider any descriptive phrase or adjective in the poem. What are the connotations? How does it relate to the rest of the poem?

Technical Notes

The poem is an ode, with the stanza rhyme scheme *a b a b c d e c d e*. The METER is predominately IAMBIC PENTAMETER.

Since this poem happens to be about both poetry and melancholy, two subjects we have already encountered, you can compare its effect on you with the effects of the first two poems, "Ode on Melancholy" and "Ars Poetica."

Gerald Francis

POETRY AND MELANCHOLY

A poem is meant to give relief,
To soothe all pangs of dread and grief.
To hear the truth of love or woe,
Then to a good poem you should go.

The poem is like a faithful friend,
It helps a broken heart to mend,
It makes a gloomy day turn bright,
Because its words have secret might.

Considerations

1. What do you think of this poem? If you like it, what makes it effective? If you dislike it, what do you think is wrong with it?

2. Can you find any metaphors here? What are the X and Y terms?

3. What are some of the essential differences between this poem and "Ode on Melancholy" and "Ars Poetica"?

4. What effect do the meter and rhyme of the poem have on you?

The poet is trying to tell us how he feels about poetry, how it brightens his life. Do we get anything new here, any depth, excitement, or discovery? Does the poet get beyond trying to convince us to agree with him?

The first stanza is straight statement, telling us what to think. The second attempts some metaphors: (1) a poem (X) is compared to a faithful friend (Y), (2) a heart (X) is identified as something which can be broken and mended (Y), and (3) the poem (X) is given the properties of sunlight (Y).

Of these, the first asserts a similarity which falls flat because there is no tension between the terms, nothing concrete in "faithful friend" to give the abstraction ("poem") life. Does the expression "faithful friend" do any more than try to persuade us that a poem is nice by comparing it to something everyone likes? This resembles a politician supporting motherhood to get votes, doesn't it? Of course, we can't be sure of the poet's intentions, but we can see the effect of the finished product. The second quasi-metaphor is an out-and-out cliché. What about the third? In each case the unlike factor is weak, and so the union of terms is not really metaphoric.

What about the form of the poem? Many people believe that if a statement rhymes and has regular meter, it is a poem. "Poetry and Melancholy" has both. After reading it, do you think the above definition of poetry is reasonable?

How do you react to the implications and levels in this little metaphor? What does it suggest about Mistress Southwell, her personality, etc.?

Robert Herrick

UPON MISTRESS SUSANNA SOUTHWELL, HER FEET

Her pretty feet
Like snails did creep
A little out, and then,
As if they played at bo-peep,
Did soon draw in again.

The poem below is an example of the simple meta-phor extended across a whole poem. Can you see how Frost transcends the literal description here?

Robert Frost

A PATCH OF OLD SNOW

There's a patch of old snow in a corner,
   That I should have guessed
Was a blow-away paper the rain
   Had brought to rest.

It is speckled with grime as if
   Small print overspread it,
The news of a day I've forgotten—
   If I ever read it.

Considerations

1. Do you see a central metaphoric comparison here? What is the snow compared to? What about the grime?
2. Do you see how the word "should" in the second line could be taken two ways?
3. Consider some of the implications of the comparison. What kind of "news" could the patch of snow indicate to the narrator?
4. Could the word "read" in the last line be taken metaphorically to mean something more? If so, what?
5. Is the poet expressing regret over not having read the news or cynicism about it? Are both views possible? If so, are they in contradiction, or do they complement each other?

This is the complete poem from which the first line was extracted as an example earlier in the chapter. Here, as in "Ars Poetica," a poet is making his case by employing a series of metaphors. Now that we have the whole poem, see how the rose comparison works in context.

Robert Burns

A RED, RED ROSE

Oh my luve is like a red, red rose,
  That's newly sprung in June:
Oh my luve is like the melodie,
  That's sweetly play'd in tune.

As fair art thou, my bonie lass,
  So deep in luve am I;
And I will luve thee still, my dear,
  Till a' the seas gang dry.

Till a' the seas gang dry, my dear,
  And the rocks melt wi' the sun;
And I will luve thee still, my dear,
  While the sands o' life shall run.

And fare thee weel, my only luve!
  And fare thee weel a while!
And I will come again, my luve,
  Tho' it were ten thousand mile!

Considerations

1. The poet writes that his "luve" is like a rose. Does "luve" mean his girl friend or his love for her? Or both? Consider how this confusion might add depth to the poem.

2. In the second, third, and fourth stanzas of the poem, the poet makes exaggerated comparisons in which the quality of his love is compared to impossible or heroic actions. How do these exaggerations contribute to the poem's effectiveness as a statement of love?

3. What would you get from the photograph accompanying this poem without the poem itself? Do you think it would be possible to convey the sense of this poem in an illustration? Why or why not?

4. Consider the rhyme and meter of the poem. How do they contribute to the poem's effectiveness as a love poem? Does this poem remind you of a song?

On the surface the next piece is a carpe diem *"seduction poem,"* in which the narrator is sup- *posedly talking a lady into surrendering her virgini-* *ty. The argument of the poem is clever and straight-* *forward. Whether it would actually accomplish its* *purpose is a matter for conjecture, but a deeper* *poetic purpose is served. The seduction framework* *becomes the poet's opportunity to discover things* *about man's relation to love and time.*

Andrew Marvell

TO HIS COY MISTRESS

Had we but world enough, and time,
This coyness, Lady, were no crime.
We would sit down, and think which way
To walk, and pass our long love's day.
Thou by the Indian Ganges' side
Should'st rubies find: I by the tide
Of Humber would complain. I would
Love you ten years before the Flood:
And you should, if you please, refuse
Till the Conversion of the Jews.
My vegetable love should grow
Vaster than empires, and more slow.
An hundred years should go to praise
Thine eyes, and on thy forehead gaze;
Two hundred to adore each breast:
But thirty thousand to the rest:
An age at least to every part,
And the last age should show your heart.
For, Lady, you deserve this state;
Nor would I love at lower rate.
—But at my back I always hear
Time's wingèd chariot hurrying near:
And yonder all before us lie
Deserts of vast eternity.
Thy beauty shall no more be found;
Nor, in thy marble vault, shall sound
My echoing song: then worms shall try
That long preserved virginity:
And your quaint honor turn to dust;
And into ashes all my lust.
The grave's a fine and private place,
But none I think do there embrace.
— Now therefore, while the youthful hue
Sits on thy skin like morning dew,
And while thy willing soul transpires
At every pore with instant fires,
Now let us sport us while we may;
And now, like am'rous birds of prey,
Rather at once our time devour,
Than languish in his slow-chapt° power.
Let us roll all our strength, and all
Our sweetness, up into one ball:
And tear our pleasures with rough strife,
Thorough the iron gates of life.
Thus, though we cannot make our sun
Stand still, yet we will make him run.
°Chewed slowly.

Considerations

The poem begins with a complicated comparison of the hours of "love's long day" (X) to the ages of history (Y) and a comparison of the local terrain of the lover's walk (X) to the geography of the world (Y). Brooks in a seventeenth-century suburban field become great rivers, the Humber and the Ganges; the lady's body becomes something that could literally take ages to properly explore. If there were time, the poet says, he could do all this.

The overall structure follows the form of a classical three-part logical argument: (1) if ("Had we but world enough . . ."), (2) but ("But at my back . . ."), and (3) therefore ("Now therefore, while . . .").

Having opened his piece by emphasizing the shortness of life, the poet moves through the second and third stages of the argument using a series of forceful local metaphors that set abstractions against concrete details. Among other things, this demonstrates how metaphors can give immediacy and uniqueness to the abstract. The major direct and indirect metaphors are listed below.

X	Y
1. Time	1. A wingëd chariot
2. Deserts	2. Vast eternity
3. Virginity	3. Something (like a corpse) that can be "tried" by worms (note the sexual implication of worms)
4. Honor	4. Quaintness, a quaint object*
5. Honor	5. Subject to decay (turning to dust)
6. Lust	6. Combustible material (since it can be turned to ashes)
7. The grave	7. Something like a bed chamber (it is a "fine and private place" except that none "do there embrace")
8. Youth (as reflected in the skin)	8. Like morning dew (which, after all, vanishes soon enough)
9. Willing soul	9. Fire burning out through the skin (probably burning off the dew)
10. The lovers	10. "Am'rous birds of prey"
11. Time	11. Something which can be devoured
12. The lovers' strength and sweetness	12. Something that can be rolled up into a ball— (like) birds rolling up into a ball when tearing their "pleasures with rough strife"
13. Life	13. Iron gates
14. Sun	14. Unspecified, probably time (though it might be love or other things as well)

8"Quaint" was also a period sexual pun.

As you can see, many of the metaphors are implicit. The point here is not to become an expert at uncovering and analyzing hidden metaphors but to see that poetic language is essentially metaphoric: to become sensitive to this level of communication.

Marvell's use of words relies, not always obviously, on the union of dissimilar things, the unlike factor. In some cases—for example, item 7 in the preceding list—the two terms are contrasted. In other cases there is comparison—*X* is (like) *Y*: youth equals morning dew (item 8), and lovers equal amorous birds of prey (item 10). Several are associations: time with wingèd chariot (item 1), life with iron gates (item 13), and honor with dust and with quaintness (items 4 and 5).

What sort of effect does the surrealist landscape sketched by the metaphors have on your understanding? Do you sense a unique perception of love and living where the "iron gates of life" open on those "deserts of vast eternity" as the two "am'rous birds of prey" roll through "tearing their pleasures"? Look at this last metaphor: Through this identification (lovers are like birds) Marvell develops a complex psychological vision with love as hunger, violence, raw survival. As often happens, there is a twist or ironic play on an old cliché here: Commonly, poetic lovers were compared to turtledoves and the like. How do you react to the savage humor of Marvell's slant? What dimension does it add to the general attitude (in the poem) about lovemaking? Remember, the piece is supposed to be arguing in favor of this love. Is the poet really making fun of it too? If we dynamically balance the basic seriousness with the mocking humor undercutting it, we discover a form of poetic irony, a surprising reversal of the general drift and expected direction of the poet's point of view.

are continually compared with images usually considered unpleasant. The effect is partly to shock Comparing romantic love to worms, graves, and ashes is one way of mocking it. Romantic images the reader into reexamining his ideas and habits of thought.

> old-fashioned
> out of date

1. Honor—generally thought of as something lofty and significant—is associated with the word "quaint." What effect does this have?
2. The lovers as birds of prey are going to "devour" time. Since what they are devouring is each other, is there an implication that the lovers *are* time themselves?
3. Consider the line "My vegetable love should grow/Vaster than empires, and more slow." What are the connotations (suggested meanings) of Marvell's association of love's growth with vegetable growth? In what ways does this metaphor relate to the central comparison of the first part of the poem, that is, the comparison of love's time to historical time?
4. Consider in detail some of the possible comments on love and time implied by the language of the poem.
5. Marvell opens the poem by suggesting that time is short. Consider the last two lines. Is there a contradiction here? What kinds of relations can you develop between the opening statements and this one?
6. What connection has the illustrator made with this poem?

Technical Notes

The poem is written in couplets of IAMBIC TETRAMETER.

Here the poet pokes fun at the exaggerated and overdone metaphors used by his fellow poets to praise their lovers. Shakespeare calls attention to the grotesqueness and absurdity of these comparisons and illustrates the dangers of misusing metaphoric language, dangers anyone who has ever tried to write poetry himself will be familiar with.

William Shakespeare

MY MISTRESS' EYES . . .

My mistress' eyes are nothing like the sun;
Coral is far more red than her lips' red:
If snow be white, why then her breasts are dun; → *neutral brownish to gray / dull grayish brown*
If hairs be wires, black wires grow on her head.
I have seen roses damask'd, red and white, → *fragrant red + pink roses*
But no such roses see I in her cheeks;
And in some perfumes is there more delight
Than in the breath that from my mistress reeks.
I love to hear her speak; yet well I know
That music hath a far more pleasing sound;
I grant I never saw a goddess go,
My mistress, when she walks, treads on the ground:
    And yet, by heaven, I think my love as rare → *unusual / Innocent (Rare Steak - not fully cooked)*
    As any she (belied) with false compare.

to disappoint or leave unfulfilled
to misrepresent falsely - lie or slander

Considerations

In the first line Shakespeare mocks a comparison which was an old favorite at that time and had been much used by earlier poets: the comparison of the mistress's eyes with the sun. The purpose of this was to exalt the woman by identifying her with lofty, impressive objects.

Here the way Shakespeare puts the metaphors makes them ridiculous; we have a lady's snow-white breast, her rosy cheeks, her lips as red as coral. But Shakespeare's phrasing stresses the real, denotative, literal aspect of the terms in each comparison—the snow, the rose, the coral—and draws our attention to the difference, the impossible difference, between these and a woman's features. So he compels us to imagine a grotesque lady, who he compares to his mistress, to the latter's definite advantage. By setting the artificial mistress created out of clumsy metaphor beside his own realistically presented, unadorned, but "rare" mistress, Shakespeare focuses on basic humanness with fresh eyes. We might explicate this structure as follows: overdone "fancy" depiction (X) + realistic description of the real mistress (Y) = fresh insight into love, language, and poetry. So cliché and absurd metaphor are made a term in Shakespeare's own very original and acute metaphor.

1. How does the poet go about making fun of the metaphors of others? What different kinds of bad or cliché metaphor is he ridiculing here?
2. What is the real purpose of his mockery of bad metaphor?

3. Consider the picture the poem gives you of Shakespeare's mistress. What details do we know about her? Consider the poet's use of the word "rare" in the last line. How does this word relate to the argument in favor of his mistress?
4. Does the word "love" in the phrase "my love as rare" have a double meaning? What are the implications of this?
5. Consider the last line. Why does the poet use the word "belied"?
6. Could Shakespeare have as effectively described his mistress's naturalness without referring to the artifice of other poets?
7. Can a photograph capture beauty? Could it capture Shakespeare's insight into beauty?
8. Compare this poem with the Burns piece.

Technical Notes

✳ This poem is a SHAKESPEAREAN SONNET written in iambic pentameter.

Mistresses, as you can see, have been a favorite poetic subject. It seems that there is nothing like love to excite a poet to finer contemplation.

In everyday speech we might talk about a woman's "flowing gown" or describe a dress as "flowing." But this comparison of the motion of water to the fit and fall of a dress has lost its impact. It is a dead metaphor (like the eye of a needle or leg of a table); it has become so common that we no longer react to it metaphorically at all. How does the poet bring the dead metaphor to life?

Robert Herrick

UPON JULIA'S CLOTHES

When as in silks my Julia goes,
Then, then (me thinks) how sweetly flowes
That liquefaction of her clothes.

Next, when I cast mine eyes and see
That brave Vibration each way free;
O how that glittering taketh me!

Considerations

1. Consider Herrick's use of "brave Vibration." How might this describe Julia's clothes? Julia herself?
2. Make the same consideration for "glittering" in the last line.
3. Consider how Herrick's overall description of Julia's clothes is a description of Julia and of Julia's effect on him.
4. Could "each way free" also suggest that she is finally naked? Suppose you read the last line with the emphasis: "Oh how *that* glittering taketh me."

Oriental poetry, particularly Japanese, has been concerned with the sudden, surprise effects of metaphoric juxtaposition. The following four short Japanese poems aim at flashes of insight. What are the terms of the metaphors here? How do the poems work on us?

Kubonta

HAIKU

Kite like a soul,
dancing,
journeying . . .
Fallen to earth.

Rendition from Japanese

Matso Bashō

HAIKU

One's life, a single
dewdrop.
Its lonely savor.

Rendition from Japanese

Fujiwara Teika (Sadaie)

TANKA

Spring night.
My dream's suspended bridge
Is shattered.
Swirling in the chasm . . .
Pale light in the east.

Rendition from Japanese

Priest Saigyō

TANKA

Everything is changing
And changes
In this fleeting world . . .
The same still light of the
Changing moon.

Rendition from Japanese

Many modern poets have been impressed by the Japanese short forms and have experimented with their own versions, using the brief, deftly put metaphor for immediate effect—for example, the contemporary poet William Packard, in the following poem.

William Packard

THESE VOICES

these voices
silver fish in the
invisible river

Considerations

1. Consider the Bashō poem. Is "lonely savor" a metaphor?
2. Do you see an apparent contradiction involved in the Saigyō piece? Is this metaphoric? How?

Technical Notes

The four Japanese poems were written in their original language in the HAIKU and TANKA forms, as indicated by the titles.

The twentieth-century poet Wallace Stevens was also attracted to the kind of Oriental poetry which looks to effect a sudden sense of insight through metaphoric contrast. One of Stevens' better-known poems in this mode is "Thirteen Ways of Looking at a Blackbird."

Wallace Stevens

THIRTEEN WAYS OF LOOKING AT A BLACKBIRD

I
Among twenty snowy mountains,
The only moving thing
Was the eye of the blackbird.

II
I was of three minds,
Like a tree
In which there are three blackbirds.

III
The blackbird whirled in the autumn winds.
It was a small part of the pantomime.

IV
A man and a woman
Are one.
A man and a woman and a blackbird
Are one.

V
I do not know which to prefer,
The beauty of inflections
Or the beauty of innuendoes,
The blackbird whistling
Or just after.

VI
Icicles filled the long window
With barbaric glass.
The shadow of the blackbird
Crossed it, to and fro.
The mood
Traced in the shadow
An indecipherable cause.

VII
O thin men of Haddam,
Why do you imagine golden birds?
Do you not see how the blackbird
Walks around the feet
Of the women about you?

VIII
I know noble accents
And lucid, inescapable rhythms;
But I know, too,
That the blackbird is involved
In what I know.

IX
When the blackbird flew out of sight,
It marked the edge
Of one of many circles.

X
At the sight of blackbirds
Flying in a green light,
Even the bawds of euphony
Would cry out sharply.

XI
He rode over Connecticut
In a glass coach.
Once, a fear pierced him,
In that he mistook
The shadow of his equipage
For blackbirds.

XII
The river is moving.
The blackbird must be flying.

XIII
It was evening all afternoon.
It was snowing
And it was going to snow.
The blackbird sat
In the cedar-limbs.

Considerations

We can assume that the poet's use of a blackbird rather than a bluebird or a sparrow, for example, was not accidental. And it is probable that he is counting on the word "blackbird" to have some enigmatic, even sinister connotations. "Black" is one of those loaded words poets love to use because they are rich with associations: death, absence of light, evil, mystery, ominousness, and so on. The intelligent use of such words can add many levels of meaning. But the problem is that words like "black" have been overworked in this way. Stevens avoids the problem by using an image that has black *in* it. On one level, the blackbird comes to suggest a concentration of some reality beyond the habits of the senses and everyday patterns of thought, a reality haunting human illusions about what is real, what is fact. The following brief discussions examine a few of the many facets of this poem.

I

In section I, the mammoth, monumentally solid, white, unmoving "twenty snowy mountains" are contrasted with the quick, intensely black, small, extremely mobile eye of the blackbird. Does this contrast strike us as an insight, something the mind almost seems to "see"? We might spend hours debating the meaning of this little description. We sense that it means *something*, that some truth has been conveyed, but we cannot pin it down or agree or disagree about it because there is no statement or opinion here. While we might argue with one another over what we *think* the truth is, there is no way to refute our individual experiences of it.

II

The abstract "three minds" are made vividly concrete by juxtaposition with the "tree in which there are three blackbirds."

III

The metaphor here is less direct and seems at first like mere description. But notice that the blackbird whirling in the winds is equated with "a small part of the pantomime." A pantomime is a story told by movement. We are drawn to wonder what that story is about.

IV

A man and a woman are identified with the abstract concept "one" (as God is one, all men are one, etc.). We tend to accept this notion because it is a virtual cliché that men and women in love can totally unite physically and spiritually. Are you startled, however, when Stevens relates this accepted association with one including the blackbird as a third term? The blackbird comes in as if to suggest some cosmic mystery, some reality, some portent, whatever rich connotations this black, ambiguous, unsettling bird introduces into the familiar world of men and women.

V

This is a simple comparison. Can you see what the terms of the comparison are? What are these inflections and innuendoes?

VI

The picture of the blackbird crossing back and forth along the window becomes the X term for the mysterious lines: "The mood/Traced in the shadow/An indecipherable cause." Stevens' use of the word "cause" for this picture raises many questions. Cause for what? The blackbird? Its shadow? Nature? Something beyond nature? The mood itself? Why is the cause "indecipherable"? Does this suggest philosophic ideas about cause and effect?

The comparison of the icicles to "barbaric glass" presents the backdrop against which we see the blackbird's shadow. The suggestive power lies in the subtle connection between the picture of the blackbird's shadow in the window and the final statement about the "indecipherable cause."

VII

Here the poet contrasts the golden birds to the blackbird. What kinds of associations do golden birds suggest? Images of the past? The golden age? Images of aspirations? Dreams? Wealth? Beauty? They could be felt as any or all of these things, or others. In the contrast we also see the poet playing off our associations with the blackbird itself. Possibly the sinister element is being stressed here since, like an omen of something impending, the blackbird walks "around the feet of the women." Other impressions of the section are equally plausible; if, for example, you see the blackbird expressing cosmic, "higher," or absolute reality, then you might say that the "men of Haddam" are living in golden dreams and missing the blunt, black fact of truth right under their noses.

VIII

The "noble accents/And lucid, inescapable rhythms" are set against the blackbird. But is the blackbird different from them (contrasted), or is it an example of them (compared)? The poet's use of the word "too" in the third line implies that he may feel they are different, but this is not clear. And if different, is the blackbird *escapable*—is it *un*lucid, *ig*noble? How? Again, the poet's metaphoric use of the blackbird makes us sense that it stands for something beyond itself, something as abstract and indefinable as those "lucid, inescapable rhythms" themselves.

IX

The blackbird's flight is associated with a circle, of which the poem claims there are "many." Since we did not see this circle until it was marked by the bird's flight, other circles are suggested, circles invisible to us until marked by something. Circles have rich associations for us: perfection, cycles of life, going around in a circle, being ringed in, the circle as a symbol of unity or infinity, etc. Metaphorically, the blackbird opens a way into understanding the complex circularities of existence.

X

It seems clear from the use of the word "even" that the "bawds of euphony" (the whores of harmonious sound) are hardened or indifferent to most sights. Their dulled sophistication is set against their reaction to "the sight of blackbirds/Flying in a green light." It is left for us to discover whether the bawds would cry out sharply from delight, fear, awe, or something else. In any event, the blackbirds suddenly alter the bawds' usual state, perhaps with the impact of something deeper than what we are habituated to, a violent truth about things.

XI

Fear, the blackbird, and the shadow of the glass coach are all intermingled and associated. Once more the blackbirds seem to be a portent. But

notice how that fear becomes transferred by association ("mistook/The shadow of his equipage/For blackbirds") to the glass coach. In this context what does the glass coach mean? Certainly it is evocative, metaphoric. What is the effect of the association of "glass" with "pierce"? Why does the poet use such archaic words as "equipage" and "coach"? How do they add to the meaning? The connotations create a tension between the various terms and seem to point at something beyond the simple description of a traveler looking out the window of his car or train at shadows. Was he frightened, for example, by the ominous shadow of truth? Is his whole existence as fragile as the glass coach?

XII

The river's movement is juxtaposed to the flying blackbird. Is there a causal relation implied between these two? Does the river move and then the blackbird fly, or are they manifestations of the same underlying natural process? Or is it a simple comparison: The river's movement is (like) the blackbird's flying? All these possibilities might be felt simultaneously. The little two-line metaphor suggests tantalizing depths we can almost plumb.

XIII

The first sentence gives us a complex image of time and movement. The snow is falling continuously; all afternoon it is evening, as if time were somehow stilled in this motion. Against this endless, static time the poet sets a bird in the cedar-limbs. Will it stay still or take flight? The black against white presents a stark visual contrast, and the blackbird, gathered into a violent stillness in the tree, contrasts with the steadily falling snow. The bird again is "haunting" the peaceful (perhaps illusory) landscape with its total, absolute "realness."

In most of the sections discussed so far, Stevens uses the bird as a metaphoric aspect of the unknown. He puts it against contrasting backgrounds—mountains, golden birds, falling snow, the shadow of the glass coach, etc.—and all this triggers in us a sense of import, urgency, and meaning. So overall the bird itself is an X for some other Y that we can only dimly sense, something beyond all the comparisons given in the poem and our attempts to discuss them. It holds something else in itself; it stands for something beyond the intellect's range and grasp. So through poetry we can sometimes glimpse a vast unknown that waits at the limits of our familiar worlds.

1. *Section I* Is twenty snowy mountains a better number than thirty or fifty? Consider some of the possible meanings for the metaphor in this section.
2. *Section II* How do you visualize this metaphor?
3. *Section III* What reasons might there be for using the word "whirled"? Do you see an ambiguity here? What possibilities of meaning can you see in the phrase "a small part of the pantomime"?
4. *Section IV* Can you visualize this metaphor? Compare your mental impression of this with your impression of the metaphor in section II.
5. *Section VI* What are some of the possible implications of the last three lines? Do you see any double meanings in the term "traced"? Is the blackbird tracing the cause or being traced *by* it? Do you see any tension in the vertical and horizontal lines of the image? What relations do the icicles have to the window?
6. *Section VII* How does the word "thin" relate to the rest of this section? Literally, Haddam is a town in Connecticut. Does Stevens' use of the word in this context make it metaphoric? Does the fact that it sounds biblical add to the meaning? What kinds of connection do you perceive here between the blackbird and women? And the thin men? Both together?
7. *Section VIII* What are some of the possible meanings for the blackbird in this fragment?
8. *Section IX* What is the significance here of the fact that the blackbird is flying "out of sight"?
9. *Section X* What are some of the implications of the phrase "bawds of euphony"? Who might they be? Why is the word "sharply" appropriate in this context? Why "green light"?
10. *Section XI* What is particularly appropriate about the poet's use of "pierced"? "Equipage"? Why or how is his equipage like the shadow of blackbirds?
11. *Section XII* Why are these lines separate sentences?
12. Can you see any logic in Stevens' arrangement of the thirteen sections of the poem? For example, what relation do you see between sections VII and VIII or between sections I and XIII?
13. Do you think you could get anything like the impact of the poem from a photograph?

Technical Notes

Stevens uses neither rhyme nor regular meter in this poem. This kind of form, or lack of rigid form, is called FREE VERSE.

The contemporary Russian poet Voznesensky plays on the metaphoric idea that this world (X) is really an antiworld (Y). See for yourself how he works this out. Notice what effect his individual metaphors have on this concept.

Andrei Voznesensky

ANTIWORLDS

The clerk Bukashkin is our neighbor:
His face is grey as blotting-paper.

But like balloons of blue or red,
Bright Antiworlds
                    float over his head!
On them reposes, prestidigitous,
Ruling the cosmos, a demon-magician,
Anti-Bukashkin the academician,
Lapped in the arms of Lollobrigidas.

But Anti-Bukashkin's dreams are the color
Of blotting-paper, and couldn't be duller.

Long live Antiworlds! They rebut
With dreams the rat-race and the rut.
For some to be clever, some must be boring.
No deserts? No oases, then.
There are no women—
                    just anti-men.
In the forests, anti-machines are roaring.
There's the dirt of the earth, as well as the salt.
If the earth broke down, the sun would halt.

Ah, my critics; how I love them.
Upon the neck of the keenest of them,
Fragrant and bald as fresh-baked bread,
There shines a perfect anti-head . . .

. . . I sleep with windows open wide;
Somewhere a falling star invites,
And skyscrapers,
                    like stalactites,

Hang from the planet's underside.
There, upside down
                    below me far,
Stuck like a fork into the earth,
Or perching like a carefree moth,
My little Antiworld,
                    there you are!

In the middle of the night, why is it
That Antiworlds are moved to visit?

Why do they sit together, gawking
At the television, and never talking?

Between them, not one word has passed.
Their first strange meeting is their last.

Neither can manage the least *bon ton.*
Oh, how they'll blush for it later on!

Their ears are burning like a pair
Of crimson butterflies, hovering there . . .

. . . A distinguished lecturer lately told me,
"Antiworlds are a total loss."

Still, my apartment-cell won't hold me;
I thrash in my sleep, I turn and toss.

And, radio-like, my cat lies curled
With his green eye tuned in to the world.

*Translation from Russian by
Richard Wilbur*

The late-eighteenth-century poet William Blake was both poet and painter,
famed for his "visionary" images. How do the metaphors work here?

William Blake

AUGURIES OF INNOCENCE

To see a World in a Grain of Sand,
And a Heaven in a Wild Flower,
Hold Infinity in the palm of your hand,
And Eternity in an hour.
A Robin Redbreast in a Cage
Puts all Heaven in a Rage.
A dove-house fill'd with Doves and Pigeons
Shudders Hell thro' all its regions.
A dog starv'd at his Master's Gate
Predicts the ruin of the State.
A Horse misus'd upon the Road
Calls to Heaven for Human blood.
Each outcry of the hunted Hare
A fibre from the Brain does tear.
A Skylark wounded in the wing,
A Cherubim does cease to sing.
The Game Cock clip'd and arm'd for fight
Does the Rising Sun affright.
Every Wolf's and Lion's howl
Raises from Hell a Human Soul.
The wild Deer, wand'ring here and there,
Keeps the Human Soul from Care.
The Lamb misus'd breeds Public Strife
And yet forgives the Butcher's knife.
The Bat that flits at close of Eve
Has left the Brain that won't Believe.
The Owl that calls upon the Night
Speaks the Unbeliever's fright.
He who shall hurt the little Wren
Shall never be belov'd by Men.
He who the Ox to wrath has mov'd
Shall never be by Woman lov'd.
The wanton Boy that kills the Fly
Shall feel the Spider's enmity.
He who torments the Chafer's Sprite
Weaves a Bower in endless Night.
The Catterpiller on the Leaf
Repeats to thee thy Mother's grief.
Kill not the Moth nor Butterfly,
For the Last Judgment draweth nigh.
He who shall train the Horse to war

Shall never pass the Polar Bar.
The Beggar's Dog and Widow's Cat,
Feed them and thou wilt grow fat.
The Gnat that sings his Summer's Song
Poison gets from Slander's tongue.
The poison of the Snake and Newt
Is the sweat of Envy's Foot.
The poison of the Honey Bee
Is the Artist's Jealousy.
The Prince's Robes and Beggar's Rags
Are Toadstools on the Miser's Bags.
A Truth that's told with bad intent
Beats all the Lies you can invent.
It is right it should be so;
Man was made for Joy and Woe;
And when this we rightly know,
Thro' the World we safely go,
Joy and Woe are woven fine,
A Clothing for the soul divine.
Under every grief and pine
Runs a joy with silken twine.
The Babe is more than Swadling Bands;
Throughout all these Human Lands
Tools were made, and Born were hands,
Every Farmer Understands.
Every Tear from Every Eye
Becomes a Babe in Eternity;
This is caught by Females bright
And return'd to its own delight.
The Bleat, the Bark, Bellow and Roar,
Are Waves that Beat on Heaven's Shore.
The Babe that weeps the Rod beneath
Writes Revenge in realms of Death.
The Beggar's Rags, fluttering in Air,
Does to Rags the Heavens tear.
The Soldier, arm'd with Sword and Gun,
Palsied strikes the Summer's Sun.
The poor Man's Farthing is worth more
Than all the Gold on Afric's Shore.
One Mite wrung from the Lab'rer's hands
Shall buy and sell the Miser's Lands;

Or, if protected from on high,
Does that whole Nation sell and buy.
He who mocks the Infant's Faith
Shall be mock'd in Age and Death.
He who shall teach the Child to Doubt
The rotting Grave shall ne'er get out.
He who respects the Infant's faith
Triumphs over Hell and Death.
The Child's Toys and the Old Man's Reasons
Are the Fruits of the Two seasons.
The Questioner, who sits so sly,
Shall never know how to Reply.
He who replies to words of Doubt
Doth put the Light of Knowledge out.
The Strongest Poison ever known
Came from Caesar's Laurel Crown.
Nought can Deform the Human Race
Like to the Armour's iron brace.
When Gold and Gems adorn the Plow
To Peaceful Arts shall Envy Bow.
A Riddle, or the Cricket's Cry,
Is to Doubt a fit Reply.
The Emmet's Inch and Eagle's Mile
Make Lame Philosophy to smile.
He who Doubts from what he sees
Will ne'er Believe, do what you Please.
If the Sun and Moon should Doubt,
They'd immediately Go Out.
To be in a Passion you Good may do,
But no Good if a Passion is in you.
The Whore and Gambler, by the State
Licensed, build that Nation's Fate.
The Harlot's cry from Street to Street
Shall weave Old England's winding Sheet.
The Winner's Shout, the Loser's Curse,
Dance before dead England's Hearse.
Every Night and every Morn
Some to Misery are Born.
Every Morn and every Night
Some are Born to Sweet Delight.
Some are Born to Sweet Delight,
Some are Born to Endless Night.
We are led to Believe a Lie
When we see not Thro' the Eye,
Which was Born in a Night to perish in a Night,
When the Soul Slept in Beams of Light.
God Appears, and God is Light,
To those poor souls who dwell in Night;
But does a Human Form Display
To those who Dwell in Realms of Day.

Considerations

Like other poets, Blake stresses his metaphors in several different ways:

Comparison: "The Bleat, the Bark, Bellow and Roar/Are Waves that Beat on Heaven's Shore."
Identification: "Runs a joy with silken twine."
Contrast: "Some are Born to Sweet Delight,/Some are Born to Endless Night."
Association: "Each outcry of the hunted Hare/A fibre from the Brain does tear."
Personification: "Poison gets from Slander's tongue."

Notice how many of the associations take the form of cause and effect. If *X*, then *Y*; if "A Robin Redbreast in a Cage," then "all Heaven in a Rage"; if a man "the Ox to wrath has moved," then he "Shall never be by Woman lov'd"; and so on. Notice also that it is by linking commonplace things (a beggar's rags, the maltreatment of a horse) with grand cosmic consequences that Blake projects his vision.

The poet says that "To see a World in a Grain of Sand,/And a Heaven in a Wild Flower," is his intention, and so he sets out to show us the great in the small, the universal in the particular, the celestial in the mundane. The contrasts are merged into metaphoric unity. Is he implying that the action of metaphor (where seemingly unlike, fragmentary things, in uniting, reveal a whole truth) is a universal, spiritual law?

In concluding, Blake extends his union of opposites—big and little—to man and God. For "those poor souls who dwell in Night" (and "night," like "black," is a loaded word that operates metaphorically connoting ignorance, evil, blindness), God appears as "light." But the ones who live in God's realms (day) observe that God is man himself. Anyone who can see a world in a grain of sand will grasp this immediately.

1. Consider how the line "And Eternity in an hour" might resemble Marvell's language in the first section of "To His Coy Mistress."
2. Consider the lines "The Game Cock clip'd and arm'd for fight/Does the Rising Sun affright." What are the similarities and differences between the two terms of this metaphor (the

game cock and the sun)? Make this kind of consideration for other metaphors in the poem.

3. What possible reasons might Blake have had for calling this poem "Auguries of Innocence"?

4. Consider any of the local metaphors in the poem. What new perceptions of things result from the metaphors?

5. Consider the last eight lines of the poem. What are some of their connections to what has gone before in the piece?

Technical Notes

The poem has a feeling of regular meter, partly because of Blake's use of couplets—most of them separate, self-contained thoughts—and partly because of his use of ACCENTUAL MEASURE, four STRESSES to a line.

The poem below is a statement of traditional Christian doctrine, but it is made through metaphors which give it a humorous twist and revitalize the idea—as well as giving you something to think about next time you crave a smoke.

Anonymous

A RELIGIOUS USE OF TAKING TOBACCO

The Indian weed withered quite,
Green at morn, cut down at night,
   Shows thy decay;
   All flesh is hay:
Thus think, then drink tobacco.

And when the smoke ascends on high,
Think thou behold'st the vanity
   Of worldly stuff,
   Gone with a puff:
Thus think, then drink tobacco.

But when the pipe grows foul within,
Think of thy soul defiled with sin.
   And that the fire
   Doth it require:
Thus think, then drink tobacco.

The ashes that are left behind,
May serve to put thee still in mind
   That into dust
   Return thou must:
Thus think, then drink tobacco.

Considerations

1. What are the terms of the major metaphoric comparison in this poem?
2. How is this comparison extended into other metaphors?
3. Would you argue about doctrine put in this way or experience the "truth" of it no matter what your beliefs? Why?
4. What are the differences between the poetic statement and the statement of the photograph accompanying the poem?

Unlike most of the poems we have looked at up to now, the one below may seem at first to be no more than a list, a series of obliquely related statements. The connections between them are not very clear until we see that violence, anger, war, death, etc., are continually being referred to.

Philip Levine

HOW MUCH CAN IT HURT?

The woman at the checkstand
Who wishes you cancer

The fat man who hates his mother
The doctor who forgets

The soup bubbling on the back of the stove
The stone staring into the sun

The girl who kisses her own arms
The girl who fries her hair

The egg turning brown under the spoon
The lemon laughing all night long

My brother in his uniform over Dresden
The single thrill of fire going for the bed

The kindergarten blowing its windows out
Chalk burning the little fingers

The newspaper waiting all weekend
Dozing in rain with the deaths smeared on its lips

The oiling and the loading and the springing
The bullets sucking quietly in their cradles

How much can it hurt in the wood
In the long nerve of lead, in the fattened head

How much can it hurt
In each ration of meat hooked and hanging

In the unfinished letter, the dried opened socket
The veil of skin flapping, the star falling

My face punctured with glass
The teeth eating themselves in dreams

Our blood refusing to breathe, refusing to sleep
Asking the wounded moon

Asking the pillow, asking, asking
How much can it hurt?

Considerations

What we really have in this poem is an extension of
the principle of covert or implied metaphoric language: The statements are comparisons, and we
have to find out what lies unstated, what connects
X to Y. As we have seen, in poetry the unstated
meanings really matter most.

There are many examples here of metaphoric
usage dealt with in previous poems, for example,
"The newspaper waiting all weekend/Dozing in
rain with deaths smeared on its lips." The newspaper is a personification, as joy is in "Ode on
Melancholy."

1. What examples of metaphoric language can
   you find in the poem?
2. "The girl who fries her hair" seems somehow
   to connect with the images of burning children
   in Dresden. (Dresden, an open city, was
   bombed by the Allies during World War II;
   100,000 civilians were killed, many of them
   women and children who had been sent there
   for safety.) Can you find other such relationships between the opening ten lines and the
   rest of the poem?
3. Consider whether it is possible to write a
   simple explication of this particular piece. If
   not, why not?

Here we see a medieval French poem that has something in common with the twentieth-century piece we have just looked at. The poet lists things—in this case the names of famous women in history—without making any overt comment. Though this list is not as studded with individual metaphors as the one in the Levine poem, there is obviously something metaphoric here. Can you see it? Remember that we are looking for a relationship that creates a tension—an X/Y.

François Villon

BALLAD OF THE LADIES
OF OLD

Tell, where, what country is Flora,
The girl who was called the fair Roman?
Or where is Archipiades,[1] or Thais,[2]
Who was her incomparable cousin?
Or Echo, who whispered of love
Over rivers and desolate marsh?
Her beauty was far more than human,
   they say.
And last year's snows, where are they?

Where is sweet Eloise, the wise,[3]
For whose love Peter Abelard endured
The loss of the flame of his manhood,
And the the pain of a monk coldly cloistered?
And where the tyrannical queen[4]
Who decreed that poor Buridan, her lover,
Be tossed in a sack in the bay?
And last year's snows, where are they?

Oh, where is the lily pale princess
Who sang in a lily pale voice?
Bertha bigfoot,[5] Alice, Beatrice,
Lady Haremburgis,[6] and others of choice?
And good Joan of Arc, where is she,
Whose brave body kept Englishmen warm?
Where *are* they, Oh Virgin, I pray?
And last year's snows, where are they?

ENVOY
Prince, don't ask me this week or this year
To divulge where these ladies have gone.
The refrain of this song's all that stays.
And last year's snows, where are they?

*Translation from French
by John Briggs*

Considerations

Notice that each group in the list is followed by a line saying simply, "They're gone, and where are yesterday's snows?" We might compare this with the Levine line: "How much can it hurt?" You *know* the answer, perhaps, but you cannot say what it is. The simple answer is unstated, and you have to bring to it your own fresh understanding of death, pain, and loss. The extension here associates and unites X (the ladies in question are all gone) and Y (where are the snows?). In a sense the poet has actually said that the women have melted away like the snow, but by keeping the connection less obvious, he produces a sense of distance, mystery, and intensity.

1. Do you think the length of the Villon poem adds anything to its effect? If so, how?
2. Are the questions asked in the Villon and the Levine poems really meant to be answered? Can they be?

[1]A celebrated Athenian woman.

[2]No doubt beautiful.

[3]Eloise was a student of Abelard, the twelfth-century philosopher. He was castrated by agents of her father; he consequently retired to a monastery, and she to a convent.

[4]The wife of Louis X.

[5]Charlemagne's mother.

[6]The twelfth- or thirteenth-century daughter of a count.

*This poem, by the contemporary poet Robert Lowell, uses metaphor to investi-
gate the self. Many individual metaphors are on the surface here, but some of the
larger, central metaphoric relationships are submerged, not directly stated. This
piece is considered a difficult poem. See how well you can get into it. As you
read, be alert to Lowell's metaphoric use of sight, vision, and seeing.*

Robert Lowell

MYOPIA: A NIGHT

Bed, glasses off, and all's
ramshackle, streaky, weird
for the near-sighted, just
a foot away.
        The light's
still on an instant. Here
are the blurred titles, here
the books are blue hills, browns,
greens, fields, or color.
           This
is the departure strip,
the dream-road. Whoever built it
left numbers, words and arrows.
He had to leave in a hurry.

I see
a dull and alien room,
my cell of learning,
white, brightened by white pipes,
ramrods of steam . . . I hear
the lonely metal breathe
and gurgle like the sick.
And yet my eyes avoid
that room. No need to see.
No need to know I hoped
its blank, foregoing whiteness
would burn away the blur,
as my five senses clenched
their teeth, thought stitched to thought,
as through a needle's eye . . .

I see the morning star . . .

Think of him in the Garden,
that seed of wisdom, Eve's
seducer, stuffed with man's
corruption, stuffed with triumph:
Satan triumphant in
the Garden! In a moment,

all that blinding brightness
changed into a serpent,
lay grovelling on its gut.

What has disturbed this household?
Only a foot away,
the familiar faces blur.
At fifty we're so fragile,
a feather . . .

The things of the eye are done.
On the illuminated black dial,
green ciphers of a new moon—
one, two, three, four, five, six!
I breathe and cannot sleep.
Then morning comes,
saying, "This was a night."

Considerations

The opening stanza seems at first just to state literally that a man with poor sight can't see clearly when he takes his glasses off. However, by the end of the second stanza, where books have become "blue *hills*, browns, greens, *fields*, or color," we begin to react to the covert metaphor: going to sleep + not seeing clearly + illusion and imagination = (in stanza three) the "departure strip" and "dream-road." This extended metaphor hints at how the mind moves into unreality, fantasy, and perhaps (as the poem later suggests) another quality of reality or at least another way of understanding it.

By the fourth stanza, the narrator's uncomfortable room has begun to function as a larger metaphor comparing the room to the body, the cage of the world imprisoning the soul, the ego, etc. The poet implies that the room is somehow *like* one's life and the world: "I see/a dull and alien room, my cell of learning." Note the metaphor within a metaphor here: Metal breaths and gurgles are "like the sick." Though it is not stated directly that the room equals body, life, etc., these lines are clues.

In his agony the speaker sees the morning star, Venus. Venus was the roman goddess of love and beauty. The morning star is also classically associated with Lucifer. From here we move to Eve, the first woman presiding at the fall of man, and the snake, the devil associated with both knowledge (going back to "my cell of learning") and the "senses" that "clenched their teeth" a few lines ago. Thus the metaphor of dark, dream, and blurring has led to a kind of vision in which the "blinding brightness" of the original perfection of Eden and the perfection of *vision* itself, sight and seeing, have fallen into night, darkness, and blurs. Think of the very title of the poem. Do you see Lucifer, as the angel of light, falling into darkness, becoming "a serpent . . . groveling on its gut"?

In the second-to-last stanza, can you find in "What has disturbed this household?" levels of association which relate "household" to all mankind, history spiritual and temporal, philosophy, etc., as well as to the house as the body of a man burning with his immediate lusts, fears, and passions?

The final stanza takes us out of the narrator's vision back to the limited view of the room; everyday life and its darkness become compressed into the glowing clockface near the bed, a one-word metaphor like "leaven" in the Christ parable. There are a great many things to consider in this piece. The ones listed below should get you started.

1. Consider the lines "Whoever built it/left numbers, words and arrows./He had to leave in a hurry" in terms of the larger comparison:

the room stands for the speaker's life and the world.

2. Consider the lines "And yet my eyes avoid/ that room. No need to see." What implications are there in these lines that the room is being compared to the speaker's life and the world?

3. Why is the metal in the fourth stanza "lonely"? How does this word operate metaphorically? (Compare this image with the Bashō poem.)

4. What are some of the implications of the narrator's seeing the morning star in the fifth stanza? Could it represent hope? Hope outside the world? How? What else? What associations would you attach to the morning star if you did not know it stood for Venus or Lucifer?

5. What connection do you see between the "foregoing whiteness" of the room in stanza four and the "blinding brightness" of stanza six? What does the narrator want here? How does this relate to the morning star?

6. How does the Eden myth relate to the narrator's situation?

7. The line "At fifty we're so fragile" is really a metaphor as in "fragile like a feather."

What kind of fragile is that? Can you find other examples of this kind of comparison in the poem?

8. What are some of the implications of the word "night" in the last stanza? Compare this with Blake's use of "night" in the last stanza of "Auguries of Innocence."

9. How does the line "The things of the eye are done" relate to the rest of the poem? Is there a pun on the word "eye"?

10. What is the significance of the poem's title? (What is myopia, for instance?)

11. The poem as a whole is held together by mood and continuing point of view. For instance, the lines "as my five senses clenched/their teeth, thought stitched to thought,/as through a needle's eye . . ." are clearly metaphoric. What terms are being juxtaposed? What connection does this metaphor have to the others in the poem? What can you say about the point of view?

Technical Notes

Iambic feet tend to predominate throughout the poem.

LINES OF INQUIRY

The following poems achieve much of their effect through the use of striking metaphors. As you read these poems, consider the following questions:

1. *What are the terms (X and Y) of individual metaphors?*
2. *What is the unlike factor in these metaphors, and how does this make them effective?*
3. *What does the individual metaphor help you perceive? What insights does it evoke?*
4. *How does the poet's use of each individual metaphor add to the overall implications of the poem?*

Edward FitzGerald

from RUBÁIYÁT OF OMAR KHAYYÁM OF NAISHÁPÚR

Come, fill the Cup, and in the fire of Spring
Your Winter-garment of Repentance fling:
　　The Bird of Time has but a little way
To flutter—and the Bird is on the Wing.

Whether at Naishápúr or Babylon,
Whether the Cup with sweet or bitter run,
　　The Wine of Life keeps oozing drop by drop,
The Leaves of Life keep falling one by one.

Each Morn a thousand Roses brings, you say;
Yes, but where leaves the Rose of Yesterday?
　　And this first Summer month that brings the Rose
Shall take Jamshyd and Kaikobád away.

Well, let it take them! What have we to do
With Kaikobád the Great, or Kaikhosrú?
　　Let Zál and Rustum bluster as they will,
Or Hátim call to Supper—heed not you.

With me along the strip of Herbage strown
That just divides the desert from the sown,
　　Where name of Slave and Sultán is forgot—
And Peace to Mahmúd on his golden Throne!

A Book of Verses underneath the Bough,
A Jug of Wine, a Loaf of Bread—and Thou
　　Besides me singing in the Wilderness—
Oh, Wilderness where Paradise enow!

Some for the Glories of This World; and som
Sigh for the Prophet's Paradise to come;
　　Ah, take the Cash, and let the Credit go,
Nor heed the rumble of a distant Drum!

Look to the blowing Rose about us—"Lo,
Laughing," she says, "into the world I blow,
　　At once the silken tassel of my Purse
Tear, and its Treasure on the Garden throw."

And those who husbanded the Golden grain,
And those who flung it to the winds like Rain
　　Alike to no such aureate Earth are turned
As, buried once, Men want dug up again.

The Worldly Hope men set their Hearts upon
Turns Ashes—or it prospers; and anon,
　　Like Snow upon the Desert's dusty Face,
Lighting a little hour or two—is gone.

David Posner

AFTER THE REVOLUTION

The blood on the windows is fresh,
Most of the windows are broken.
Walls slough their cracks.
As the wounds close
My enemies
Tighten in my arms like burnt flesh.
A pair of trousers billows down the gutter
Making an obscene joke.
Far off, a wheel sighs
On the other side of the moon.
In the house across the street
   the empty rooms
Have murdered each other.
Water whispers through the drains
Into my hands.
I lean my sail, ready
To break records, move darkness into light;
Shove my arms in the barrel
For a treasure like snow, like the sea, the sun;
Come up salty, clutching a dead fish—
Its mouth open,
Its eyes pickled.
There's time to sleep before morning.
I roll back the stone from my tomb,
And let the dead day rise.

Anonymous

I HAVE A LITTLE LOVE

I have a little love
across the sea,
and countless signs of love
she's sent to me.

She sent a cherry
with no stone;
sent a dove
with no bones;

a tree without
branches or leaves;
told me of a lover
who never grieves.

Can there be a cherry
without a stone?
A dove without bones?

Can there be a tree
branchless, without a leaf?
Can I love
without grief?

The blossom of a cherry
has no stone;
the egg of a dove
no bones;

the seed of a tree
shows no branch or leaf,
a lover when he's loving
has no grief.

Rendition from Middle English

Gwendolyn Brooks

MY DREAMS, MY WORKS, MUST WAIT TILL AFTER HELL

I hold my honey and I store my bread
In little jars and cabinets of my will.
I label clearly, and each latch and lid
I bid, Be firm till I return from hell.
I am very hungry. I am incomplete.
And none can tell when I may dine again.
No man can give me any word but Wait,
The puny light. I keep eyes pointed in;
Hoping that, when the devil days of my hurt
Drag out to their last dregs and I resume
On such legs as are left me, in such heart
As I can manage, remember to go home,
My taste will not have turned insensitive
To honey and bread old purity could love.

Anne Sexton

THE MOSS OF HIS SKIN

*"Young girls in old Arabia were often buried alive
next to their dead fathers, apparently as sacrifice
to the goddesses of the tribes. . . ." Harold
Feldman, "Children of the Desert,"*
Psychoanalysis and Psychoanalytic Review, *Fall
1958.*

It was only important
to smile and hold still,
to lie down beside him
and to rest awhile,
to be folded up together
as if we were silk,
to sink from the eyes of mother
and not to talk.
The black room took us
like a cave or a mouth
or an indoor belly.
I held my breath
and daddy was there,
his thumbs, his fat skull,
his teeth, his hair growing
like a field or a shawl.
I lay by the moss
of his skin until
it grew strange. My sisters
will never know that I fall
out of myself and pretend
that Allah will not see
how I hold my daddy
like an old stone tree.

Henry Vaughan

THEY ARE ALL GONE INTO
THE WORLD OF LIGHT

They are all gone into the world of light!
   And I alone sit lingring here;
Their very memory is fair and bright,
    And my sad thoughts doth clear.

It glows and glitters in my cloudy brest
   Like stars upon some gloomy grove,
Or those faint beams in which this hill is drest,
    After the Sun's remove.

I see them walking in an Air of glory,
   Whose light doth trample on my days:
My days, which are at best but dull and hoary,
    Meer glimering and decays.

O holy hope! and high humility,
   High as the Heavens above!
These are your walks, and you have shew'd them me
    To kindle my cold love,

Dear, beauteous death! the Jewel of the Just,
   Shining no where, but in the dark;
What mysteries do lie beyond thy dust;
    Could man outlook that mark!

He that hath found some fledg'd birds nest, may know
   At first sight, if the bird be flown;
But what fair Well, or Grove he sings in now,
    That is to him unknown.

And yet, as Angels in some brighter dreams
   Call to the soul, when man doth sleep:
So some strange thoughts transcend our wonted theams,
    And into glory peep.

If a star confin'd into a Tomb
   Her captive flames must needs burn there;
But when the hand that lockt her up, gives room,
    She'l shine through all the sphære.

O Father of eternal life, and all
   Created glories under thee!
Resume thy spirit from this world of thrall
    Into true liberty.

Either disperse these mists, which blot and fill
   My perspective (still) as they pass,
Or else remove me hence unto that hill
   Where I shall need no glass.

The next few poems are based almost entirely on one metaphor or one metaphoric idea. As you read them, consider the following:

1. *What things are being associated, contrasted, or compared to make the metaphor?*
2. *What is the unlike factor in these associations? How does this make the metaphors effective?*
3. *How many different ways is the central metaphor being expressed?*

Anonymous

from THE PEARL

In this early English poem the poet laments the loss of his young daughter and likens her to a lost pearl. What other things might the pearl stand for? The entire poem, of which these two stanzas are a modern translation, contains 100 stanzas, each twelve lines long. In the poem the poet dreams he finds his pearl in the heavenly kingdom.

I
Perfect pearl, a pleasure for princes
To cleanly enclose in gold so clear,
Not in the orient, am I convinced,
Can any preciousness equal her,
So round, so right in every way,
So small, so smooth her curvings were,
Of every jewel I've seen, I say,
I call her clearly beyond compare.
   Alas! in an arbor I lost her;
   Hidden in the high tangled grass;
   For love's lost soul my griefs were:
   Pearl, spotless, perfect, peerless.

II
Since in that spot it from me fell,
I have often stood still, dreaming
Of the good that's gone, my wealth
Weighs on my worn heart false, seeming;
Within I swell and burn and strain.
Yet such a sweet song stays
From that hushed hour, pain
Seems soothed in dreams of other days;
   Images float past in fierce distress:
   To see her set in sullen dirt!
   O earth you stain that sweetness—
   My pearl without a spot or hurt.

Translated from Middle English
by Richard Monaco

Tu Fu

AT THE OUTSKIRTS
OF THE WORLD

I am outside of all mountain ranges.
A wind-rent cloud at the outskirts of the world.
Year on year of strangeness and alien weathers.
The end of every road.
I am Prince of ruin and solitary loss:
An exile in any kind of country.
Even at home I was behind mountains.
Hour by hour I walk my empty road.

Rendition from Chinese by
Richard Monaco

Anonymous

A DULL MAN MIGHT THINK

A dull man might think
a lady a leech;
a sharp one can see
this is false.

A leech only drinks your blood,
swells and is content.
A woman leaves nothing
but the picked bones.

Rendition from Sanskrit

Emily Dickinson

THE AUCTIONEER OF PARTING

The Auctioneer of Parting
His "Going, going, gone"
Shouts even from the Crucifix,
And brings his Hammer down—
He only sells the Wilderness,
The prices of Despair
Range from a single human Heart
To Two—not any more—

Fedérico García Lorca

THE SONG WANTS
TO BE LIGHT

The song wants to be light.
In the darkness the song waits,
phosphorous filaments and pale threads
of moon.
Lucidity not sure of what it wants.
But in its pure limits
it encounters itself,
so is born.

Rendition from Spanish

Edmund Spenser

ONE DAY I WROTE HER NAME
UPON THE STRAND

One day I wrote her name upon the strand,[1]
but came the waves and washed it away:
again I wrote it with a second hand,
but came the tide, and made my pains his pray.
Vain man, said she, that doest is vain assay,
a mortal thing so to immortalize,
for I my self shall like to this decay,
and eke[2] my name be wiped out likewise.
Not so, (quod I) let baser things devise
to die in dust, but you shall live by fame:
my verse your virtues rare shall eternalize,
and in the heavens write your glorious name.
   Where whenas death shall all the world subdue,
   our love shall live, and later life renew.

[1]shore
[2]also

In the next few poems, metaphoric language is spun around subjects that include time, love, and death. As you read the poems, try to see how the poet is metaphorically carrying you beyond his description and statements into deeper awareness.

Dylan Thomas

A REFUSAL TO MOURN THE DEATH, BY FIRE, OF A CHILD IN LONDON

Never until the mankind making
Bird beast and flower
Fathering and all humbling darkness
Tells with silence the last light breaking
And the still hour
Is come of the sea tumbling in harness

And I must enter again the round
Zion of the water bead
And the synagogue of the ear of corn
Shall I let pray the shadow of a sound
Or sow my salt seed
In the least valley of sackcloth to mourn

The majesty and burning of the child's death.
I shall not murder
The mankind of her going with a grave truth
Nor blaspheme down the stations of the breath
With any further
Elegy of innocence and youth.

Deep with the first dead lies London's daughter,
Robed in the long friends,
The grains beyond age, the dark veins of her mother,
Secret by the unmourning water
Of the riding Thames.
After the first death, there is no other.

Gerard Manley Hopkins

I WAKE AND FEEL THE FELL OF DARK

I wake and feel the fell of dark, not day.
What hours, O what black hoúrs
  we have spent
This night! what sights you, heart, saw;
  ways you went!
And more must, in yet longer light's delay.
  With witness I speak this. But where I say
Hours I mean years, mean life.
  And my lament
Is cries countless, cries like dead letters sent
To dearest him that lives alas! away.

   I am gall, I am heartburn. God's most
    deep decree
Bitter would have me taste: my taste was me;
Bones built in me, flesh filled,
  blood brimmed the curse.
  Selfyeast of spirit a dull dough sours. I see
The lost are like this, and their scourge to be
As I am mine, their sweating selves;
  but worse.

Anonymous

SPRING SONG

Lent with love to town is coming,
With blossoms and with birds singing,
All this bliss bringeth;
Daisies in these dales,
Notes sweet of nightingales,
Each bird his song singeth.
The threstelcocks insist: Oh,
Away is their winter woe,
When woodruff bloometh.
So many, many sing
And know the wealth of spring
That all the wood ringeth.

The roses in their colors gleam,
The leaves on the light wood seem
Filling with delight.
The radiant moon is blooming,
The lily's lovely being,
Fennel and fille gleam in the night.
The wild, wooing drakes
Bring joy to their mates,
On flowing streams still and bright.
Hear the lovers complain,
I know I feel that pain,
Sharp passion's cut and bite.

The moon fills, gleaming,
The sweet sun blazes, beaming,
Over bird sounds clear.
Dews moisten the downs;
Beasts whisper secret sounds
And settle love-troubles here.
Under the earth worms woo,
The pride of women should astound you,
That it gives them so much cheer.
If I can have no woman now,
All these rich joys I'll leave, I vow,
And live, a lost creature, in the forest here.

*Translation from
Middle English*

John Donne

HOLY SONNET I

Thou hast made me, And shall thy worke decay?
Repaire me now, for now mine end doth haste,
I runne to death, and death meets me as fast,
And all my pleasures are like yesterday;
I dare not move my dimme eyes any way,
Despaire behind, and death before doth cast
Such terrour, and my feeble flesh doth waste
By sinne in it, which it t'wards hell doth weigh;
Onely thou art above, and when towards thee
By thy leave I can looke, I rise againe;
But our old subtle foe so tempteth me,
That not one houre my selfe I can sustaine;
    Thy Grace may wing me to prevent his art,
    And thou like Adamant draw mine iron heart.

Pablo Neruda

NOTHING BUT DEATH

There are cemeteries that are lonely,
graves full of bones that do not make a sound,
the heart moving through a tunnel,
in it darkness, darkness, darkness,
like a shipwreck we die going into ourselves,
as though we were drowning inside our hearts,
as though we lived falling out of the skin into the soul.

And there are corpses,
feet made of cold and sticky clay,
death is inside the bones,
like a barking where there are no dogs,
coming out from bells somewhere, from graves somewhere,
growing in the damp air like tears or rain.

Sometimes I see alone
coffins under sail,
embarking with the pale dead, with women that have dead
    hair,
with bakers who are as white as angels,
and pensive young girls married to notary publics,
caskets sailing up the vertical river of the dead,
the river of dark purple,
moving upstream with sails filled out by the sound of
    death,
filled by the sound of death which is silence.

Death arrives among all that sound
like a shoe with no foot in it, like a suit with no man in it,
comes and knocks, using a ring with no stone in it, with no
   finger in it,
comes and shouts with no mouth, with no tongue, with no
   throat.
Nevertheless its steps can be heard
and its clothing makes a hushed sound, like a tree.

I'm not sure, I understand only a little, I can hardly see,
but it seems to me that its singing has the color of damp
   violets,
of violets that are at home in the earth,
because the face of death is green,
and the look death gives is green,
with the penetrating dampness of a violet leaf
and the somber color of embittered winter.

But death also goes through the world dressed as a broom,
lapping the floor, looking for dead bodies,
death is inside the broom,
the broom is the tongue of death looking for corpses,
it is the needle of death looking for thread.

Death is inside the folding cots:
it spends its life sleeping on the slow mattresses,
in the black blankets, and suddenly breathes out:
it blows out a mournful sound that swells the sheets,
and the beds go sailing toward a port
where death is waiting, dressed like an admiral.

Translation from Spanish by Robert Bly

Robert Southwell

TIMES GOE BY TURNES

The lopped tree
  In time may grow againe,
Most naked plants
  Renew both fruit and flowre:
The sorriest wight[1]
  May finde release of paine,
The dryest soile
  Suck in some moistning showre.
Times goe by turnes,
  And chances change by course,
From foule to faire,
  From better hap[2] to worse.

The Sea of Fortune
  Doth not ever flow,
She drawes her favours
  To the lowest ebbe;
Her tides have equall times
  To come and goe,
Her Loome doth weave
  The fine and coursest webbe;
No joy so great,
  But runneth to an end:
No hap so hard,
  But may in fine amend.

Not always Fall of leafe,
  Nor ever Spring,
No endlesse night,
  Nor yet eternall day:
The saddest Birds
  A season finde to sing,
The roughest storme
  A calme may soone allay.
Thus with succeeding turnes
  God tempereth all;
That man may hope to rise,
  Yet feare to fall.

A chance may winne
  That by mischance was lost,
That net that holds no great,
  Takes little fish;
In some things all,
  In all things none are crost:
Few all they need,
  But none have all they wish.

Unmedled joyes
  Here to no man befall:
Who least, hath some,
  Who most, hath never all.

[1]creature
[2]circumstance

Eduard Mörike

IM FRÜHLING

Spring lives on this hill around me.
I'm free among clouds and the vivid
Veering of a bird.
Tell me, my single love,
Where are you? I must be with you!
But you live where the wind lives.

My mind and the sunflowers open,
Longing,
Longing upward,
In love and hope.
Spring, why drain me?
What will fill me?

Clouds and the river move,
The sun kisses my blood,
Darkness pulls my eyes,
Sleep presses soft and deep . . .
Only my ear is awake,
Follows the wisping of a bee . . .

My mind unfolds like a cloud:
I wish, I want, I need . . .
What? The hurt and healing.
What? My heart in the shadow
Of goldengreen branches,
The knots and the crossings
Tangle memory,
Old, wordless days . . .

Rendition from German by
Richard Monaco

W. D. Snodgrass

SEEING YOU HAVE . . .

Seeing you have a woman
Whose loves grow thick as the weeds
That keep songsparrows through the year,
Why are you envious of boys
Who prowl the streets all night in packs
So they are equal to the proud
Slender girls they fear?

She's like the tall grass, common,
That sends roots, where it needs,
Six feet into the prairies.
Why do you teach yourself the loud
Hankering voices of blue jays
That quarrel branch by branch to peck
And spoil the bitter cherries?

NOTE ON ILLUSTRATIONS

Do you find you are more interested in reading the poems accompanied by drawings or photographs? Something visual, immediate, and clear is very attractive to most of us. Unfortunately, we often think the opposite of poetry—consider it round-about, abstract, and vague. But in fact the poet's purpose is not unlike the artist's or photographer's: to present an immediate, concrete, "seeable" vision of things. Are you beginning to "see" poetry? As you look at the other illustrations in the book, you might think about the following points:

1. What are the advantages or limitations of seeing the unvarnished object in a photograph? What are the advantages or limitations of seeing an abstract rendering in a drawing?
2. In what sense does the illustrator *illustrate* the poem?
3. Do you have any new insight about the piece as a result of the illustration?
4. Does the illustration tend to fix your experience of the poem, add to it, or detract from it, or is it another experience entirely, essentially unrelated to the poem?

CHAPTER 2
METAPHORIC
LANGUAGE
IN POETRY

We have seen how the metaphoric experience goes beyond poetic subject matter (mistresses, roads, melancholy) and can excite an awareness, an intuitive state, in the mind. Now, to go further, let's consider some varieties of metaphoric language in order to understand the overall mood, effect, and atmosphere of a poem—what is called TONE.

All the fairly simple metaphors we have seen fall into three basic categories. In these we compare, contrast, associate, or identify:

1. An *abstraction* with something *concrete* (or vice versa), e.g., joy/grape, time/wingëd chariot. Most simple metaphors are of this type, though sometimes the second term is unstated, like the overall metaphor of the blackbird in the Stevens poem, where we have a concrete *X* we must connect to *Y* abstractions ourselves.
2. Something *concrete* with something *concrete*, e.g., Keat's "yewberries" (*X*) and the "ruby grape of Proserpine" (*Y*). This is not a very common usage.
3. An *abstraction* with an *abstraction*. This is rarer still; we will see one in Donne's "A Valediction: Forbidding Mourning," where ordinary lovers' souls are said to be "like sense." Usually at least one of the terms is arranged to *seem* concrete.

In the case of combination 1 the abstract term is generally the main subject—the focus of the metaphor (Joy, Time, etc.)—but in combinations 2 or 3 it may be more difficult to tell. For instance, suppose we turn our example around and say: "This red, red rose is like my luve." What is the main subject here? It could still be "my luve," but it might alternatively be the rose. Only the context, the situation in which the statement is made, can tell us for certain which term is the main one. Notice how the main subject directs the metaphor. Sometimes we can discover the subject only through the context, or tone.

What if we said, "The red rose of my luve"? The same *X/Y* relationship would exist, but there's a new angle. Now love is *clearly* abstract. (Of course, we're assuming a context that doesn't refer to a flower on her evening dress.) Then if we alter our choice of words slightly, using more conversational or colloquial diction, we might say: "My girl friend's a real rose." Each of these changes affects the metaphor and how we take it. *Tone* is considered to be the attitude of the poet (as expressed in any one piece) toward his subject matter, and so the way a given metaphor is "put" reflects or expresses the tone.

Another expression or reflection of tone is IRONY. People have talked about socratic irony, verbal irony, cosmic irony, tragic irony, and so on, but what is really taking place in an ironic statement? Perhaps it is not too complicated: "If you don't smoke enough cigarettes, you'll never get lung cancer." The writer says one thing (*X*) but really means something else (*Y*), though, as in this example, the words of the statement might be perfectly true. Irony has to do with being aware of the speaker's intentions in making his statement. It works more or less like metaphor: There is a tension between the literal level and the connotations—for instance, "Nations have been known to make war from time to time." You might call that an ironic UNDERSTATEMENT. It plays off the fact that men have been continually fighting for thousands of years. But because this is not just said outright, the unlike factor between our knowledge of the seriousness of man's continual war making (*X*) and a statement of it as if it were a trivial matter (*Y*) intensifies the statement, puts it in a new light, makes us stop and see it freshly for a moment.

There are many forms of irony. For instance, in understatement the expressed meaning is mild and the intended meaning is intense, as above, while in ironic overstatement (HYPERBOLE) the reverse is true. In some irony a character or statement considered foolish may actually prove wise, or an apparently wise one may prove foolish. In dramatic irony a character may think he is doing one thing while he is really doing something else (Oedipus, when he looks for his father's murderer, is really finding out that the murderer is himself), or something may have one meaning in its immediate context and then turn out to mean something else later on (ironic FORESHADOWING). In heavy irony, called SARCASM, apparent praise is actually dispraise (for example, a conservative commenting on a liberal President: "Oh, he's a *great* man for the White House!"). So in all irony there is a difference, a tension between what a thing means on the surface (*X*) and its recognized "real" meaning (*Y*).

If a poem is consistently ironical, a tone of irony conditions the way it is read and understood. Compare the total sincerity of Blake's "Auguries of Innocence," in the previous chapter, with Marvell's "To His Coy Mistress." In the first case, the metaphors operate within a tone of visionary truth; in the second, the atmosphere is always amusing, and truth is understood with an ironic smile. If we take several metaphors out of each poem and examine them separately, we lose this sense of direction, of tone, in which case Blake might seem funny, or Marvell deadly serious.

Other elements that help establish a poem's tone are pun and paradox. A pun, which we have already touched on, works similarly to irony and metaphor: "Would he had been one of my rank!" one of Shakespeare's characters says, and another replies, "To have smell'd like a fool." So rank as status (*X*) is juxtaposed to rank as a bad smell

(Y). The similarity between X and Y (they are the same word) emphasizes the *unlike factor*, the contrast, between them.

In a PARADOX, X is set up to be equal to the *opposite* of X; thus Y in such cases is the same as X's contradiction, as in Marvell's line (from "Eyes and Tears"), "Yet happy they whom *grief* does bless." So in the paradox, too, the unlike factor gives power to the asserted similarity.

The Shakespeare and Marvell examples of pun and paradox are also examples of irony. Pun and paradox frequently have an ironic effect.

Poetic IMAGES refer to something perceived by the human senses. These are sometimes called *word pictures*, although there are images of sound, touch, taste, and smell as well.

An image, in itself, is a *description*—for example, the wind blowing, a river flowing, the smell or feel of grass or earth, the sound of a gun. At the very least it is a noun: wind, river, grass, gun—in other words, a sound, sight, taste, smell, or touch. The act of poetry is to make the images of experience or imagination (an imaginary animal or place, for instance) metaphoric, that is, to make them mean things they *cannot* describe. This is done either by (1) combining the image into a metaphor (associating time to the image "wingèd chariot," for example) or by (2) placing it in a context where it *functions* as a metaphor (i.e., the description "foregoing whiteness" in Lowell's "Myopia" (page 34) functions as an X with such unstated Y's as innocence, numbness, death, eternity).

The type of image helps determine tone. In order to see this more clearly, let's look at the various types of images possible.

1. *Natural images*   These employ objects in the world, such as flowers, the sea, and the stars, that have intrinsic connotative depth and mystery for the observer regardless of how familiar they are to him.
2. *Technological images*   These involve objects that are fashioned for a particular purpose, such as typewriters, guns, and washing machines, and which have little resonance or depth in themselves since familiarity and science define and explain them thoroughly for the most part. They can become metaphoric, however.
3. *Literary-technological images*   These involve technological objects that possess a kind of *imposed* depth and connotation because they have been used in literature so often—for example, a lyre, an urn, a sword, or a bow. We can even, in certain cases, speak of CONVENTIONAL IMAGES or CLICHÉ images, such as Cupids' arrow.
4. *Literary-natural images*   These involve the use of specific natural images that have added color because of their association with myth, religion, or historical events—for instance, the Styx, holly or yew-berries, and Olympus. Often they are ALLUSIONS, references to a person, place, or event with which the reader is assumed to be familiar, such as the Styx and Olympus.

5. *Natural, nonliterary images, infrequently occurring in literature*
   These involve things which are generally thought of as being prosaic, ugly, unpleasant, and/or lacking in depth and mystery *in themselves*. Obviously, if they are used skillfully in a poem they work as well as anything else. These images include things like fecal matter, zinc oxide, and fungus.

Now, if we were to use these types of images to make simple metaphors, we might have something like:

1. *Natural*   Grandma is (like) a rose.
2. *Technological*   Grandma is (like) a sewing machine.
3. *Literary-technological*   Grandma is (like) a lyre.
4. *Literary-natural*   Grandma is (like) Venus.
5. *Natural, nonliterary*   Grandma is (like) cabbage.

Again, imagery when used as (*a*) contrast, comparison, association, or identification or (*b*) in a context where the tone suggests that we ought to be comparing, associating, etc. becomes metaphoric language. So even putting an individual metaphor in the *X/Y* form (as in the above examples) may not be enough to highlight the similarities and differences and cause the terms to interact. In example 1 the relationship is obvious, but in example 2 it isn't since a sewing machine does not have basic poetic associations for us, the way a rose does. The relationship between it and Grandma is obscure. We need a clearer context, a background, an attitude to establish in what way she is like a sewing machine. Does she stitch her life together? Taken alone, the sentence lacks direction. Try writing a few lines that might bring this image to metaphoric life. For example, what happens if you add the word "rusty"?
Notice that because there is no context, example 1 is rather vague and general, whereas example 2 is virtually nonmetaphoric, though it has possibilities. So in a sense, tone directs, focuses. For instance, if we were to write a poem obviously suggesting that warfare is dreadful and if we capped it with natural images expressed as metaphor—"The soldier's blood like dew upon the grass"—the tone (war is horrible) would condition how we associated the terms of the metaphor. If our imaginary poem treated war as a "glorious struggle, honorable necessity, grim beauty," and so on, the same metaphor would have quite different connotations, suggesting some mystical beauty associated with dying, or the like.
In example 3 we can make some connections to the lyre of Orpheus and so the metaphor, as with examples 1 and 4, is there, if vague and unfocused. Example 5 certainly needs focus, as example 2 does.
So, unlike everyday language, which demands logical, obvious relationships, poetry can contain virtually any number of things

linked as *X/Y*. For example, fill in the blank in "Grandma is like
_____." Provide a context, set up an unlike factor (*X*), and see how it
works. You do not have to write great poetry to test this principle.

A "white dove" is a natural image. If we had the white dove
"circling the bloody battlefield," we would create a tone of violent
contrast: innocent bird (*X*) contrasted to carnage (*Y*). So through this
contextual association we might have a kind of metaphor developed by
contrast. But, someone may point out, a dove *stands for* (is a symbol
of) peace, and thus another kind of meaning is involved. We associate
doves with peace, and so in another sense the fact that we have
chosen a dove to float over the combat (a canary would not do, clearly)
provides an additional contrast, peace versus war. We might say that a
SYMBOL is an image that has meanings *asserted* of it. We just *say* that
the dove means peace; it is a special connotation for the word. Except
in a few cases, all symbols are *conventional*. Various examples are the
cross, the hammer and sickle, the Magen David, the hourglass, and
the scythe. We know pretty well what these symbols stand for, and
so when we assert that dove = peace, we are making the image
"dove" a kind of code word for an idea. Remember that an image
without a context is not metaphoric, but it might be a symbol. For
example, "I'm thinking of a dove" *might* mean "I'm considering
peace." But there is clearly no metaphor. A poetic context might be:
"The soldier with a mind of razor steel is thinking of a dove," where
the image is obviously to be contrasted: steel thoughts (*X*) with soft
dove qualities (*Y*). This context then also *includes* the symbol for
peace.*

Symbol and metaphor, like image and metaphor, are terms often
used interchangeably. What we have called *metaphors with unstated Y
terms*, like the overall metaphor of Stevens' blackbird, are sometimes
called *symbols*.

In order to avoid confusion, we can define "symbol" in a way
commonly agreed on: *In a symbol the Y term is always obvious*, that is,
once you know what meanings or connotations have been assigned to
the image, such as that a dove stands for peace. Paradoxically, you
have to know it is a symbol to get the meaning, and you must know
what it means to see that it is a symbol.

When a poet drops a conventional symbol into a poetic context, it
turns metaphoric, just as an image does. For instance, the natural
image of the beetle is sometimes considered a symbol of death, but in
Keats's "Ode on Melancholy" this image-symbol is metaphoric
because of its general relationship to "melancholy," and its specific
one to "mournful Psyche," and because Keats relies not only on its

---

*On the other hand, suppose we had a nightingale flying over our supposed battlefield.
There is no metaphoric action unless we know that the nightingale is a symbol of
eternal sorrow, grief, immortality. Then we have eternal sorrow (represented by the
bird) associated with the local carnage. Many technological and literary-natural images
have symbolic connotations attached to them.

assigned symbolic meaning (death) but also on its connotations (the insectlike quality).

Suppose we write: "She is in the Lethean forest." Lethe is an *allusion* to classical mythology; it was the river of forgetfulness, from which the dead drank upon their entrance into Hades. Lethe is a symbol because it has come to *stand for* forgetfulness. A sip of its waters, and you forgot all you had known and been in life. But there is an implicit comparison here. She is in a forest which is (like) (1) the shadowy trees around Lethe, (2) a wood of death, (3) a place of forgetfulness, and so on. So Lethe is metaphoric. If you are familiar with the allusion, you pick up meanings like the first two listed above, but unless you know that Lethe is a symbol, meanings along the line of the third one are lost. If you don't know that it's an allusion *or* a symbol, there is no metaphoric effect at all. The tension, the unlike factor, comes in only when you perceive the strain between what Lethe refers to and what an ordinary forest is. Similarly, in reading Lowell's "Myopia: A Night" (page 34), you would have to know that the morning star is Venus, as well as who Venus was, or that it might symbolize Lucifer in order to link those meanings to the poem; however, even if you did not know all this, the morning star could still stand metaphorically as a contrast between the poet's room and something outside it, meanings we'd get from the rich connotations of the natural images of "morning" and "star."

In addition to conventional symbols, with which we are all supposed to be familiar, poets sometimes use symbols of their own devising—PRIVATE SYMBOLS. The principle is the same: The poet (often over the course of his career) *assigns* some specific meaning or meanings to an image, or he may take a conventional symbol and extend it. The important thing is to experience how it becomes metaphoric.

Look at the following extracts from a work by W. B. Yeats (for entire poem see page 317):

III

O sages standing in God's holy fire
As in the gold mosaic of a wall,
Come from the holy fire, perne in a gyre,
And be the singing masters of my soul.

. . . .

IV

Once out of nature I shall never take
My bodily form from any natural thing,
But such a form as Grecian goldsmiths make
Of hammered gold and gold enamelling

To keep a drowsy Emperor awake;
Or set upon a golden bough* to sing
To lords and ladies of Byzantium
Of what is past, or passing, or to come.

There are a number of images here that might be symbols: "perne in a *gyre*," "God's holy fire," and "Byzantium" itself. Sometimes we "feel" that something is a symbol because we sense that if we just knew more about the image, there would be metaphoric action. You might feel that here, with good reason. Let's just consider "Byzantium." Probably we all know something about what that city was and when it was. The poem itself might even suggest things to us about a way of life and a certain time. But only if we study Yeats's works do we discover that it had a special, private symbolic meaning for him (representing, among other things, the poetic imagination). Notice, however, that you do *not* have to know this to experience the poem on a great many levels.

Another element of tone is the sound and pattern of the poem's language: whether the poet uses meter or rhyme or words with similar consonant or vowel sounds. In practice this aspect cannot really be separated from other elements (metaphor, irony, images, symbols, etc.). For example, in Shakespeare's line (from *Macbeth*), "Life's but . . . a poor player that struts and frets his hour upon the stage," can we really say whether Shakespeare chose "struts" and "frets" because of their sound or because of their meaning? Obviously, the sound and the meaning are one unit. The connotation of any word *includes* its sound (i.e., "small" and "tiny"). Similarly, on one level, arranging words in a regular pattern (meter) or repeating similar sounds (rhyme) in a line pattern (verse form) is one way poets shape and direct connotations, a written version of our inflecting or stressing certain words when we talk. In most cases, a poet may use rhyme and meter (or not use it) largely because it is traditional to do so. Sometimes the rhyme-meter form may have a more immediate effect of tone; a singsong meter and clever rhyme might connote irony, humor, or satire, for example, and so become a kind of metaphor where the mechanical sound (X) plays off the mechanical attitudes or gestures of the ridiculed object (Y). In addition, meter, rhyme, measure, stress, or other aspects of sound may serve to give a sense of order to a poem—and by establishing a sound pattern and then varying or contrasting it, emphasis and tension can be produced. Certainly, the ordering of sound as words in poetry (by whatever techniques) sets the poem dynamically off from ordinary speech and other writing. The poetic sound pattern, then, adds intensity to the

*The Golden Bough is a conventional literary symbol connoting special privilege, sovereignty, the key to seeing the world beyond.

way metaphoric language is put. A further inquiry into sound is presented at the end of the book.

So everything we have been discussing helps determine tone. A poem's tone is clearly a composite of many factors—irony, sincerity, metaphor types, intensity, use of symbols, puns, and the choice of words and their particular order or sound. There is no mechanical way to define tone. You have to pick it up the same way you do the levels of meaning in the various metaphoric constructions.

This poem contains so few of the familiar poetic devices that it seems only to describe attending a lecture. Unlike the simple-seeming Frost poem, "A Patch of Old Snow," this one doesn't even include traditional meter or rhyme to make you think of poetry when you read it. Only the way it is printed on the page suggests a relationship to poetic tradition. What is the poet's tone here?

Walt Whitman

WHEN I HEARD THE LEARN'D ASTRONOMER

When I heard the learn'd astronomer,
When the proofs, the figures, were ranged in columns before me,
When I was shown the charts and diagrams, to add, divide, and measure
   them,
When I sitting heard the astronomer where he lectured with much applause
   in the lecture-room,
How soon unaccountable I became tired and sick,
Till rising and gliding out I wander'd off by myself,
In the mystical moist night-air, and from time to time,
Look'd up in perfect silence at the stars.

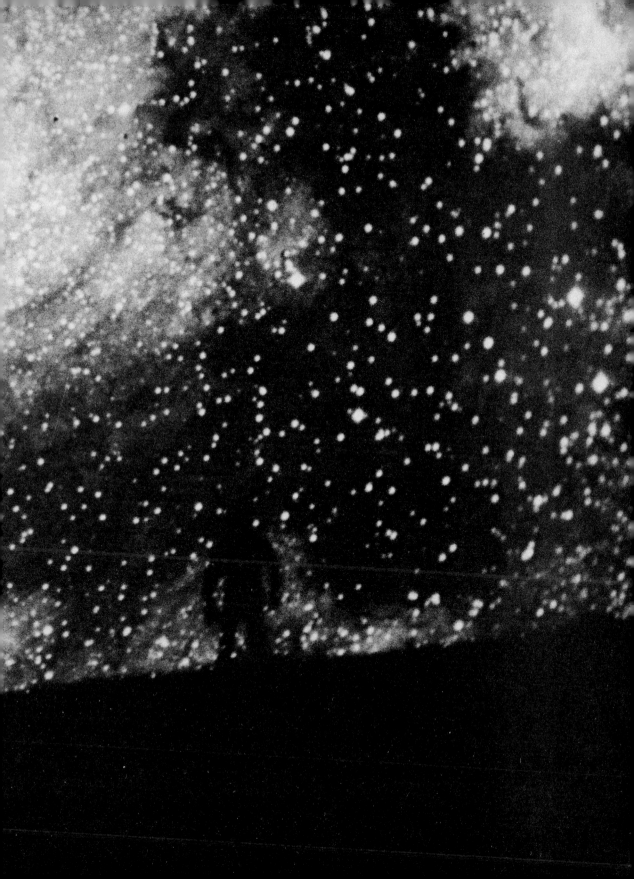

Considerations

Can you discover a metaphor that works the way those we discussed in Chapter 1 did? There doesn't seem to be one, does there? How, then, do we get into this piece?

The whole point, climax, and impact of this poem lie in intense *metaphoric irony*. In this case, it is totally *serious* irony. The astronomer's theories, the limited logic of the human brain (*X*), are contrasted with the vast, absolute reality of the universe (*Y*), which is overwhelmingly visible to anyone who takes the trouble simply to look at it without prejudice, without some theory to expound. This contrast, made through simple, descriptive images with virtually no comment, appears totally to demolish the pedantic, speculative, limited world of the lecturer and, at the same time, to expand our sense of awe. The poet does not overtly say anything negative about the astronomer. The reader has to pick up on that for himself. Whitman apparently does not even want to dignify what men can say about reality to the extent of making any kind of argument in the manner of, say, Marvell or Blake. In effect, he says: "I couldn't listen to it; I went outside and looked at the sky." This is put very subtly: "Looked up in perfect silence at the stars." Notice the contrast of the droning lecture with the "perfect silence." So the comparison that makes the metaphor here is between man's presumptions and the vast, unfathomable universe. The tone results from seemingly artless speech plus deep irony. If you didn't feel the tension between the two areas that are compared, the poem wouldn't have much impact. It would be little more than a description of an evening out.

1. How does the use of the word "learn'd" add to the ironic tone?
2. Is there any irony in the poet's use of the word "unaccountable"?
3. Throughout the poem, Whitman gives us images of what he saw. How do these images react with one another? For example, how does the image "mystical moist night-air" contrast with the astronomer's lecture?
4. What would the effect of this poem have been if the poet had actually drawn attention to the irony? Would it have remained ironic?

Technical Notes

This poem is in free verse, which Whitman popularized.

You should not have any trouble spotting the colossally ironic tone in this poem.

Percy Bysshe Shelley

OZYMANDIAS

I MET a traveller from an antique land
Who said: Two vast and trunkless legs of stone
Stand in the desert . . . Near them, on the sand,
Half sunk, a shattered visage lies, whose frown,
And wrinkled lip, and sneer of cold command,
Tell that its sculptor well those passions read
Which yet survive, stamped on these lifeless things,
The hand that mocked them, and the heart that fed:
And on the pedestal these words appear:
'My name is Ozymandias, king of kings:
Look on my works, ye Mighty, and despair!'
Nothing beside remains. Round the decay
Of that colossal wreck, boundless and bare
The lone and level sands stretch far away.

Considerations

1. What is ironic about the legend on the pedestal
   of Ozymandias's statue?
2. What are the implications of the image in the
   final two lines?

In this poem, a contemporary poet uses metaphoric irony derived from metaphoric imagery which takes us beyond description into some complex emotional territory.

James Merrill

LABORATORY POEM

Charles used to watch Naomi, taking heart > dissect
And a steel saw, open up turtles, live.
While she swore they felt nothing, he would gag
At blood, at the blind twitching, even after
The murky dawn of entrails cleared, revealing
Contours he knew, egg-yellows like lamps paling.

Well then. She carried off the beating heart
To the kymograph and rigged it there, a rag
In fitful wind, now made to strain, now stopped
By her solutions tonic or malign ⇒ injurous
                    Refreshing
Alternately in which it would be steeped.
What the heart bore, she noted on a chart,
            beat

For work did not stop only with the heart.
He thought of certain human hearts, their climb → journey
Through violence into exquisite disciplines
Of which, as it now appeared, they all expired.
Soon she would fetch another and start over,
Easy in the presence of her lover.

Kymograph – records
pressure vibrations

Considerations

In this poem we view a gruesome scene in a biology lab and observe and participate in Charles's reaction to the dissection. Here, through careful use of detail, the poet subtly and ironically juxtaposes love (X) to the procedures Naomi performs on the turtles (Y).

As the poem opens, we find her taking "heart and a steel saw" to begin the dissection. The word "heart" is central: It is an idiom here, as in "You have to have the heart to do it" or "Don't give up, take heart," but we soon discover the pun—Naomi is "taking heart" another way too.

Naomi tells Charles that the turtles feel no pain; nevertheless, he is upset by the sight: "he would gag/At blood, at the blind twitching." "Blood" and "blind twitching" are literal descriptive images of what Charles sees, but notice that already *we* begin to see that something more is involved. Perhaps we feel the impact of the words' associations and connotations: blood as a symbol for life and pain; "blindness" to others and ourselves; the blind fate in which we all "twitch," etc. Naomi's opening up the turtles lays bare a whole area of questions and feelings we have about existence. Do we begin to sense that what Charles sees has something to do with his love for Naomi too?

The image that follows (line five) takes us further into life/death/love implications. "The murky dawn of entrails" is actually a covert metaphor; that is, the turtles' entrails (X) are (like) a "murky dawn'' (*Y*). Both terms of the comparison associate richly with questions of life and death: We commonly connect entrails with emotions or feelings: ''I feel it in my guts''; or with basics: ''the guts of something.'' We connect dawning with coming into being or awareness, as in ''the dawn of life'' or ''it dawned on me.'' Perhaps the meaning of the dissection itself is dawning on Charles.

When the ''dawn of entrails'' clears, what Charles observes is ''contours he knew.'' The word ''contours'' becomes an *X* for a number of possible *Y*'s. What contours? The shape of his relation to Naomi? Of love? Of life? Of death? Of violence? The image of the ''egg-yellow'' color of the entrails like ''lamps paling'' is a double comparison: eggs (*X*) to entrails (*Y*) and then entrails (*X*) to paling lamps (*Y*). What possibilities of meaning do you see here?

 The entrails/lamps metaphor also continues a tension introduced earlier by the ''steel saw'': a tension between the cold technological world of dissection and the organic world of life and death.

Stanza two extends this juxtaposition of the technological to the organic as Naomi carries the ''beating heart'' to a ''kymograph.'' We do not have to know what a kymograph is to sense its passionless, calculating purpose. The whole process of the dissection is being carried out with an inhuman efficiency symbolized by this machine, which measures and tests the disembodied heart for its responses but ignores its essence—life.

The heart subjected to this fatal observation is no more than a ''rag in a fitful wind.'' In Naomi's scientific and logical hands it is ''now made to strain, now stopped/By her solutions tonic or malign'' and watched for reactions. Note the pun on ''solutions.'' Literally they are chemical solutions to speed up or depress the heart's action, but figuratively what are they? Her solutions to life? Her solutions to love? Something she manifests that affects her lover: different moods, etc.? The phrase ''What the heart bore'' refers literally to the turtle's heart, but metaphorically what does it imply?

Stanza three breaks away more sharply from the descriptive tone to reveal the poem's metaphoric intent: the dissection of the turtle's heart (*X*) is associated directly with ''human hearts'' (*Y*). And the ''violence'' and ''exquisite discipline'' of Naomi's skill at dissection are identified with death (''they all expired''). But what kind of death?

Physical? Psychological? Moral? Spiritual? Does ''they'' refer to her past lovers? She ''broke'' all their hearts? What or who is it really that is expiring? Obviously, this is all complexly metaphoric. Though it is never really stated, we feel that what Naomi is doing to the turtles she also does with life and love, and Charles.

The poem's major irony comes clear in the last line. Despite Naomi's cold violence as she slices the turtles, she is ''easy in the presence of her lover.'' But the dissecting skill which she has mastered and which puts her at ease with Charles makes him decidedly *un*easy with her. Love is mentioned for the first time in this line: a word which connotes unity and tenderness here ironically set.

So the tone of the poem is largely the result of (1) a conversational description of the dissection and Charles's reaction to it, (2) a contrast of the mechanical elements of the dissection (*X*) with the organic elements of the thing dissected (*Y*), and (3) the central implied comparison of the dissection (*X*) to love (*Y*). Of course we do not know anything at all about the ''love'' between these lovers *except* through the description of Charles's reaction to the dissection. But we fill in the gaps as the poem begins to extend past the literal statements and images.

1. The egg is associated with birth. Consider the implications of Merrill's identifying the egg with the entrails of the turtle and with ''lamps paling.''
2. Could the word ''dissection'' itself be taken metaphorically (as an *X*)? Aside from the literal cutting into bodies, are other kinds of dissection possibly suggested here?
3. Look at the verb tenses in which this poem is written. What do they tell you?
4. Consider the lines ''tonic or malign/Alternately in which it would be steeped.'' What are some of the metaphoric possibilities here? In other words, what thoughts, feelings, and ideas could this refer to?
5. What insights do you gain from this poem?

Technical Notes

The poem includes exact rhymes (heart–chart, gag–rag) and some slant rhymes (revealing–paling). Iambic meter is the background.

The tone here is obviously not ironic, but clear and straightforward. The poem can be taken only as a sincere, direct inspirational statement based on "inspired" metaphoric imagery. In fact, the poem became a standard hymn in English liturgy.

William Blake

from MILTON

And did those feet in ancient time
Walk upon England's mountains green?
And was the holy Lamb of God
On England's pleasant pastures seen?

And did the Countenance Divine
Shine forth upon our clouded hills?
And was Jerusalem builded here
Among these dark Satanic Mills?

Bring me my Bow of burning gold!
Bring me my Arrows of desire!
Bring me my Spear! O clouds unfold!
Bring me my Chariot of fire!

I will not cease from Mental Fight,
Nor shall my Sword sleep in my hand,
Till we have built Jerusalem
In England's green and pleasant Land.

Considerations

Look at the line "Bring me my Bow of burning gold!" How is it metaphoric? It is obviously an image we can picture; for example, we can imagine a Walt Disney cartoon of a burning golden bow. It is not a picture of something real, of course; it can be put together *only* by the imagination. Notice that this line contains an implicit comparison of the form "the bow is (like) burning gold." The bow could be made of burning wood, and though it would be hard to hold, it would not be a metaphor. Can you see why not? Because a mental picture is drawn, the *image itself*, apart from the metaphoric relationship of bow to gold, becomes an X, and we have Y levels such as a glorious war, a war of gold, fire and light, a spiritual war.

In the "arrows of desire" metaphor, mentioned before, you cannot actually imagine arrows which are (like) desires. You can only sense this combination; there is no picture. So we discover that the effect of linking a *concrete* term with a *concrete* term, as with the bow and gold, can produce a picture (and it might, in other cases, cause us to imagine sounds or smells, etc.), while linking an *abstract* with a *concrete* term (desires, arrows) has a different impact, perhaps more interesting, because it forces the mind instantly to give up its familiar patterns of association—like imagining pictures, for instance. Poetry, for the most part, aims at this dynamic state of awareness.

What about "these dark Satanic Mills"? What do we "see" here? Does "Satanic Mills" mean mills that are *like* Satan? Mills that Satan operates? Blake says they are in England, but did they come from hell? Are they incarnate evil ideas? Are workers there in a kind of hell? "Satanic" might call up images of fire and brimstone: imagine in the lush English countryside the sight of squat, soot-darkened factories belching black smoke and orange flame. It might recall paintings of hell. So there is a kind of *concrete* term in "Satanic." But, on the other hand, we have never actually seen what this *literary image* refers to (unlike gold, burning or otherwise), and much of the metaphor's suggestive intensity results from linking an *abstract* with a *concrete* term.

In the last line, "built Jerusalem" is another kind of symbol-metaphor. Jerusalem has traditional connotations, and these are applied to the context.

Certainly the poet does not mean to move the actual city to England. What *does* he mean?

1. Do you think the last two lines of the poem are as intense as the bow-and-arrow pair? How does this affect the tone?
2. What is meant by "Mental Fight"?
3. Does the metaphoric image "bow of burning gold" seem symbolic to you, as if it had conventional meanings assigned to it, as if the poet had said, "Bring me my cross"? Part of the symbolic feeling of this metaphoric image is the result of the poem's tone. Can you see how?

Technical Notes

The second and fourth lines of each stanza rhyme—a BALLAD STANZA. Note in the last stanza the additional slant rhyme of "land" and "Jerusalem." The background rhythm is iambic.

The next piece uses metaphoric image in the context of a direct and philosophic tone—as if the poet wants to explain some ideas about "the knowledge of silence," to express what it is. But while a philosopher might take hundreds of pages and invent a complicated logical system to explain the relation of silence to self, the poet does it in a few lines. And while the philosopher's system might be refuted in argument, the poet has no system to refute. Since he does not start with a premise, he has no conclusions. He offers instead images and metaphors which point at what he sensed, at the momentary flash of truth which is understood not as thought but as living experience.

Alfred Dorn
THE KNOWLEDGE OF SILENCE

Silence is not an empty room
Where entering mind grows void in vacancy,
But a museum where the self collects
Its past in marble.
          Here is yet the bloom
Of vanished laughter held in tinted stone,
For here is all that sculpting mind has known.
Here is the white lucidity of tasks
Perfected; here stand jagged blocks of pain
Broken from time.
          And here the mind at last
Endures the pitiless light beneath its masks.

Considerations

1. Consider the opening line. Although the poet denies that silence (X) is like an empty room (Y), are these terms united in some way? How?
2. Consider the images in the poem (such as "vanished laughter held in tinted stone" or "the white lucidity of tasks"). Are these also metaphors?
3. How do all the metaphors and metaphoric images relate to one another in this poem? What things is the marble related to, for example?
4. What are the masks, and what do they have to do with sculpture and silence? Do you see how, in effect, the last two lines are juxtaposed to the rest of the poem as an X to a Y? What is the "pitiless light"?
5. What is the "knowledge" of silence?
6. Though this poem does not have the if-then logician's tone of "To His Coy Mistress," there is a definite feeling of reasonableness about it. Can you account for this tone?

Technical Notes

Although not a regular pattern, the rhyme scheme of the poem is *a b c d a a a e f f e e*. Note the use of INTERNAL RHYME. Rhyme is employed to give the poem a sense of closure and adds to the "reasonable" tone, as if the thoughts were neat and complete. Note the slant rhyme at the end. All lines except the third are iambic pentameter.

This Wallace Stevens poem takes as its ostensible subject metaphoric imagery itself. In "Thirteen Ways of Looking at a Blackbird" we found that, overall, the blackbird was an X with many possible Y's. Here, Stevens envisions the world as full of images that stand as the metaphoric X. What is the tone of this poem?

Wallace Stevens

THE MOTIVE FOR METAPHOR

You like it under the trees in autumn,
Because everything is half dead.
The wind moves like a cripple among the leaves
And repeats words without meaning.

In the same way, you were happy in spring,
With the half colors of quarter-things,
The slightly brighter sky, the melting clouds,
The single bird, the obscure moon—

The obscure moon lighting an obscure world
Of things that would never be quite expressed,
Where you yourself were never quite yourself
And did not want nor have to be,

Desiring the exhilarations of changes:
The motive for metaphor, shrinking from
The weight of primary noon,
The A B C of being,

The ruddy temper, the hammer
Of red and blue, the hard sound—
Steel against intimation—the sharp flash,
The vital, arrogant, fatal, dominant X.

Considerations

Who is the "you" the poet addresses in the first line? The reader? The poet himself? Another poet? Perhaps all these. But whoever it is, the narrator (or VOICE) of the poem obviously treats the "you" in an ironic tone, approaching sarcasm. The irony comes out of contrasting the you's rather pale, timid preference for "half colors" and "quarter-things" (X) with a hard, vital, dominant reality (Y)

represented as the "weight of primary noon,/The ABC of being." In the face of this reality the "you" and his "motive for metaphor" are "shrinking."

Notice Stevens' use of images: "The slightly brighter sky, the melting clouds,/The single bird, the obscure moon." Sky, clouds, birds, and the moon are natural images that already have a great many associations for us. On one level, Stevens is showing us that they are potential metaphoric terms, and the list suggests that the world is alive with such things: the raw material of the poet's trade. Stanza three describes the tone of this world of potential metaphor; it could as well be a description of our reaction to a good poem: "Of things that would never be quite expressed,/Where you yourself were never quite yourself/And did not want nor have to be."

Against this poetic world of "intimation" the poet contrasts the world of "steel" in the final stanza, a world where things are clear, hammered out, "vital, arrogant, fatal, dominant." One way of seeing this is to take Stevens' poem as contrasting the blunt, undeniable facts of reality (X) with vague, shadowy "intimation" (Y), a kind of shrinking back from reality. But could we also see this whole idea as subtly ironic? Isn't this reality, the "dominant X," presented not as itself but through metaphor? Isn't the letter "X" itself a metaphor? Can you see this? Obviously, we can get at the reality, "X," only through metaphoric images such as those Stevens has given us (in this case, technological): the red and blue hammer, the steel, the "weight of primary noon." So from this angle the motive for metaphor may be the desire not to shrink from reality but to *discover* it, though this comes about only through "intimation," indirectly, because the image-metaphors are never the Absolute; they can only suggest it. Seen this way, the time of moons and birds and the one of steel and primary noon are really the same, though one is a gentle season, and the other is harsh. So these metaphoric images become tools for discovering the unknown, the "dominant X."

1. Can you see other ways in which the ironic contrast between the gentle and harsh worlds account for this poem's tone? What effect do the ironies have on our interpretations?

2. What do you think the motive for metaphor is? Can we ever give a final answer to this?

3. Can we really tell whether Stevens' "X" refers to the blunt outward facts of existence or to the unknown that lies behind existential facts? Or both? Are these two ways of looking at the poem really contradictory?

4. Who do you feel the "you" of the poem is? Why?

5. Consider individual lines and phrases, such as "The wind moves like a cripple among the leaves" or "Desiring the exhilarations of changes." What relation do they bear to the central metaphor, which juxtaposes the poet's world to reality? What are the levels of meaning?

6. Consider the line "And repeats words without meaning." What are some of the possible implications of this line in terms of the whole poem?

7. Why is the "you" of the poem said to be "happy" in the autumn and spring?

8. Stevens used the color blue in many of his poems as a private symbol for the aesthetic or artistic function. How does the color relate to this particular poem if that meaning is added? What do you associate with blue? Do you have other associations that might be relevant here? What about red?

9. Might the seasons themselves be private symbols for Stevens? Do you sense this possibility here? Find out what Stevens wanted these symbols to stand for.

Technical Notes

Note the use of ASSONANCE (spring–slightly–bright–bird–melting). The rhythm is a recurrent accentual TRIMETER.

Here an early-twentieth-century poet uses conventional symbols to enrich his brief, violent vision of modern life.

Hart Crane

MOMENT FUGUE

The syphilitic selling violets calmly
    and daisies
By the subway news-stand knows
        how hyacinths

This April morning offers
    hurriedly
In bunches sorted freshly—
        and bestows
On every purchaser
          (of heaven perhaps)

His eyes—
        like crutches hurtled against glass
Fall mute and sudden (dealing change
    for lilies)
Beyond the roses that no flesh can pass.

Considerations

A man suffering from a sexual disease is selling flowers. The tone of violent vision results largely from the clashing ironic juxtaposition of disease (*X*) with (*Y*) fresh flowers, natural objects considered pure, sweet, delicate.

The flowers are obviously metaphoric, an *X* we are meant to connect with some *Y* or *Y*'s. In the last line of the second stanza the poet gives us one possible connection: flowers stand for heaven ("perhaps").

In the third stanza, the flowers are used symbolically, as discussed earlier in the chapter: lilies are the conventional symbol for death and resurrection, and roses are the symbol for God, love, redemption. Could April also be a symbol? Thus the basic metaphoric association of the flowers with heaven is extended here by specific symbolic associations.

1. Consider some of the implications of the fact that it is a "syphilitic" selling these flowers. What kinds of things has the flower seller come to represent by the end of the poem?
2. Why might the flower seller be offering his flowers "hurriedly"?
3. What are some of the implications of the line "His eyes—/like crutches hurled against glass/Fall mute and sudden"?
4. Can you see several puns in this poem? If so, what levels do they add?
5. Look at the title of the poem. What is a fugue? Why is the poem a "moment fugue"? (You will probably want to look at the poem's shape and line arrangement when you consider this.) How do the meter and grammatical structures intensify this piece?
6. What are some of the possible levels of meaning in the last line?
7. Do you see any symbols here? What is their effect?

Technical Notes

The poem employs iambic pentameter irregularly broken into HEMISTICHES. Only the final line is whole. There are occasional rhymes (eyes–lilies, glass–pass).

In this poem the familiar rose is obviously metaphoric, but Blake also had some specific private symbolic meanings in mind. First see how much you can get from the poem directly; then you might want to find out what specific things Blake wanted his sick rose to stand for. Does the idea of a sick rose itself contribute to the poem's tonal effect?

William Blake

THE SICK ROSE

O Rose, thou art sick!
The invisible worm
That flies in the night,
In the howling storm,

Has found out thy bed
Of crimson joy,
And his dark secret love
Does thy life destroy.

Baudelaire was the first great French "symbolist" poet. He believed that the phenomena of the world were symbols through which we could contact spiritual realities and transform our sense perceptions. So he used many private and conventional symbols in his poems. But whatever symbolic meanings he assigned to his images, we can see in this poem how they combine into metaphors, and we can understand the piece well enough without knowing what Baudelaire wanted his symbols to mean. How would you describe the tone of this piece?

Charles Baudelaire

CORRESPONDENCES

The whole world is a temple from whose living columns
Issue forth at times a host of commingled words;
Man passes through, surrounded by such forests of symbols,
Symbols that watch him out of kindred interest.
As, at a distance, overlapping echoes merge
To mingle in a unity of depth and shadow,
Vast as the night, vast as the effulgence of the day,
So scents and sounds and colors tally with one another.

Perfumes there are, fresh and cool as the flesh of children,
Sweet to the taste as oboes, green as meadows—
And there are other perfumes, rich, corrupt, triumphant,
Able to expand in space like infinite things:

    Musk and amber, benjamin and frankincense.
    These are what sing the ecstasies of soul and sense.

Translation from French by Christopher Collins

Considerations

1. Obviously, the key metaphor of the poem is that the terrain of the world (*X*) is a living (organic) temple of symbols (*Y*). What are the other metaphors based on this one?
2. Consider in detail some of these secondary metaphors, for example, the one beginning "As, at a distance. . . ." What kinds of levels does the word "tally" add to this metaphor? How are these secondary metaphors linked to the main one? What part do all the metaphors play in creating the tone of the poem?
3. Consider the thesis of the poem. Is the world full of symbols? If so, in what way? What part does the thesis play in the tone of the poem?
4. You might want to do some research to find out what private symbols Baudelaire used in this poem and then reread it to see what

meaning your knowledge of these symbols adds to the poem.
5. What are the many possibilities in the line "Able to expand in space like infinite things"?
6. Compare this piece to "Motive for Metaphor." Stevens showed us the intimate relation between *image* and metaphor; how does this Baudelaire poem demonstrate the connection between *symbol* and metaphor?

Technical Notes

The poem in the original French is a SONNET. In this translation the rhymes have been omitted, but the original iambic HEXAMETER (ALEXANDRINES) has been retained.

The tone of this poem is based on a series of puns.

Stephen Spender
SUBJECT: OBJECT: SENTENCE

A subject thought: because he had a verb
With several objects, that he ruled a sentence.
Had not Grammar willed him these substantives
Which he came into, as his just inheritance?

His objects were *wine, women, fame* and *wealth,*
And a subordinate clause—*all life can give.*
He grew so fond of having these that, finally,
He found himself becoming quite subjective.

Subject, the dictionary warned means *someone ruled by
Person or thing.* Was he not *having's* slave?
To achieve detachment, he must be *objective*
Which meant to free himself from the verb *have.*

Seeking detachment, he studied the context
Around his sentence, to place it in perspective:
Paraphrased, made a critical analysis,
And then re-read it, feeling more *objective.*

Then, with a shock, he realized that *sentence*
Like *subject-object* is treacherously double.
A sentence is condemned to stay as stated—
As in *life-sentence, death-sentence,* for example.

Considerations

1. What puns do you see here, and how does the
   poet play on the double meanings of these
   words?
2. Besides using direct puns, in what ways does
   the poet play off grammar itself in order to
   evoke levels of meaning?

In this piece, the poet is employing sound as a metaphoric device, juxtaposing tightly held meter and rhyme patterns (X) with a complaint against them (Y). A humorous tone results.

Ben Jonson

A FIT OF RIME AGAINST RIME

Rime, the rack of finest wits,
That expresseth but by fits,
                    True Conceipt,[1]
Spoyling Senses of their Treasure,
Cosening Judgement with a measure,
                    But false weight.
Wresting words, from their true calling;
Propping Verse, for feare of falling
                    To the ground.
Joynting Syllabes, drowning Letters,
Fastning Vowells, as with fetters
                    They were bound!
Soone as lazie thou wert knowne,
All good Poëtrie hence was flowne,
                    And Art banish'd.
For a thousand yeares together,
All *Parnassus*[2] Greene did wither,
                    And wit vanish'd.
Pegasus[3] did flie away,
At the Wells no Muse did stay,
                    But bewailed
So to see the Fountaine drie,
And *Apollo's*[4] Musique die,
                    All light failed!
Starveling rimes did fill the Stage,
Not a Poët in an Age,
                    Worth a crowning.
Not a worke deserving Baies,[5]
Nor a lyne deserving praise,
                    Pallas[6] frowning.

Greeke was free from Rimes infection,
Happy Greeke, by this protection,
                    Was not spoyled.
Whilst the Latin, Queene of Tongues,
Is not yet free from Rimes wrongs,
                    But rests foiled.
Scarce the Hill againe doth flourish,
Scarce the world a Wit doth nourish,
                    To restore
Phoebus[7] to his Crowne againe;
And the Muses to their braine:
                    As before.
Vulgar Languages that want
Words, and sweetnesse, and be scant
                    Of true measure,
Tyran[8] Rime hath so abused,
That they long since have refused
                    Other ceasure.
He that first invented thee,
May his joynts tormented bee,
                    Cramp'd for ever;
Still may Syllabes jarre with time,
Still may reason warre with rime,
                    Resting never.
May his Sense, when it would meet
The cold tumor in his feet,
                    Grow unsounder.
And his Title be long foole,
That in rearing such a Schoole,
                    Was the founder.

[1]Conceit: poetic conception, possible pun
[2]Mountain in Greece, symbolic of poetic inspiration
[3]Winged horse; symbolic of poetry
[4]Greek god of poetry
[5]Bays—prize for excellence
[6]Athena, Greek goddess of the arts

[7]Apollo
[8]Tyrant

Considerations

1. In what ways is Jonson's technique in this poem similar to Spender's in "Subject: Object: Sentence"?
2. What things does Jonson associate with rhyme ("rime") in this poem?
3. In what ways does Jonson's own use of rhyme add to the meaning of the poem?
4. What is Jonson's complaint against rhyme? Is that complaint ironic? That is, is there a sense in which he is really praising rhyme too? Consider the title.
5. Notice the poet's use of allusions (references) to Greek mythology (Pegasus, Apollo, Pallas, etc.). What implicit connections does this make between poetry and myth?

A central paradox sparks the Earl of Rochester's witty tone and creates surprising reversals and twists of association. We said that a paradox is like a metaphoric relationship except that instead of X/Y, we have X equals not-X. In other words, paradoxical statements seem self-contradictory. You should be able to spot the major paradox in this poem fairly easily.

John Wilmot, Earl of Rochester

UPON NOTHING

Nothing! thou Elder Brother ev'n to Shade,
Thou hadst a being ere the World was made,
And (well fixt) art alone, of Ending not afraid.

Ere Time and Place were, Time and Place were not,
When Primitive *Nothing* something streight begot,
Then all proceeded from the great united—What.

Something, the gen'ral Attribute of all,
Sever'd from thee, its sole Original.
Into thy boundless self must undistinguish'd fall.

Yet Something did thy mighty Pow'r command,
And from thy fruitful Emptiness's Hand,
Snatch'd Men, Beasts, Birds, Fire, Air, and Land.

Matter, the wickedest Off-spring of thy Race,
By Form assisted, flew from thy Embrace,
And Rebel Light obscur'd thy reverend dusky Face.

With Form and Matter, Time and Place did join;
Body, thy Foe, with thee did Leagues combine,
To spoil thy peaceful Realm, and ruin all thy Line.

But Turn-Coat Time assists the Foe in vain,
And, brib'd by thee, assists thy short-liv'd Reign,
And to thy hungry Womb drives back thy Slaves again.

Tho' Mysteries are barr'd from Laick⁰ Eyes,
And the Divine alone, with Warrant, pries
Into thy Bosom, where the Truth in private lies:

Yet this of thee the Wise may freely say,
Thou from the Virtuous nothing tak'st away,
And to be part with thee the Wicked wisely pray.

Great Negative, how vainly wou'd the Wise
Enquire, define, distinguish, teach, devise?
Didst thou not stand to point their dull Philosophies.

Is, or *is not*, the Two great Ends of Fate,
And, true or false, the Subject of Debate,
That perfect, or destroy, the vast Designs of Fate;

When they have rack'd the *Politician's* Breast,
Within thy Bosom most securely rest,
And, when reduc'd to thee, are least unsafe and best.

But, *Nothing*, why does *Something* still permit,
That Sacred Monarchs should at Council sit,
With Persons highly thought at best for nothing fit.

Whilst weighty *Something* modestly abstains,
From Princes Coffers, and from Statesmen's Brains
And Nothing there like stately *Nothing* reigns.

Nothing, who dwell's with Fools in grave Disguise,
For whom they reverend Shapes, and Forms devise,
Lawn Sleeves, and Furrs, and Gowns, when they like
    thee look wise.

French Truth, *Dutch* Prowess, *British* Policy,
Hibernian Learning, *Scotch* Civility,
Spaniards Dispatch, *Danes* Wit, are mainly seen in thee.

The Great Man's Gratitude to his best Friend,
Kings Promises, Whores Vows, towards thee they bend,
Flow swiftly into thee, and in thee ever end.

⁰layman's

Considerations

The trick is, of course, that the poet has personified the abstraction "nothing" as if it were some god and so has turned *nothing* into *something*. This something/nothing becomes the creator whose creations are all reversed: "And from thy fruitful Emptiness's Hand,/Snatch'd men, Beasts, Birds, Fire, Air, and Land." The tone of praise for this god becomes SATIRE, in which the poet undercuts the vanities (the somethings) of scholars and philosophers and virtually everything we accept as substance—because we ironically see it all as nothing. So though the poem is humorous, it points to a rather serious insight.

1. Consider the paradoxical elements of "And Rebel Light obscur'd thy reverend dusky Face." The implicit terms of this metaphor-paradox rely on the simple reversal: light (*X*) = darkness (*Y*), since we normally think of darkness as obscuring things. Find other examples of metaphor relying on this kind of reversal. What might "Rebel" in "Rebel Light" be an allusion to?

2. Beyond satire, what are some of the other implications of the poet's identification of nothing with the various somethings of the poem? What levels of meaning does he generate through this paradox?

This Marvell poem is laced with paradox. What other dimensions of tone do you perceive?

Andrew Marvell

EYES AND TEARS

How wisely Nature did decree,
With the same eyes to weep and see!
That, having viewed the object vain,
They might be ready to complain.

And, since the self-deluding sight,
In a false angle takes each height;
These tears which better measure all,
Like wat'ry lines and plummets fall.

Two tears, which sorrow long did weigh
Within the scales of either eye,
And then paid out in equal poise,
Are the true price of all my joys.

What in the world most fair appears,
Yea even laughter, turns to tears:
And all the jewels which we prize,
Melt in these pendants of the eyes.

I have through every garden been,
Amongst the red, the white, the green;
And yet, from all the flowers I saw,
No honey, but these tears could draw.

So the all-seeing sun each day
Distills the world with chemic ray;
But finds the essence only showers,
Which straight in pity back he pours.

Yet happy they whom grief doth bless,
That weep the more, and see the less:
And, to preserve their sight more true,
Bathe still their eyes in their own dew.

So Magdalen, in tears more wise
Dissolved those captivating eyes,
Whose liquid chains could flowing meet
To fetter her Redeemer's feet.

Not full sails hasting loaden home,
Nor the chaste lady's pregnant womb,
Nor Cynthia teeming shows so fair,
As two eyes swoln with weeping are.

The sparkling glance that shoots desire,
Drenched in these waves, does lose its fire.
Yea oft the Thund'rer pity takes
And here the hissing lightning slakes.

The incense was to Heaven dear,
Not as a perfume, but a tear.
And stars show lovely in the night,
But as they seem the tears of light.

Ope then mine Eyes your double Sluice,
And practise so your noblest Use.
For others too can see, or sleep;
But only humane Eyes can weep.

Now like two Clouds dissolving, drop,
And at each Tear in distance stop:
Now like two Fountains trickle down:
Now like two floods o'return and drown.

Thus let your Streams o'reflow your Springs,
Till Eyes and Tears be the same things:
And each the other's difference bears;
Those weeping Eyes, those seeing Tears.

Considerations

Paradox and irony can be very close, as witness the opening stanza here. The poet says that ironically, almost paradoxically, nature gives us eyes to see the world *in order to weep* because the world we see is utterly vain. Moving through the poem, you discover that this ironic-paradoxical tone persists to the very end.

Alternately and together, "eyes" and "tears" are terms of individual metaphors throughout the piece. In the last stanzas, they are united as in the opening lines: Eyes become tears, which is to say that eyes = tears, a paradoxical relationship. Marvell's paradox conveys profound seriousness without losing distance: "Those weeping eyes, those seeing tears." How is the intensity of those last three words bound up with the very paradox of the statement? One level of "those seeing tears" might be paraphrased as "Grief or grieving allows us to 'see' things as they really are." In various ways the whole poem echoes this.

1. Identify the paradoxes.
2. Try putting the irony here into words.
3. What can you say about the tone? Is it really serious? Funny?
4. Consider the different things the poet relates metaphorically to eyes and/or tears. What levels of meaning do you get from each of these metaphoric relationships?
5. Is the word "garden" in the fifth stanza a metaphor? Could it also be a symbol?
6. In the last stanza, what kinds of things does the poet mean by "And each the other's difference bears"? How is that related to the eyes/tears paradox?

The tone of this poem is established by the voice of a man thoughtfully talking about his sense of approaching death. The overall attitude of the speaker is easy to perceive and is conveyed through several direct metaphors which give the ideas great force.

William Shakespeare

THAT TIME OF YEAR . . .

That time of year thou mayst in me behold
When yellow leaves, or none, or few, do hang
Upon those boughs which shake against the cold,
Bare ruined choirs, where late the sweet birds sang.
In me thou see'st the twilight of such day
As after sunset fadeth in the west,
Which by and by black night doth take away,
Death's second self that seals up all in rest.
In me thou see'st the glowing of such fire,
That on the ashes of his youth doth lie,
As the death-bed, whereon it must expire
Consumed with that which it was nourished by.
   This thou perceiv'st, which makes thy love more strong
   To love that well, which thou must leave ere long.

Considerations

1. Notice that the narrator of the poem implicitly compares life (*X*) to a year (*Y*). This spring/youth, winter/age, is almost cliché poetic association. How does Shakespeare put life into it?

2. Consider the metaphor of the fire and ashes. Is it a paradox?

3. What is the relation of the final couplet to the rest of the poem?

contradictory statement that may none the less be true

Contrast the previous poems in this chapter with this one. What is the tone here? How is it achieved? Does the moon function metaphorically here?

George Gordon, Lord Byron

SO WE'LL GO NO MORE A-ROVING

1
So we'll go no more a-roving
  So late into the night,
Though the heart be still as loving,
  And the moon be still as bright.

2
For the sword outwears its sheath,
  And the soul wears out the breast,
And the heart must pause to breathe,
  And Love itself have rest.

3
Though the night was made for loving,
  And the day returns too soon,
Yet we'll go no more a-roving
  By the light of the moon.

In this next poem the seventeenth-century poet John Donne achieves a remarkable tone by consciously and artfully keeping the distance between the X *and* Y *terms so great that the unlike factor borders on being absurd.*

This poem is considered particularly difficult. Chapter 7 deals with poems of this order, but let's see how far we can go into it with the experience we already have.

John Donne

A VALEDICTION: FORBIDDING MOURNING

As virtuous men passe mildly away,
  And whisper to their soules, to goe,
Whilst some of their sad friends doe say,
  The breath goes now, and some say, no:

So let us melt, and make no noise,
  No teare-floods, nor sigh-tempests move,
T'were prophanation of our joyes
  To tell the layetie our love.

Moving of th'earth brings harmes and feares,
  Men reckon what it did and meant,
But trepidation of the spheares,
  Though greater farre, is innocent.

Dull sublunary lovers love
  (Whose soule is sense) cannot admit
Absence, because it doth remove
  Those things which elemented it.

But we by a love, so much refin'd,
  That our selves know not what it is,

Inter-assured of the mind,
  Care lesse, eyes, lips, and hands to misse.

Our two soules therefore, which are one,
  Though I must goe, endure not yet
A breach, but an expansion,
  Like gold to airy thinnesse beate.

If they be two, they are two so
  As stiffe twin compasses are two,
Thy soule the fixt foot, makes no show
  To move, but doth, if th'other doe.

And though it in the center sit,
  Yet when the other far doth rome,
It leanes, and hearkens after it,
  And growes erect, as that comes home.

Such wilt thou be to mee, who must
  Like th'other foot, obliquely runne;
Thy firmnes drawes my circle just,
  And makes me end, where I begunne.

Considerations

The important tonal elements are immediately apparent in this poem: (1) exaggeration (a characteristic of Donne's poetry) and (2) an exposition that *seems* logical. Remember we also saw this poetic logic, as well as exaggerated or strange metaphors, in "To His Coy Mistress." Poets who used these techniques in the seventeenth-century came to be called METAPHYSICAL POETS. Both Marvell and Donne are prime exponents of this STYLE.

In order to keep his exaggerations from becoming absurd, Donne speaks (in the poem) as though he were making a reasoned argument. In the first two stanzas he says, in effect, "*Since* good men die peacefully in a subtle way, *therefore* he and his lady should part without weeping or showing their feelings." If you separate this argument from the poem, it's clearly not very convincing, but is it really meant to convince?

Donne maintains the premise-conclusion form (since-therefore, if-then) for almost the entire poem. In addition, he maintains exaggeration on at least two levels: (1) the distance between the things compared (dying men to lovers, compasses to lovers, etc.) and (2) exaggeration of emotion and idea ("virtuous men" whispering to their souls or Donne telling his lover to produce no "teare-floods, no sigh-tempests"). This kind of intensification cannot be reduced to something like: "Don't be upset when I leave, honey, because I'll love you wherever I am." Donne goes deeply into the idea and experience of love and parting while still keeping his sense of humor and irony. This

attitude also helps prevent the extremes from becoming silly: he establishes the tone by revealing his feelings without losing a certain distance and perspective. Compare this with the Burns rose poem, where the voice of the poet becomes increasingly melodramatic and sentimental.

Though in the first two stanzas the speaker has not actually said he is parting from his lover, the idea of separation is certainly implicit: The image of the soul leaving the body (*X*) in stanza one is compared to the second-stanza image of lover parting from lover (*Y*). Through this relationship a sense of quiet beauty and holiness, sadness and virtue, is suggested. The most important meanings in this relationship are actually unstated. They exist, as in other examples, as a sum of *X* + *Y*. When we paraphrase them, they instantly lose their power, and the poetic tension dissipates. Since poetic tension is a state of insight, coming to a conclusion (paraphrase) puts an end to that state.

In the second stanza, we also have an example of a single word acting as metaphor: "layetie," which means laymen, worldly people. Would this term have much force if instead Donne had said "other people"? Not only does "layetie" connect with the mood of sacredness already established, but it also suggests that only other lovers in the purest state of love, only those who truly love (without worldly, egotistical desires), are fit to hear of these feelings or capable of understanding them. Notice that you can perceive and experience this immediately in the poem, but to discuss it takes a disproportionate amount of space and time.

Right from the first two stanzas the idea of spirit versus flesh is being played on. Donne keeps hinting that even if bodies are apart, souls remain in touch. In the third stanza we are told that the earth (which is physical *like* the body—a covert metaphor) moves (experiences earthquakes, tidal waves, etc.); we are also told that when the spheres* tremble, though their motion is as vast as

*Spheres were considered to be invisible forces that sustain and shape the visible universe, each one defined by the orbit of a particular planet; thus there was a "lower" sphere, like the sphere of the moon, and a higher sphere—the sphere of Jupiter, for example.

space and proportionately profound, it is undetectably subtle and troubles no one. So from this angle we have returned to the idea that souls are mild and gentle and cause no problems when they act. Desires (particularly physical desires) cause trouble. This, same basic metaphoric relationship has been extended from stanza one.

In the fourth stanza the expression "sublunary lovers" continues the metaphoric contrast between earth/body (X) and soul/heaven (Y). "Sublunary" (under the moon) refers not only to the earth—earthly concerns—but also to the place ruled by the moon (from astrology), where there is birth, death, and corruption. The sublunary was the lowest of the spheres. Here Donne continues the "logical," reasonable tone: "Dull sublunary lovers love/(Whose soule is sense) cannot admit/Absence, because it doth remove/Those things which elemented it." In other words, things bound to the senses in the physical world perish, and so if all you want is your lover's body, then when she's gone—when you have parted from each other—you have nothing. The fifth stanza completes the contrast of spirit versus flesh begun in stanza four by showing that the narrator and his lover are beyond these worldly miseries, having arrived at a higher state or point of view.

In stanza six we see the first explicit metaphor of the poem. Souls parting from each other are compared to beaten gold. What was hidden before, suggested by covert metaphoric operations, is now (as a kind of dramatic conclusion) being exposed in open form. All the previous suggestions are united in a single, complex extended metaphor* possessing added meaning because of the extensive build-up. Because of all the levels of meaning already in the air, the tension between "compasses" (X) on the one hand (a *technological* image, very unpoetic by most standards—like a TV set or washing machine) and lovers (Y) on the other pulls these meanings together with great force. The feeling of "truth" that comes out of this rather bizarre association can't be stated. It has to be sensed, intuited, or "felt." The most abstract of concepts (soul, love, etc.) are tied to the most dead and concrete of objects. This is *extreme* metaphor and results in an extreme, almost shocking tone. And

*These are sometimes called CONCEITS today, though the term originally meant metaphors with extreme stress on the unlike factor.

since the two terms are incredibly far apart, almost as a function of this distance the piece gains terrific, surprising depth and impact.

1. Can you see any further parallels between the situation in the poem and the pair of compasses?
2. In what ways does Donne refer to the world (the earth)? How are the "teare-floods" and "sigh-tempests" related to the world? How is the compass conceit related to the world? What kinds of meanings does the world take on in this poem?
3. Consider the second line in the fourth stanza. In what ways do the "dull sublunary lovers" have souls that are sense?
4. If other people are the "layetie" (lay people, nonchurchmen), what are the lovers implicitly compared to?
5. In stanza five, why don't the lovers know what their love is?
6. Consider the implications of each of the details in the metaphor of the compasses. "Thy firmness draws my circle just," for example. What are some of the possibilities in the word "circle"? (Remember section IX of Stevens' blackbird poem.) What does it refer to? What might it mean? You can make these kinds of considerations for many of the words in the poem.
7. Consider the different effect when metaphors are made, as in "Ode on Melancholy," with "poetic" literary or natural images (goddesses, grapes) and with the "unpoetic" technological objects here. How does the type of image seem to affect the tone of each kind of poem?
8. Consider the two lines "Inter-assured of the mind,/Care lesse, eyes, lips, and hands to misse." How does the stress pattern in the first line contrast with the stress pattern in the second? How does this reflect the sense of the lines? Can you find other examples of this kind of metric contrast in the poem?
9. Does Donne's "distance" necessarily show a lack of deep feeling? Would you imagine a poet feels more intensely just because he *says* he does? How can we gauge his feeling?

Technical Notes

The rhyme scheme is simple *a b a b*. The meter is iambic tetrameter.

Compare this next poem with the Donne piece. Notice the same type of exaggerated metaphoric comparisons. What is the effect of the tone in the Wills piece?

William Wills

IN PRAISE OF MARRIAGE

Just as this ruler measures off the floor
In inches and feet, where I the carpet lay,
So you, my bride, are the measure of me.

My love is like the rug I struggle with:
It must be cut and fitted to your needs;
It must be shaped to the room of our life;

It must cover the bare boards,
The imperfections and the old shellac,
Brushed on by others, and the worn-out

Places where other boots have scraped.
O take the scissors and the hammer, love,
Square me off and nail me into place!

Considerations

1. Is the poet being witty or sincere? Can you find any clues to his attitude, the mood, or the atmosphere? How are we supposed to take this poem?
2. Is the writing overdone? If so, can you give clear reasons why? If not, what are its merits?
3. Do you see a difference between this and the Donne piece in terms of the depth and intensity of insight? If so, how do you account for it?

What would you say about the tone here? What does it depend on? At first this piece may seem more complex than it actually is. The relation between the hour-glass (X) and what it is associated with (Y) is fairly simple, and you should be able to work it out without much trouble.

Ben Jonson

THE HOURE-GLASSE

Doe but consider this small dust,
  Here running in the Glasse,
    By Atomes mov'd;
  Could you beleeve, that this,
    The body was
      Of one that lov'd?
And in his Mistris flame, playing like a flye,
  Turn'd to cinders by her eye?
    Yes; and in death, as life unblest,
      To have't exprest,
  Even ashes of lovers find no rest.

Considerations

1. Contrast the humorous irony here with the deadly serious, exalted feeling of "When I Heard the Learn'd Astronomer." How much of this difference in effect is due to Jonson's use of the technological image of the hourglass?
2. Consider the individual images and metaphors of the poem. How do they affect the tone (for example, the fly metaphor)? What insights do they generate?
3. Consider the last statement. Try stressing "lovers" and then try stressing "ashes." How does this alter the tone?
4. Do you see a connection between the continuous movement in the hourglass and the process of love? Could the metaphor be suggesting that the lovers are continually afflicting their minds with doubt and hope, sighing, weeping, etc.? How? What does the fact that this all takes place in an *hourglass* add?

These three poems are examples of how tone can become a theme in itself. The Raleigh and the Donne pieces both play off Marlowe's tone in the original.

Christopher Marlowe

THE PASSIONATE SHEPHERD TO HIS LOVE

Come live with me and be my love,
And we will all the pleasures prove,
That hills and valleys, dales and fields,
And all the craggy mountains yields.

There we will sit upon the rocks,
And see the shepherds feed their flocks,
By shallow rivers to whose falls
Melodious birds sing madrigals.

And I will make thee beds of roses
With a thousand fragrant posies,
A cap of flowers, and a kirtle
Embroidered all with leaves of myrtle;

A gown made of the finest wool
Which from our pretty lambs we pull;
Fair lined slippers for the cold,
With buckles of the purest gold;

A belt of straw and ivy buds,
With coral clasps and amber studs:
And if these pleasures may thee move,
Come live with me and be my love.

The shepherds' swains shall dance and sing
For thy delight each May morning:
If these delights thy mind may move,
Then live with me and be my love.

Sir Walter Raleigh

THE NYMPH'S REPLY TO THE SHEPHERD

If all the world and love were young,
And truth in every shepherd's tongue,
These pretty pleasures might me move,
To live with thee, and be thy love.

Time drives the flocks from field to fold,
When rivers rage, and rocks grow cold,
And Philomel° becometh dumb,
The rest complains of cares to come.

The flowers do fade, and wanton fields,
To wayward winter reckoning yields,
A honey tongue, a heart of gall,
Is fancy's spring, but sorrow's fall.

Thy gowns, thy shoes, thy beds of roses,
Thy cap, thy kirtle, and thy posies,
Soon break, soon wither, soon forgotten:
In folly ripe, in reason rotten.

Thy belt of straw and ivy buds,
Thy coral clasps and amber studs,
All these in me no means can move,
To come to thee, and be thy love.

But could youth last, and love still breed,
Had joys no date, nor age no need,
Then these delights my mind might move,
To live with thee and be thy love.

°A figure in Greek mythology (see page 172).

John Donne

THE BAITE

Come live with mee, and bee my love,
And wee will some new pleasures prove
Of golden sands, and crystal brookes,
With silken lines, and silver hookes.

There will the river whispering runne
Warm'd by thy eyes, more than the Sunne.
And there th'inamor'd fish will stay,
Begging themselves they may betray.

When thou wilt swimme in that live bath,
Each fish, which every channell hath,
Will amorously to thee swimme,
Gladder to catch thee, than thou him.

If thou, to be so seene, beest loath,
By Sunne, or Moone, thou darknest both,
And if my selfe have leave to see,
I need not their light, having thee.

Let others freeze with angling reeds,
And cut their legges, with shells and weeds,
Or treacherously poore fish beset,
With strangling snare, or windowie net:

Let coarse bold hands, from slimy nest
The bedded fish in banks out-wrest,
Or curious traitors, sleavesilke flies
Bewitch poore fishes wandring eyes.

For thee, thou needst no such deceit,
For thou thy selfe art thine owne bait;
That fish, that is not catch'd thereby,
Alas, is wiser farre than I.

Considerations

As you see, the Marlowe piece is serious and
straightforward. The poet speaks with a shepherd's voice, associating his love with an ideal or
mythical world. Implicit in this is a comparison of
his contemporary environment with a place or
state of perfection. Poets have done this for ages
and still do. In the Marlowe and Raleigh poems we
have the shepherd's world (*X*) expressing the
poet's world (*Y*). This metaphoric technique has
been used so often that it is called a LITERARY
CONVENTION, something like a dead metaphor.
Unless handled with consummate skill and energy,
a literary convention is always in danger of becoming a stylistic cliché. If everybody is comparing his
love relationships to the affairs of shepherds and
nymphs, there is little that is vital or fresh about
the idea.

Marlowe's poem is an example of a fairly clever
use of convention, but few would call it outstanding. Raleigh read it and reacted, it would seem, to
the tone of simple sincerity and (he must have
thought) excessive optimism. So Raleigh stays
within the convention, but gives it a whole new
twist. The basic difference in tone has nothing to
do with metaphors, images, diction, or technique
(the styles are similar); instead it is established by
a note of cynicism against a background of realistic
appraisal of the facts of life. Notice how the effect
of the convention is completely changed by this. If
you read the Marlowe poem first and it seems
dead, when you follow up with the Raleigh poem
the metaphoric situation comes to life. It suddenly
has bite and depth.

Donne goes further: He extends the cynical tone
and mocks the convention itself, and he creates a
totally independent poem. Raleigh's piece is literally an answer to the Marlowe poem and thus
depends on it for full value. Donne sets up an
atmosphere of absurd humor together with a very
sophisticated sense of the reality of love.

1. How do Donne's references to "slimy nest"
   and "flies" affect the contrast between the first
   two poems and his own? What does the comparison of lovers to fish do?
2. Compare the tone of the first two poems with
   Donne's tone, the result of striking, even
   grotesque *natural, nonliterary* images against
   natural and *literary-natural* images. What is
   the effect of this on the convention he is
   mocking?

Technical Notes

The poems are all written in what amounts to
iambic tetrameter. The rhyme schemes are obviously parallel.

This long poem, one of the wittiest in the language, is satiric in tone. Pope, who flourished in a cultured eighteenth-century English social atmosphere, aims barb after barb at London high society and hits home by making clever juxtapositions that set the capricious, petty concerns and foolishness of the local upper classes against eternal EPIC *drama: the trivial (X) to the heroic (Y). A gentleman's idle prank on a young lady is treated as if it were an event in the battle of Troy. In his dedication Pope said: "For the ancient Poets are in one respect like many modern Ladies: Let an Action be never so trivial in it self, they always make it appear of the utmost Importance." Pope was not being negative about the ancient poets; he admired them greatly, and so the dedication is ironic: he is pointing out that his representation of London society (in which its trivia are treated as important) is equivalent to its own self-image, the difference being that he sees it as absurd comedy. Pope's descriptions of insignificant doings at court, in the manner of Homer and Virgil, form the structure supporting this satire: In the* Iliad *great battles are fought; in London society the battles consist of playing card games (games of "Ombre") and throwing snuff. The battle of Troy was ignited by the abduction of Helen; in London society war is waged because the Baron snipped off a lock of Belinda's hair. In Virgil's* Aeneid, *Queen Dido performs rites before immolating herself for love of the hero, Aeneas. In "The Rape of the Lock," Belinda performs the "rites of pride" at her dressing table. In the epics, universal Olympian gods and goddesses take sides and offer aid to the heroes in the great human battles. In Pope's poem, spiteful gnomes and prankish sprights and sylphs, spirits of vanity, guard Belinda's earrings and pamper her sacred lock.*

Don't be intimidated if you miss many of the things the poet refers to. One of the beauties of this poem is its richness. You don't even have to be very familiar with the epics Pope is playing off to appreciate much of the humor here. No matter how much you miss, there is always more to enjoy and more to gain on succeeding readings. But even on the first reading you should be able to appreciate that beneath the witty surface, Pope penetrates into the nature of human values, going past London society and epic legends to present an incisive vision of human folly and pretentiousness.

Alexander Pope

THE RAPE OF THE LOCK

CANTO I
What dire Offence from am'rous Causes springs,
What mighty Contests rise from trivial Things,
I sing—This Verse to *Caryll*,[1] Muse! is due;
This, ev'n *Belinda* may vouchsafe to view:
Slight is the Subject, but not so the Praise,
If She inspire, and He approve my Lays.
   Say what strange Motive, Goddess! cou'd compel
A well-bred *Lord* t'assault a gentle *Belle*?
Oh say what stranger Cause, yet unexplor'd,
Cou'd make a gentle *Belle* reject a *Lord*?
In Tasks so bold, can Little Men engage,
And in soft Bosoms dwells such mighty Rage?

[1]A friend of Pope

Sol thro' white Curtains shot a tim'rous Ray,
And op'd those Eyes that must eclipse the Day;
Now Lapdogs give themselves the rowzing Shake,
And sleepless Lovers, just at Twelve, awake:
Thrice rung the Bell, the Slipper knock'd the Ground,[2]
And the press'd Watch return'd a silver Sound.[3]
Belinda still her downy Pillow prest,
Her Guardian *Sylph* prolong'd the balmy Rest.
'Twas he had summon'd to her silent Bed
The Morning-Dream that hover'd o'er her Head.
A Youth more glitt'ring than a *Birth-night Beau*,[4]
(That ev'n in Slumber caus'd her Cheek to glow)
Seem'd to her Ear his winning Lips to lay,
And thus in Whispers said, or seem'd to say.
  Fairest of Mortals, thou distinguish'd Care
Of thousand bright Inhabitants of Air!
If e'er one Vision touch'd thy infant Thought,
Of all the Nurse and all the Priest have taught,
Of airy Elves by Moonlight Shadows seen,
The silver Token, and the circled Green,
Or Virgins visited by Angel-Pow'rs,
With Golden Crowns and Wreaths of heavn'ly Flow'rs,
Hear and believe! thy own Importance know,
Nor bound thy narrow Views to Things below.
Some secret Truths from Learned Pride conceal'd,
To Maids alone and Children are reveal'd:
What tho' no Credit doubting Wits may give?
The Fair and Innocent shall still believe.
Know then, unnumber'd Spirits round thee fly,
The light *Militia* of the lower Sky;
These, tho' unseen, are ever on the Wing,
Hang o'er the *Box*, and hover round the *Ring*.[5]
Think what an Equipage thou hast in Air,
And view with scorn *Two Pages* and a *Chair*.[6]
As now your own, our Beings were of old,
And once inclos'd in Woman's beauteous Mold;
Thence, by a soft Transition, we repair
From earthly Vehicles to these of Air.
Think not, when Woman's transient Breath is fled,
That all her Vanities at once are dead:
Succeeding Vanities she still regards,
And tho' she plays no more, o'erlooks the Cards.
Her Joy in gilded Chariots, when alive,

[2]Belinda's handbell unanswered, she knocked with her slipper
[3]The watch sounded the quarters of the hour when pressure was applied to the pin near the pendant.
[4]Birthday dress
[5]A fashionable parade for coaches in Hyde Park
[6]A sedan chair

And Love of *Ombre*,[7] after Death survive.
For when the Fair in all their Pride expire,
To their first Elements their Souls retire:
The Sprights of fiery Termagants[8] in Flame
Mount up, and take a *Salamander*'s Name.
Soft yielding Minds to Water glide away,
And sip with *Nymphs*, their Elemental Tea.
The graver Prude sinks downward to a *Gnome*,
In search of Mischief still on Earth to roam.
The light Coquettes in *Sylphs* aloft repair,
And sport and flutter in the Fields of Air.
  Know farther yet; Whoever fair and chaste
Rejects Mankind, is by some *Sylph* embrac'd:
For Spirits, freed from mortal Laws, with ease
Assume what Sexes and what Shapes they please.
What guards the Purity of melting Maids,
In Courtly Balls, and Midnight Masquerades,
Safe from the treach'rous Friend, the daring Spark,[9]
The Glance by Day, the Whisper in the Dark;
When kind Occasion prompts their warm Desires,
When Musick softens, and when Dancing fires?
'Tis but their *Sylph*, the wise Celestials know,
Tho '*Honour* is the Word with Men below.
  Some Nymphs there are, too conscious of their Face,[10]
For Life predestin'd to the *Gnomes*' Embrace.
These swell their Prospects and exalt their Pride,
When Offers are disdain'd, and Love deny'd.
Then gay Ideas crowd the vacant Brain;
While Peers and Dukes, and all their sweeping Train,
And Garters, Stars and Coronets appear,
And in soft Sounds, *Your Grace* salutes their Ear.
'Tis these that early taint the Female Soul,
Instruct the Eyes of young *Coquettes* to roll,
Teach Infant-Cheeks a bidden Blush[11] to know,
And little Hearts to flutter at a *Beau*.
  Oft when the World imagine Women stray,
The *Sylphs* thro' mystick Mazes guide their Way,
Thro' all the giddy Circle they pursue,
And old Impertinence[12] expel by new.
What tender Maid but must a Victim fall
To one Man's Treat,[13] but for another's Ball?
When *Florio* speaks, what Virgin could withstand,

[7]A card game like bridge
[8]An overbearing, nagging woman
[9]A lively, showy, fellow. A term of contempt
[10]Their beauty
[11]With rouge
[12]Trifle
[13]An entertainment of food and drink

If gentle *Damon* did not squeeze her Hand?
With varying Vanities, from ev'ry Part,
They shift the moving Toyshop of their Heart;
Where Wigs with Wigs, with Sword-knots Sword-knots[14] strive,
Beaus banish Beaus, and Coaches Coaches drive.
This erring Mortals Levity may call,
Oh blind to Truth! the *Sylphs* contrive it all.
   Of these am I, who thy Protection claim,
A watchful Sprite, and *Ariel* is my Name.
Late, as I rang'd the Crystal Wilds of Air,
In the clear Mirror of thy ruling *Star*
I saw, alas! some dread Event impend,
Ere to the Main this Morning Sun descend.
But Heav'n reveals not what, or how, or where:
Warn'd by thy *Sylph*, oh Pious Maid beware!
This to disclose is all thy Guardian can.
Beware of all, but most beware of Man!
   He said; when *Shock*, who thought she slept too long,
Leapt up, and wak'd his Mistress with his Tongue.
'Twas then *Belinda*! if Report say true,
Thy Eyes first open'd on a *Billet-doux*;
Wounds, Charms, and *Ardors,* were no sooner read,
But all the Vision vanish'd from thy Head.
   And now, unveil'd, the *Toilet* stands display'd,
Each Silver Vase in mystic Order laid.

[14]A ribbon tied to the hilt of a sword

First, rob'd in White, the Nymph intent adores
With Head uncover'd, the *Cosmetic* Pow'rs.
A heav'nly Image in the Glass appears,
To that she bends, to that her Eyes she rears;
Th'inferior Priestess, at her Altar's side,
Trembling, begins the sacred Rites of Pride.
Unnumber'd Treasures ope at once, and here
The various Off'rings of the World appear;
From each she nicely culls with curious Toil,
And decks the Goddess with the glitt'ring Spoil.
This Casket *India*'s glowing Gems unlocks,
And all *Arabia* breathes from yonder Box.
The Tortoise here and Elephant unite,
Transform'd to *Combs*, the speckled and the white.
Here Files of Pins extend their shining Rows,
Puffs, Powders, Patches, Bibles, Billet-doux.
Now awful Beauty puts on all its Arms;
The Fair each moment rises in her Charms,
Repairs her Smiles, awakens ev'ry Grace,
And calls forth all the Wonders of her Face;
Sees by Degrees a purer Blush arise,
And keener Lightnings quicken in her Eyes.[15]
The busy *Sylphs* surround their darling Care;
These set the Head, and those divide the Hair,
Some fold the Sleeve, whilst others plait the Gown;
And *Betty's* prais'd for Labours not her own.

CANTO II
Not with more Glories, in th' Etherial Plain,
The Sun first rises o'er the purpled Main,
Than issuing forth, the Rival of his Beams
Lanch'd on the Bosom of the Silver *Thames*.
Fair Nymphs, and well-drest Youths around her shone,
But ev'ry Eye was fix'd on her alone.
On her white Breast a sparkling *Cross* she wore,
Which *Jews* might kiss, and Infidels adore.
Her lively Looks a sprightly Mind disclose,
Quick as her Eyes, and as unfix'd as those:
Favours to none, to all she Smiles extends,
Oft she rejects, but never once offends.
Bright as the Sun, her Eyes the Gazers strike,
And, like the Sun, they shine on all alike.
Yet graceful Ease, and Sweetness void of Pride,
Might hide her Faults, if *Belles* had Faults to hide:
If to her share some Female Errors fall,
Look on her Face, and you'll forget 'em all.

[15]She is using either eyeshadow or the juice of belladona
(nightshade), which enlarges the pupils of the eyes and
was popular in the eighteenth century.

This Nymph, to the Destruction of Mankind,
Nourish'd two Locks, which graceful hung behind
In equal Curls, and well conspir'd to deck
With shining Ringlets the Smooth Iv'ry Neck.
Love in these Labyrinths his Slaves detains,
And mighty Hearts are held in slender Chains.
With hairy Sprindges we the Birds betray,
Slight Lines of Hair surprize the Finny Prey,
Fair Tresses Man's Imperial Race insnare,
And Beauty draws us with a single Hair.
  Th' Adventrous *Baron* the bright Locks admir'd,
He saw, he wish'd, and to the Prize aspir'd:
Resolv'd to win, he meditates the way,
By Force to ravish, or by Fraud betray;
For when Success a Lover's Toil attends,
Few ask, if Fraud or Force attain'd his Ends.
  For this, ere *Phœbus* rose, he had implor'd
Propitious Heav'n, and ev'ry Pow'r ador'd,
But chiefly *Love*—to *Love* an Altar built,
Of twelve vast *French* Romances, neatly gilt.
There lay three Garters, half a Pair of Gloves;
And all the Trophies of his former Loves.
With tender *Billet-doux* he lights the Pyre,
And breathes three am'rous Sighs to raise the Fire.
Then prostrate falls, and begs with ardent Eyes
Soon to obtain, and long possess the Prize:
The Pow'rs gave Ear, and granted half his Pray'r,
The rest, the Winds dispers'd in empty Air.
  But now secure the painted Vessel glides,
The Sun-beams trembling on the floating Tydes,
While melting Musick steals upon the Sky,
And soften'd Sounds along the Waters die.
Smooth flow the Waves, the Zephyrs gently play,
Belinda smil'd, and all the World was gay.
All but the *Sylph*—With careful Thoughts opprest,
The 'impending Woe sate heavy on his Breast.
He summons strait his Denizens of Air;
The lucid Squadrons round the Sails repair:
Soft o'er the Shrouds Aerial Whispers breathe,
That seem'd but *Zephyrs* to the Train beneath.
Some to the Sun their Insect-Wings unfold,
Waft on the Breeze, or sink in Clouds of Gold.
Transparent Forms, too fine for mortal Sight,
Their fluid Bodies half dissolv'd in Light.
Loose to the Wind their airy Garments flew,
Thin glitt'ring Textures of the filmy Dew;
Dipt in the richest Tincture of the Skies,
Where Light disports in ever-mingling Dies,
While ev'ry Beam new transient Colours flings,
Colours that change when'er they wave their Wings.
Amid the Circle, on the gilded Mast,

Superior by the Head, was *Ariel* plac'd;
His Purple Pinions opening to the Sun,
He rais'd his Azure Wand, and thus begun.

   Ye *Sylphs* and *Sylphids*, to your Chief give Ear,
Fays, Fairies, Genii, Elves, and *Dæmons* hear!
Ye know the Spheres and various Tasks assign'd,
By Laws Eternal, to th' Aerial Kind.
Some in the Fields of purest *Æther* play,
And bask and whiten in the Blaze of Day.
Some guide the Course of wandring Orbs on high,
Or roll the Planets thro' the boundless Sky.
Some less refin'd, beneath the Moon's pale Light
Pursue the Stars that shoot athwart the Night,
Or suck the Mists in grosser Air below,
Or dip their Pinions in the painted Bow,
Or brew fierce Tempests on the wintry Main,
Or o'er the Glebe distill the kindly Rain.
Others on Earth o'er human Race preside,
Watch all their Ways, and all their Actions guide:
Of these the Chief the Care of Nations own,
And guard with Arms Divine the *British Throne.*

   Our humbler Province is to tend the Fair,
Not a less pleasing, tho' less glorious Care.
To save the Powder from too rude a Gale,
Nor let th' imprison'd Essences exhale,
To draw fresh Colours from the vernal Flow'rs,
To steal from Rainbows ere they drop in Show'rs
A brighter Wash; to curl their waving Hairs,
Assist their Blushes, and inspire their Airs;
Nay oft, in Dreams, Invention we bestow,
To change a *Flounce,* or add a *Furbelo.*[16]

   This Day, black Omens threat the brightest Fair
That e'er deserv'd a watchful Spirit's Care;
Some dire Disaster, or by Force, or Slight,
But what, or where, the Fates have wrapt in Night.
Whether the Nymph shall break *Diana's* Law,
Or some frail *China* Jar receive a Flaw,
Or stain her Honour, or her new Brocade,
Forget her Pray'rs, or miss a Masquerade,
Or lose her Heart, or Necklace, at a Ball;
Or whether Heav'n has doom'd that *Shock* must fall.
Haste then ye Spirits! to your Charge repair;
The flutt'ring Fan be *Zephyretta's* Care;
The Drops to thee,[17] *Brillante,* we consign;
And, *Momentilla,* let the Watch be thine;
Do thou, *Crispissa,* tend her fav'rite Lock;
Ariel himself shall be the Guard of *Shock.*

[16]A piece of material plaited and puckered together,
either below or above, on women's petticoats or gowns

[17]Diamond(s) hanging in the ear

To Fifty chosen *Sylphs*, of special Note,
We trust th' important Charge, the *Petticoat*:
Oft have we known that sev'nfold Fence to fail,
Tho' stiff with Hoops, and arm'd with Ribs of Whale.
Form a strong Line about the Silver Bound,
And guard the wide Circumference around.
    Whatever Spirit, careless of his Charge,
His Post neglects, or leaves the Fair at large,
Shall feel sharp Vengeance soon o'ertake his Sins,
Be stopt in *Vials*, or transfixt with *Pins*;
Or plung'd in Lakes of bitter *Washes* lie,
Or wedg'd whole Ages in a *Bodkin*'s Eye:[18]
Gums and *Pomatums* shall his Flight restrain,
While clog'd he beats his silken Wings in vain;
Or Alom-*Stypticks* with contracting Power
Shrink his thin Essence like a rivell'd Flower.[19]
Or as *Ixion* fix'd, the Wretch shall feel
The giddy Motion of the whirling Mill,
In Fumes of burning Chocolate shall glow,
And tremble at the Sea that froaths below!
    He spoke; the Spirits from the Sails descend;
Some, Orb in Orb, around the Nymph extend,
Some thrid the mazy Ringlets of her Hair,
Some hang upon the Pendants of her Ear;
With beating Hearts the dire Event they wait,
Anxious, and trembling for the Birth of Fate.

CANTO III
Close by those Meads for ever crown'd with Flow'rs,
Where *Thames* with Pride surveys his rising Tow'rs,
There stands a Structure of Majestick Frame,
Which from the neighb'ring *Hampton* takes its Name.
Here *Britain*'s Statesmen oft the Fall foredoom
Of Foreign Tyrants, and of Nymphs at home;
Here Thou, Great *Anna*![20] whom three Realms obey,
Dost sometimes Counsel take—and sometimes *Tea*.
    Hither the Heroes and the Nymphs resort,
To taste awhile the Pleasures of a Court;
In various Talk th' instructive hours they past,
Who gave the *Ball*, or paid the *Visit* last:
One speaks the Glory of the *British Queen*,
And one describes a charming *Indian Screen*;
A third interprets Motions, Looks, and Eyes;
At ev'ry Word a Reputation dies.
Snuff, or the *Fan*, supply each Pause of Chat,
With singing, laughing, ogling, and all that.

[18]Pope plays on the various meanings of "bodkin: (1) a blunt-pointed needle; (2) a hair ornament; and (3) a dagger.

[19]Contracted into wrinkles and corrugations

[20]Queen Anne of England

Mean while declining from the Noon of Day,
The Sun obliquely shoots his burning Ray;
The hungry Judges soon the Sentence sign,
And Wretches hang that Jury-men may Dine;
The Merchant from th' *Exchange* returns in Peace,
And the long Labours of the *Toilette* cease—
Belinda now, whom Thirst of Fame invites,
Burns to encounter two adventrous Knights,
At *Ombre* singly to decide their Doom;
And swells her Breast with Conquests yet to come.
Strait the three Bands prepare in Arms to join,
Each Band the number of the Sacred Nine.
Soon as she spreads her Hand, th' Aerial Guard
Descend, and sit on each important Card:
First *Ariel* perch'd upon a *Matadore*,
Then each, according to the Rank they bore;
For *Sylphs*, yet mindful of their ancient Race,
Are, as when Women, wondrous fond of Place.
   Behold, four *Kings* in Majesty rever'd,
With hoary Whiskers and a forky Beard;
And four fair *Queens* whose hands sustain a Flow'r,
Th' expressive Emblem of their softer Pow'r;
Four *Knaves* in Garbs succinct, a trusty Band,
Caps on their heads, and Halberds in their hand;
And Particolour'd Troops, a shining Train,
Draw forth to Combat on the Velvet Plain.
   The skilful Nymph reviews her Force with Care;
Let Spades be Trumps! she said, and Trumps they were.[21]
   Now move to War her Sable *Matadores*,
In Show like Leaders of the swarthy *Moors*.
Spadillio first, unconquerable Lord!
Led off two captive Trumps, and swept the Board.
As many more *Manillio* forc'd to yield,
And march'd a Victor from the verdant Field.
Him *Basto* follow'd, but his Fate more hard
Gain'd but one Trump and one *Plebeian* Card.
With his broad Sabre next, a Chief in Years,
The hoary Majesty of *Spades* appears;
Puts forth one manly Leg, to sight reveal'd;
The rest his many-colour'd Robe conceal'd.
The Rebel-*Knave*, who dares his Prince engage,
Proves the just Victim of his Royal Rage.
Ev'n mighty *Pam* that Kings and Queens o'erthrew,
And mow'd down Armies in the Fights of *Lu*,
Sad Chance of War! now, destitute of Aid,
Falls undistinguish'd by the Victor *Spade*!
   Thus far both Armies to *Belinda* yield;
Now to the *Baron* Fate inclines the Field.
His warlike *Amazon* her Host invades,

[21]Remember Gen. 1:3: "And God said, 'Let there be light:' and there was light."

Th' Imperial Consort of the Crown of *Spades*.
The *Club's* black Tyrant first her Victim dy'd,
Spite of his haughty Mien, and barb'rous Pride:
What boots the Regal Circle on his Head,
His Giant Limbs in State unwieldy spread?
That long behind he trails his pompous Robe,
And of all Monarchs only grasps the Globe?

   The *Baron* now his *Diamonds* pours apace;
Th' embroider'd *King* who shows but half his Face,
And his refulgent *Queen*, with Pow'rs combin'd,
Of broken Troops an easie Conquest find.
Clubs, Diamonds, Hearts, in wild Disorder seen,
With Throngs promiscuous strow the level Green.
Thus when dispers'd a routed Army runs,
Of *Asia's* Troops, and *Africk's* Sable Sons,
With like Confusion different Nations fly,
Of various Habit and of various Dye,

The pierc'd Battalions dis-united fall,
In Heaps on Heaps; one Fate o'erwhelms them all.
  The *Knave of Diamonds* tries his wily Arts,
And wins (oh shameful Chance!) the *Queen of Hearts.*
At this, the Blood the Virgin's Cheek forsook,
A livid Paleness spreads o'er all her Look;
She sees, and trembles at th' approaching Ill,
Just in the Jaws of Ruin, and *Codille.*
And now, (as oft in some distemper'd State)
On one nice *Trick*[22] depends the gen'ral Fate.
An *Ace* of Hearts steps forth: The *King* unseen
Lurk'd in her Hand, and mourn'd his captive *Queen.*
He springs to Vengeance with an eager pace,
And falls like Thunder on the prostrate *Ace.*
The Nymph exulting fills with Shouts the Sky,
The Walls, the Woods, and long Canals reply.
  Oh thoughtless Mortals! ever blind to Fate,
Too soon dejected, and too soon elate!
Sudden these Honours shall be snatch'd away,
And curs'd for ever this Victorious Day.
  For lo! the Board with Cups and Spoons is crown'd,
The Berries crackle, and the Mill turns round.
On shining Altars of *Japan*[23] they raise
The silver Lamp; the fiery Spirits blaze.
From silver Spouts the grateful Liquors glide,
While *China*'s Earth receives the smoking Tyde.
At once they gratify their Scent and Taste,
And frequent Cups prolong the rich Repast.
Strait hover round the Fair her Airy Band;
Some, as she sip'd, the fuming Liquor fann'd,
Some o'er her Lap their careful Plumes display'd,
Trembling, and conscious of the rich Brocade.
Coffee,[24] (which makes the Politician wise,
And see thro' all things with his half-shut Eyes)
Sent up in Vapours to the *Baron*'s Brain
New Stratagems, the radiant Lock to gain.
Ah cease rash Youth! desist ere 'tis too late,
Fear the just Gods, and think of *Scylla*'s Fate!
Chang'd to a Bird, and sent to flit in Air,
She dearly pays for *Nisus*' injur'd Hair![25]

[22] A pun

[23] Lacquered tables

[24] Coffeehouses were frequented by amateur politicians.

[25] King Nisus' daughter Scylla, fell in love with Minos.
The safety of Nisus' kingdom was known to depend on a
purple hair which grew on his head. Scylla plucked out
the hair and took it to Minos, but met with nothing but
horror for her action. After Minos's victory he sailed
away; Scylla attempted to cling to his ship till, beaten off
by Nisus, who had become an osprey; she also became a
bird.

But when to Mischief Mortals bend their Will,
How soon they find fit Instruments of Ill!
Just then, *Clarissa* drew with tempting Grace
A two-edg'd Weapon from her shining Case;[26]
So Ladies in Romance assist their Knight,
Present the Spear, and arm him for the Fight.
He takes the Gift with rev'rence, and extends
The little Engine on his Fingers' Ends,
This just behind *Belinda's* Neck he spread,
As o'er the fragrant Steams she bends her Head:
Swift to the Lock a thousand Sprights repair,
A thousand Wings, by turns, blow back the Hair,
And thrice they twitch'd the Diamond in her Ear,
Thrice she look'd back, and thrice the Foe drew near.
Just in that instant, anxious *Ariel* sought
The close Recesses of the Virgin's Thought;
As on the Nosegay in her Breast reclin'd,
He watch'd th' Ideas rising in her Mind,
Sudden he view'd, in spite of all her Art,
An Earthly Lover lurking at her Heart.
Amaz'd, confus'd, he found his Pow'r expir'd,
Resign'd to Fate, and with a Sigh retir'd.
   The Peer now spreads the glitt'ring *Forfex* wide,
T'inclose the Lock; now joins it, to divide.
Ev'n then, before the fatal Engine clos'd,
A wretched *Sylph* too fondly interpos'd;
Fate urg'd the Sheers, and cut the *Sylph* in twain,
(But Airy Substance soon unites again)
The meeting Points the sacred Hair dissever
From the fair Head, for ever and for ever!
   Then flash'd the living Lightning from her Eyes,
And Screams of Horror rend th' affrighted Skies.
Not louder Shrieks to pitying Heav'n are cast,
When Husbands or when Lap-dogs breathe their last,
Or when rich *China* Vessels, fal'n from high,
In glittring Dust and painted Fragments lie!
   Let Wreaths of Triumph now my Temples twine,
(The Victor cry'd) the glorious Prize is mine!
While Fish in Streams, or Birds delight in Air,
Or in a Coach and Six the *British* Fair,
As long as *Atalantis*[27] shall be read,
Or the small Pillow grace a Lady's Bed,
While *Visits* shall be paid on solemn Days,
When numerous Wax-lights in bright Order blaze,
While Nymphs take Treats, or Assignations give,
So long my Honour, Name, and Praise shall live!

[26]Tweezer case

[27]Mrs. Manley's *Secret Memories and Manners of Several
Persons of Quality, of Both Sexes. From the New Atalantis, an Island in the Mediterranean,* 1700

What Time wou'd spare, from Steel receives its date,
And Monuments, like Men, submit to Fate!
Steel cou'd the Labour of the Gods destroy,
And strike to Dust th' Imperial Tow'rs of *Troy*;
Steel cou'd the Works of mortal Pride confound,
And hew Triumphal Arches to the Ground.
What Wonder then, fair Nymph! thy Hairs shou'd feel
The conqu'ring Force of unresisted Steel?

CANTO IV
But anxious Cares the pensive Nymph opprest,
And secret Passions labour'd in her Breast.
Not youthful Kings in Battel seiz'd alive,
Not scornful Virgins who their Charms survive,
Not ardent Lovers robb'd of all their Bliss,
Not ancient Ladies when refus'd a Kiss,
Not Tyrants fierce that unrepenting die,
Not *Cynthia* when her *Manteau's*[28] pinn'd awry,
E'er felt such Rage, Resentment and Despair,
As Thou, sad Virgin! for thy ravish'd Hair.
    For, that sad moment, when the *Sylphs* withdrew,
And *Ariel* weeping from *Belinda* flew,
Umbriel, a dusky melancholy Spright,
As ever sully'd the fair face of Light,
Down to the Central Earth, his proper Scene,
Repair'd to search the gloomy Cave of *Spleen*.[29]
    Swift on his sooty Pinions flitts the *Gnome*,
And in a Vapour reach'd the dismal Dome.
No cheerful Breeze this sullen Region knows,
The dreaded *East* is all the Wind that blows.[30]
Here, in a Grotto, sheltred close from Air,
And screen'd in Shades from Day's detested Glare,
She sighs for ever on her pensive Bed,
Pain at her Side, and *Megrim*[31] at her Head.
    Two Handmaids wait the Throne: Alike in Place,
But diff'ring far in Figure and in Face.
Here stood *Ill-nature* like an *ancient Maid*,
Her wrinkled Form in *Black* and *White* array'd;
With store of Pray'rs, for Mornings, Nights, and Noons,
Her hand is fill'd; her Bosom with Lampoons.
    There *Affectation* with a sickly Mien
Shows in her Cheek the Roses of Eighteen,
Practis'd to Lisp, and hang the Head aside,
Faints into Airs, and languishes with Pride;
On the rich Quilt sinks with becoming Woe,

[28]A loose upper garment worn by women
[29]Name for an ancient malady of malice
[30]The east wind was thought to provoke ill will.
[31]A severe headache

Wrapt in a Gown, for Sickness, and for Show.
The Fair-ones feel such Maladies as these,
When each new Night-Dress gives a new Disease.
   A constant *Vapour* o'er the Palace flies;
Strange Phantoms rising as the Mists arise;
Dreadful, as Hermit's Dreams in haunted Shades,
Or bright as Visions of expiring Maids.
Now glaring Fiends, and Snakes on rolling Spires,[32]
Pale Spectres, gaping Tombs, and Purple Fires:
Now Lakes of Liquid Gold, *Elysian* Scenes,
And Crystal Domes, and Angels in Machines.[33]
   Unnumber'd Throngs on ev'ry side are seen
Of Bodies chang'd to various Forms by *Spleen.*
Here living *Teapots* stand, one Arm held out,
One bent; the Handle this, and that the Spout:
A Pipkin[34] there like *Homer's Tripod* walks;
Here sighs a Jar, and there a Goose-pye talks;
Men prove with Child, as pow'rful Fancy works,
And Maids turn'd Bottels, call aloud for Corks.
   Safe past the *Gnome* thro' this fantastick Band,
A Branch of healing *Spleenwort* in his hand.
Then thus addrest the Pow'r—Hail wayward Queen!
Who rule the Sex to Fifty from Fifteen,
Parent of Vapours and of Female Wit,
Who give th' *Hysteric* or *Poetic* Fit,
On various Tempers act by various ways,
Make some take Physick, others scribble Plays;
Who cause the Proud their Visits to delay,
And send the Godly in a Pett, to pray.
A Nymph there is, that all thy Pow'r disdains,
And thousands more in equal Mirth maintains.
But oh! if e'er thy *Gnome* could spoil a Grace,
Or raise a Pimple on a beauteous Face,
Like Citron-Waters Matrons' Cheeks inflame,
Or change Complexions at a losing Game;
If e'er with airy Horns I planted Heads,
Or rumpled Petticoats, or tumbled Beds,
Or caus'd Suspicion when no Soul was rude,
Or discompos'd the Head-dress of a Prude,
Or e'er to costive Lap-Dog gave Disease,
Which not the Tears of brightest Eyes could ease:
Hear me, and touch *Belinda* with Chagrin;
That single Act gives half the World the Spleen.
   The Goddess with a discontented Air
Seems to reject him, tho' she grants his Pray'r.
A wondrous Bag with both her Hands she binds,

[32]Coils

[33]A satiric catalog of the scenic effects of contemporary
opera and pantomime

[34]A small earthen boiler

Like that where once *Ulysses* held the Winds;
There she collects the Force of Female Lungs,
Sighs, Sobs, and Passions, and the War of Tongues.
A Vial next she fills with fainting Fears,
Soft Sorrows, melting Griefs, and flowing Tears.
The *Gnome* rejoicing bears her Gifts away,
Spreads his black Wings, and slowly mounts to Day.
   Sunk in *Thalestris'*[35] Arms the Nymph he found,
Her Eyes dejected and her Hair unbound.
Full o'er their Heads the swelling Bag he rent,
And all the Furies issued at the Vent.
Belinda burns with more than mortal Ire,
And fierce *Thalestris* fans the rising Fire.
O wretched Maid! she spread her Hands, and cry'd,
(While *Hampton's* Ecchos, wretched Maid! reply'd)
Was it for this you took such constant Care
The *Bodkin*, *Comb*, and *Essence* to prepare;
For this your Locks in Paper-Durance bound,
For this with tort'ring Irons wreath'd around?
For this with Fillets strain'd your tender Head,
And bravely bore the double Loads of Lead?[36]
Gods! shall the Ravisher display your Hair,
While the Fops envy, and the Ladies stare!
Honour forbid! at whose unrival'd Shrine
Ease, Pleasure, Virtue, All, our Sex resign.
Methinks already I your Tears survey,
Already hear the horrid things they say,
Already see you a degraded Toast,[37]
And all your Honour in a Whisper lost!
How shall I, then, your helpless Fame defend?
'Twill then be Infamy to seem your Friend!
And shall this Prize, th' inestimable Prize,
Expos'd thro' Crystal to the gazing Eyes,
And heighten'd by the Diamond's circling Rays,
On that Rapacious Hand for ever blaze?
Sooner shall Grass in *Hide*-Park *Circus* grow,
And Wits take Lodgings in the Sound of *Bow*;
Sooner let Earth, Air, Sea, to *Chaos* fall,
Men, Monkies, Lap-dogs, Parrots, perish all!
   She said; then raging to *Sir Plume* repairs,
And bids her *Beau* demand the precious Hairs:
(*Sir Plume*, of *Amber Snuff-box* justly vain,
And the nice Conduct of a *clouded Cane*)[38]
With earnest Eyes, and round unthinking Face,
He first the Snuff-box open'd, then the Case,

[35]Thalestris was Queen of the Amazons.

[36]The curl papers for ladies' hair were fastened with strips
of pliant lead.

[37]As in drinking a toast

[38]With dark veins

And thus broke out—'My Lord, why, what the Devil?
Z—ds! damn the Lock! 'fore Gad, you must be civil!
Plague on't! 'tis past a Jest—nay prithee, Pox!
Give her the Hair'—he spoke, and rapp'd his Box.
  It grieves me much (reply'd the Peer again)
Who speaks so well shou'd ever speak in vain.
But by this Lock, this sacred Lock I swear,
(Which never more shall join its parted Hair,
Which never more its Honours shall renew,
Clipt from the lovely Head where late it grew)
That while my Nostrils draw the vital Air,
This Hand, which won it, shall for ever wear.
He spoke, and speaking, in proud Triumph spread
The long-contended Honours of her Head.
  But *Umbriel*, hateful *Gnome*! forbears not so;
He breaks the Vial whence the Sorrows flow.
Then see! the *Nymph* in beauteous Grief appears,
Her Eyes half-languishing, half-drown'd in Tears;
On her heav'd Bosom hung her drooping Head,
Which, with a Sigh, she rais'd; and thus she said.
  For ever curs'd be this detested Day,
Which snatch'd my best, my fav'rite Curl away!
Happy! ah ten times happy, had I been,
If *Hampton-Court* these Eyes had never seen!
Yet am not I the first mistaken Maid,
By Love of *Courts* to num'rous Ills betray'd.
Oh had I rather un-admir'd remain'd
In some lone Isle, or distant *Northern* Land;
Where the gilt *Chariot* never marks the Way,
Where none learn *Ombre*, none e'er taste *Bohea*!
There kept my Charms conceal'd from mortal Eye,
Like Roses that in Desarts bloom and die.
What mov'd my Mind with youthful Lords to rome?
O had I stay'd, and said my Pray'rs at home!
'Twas this, the Morning *Omens* seem'd to tell;
Thrice from my trembling hand the *Patch-box* fell;
The tott'ring *China* shook without a Wind,
Nay, *Poll* sate mute, and *Shock* was most Unkind!
A *Sylph* too warn'd me of the Threats of Fate,
In mystic Visions, now believ'd too late!
See the poor Remnants of these slighted Hairs!
My hands shall rend what ev'n thy Rapine spares:
These, in two sable Ringlets taught to break,
Once gave new Beauties to the snowie Neck.
The Sister-Lock now sits uncouth, alone,
And in its Fellow's Fate foresees its own;
Uncurl'd it hangs, the fatal Sheers demands;
And tempts once more thy sacrilegious Hands.
Oh hadst thou, Cruel! been content to seize
Hairs less in sight, or any Hairs but these!

CANTO V

She said: the pitying Audience melt in Tears,
But *Fate* and *Jove* had stopp'd the *Baron*'s Ears.
In vain *Thalestris* with Reproach assails,
For who can move when fair *Belinda* fails?
Not half so fixt the *Trojan* cou'd remain,
While *Anna* begg'd and *Dido* rag'd in vain.
Then grave *Clarissa* graceful wav'd her Fan;
Silence ensu'd, and thus the Nymph began.

   Say, why are Beauties prais'd and honour'd most,
The wise Man's Passion, and the vain Man's Toast?
Why deck'd with all that Land and Sea afford,
Why Angels call'd, and Angel-like ador'd?
Why round our Coaches crowd the white-glov'd Beaus,
Why bows the Side-box from its inmost Rows?
How vain are all these Glories, all our Pains,
Unless good Sense preserve what Beauty gains:
That Men may say, when we the Front-box grace,
Behold the first in Virtue, as in Face!
Oh! if to dance all Night, and dress all Day,
Charm'd the Small-pox, or chas'd old Age away;
Who would not scorn what Huswife's Cares produce,
Or who would learn one earthly Thing of Use?
To patch, nay ogle, might become a Saint,
Nor could it sure be such a Sin to paint.
But since, alas! frail Beauty must decay,
Curl'd or uncurl'd, since Locks will turn to grey,
Since painted, or not painted, all shall fade,
And she who scorns a Man, must die a Maid;
What then remains, but well our Pow'r to use,
And keep good Humour still whate'er we lose?
And trust me, Dear! good Humour can prevail,
When Airs, and Flights, and Screams, and Scolding fail.
Beauties in vain their pretty Eyes may roll;
Charms strike the Sight, but Merit wins the Soul.

   So spoke the Dame, but no Applause ensu'd;
Belinda frown'd, *Thalestris* call'd her Prude.
To Arms, to Arms! the fierce Virago[39] cries,
And swift as Lightning to the Combate flies.
All side in Parties, and begin th' Attack;
Fans clap, Silks russle, and tough Whalebones crack;
Heroes' and Heroins' Shouts confus'dly rise,
And base, and treble Voices strike the Skies.
No common Weapons in their Hands are found,
Like Gods they fight, nor dread a mortal Wound.

   So when bold *Homer* makes the Gods engage,
And heav'nly Breasts with human Passions rage;
'Gainst *Pallas*, *Mars*; *Latona*, *Hermes* arms;
And all *Olympus* rings with Loud Alarms.
Jove's Thunder roars, Heav'n trembles all around;

[39]A female warrior

Blue *Neptune* storms, the bellowing Deeps resound;
Earth shakes her nodding Tow'rs, the Ground Gives way;
And the pale Ghosts start at the Flash of Day!
　　Triumphant *Umbriel* on a Sconce's Height
Clapt his glad Wings, and sate to view the Fight:
Propt on their Bodkin Spears, the Sprights survey
The growing Combat, or assist the Fray.
　　While thro' the Press enrag'd *Thalestris* flies,
And scatters Deaths around from both her Eyes,
A *Beau* and *Witling* perish'd in the Throng,
One dy'd in *Metaphor*, and one in *Song*.
O cruel Nymph! a living Death I bear,
Cry'd *Dapperwit*, and sunk beside his Chair.
A mournful Glance Sir *Fopling* upwards cast,
Those Eyes are made so killing—was his last:
Thus on *Meander*'s flow'ry Margin lies
Th' expiring Swan, and as he sings he dies.
　　When bold Sir *Plume* had drawn *Clarissa* down,
Chloe stept in, and kill'd him with a Frown;
She smil'd to see the doughty Hero slain,
But at her Smile, the Beau reviv'd again.
　　Now *Jove* suspends his golden Scales in Air,
Weighs the Men's Wits against the Lady's Hair;
The doubtful Beam long nods from side to side;
At length the Wits mount up, the Hairs subside.
　　See fierce *Belinda* on the *Baron* flies,
With more than usual Lightning in her Eyes;
Nor fear'd the Chief th' unequal Fight to try,
Who sought no more than on his Foe to die.
But this bold Lord, with manly Strength indu'd,
She with one Finger and a Thumb subdu'd:
Just where the Breath of Life his Nostrils drew,
A Charge of *Snuff* the wily Virgin threw;
The *Gnomes* direct, to ev'ry Atome just,
The pungent Grains of titillating Dust.
Sudden, with starting Tears each Eye o'erflows,
And the high Dome re-ecchoes to his Nose.
　　Now meet thy Fate, incens'd *Belinda* cry'd,
And drew a deadly *Bodkin* from her Side.
(The same, his ancient Personage to deck,
Her great great Grandsire wore about his Neck
In three *Seal-Rings*; which after, melted down,
Form'd a vast *Buckle* for his Widow's Gown:
Her infant Grandame's *Whistle* next it grew,
The *Bells* she gingled, and the *Whistle* blew;
Then in a *Bodkin* grac'd her Mother's Hairs,
Which long she wore, and now *Belinda* wears.)
　　Boast not my Fall (he cry'd) insulting Foe!
Thou by some other shalt be laid as low.
Nor think, to die dejects my lofty Mind;
All that I dread, is leaving you behind!
Rather than so, ah let me still survive,

And burn in *Cupid*'s Flames,—but burn alive.
   Restore the Lock! she cries; and all around
Restore the Lock! the vaulted Roofs rebound.
Not fierce *Othello* in so loud a Strain
Roar'd for the Handkerchief that caus'd his Pain.
But see how oft Ambitious Aims are cross'd,
And chiefs contend 'till all the Prize is lost!
The Lock, obtain'd with Guilt, and kept with Pain,
In ev'ry place is sought, but sought in vain:
With such a Prize no Mortal must be blest,
So Heav'n decrees! with Heav'n who can contest?
   Some thought it mounted to the Lunar Sphere,
Since all things lost on Earth, are treasur'd there.
There Heroes' Wits are kept in pondrous Vases,
And Beaus' in *Snuff-boxes* and *Tweezer-Cases*.
There broken Vows, and Death-bed Alms are found,
And Lovers' Hearts with Ends of Riband bound;
The Courtier's Promises, and Sick Man's Pray'rs,
The Smiles of Harlots, and the Tears of Heirs,
Cages for Gnats, and Chains to Yoak a Flea;
Dry'd Butterflies, and Tomes of Casuistry.
   But trust the Muse—she saw it upward rise,
Tho' mark'd by none but quick Poetic Eyes:
(So *Rome*'s great Founder to the Heav'ns withdrew,
To *Proculus* alone confess'd in view.)
A sudden Star, it shot thro' liquid Air,
And drew behind a radiant *Trail of Hair.*
Not *Berenice*'s Locks first rose so bright,
The Heav'ns bespangling with dishevel'd Light.
The *Sylphs* behold it kindling as it flies,
And pleas'd pursue its Progress thro' the Skies.
   This the *Beau-monde* shall from the *Mall*[40] survey,
And hail with Musick its propitious Ray.
This, the blest Lover shall for *Venus* take,
And send up Vows from *Rosamonda*'s[41] Lake.
This *Partridge*[42] soon shall view in cloudless Skies,
When next he looks thro' *Galilæo*'s Eyes;
And hence th' Egregious Wizard shall foredoom
The Fate of *Louis*, and the Fall of *Rome.*
   Then cease, bright Nymph! to mourn thy ravish'd Hair
Which adds new Glory to the shining Sphere!
Not all the Tresses that fair Head can boast
Shall draw such Envy as the Lock you lost.
For, after all the Murders of your Eye,
When, after Millions slain, your self shall die;
When those fair Suns shall sett, as sett they must,
And all those Tresses shall be laid in Dust;
This Lock, the Muse shall consecrate to Fame,
And mid'st the Stars inscribe *Belinda*'s Name!

[40]An enclosed walk in St. James's Park

[41]A pond in St. James's Park

[42]John Partridge was a ridiculous Star-gazer, who in his Almanacks every year, never fail'd to predict the downfall of the Pope and the King of France, then at war with the English. [Pope]

Considerations

"The Rape of the Lock" contains a remarkable store of shrewd poetic strategy. To discuss in detail all the examples and varieties of metaphoric language Pope employs would take a book. Here are a few instances to demonstrate the range of his technique:

Irony "Here Thou, Great *Anna* [Queen Anne]! whom three Realms obey,/Dost sometimes Counsel take—and sometimes *Tea.*" The juxtaposition of counsel (*X*) and tea (*Y*) produces an amused vision of a world where the two virtually contradictory enterprises—taking tea and conducting the affairs of state—have equal importance.

Metaphor Spleen's bag, in which the Goddess of Spleen "collects the Force of Female Lungs,/ Sighs, Sobs, and Passions, and the War of Tongues." In these covert metaphors sighs, sobs, passions, etc. (*X*) are treated as if they were objects (*Y*) to make them seem foolish, among other things.

Image, personification "From silver Spouts the grateful Liquors glide." The image is also a covert metaphor of personification: Liquors (*X*) are personified as persons capable of gratitude (*Y*).

Pun, irony During the card game, before the Baron has performed his evil act, Pope writes: "On one nice *Trick* depends the gen'ral Fate." "Trick" refers to the card game as well as, ironically, to the trick that is about to be played on Belinda's favorite lock of hair.

Symbol, image, metaphor "Now *Jove* suspends his golden Scales in Air,/Weighs the Men's Wits against the Lady's Hair." Jove holds up the scales symbolizing justice. Notice that the image of scales, with Belinda's lock on one side and "wits" on the other, is a description that can be visualized, except for the wits. The symbol-image functions as a metaphor comparing the argument between the men and Belinda over the lock (*X*) to Jove's scales (*Y*).

Allusion, image The poem contains overt and covert allusions to classical epics and mythology. The covert allusions are interesting, though we may need a scholar to point some of them out to us—for example, where Pope describes Belinda's petticoat: "Tho' stiff with Hoops, and arm'd

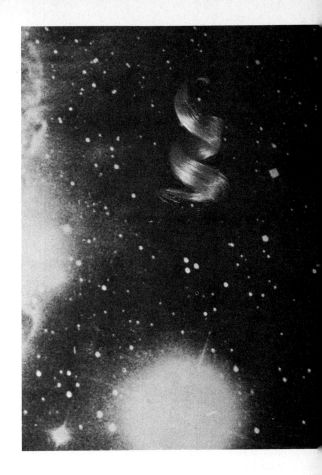

with Ribs of Whale./Form a strong Line about the Silver Bound/And guard the wide Circumference around." In this description Pope mimics Vulcan making Achilles' shield in the *Iliad*. The allusion is almost completely concealed, but it adds a dimension to the poem if you discover it—though the situation has plenty to offer even if you do not.

As we can see, Pope spares no possible technique, and for all practical purposes his poem is inexhaustible.

1. What has the lock of hair become by the end of the poem? What kinds of meanings and associations are attached to it?

2. Consider any small or large section of the poem and its relation to the rest of the piece. As an example, you could consider what effect the ongoing pun on "Ombre" has on the poem (Ombre is the name of the card game and is also the French word for "shadow").

3. What effect do the rhyme and meter have in this poem? How do they add to the tone?

Technical Notes

The poem is written in iambic pentameter, in HEROIC COUPLETS, which Pope made famous.

As we have observed, experiencing the tone of a poem is a matter of understanding the attitude taken toward the subject and of picking up on connotations. This means being open to the effects of metaphors, images, irony, and the rest. To test your ability to respond to metaphoric language and tone, read this poem by the contemporary poet Richard Wilbur and, without looking at the answers, see whether you can fill in the blank spaces with the words Wilbur actually used in the piece. Keep in mind that each choice should relate to the other aspects throughout the poem. There should be a kind of internal tonal "logic."

Richard Wilbur

A FIRE TRUCK

Right down the ____1____ street with a siren-blast
That sends all else skittering to the curb,
Redness, brass, ladders and hats hurl past,
   Blurring to sheer ____2____,

Shift at the corner into uproarious gear
And make it around the turn in a squall of traction,
The ____3____ bell maintaining sure and clear,
   Thought is ____4____ action!

Beautiful, heavy, unweary, loud, ____5____ thing!
I stand here purged of nuance, my mind blank.
All I was brooding on has taken wing,
   And I have you to thank.

As you howl beyond hearing I carry you into my mind,
Ladders and brass and all, there to admire
Your phoenix-red ____6____, enshrined
   In that not ____7____ fire.

1. quiet, lonely, forgotten, last, shocked
2. word, loud, heard, verb, absurd
3. headlong, clamorous, loud, sharp, piercing
4. forgotten, remembered, degraded, completed, defeated
5. useless, foolish, crazy, bold, obvious
6. futility, simplicity, quickness, brashness
7. extinguished, fed, hot, finished, ended

Considerations

1. Try "shocked" here. Don't the other choices seem out of tone—too weak or "intellectual" to describe the forceful, vital effect of the fire truck as represented in the rest of the poem?
2. "Verb" makes a particularly sharp metaphor: Fire truck (X) equals (Y) the grammatical term meaning "action word." This also sets up the metaphoric tension between *thought* (which is verbal) and *action*. We see this tension stated explicitly in stanza two.
3. "Headlong" continues the action aspect of the fire truck and also provides a pun; again, thought (a product of the *head*) is being juxtaposed to action. Note that if you chose "pierce," for example, you would have difficulty finding other "piercing" things in the poem, whereas "headlong" clearly works with the other elements.
4. "Degraded," in terms of diction, is the strongest here, once more elevating action over thought, since compared to the fire truck thought suddenly has lowered status. Does the tone give you the impression that the narrator of the poem feels he has been overintellectual? If that is the case, wouldn't "degrading" thought (humiliating it) be somehow worse for the narrator than "defeating" it?
5. "Obvious" paves the way for the voice of the poem to be "purged of nuance" in the next line, because "obvious" is the opposite of "nuance." Do you find an ironic twist in the last two stanzas? Has the fire truck itself become an object of thought? What has happened to the action of the first two stanzas? Is the narrator already summing up a past event?
6. "Simplicity" is consistent with "obvious" and with the continued tension between thought and action (which is simple and uncomplicated).

7. "Extinguished" completes the paradox. Why do you think "ended" or "finished" was not used? Are they weaker? Out of keeping somehow?

Note that there are no "correct" choices in a poem; the purpose here is to give you an idea of why and how a poet makes very apt or strong ones.

Wilbur's piece might have been called "Ode to a Fire Truck": the overall tone is one of praise. This praising develops contrast between the qualities of thought and action. The fire truck seems to work something like the X in Stevens' "Motive for Metaphor": the reality beyond thought.

1. "Phoenix" is an allusion to the mythological symbol of rebirth: the bird reborn out of its own ashes. It is also a pun: phoenix red is a color. What effect does the symbol have on the meaning levels in the poem? Why does it make "extinguished" a particularly apt choice?
2. Do you see a pun on "brass"? What other puns do you notice?
3. What are some other aspects of Wilbur's use of language in this poem that make it particularly effective? What does it add to our sense of the fire truck's "meaning"? (Consider, for instance, phrases like "howl beyond hearing" or "skittering to the curb." In the context of the fire truck could these be X's with Y levels?)

Technical Notes

The rhyme scheme, in QUATRAINS, is $a\,b\,a\,b$. There is a liberal use of SPONDEES for emphasis.

You might want to compare the way the next two poems use metaphoric images as structure. What are the similarities and differences in tone between these two pieces?

William Butler Yeats

CRAZY JANE AND JACK THE JOURNEYMAN

I know, although when looks meet
I tremble to the bone,
The more I leave the door unlatched
The sooner love is gone,
For love is but a skein unwound
Between the dark and dawn.

A lonely ghost the ghost is
That to God shall come;
I—love's skein upon the ground,
My body in the tomb—
Shall leap into the light lost
In my mother's womb.

But were I left to lie alone
In an empty bed,
The skein so bound us ghost to ghost
When he turned his head
Passing on the road that night,
Mine must walk when dead.

Judith Thurman

SEWING

All night the river rustles,
a thread shirring a silk garment,
barely visible upon the dark embankment,
its stitch of the same color.

It catches the earth
by the fine hairs of its body,
basting it to the flow,
and some of the flesh pulling
to go with it.

I, too, am gathered
by what flows through me,
pleating the past softly,
drawing part of it away from me,
giving it a form,
something that can be worn.

LINES OF INQUIRY

The following poems make extensive use of metaphoric images in addition to simple metaphor. As you read, you might want to consider what kinds of images and metaphors are being used (natural, technological, etc.) and whether you think the images condition the poem's tone or whether the tone has conditioned the choice of images.

Leigh Hunt

THE FISH, THE MAN, AND THE SPIRIT

TO A FISH

You strange, astonished-looking, angle-faced,
  Dreary-mouthed, gaping wretches of the sea,
  Gulping salt-water everlastingly,
Cold-blooded, though with red your blood be graced,
And mute, though dwellers in the roaring waste;
  And you, all shapes beside, that fishy be,—
  Some round, some flat, some long, all devilry,
Legless, unloving, infamously chaste:—

O scaly, slippery, wet, swift, staring wights,
  What is't ye do? What life lead? eh, dull goggles?
How do ye vary your vile days and nights?
  How pass your Sundays? Are ye still but joggles
In ceaseless wash? Still nought but gapes and bites,
  And drinks, and stares, diversified with boggles?

A FISH ANSWERS

Amazing monster! that, for aught I know,
  With the first sight of thee didst make our race
  For ever stare! O flat and shocking face,
Grimly divided from the breast below!
Thou that on dry land horribly dost go
  With a split body and most ridiculous pace,
  Prong after prong, disgracer of all grace,
Long-useless-finned, haired, upright, unwet, slow!

O breather of unbreathable, sword-sharp air,
  How canst exist? How bear thyself, thou dry
And dreary sloth? What particle canst share
  Of the only blessed life, the water?
I sometimes see of ye an actual *pair*
  Go by! linked fin by fin! most odiously.

THE FISH TURNS INTO A MAN, AND THEN
INTO A SPIRIT, AND AGAIN SPEAKS
Indulge thy smiling scorn, if smiling still,
   O man! and loathe, but with a sort of love;
   For difference must its use by difference prove,
And, in sweet clang, the spheres with music fill.
One of the spirits am I, that at his will
   Live in whate'er has life—fish, eagle, dove—
   No hate, no pride, beneath nought, nor above,
A visitor of the rounds of God's sweet skill.

Man's life is warm, glad, sad, 'twixt loves and graves,
   Boundless in hope, honoured with pangs austere,
Heaven-gazing; and his angel-wings he craves:—
   The fish is swift, small-needing, vague yet clear,
A cold, sweet, silver life, wrapped in round waves,
   Quickened with touches of transporting fear.

David Posner

BUILDING

For Olivia

A beam so balanced needs no help:
The cantilever like the rods upon a clock.
Churches are built from it and great glass windows.

Suspending the dark
At intervals as a word throws light
Or the shored sea sings,

When order is natural
The world rings
Like the body of a bell—

Though what stress hides
Inside our effortless
Love, to keep a man from breaking,

Only you and I, under one roof,
Know as we watch the naked air between us
Sob at your touch.

William Blake

THE MENTAL TRAVELLER

I travel'd thro' a Land of Men,
A Land of Men and Women too,
And heard and saw such dreadful things
As cold Earth-wanderers never knew.

For there the Babe is born in joy
That was begotten in dire woe;
Just as we reap in joy the fruit
Which we in bitter tears did sow.

And if the Babe is born a Boy
He's given to a Woman Old,
Who nails him down upon a rock,
Catches his Shrieks in Cups of gold.

She binds iron thorns around his head,
She pierces both his hands and feet,
She cuts his heart out at his side
To make it feel both cold and heat.

Her fingers number every Nerve,
Just as a Miser counts his gold;
She lives upon his shrieks and cries,
And she grows young as he grows old.

Till he becomes a bleeding youth,
And she becomes a Virgin bright;
Then he rends up his Manacles
And binds her down for his delight.

He plants himself in all her Nerves,
Just as a Husbandman his mould;
And she becomes his dwelling-place
And Garden fruitful seventy-fold.

An Agèd Shadow, soon he fades,
Wand'ring round an Earthly Cot,
Full-fillèd all with gems and gold
Which he by industry had got.

And these are the gems of the Human Soul,
The rubies and pearls of a love-sick eye,
The countless gold of the akeing heart,
The martyr's groan and the lover's sigh.

They are his meat, they are his drink;
He feeds the Beggar and the Poor
And the wayfaring Traveller:
For ever open is his door.

His grief is their eternal joy;
They make the roofs and walls to ring.
Till from the fire on the hearth
A little Female Babe does spring;

And she is all of solid fire
And gems and gold, that none his hand
Dares stretch to touch her Baby form,
Or wrap her in his swaddling band.

But She comes to the Man she loves,
If young or old, or rich or poor;
They soon drive out the agèd Host,
A Beggar at another's door.

He wanders weeping far away,
Until some other take him in;
Oft blind and age-bent, sore distrest,
Until he can a Maiden win.

And to allay his freezing Age,
The Poor Man takes her in his arms;
The Cottage fades before his sight,
The Garden and its lovely Charms.

The Guests are scatter'd thro' the land,
For the Eye altering alters all;
The Senses roll themselves in fear,
And the flat Earth becomes a Ball;

The Stars, Sun, Moon, all shrink away,
A desart vast without a bound,
And nothing left to eat or drink,
And a dark desart all around.

The honey of her Infant lips,
The bread and wine of her sweet smile,

The wild game of her roving Eye,
Does him to Infancy beguile;

For as he eats and drinks he grows
Younger and younger every day;
And on the desart wild they both
Wander in terror and dismay.

Like the wild Stag she flees away,
Her fear plants many a thicket wild;
While he pursues her night and day,
By various arts of love beguil'd,

By various arts of Love and Hate,
Till the wide desart planted o'er
With Labyrinths of wayward Love,
Where roam the Lion, Wolf, and Boar,

Till he becomes a wayward Babe,
And she a weeping Woman Old.
Then many a Lover wanders here;
The Sun and Stars are nearer roll'd;

The trees bring forth sweet extacy
To all who in the desert roam;
Till many a City there is Built,
And many a pleasant Shepherd's home.

But when they find the frowning Babe,
Terror strikes thro' the region wide:
They cry "The Babe! the Babe is Born!"
And flee away on Every side.

For who dare touch the frowning form,
His arm is wither'd to its root;
Lions, Boars, Wolves, all howling flee,
And every Tree does shed its fruit.

And none can touch that frowning form,
Except it be a Woman Old;
She nails him down upon the Rock,
And all is done as I have told.

Francesco Petrarca (Petrarch)

THE IMAGE IN MY MIND . . .

The image in my mind deadens the world
And cuts me off from every other being;
Alone in shadowy life with vivid thoughts
I search for her whom I should try to lose
Like a fox seeking the hounds and the terrible teeth:
I see her pass in sweet deadliness
Leading a pack of sighs like fangs,
This superb, carnivorous woman.

I may only imagine there is a light in her
Of pity but a brightness reflects in me,
And so I try again to tell her,
Among the shadows in the light of love:

But there is too much to be said
And time is too real.

Translation from Italian by
Richard Monaco

John Milton

ON THE DEATH OF A FAIR
INFANT DYING OF A COUGH

1
O fairest flower no sooner blown but blasted,
Soft silken Primrose fading timesslie,
Summers chief honour if thou hadst out-lasted,
Bleak winters force that made thy blossome drie;
For he being amorous on that lovely die
　　That did thy cheek envermeil, thought to kiss
But kill'd alas, and then bewail'd his fatal bliss.

2
For since grim Aquilo his charioter
By boistrous rape th'Athenian damsel got,
He thought it toucht his Deitie full near,
If he likewise he some fair one wedded not,
Thereby to wipe away th'infamous blot,
　　Of long-uncoupled bed, and childless eld[1],
Which 'mongst the wanton gods a foul reproach was held
[1]Old age

3

So mounting up in icie-pearled carr,
Through middle empire of the freezing aire
He wanderd long, till thee he spy'd from farr,
There ended was his quest, there ceast his care.
Down he descended from his Snow-soft chaire,
   But all unwares with his cold-kind embrace
Unhous'd thy Virgin Soul from her fair biding place.

4

Yet art thou not inglorious in thy fate;
For so *Apollo*, with unweeting[2] hand
Whilome[3] did slay his dearly-loved mate
Young *Hyacinth* born on *Eurota's* strand,
Young *Hyacinth* the pride of *Spartan* land;
   But then transform'd him to a purple flower
Alack that so to change thee winter had no power.

5

Yet can I not perswade me thou art dead
Or that thy coarse corrupts in earths dark wombe,
Or that thy beauties lie in wormie bed,
Hid from the world in a low delved tombe;
Could Heav'n for pittie thee so strictly doom?
   Oh no? for something in thy face did shine
Above mortalitie that shew'd thou wast divine.

6

Resolve me then oh Soul most surely blest
(If so it be that thou these plaints dost hear)
Tell me bright Spirit where e're thou hoverest
Whether above that high first-moving Spheare
Or in the Elisian fields (if such there were.)
   Oh say me true if thou wert mortal wight
And why from us so quickly thou didst take thy flight.

7

Wert thou some Starr which from the ruin'd roofe
Of shak't Olympus by mischance didst fall;
Which carefull *Jove* in natures true behoofe
Took up, and in fit place did reinstall?
Or did of late earths Sonnes besiege the wall
   Of sheenie Heav'n, and thou some goddess fled
Amongst us here below to hide thy nectar'd head.

8

Or wert thou that just Maid who once before
Forsook the hated earth, O tell me sooth
And cam'st again to visit us once more?
Or wert thou that sweet smiling Youth?
Or that crown'd Matron sage white-robed truth?
   Or any other of that heav'nly brood
Let down in clowdie throne to do the world some good.
[2]Unyielding

9

Or wert thou of the golden-winged hoast,
Who having clad thy self in humane weed,
To earth from thy prefixed seat didst post,
And after short abode flie back with speed,
As if to shew what creatures Heav'n doth breed,
    Thereby to set the hearts of men on fire
To scorn the sordid world, and unto Heav'n aspire.

10

But oh why didst thou not stay here below
To bless us with thy heav'n-lov'd innocence,
To slake his wrath whom sin hath made our foe
To turn Swift-rushing black perdition hence,
Or drive away the slaughtering pestilence,
    To stand 'twixt us and our deserved smart?
But thou canst best perform that office where thou art.

11

Then thou the mother of so sweet a child
Her false imagin'd loss cease to lament,
And wisely learn to curb thy sorrows wild;
Think what a present thou to God hast sent,
And render him with patience what he lent;
    This if thou do he will an off-spring give,
That till the world's last-end shall make thy name to live.

Luis de Gongora

ON THE TRICKY BREVITY OF LIFE

Almost unknowingly, the swift arrow left its bow,
but it will bite its destined mark, nonetheless.
The games' cart trundles through the arena of change,
surrounded by applause, toward its silent objective.

With secret and tricky speed we travel to the
end of our days. Who struggles against it,
with the beast of his reason, still
falls like the sun toward his dusk.

Even Carthage has fallen. Can you stand?
Your flight is dangerous, Licio, if you persist
in following shadows and embracing your briefness.

Time will not pardon us in our last hours,
hours that gnaw away at days,
days that swallow years.

                    Translation from Spanish

Samuel Daniel

BEAUTY, SWEET LOVE

Beauty, sweet love, is like the morning dew,
Whose short refresh upon the tender green,
Cheers for a time, but till the sun doth show,
And straight 'tis gone as it had never been.

Soon doth it fade that makes the fairest flourish,
Short is the glory of the blushing rose:
The hue which thou so carefully dost nourish,
Yet which at length thou must be forc'd to lose.

When thou, surcharg'd with burthen of thy years,
Shall bend thy wrinkles homeward to the earth,
And when in beauty's lease, expir'd, appears
The date of age, the calends of our death—
But ah! no more—this must not be foretold,
For women grieve to think they must be old.

*The following few poems use irony and/or paradox to achieve a major part of
their effect. As you read the poems, see whether you can feel what this effect is.*

Matthew Arnold

THE LAST WORD

Creep into thy narrow bed,
Creep, and let no more be said!
Vain thy onset! all stands fast.
Thou thyself must break at last.

Let the long contention cease!
Geese are swans, and swans are geese.
Let them have it how they will!
Thou art tired; best be still.

They out-talked thee, hissed thee, tore thee?
Better men fared thus before thee;
Fired their ringing shot and pass'd,
Hotly charged—and broke at last.

Charge once more, then, and be dumb!
Let the victors, when they come,
When the forts of folly fall,
Find thy body by the wall!

Andrew Marvell

THE DEFINITION OF LOVE

My Love is of a birth as rare
As 'tis for object strange and high:
It was begotten by Despair
Upon Impossibility.

Magnanimous Despair alone
Could show me so divine a thing,
Where feeble Hope could ne'er have flown
But vainly flapt its tinsel wing.

And yet I quickly might arrive
Where my extended soul is fixt,
But Fate does iron wedges drive,
And always crowds itself betwixt.

For Fate with jealous eye does see
Two perfect loves; nor lets them close:
Their union would her ruin be,
And her tyrannic power depose.

And therefore her decrees of steel
Us as the distant poles have placed
(Though Love's whole world on us doth wheel),
Not by themselves to be embraced:

Unless the giddy heaven fall,
And earth some new convulsion tear;
And, us to join, the world should all
Be cramped into a planisphere.°

As lines so loves oblique may well
Themselves in every angle greet:
But ours so truly parallel,
Though infinite can never meet.

Therefore the Love which us doth bind,
But Fate so enviously debars,
Is the conjunction of the mind,
And opposition of the stars.

°A polar projection of the sphere on a plane

James Russell Lowell

SIXTY-EIGHTH BIRTHDAY

As life runs on, the road grows strange
With faces new, and near the end
The milestones into headstones change,
'Neath every one a friend.

Joachim du Bellay

ROME

Thou stranger, which for Rome in Rome here seekest,
And nought of Rome in Rome perceiv'st at all,
These same olde walls, olde arches, which thou seest,
Olde Palaces, is that which Rome men call.
Behold what wreake, what ruine, and what wast,
And how that she, which with her mightie power
Tam'd all the world, hath tam'd herselfe at last,
The prey of time, which all things doth devour.
Rome now of Rome is th'onely funerall,
And onely Rome of Rome hath victorie;
Nor aught save Tyber hastning to his fall
Remaines of all: O world's inconstancie.
That which is firme doth flit and fall away,
And that is flitting, doth abide and stay.

Translation from Italian
by Edmund Spenser

John Donne

HOLY SONNET X

Death be not proud, though some have called thee
Mighty and dreadfull, for, thou art not soe,
For, those, whom thou think'st, thou dost overthrow,
Die not, poore death, nor yet canst thou kill mee.
From rest and sleepe, which but thy pictures bee,
Much pleasure, then from thee, much more must flow,
And soonest our best men with thee doe goe,
Rest of their bones, and soules deliverie.
Thou art slave to Fate, Chance, kings, and desperate men,
And dost with poison, warre, and sicknesse dwell,
And poppie, or charmes can make us sleepe as well,
And better than thy stroake; why swell'st thou then?
  One short sleepe past, wee wake eternally,
  And death shall be no more; death, thou shalt die.

Hugo von Hofmannstal

TRANSIENCE

I still can feel their breath upon my cheeks:
How can it be that they are gone and past,
Completely gone, these last few days and weeks?

This is a thing our minds can never grasp,
A thing too hideous even to lament:
That all things slip away and nothing lasts,

That what I call my "self" untrammeled went
Gliding out of a child to reach me here,
A child now mute and strange as a dog. And then:

That centuries ago I too was there.
And all my forebears, shrouded in cerements,
They are akin to me as my own hair,

Connected to me like my very hair.

Translation from German by
Christopher Collins

John Lydgate

from THE DANCE OF DEATH*

DEATH TO THE SERGEANT
Come forth, sir sergeant, with your stately mace:
Make no defense nor no rebellion.
Not may avail to grumble in this case
Though ye be haughty of condition;
For no appeal nor protection
May you franchise to do nature wrong,
For there is none so sturdy champion,
Though he be mighty, another is as strong.

THE SERGEANT ANSWERS
How dare this death set on me arrest
That am the king's chosen officer,
Which yesterday both east and west
Mine office did put all in fear?
But now this day I am arrested here,
And may not flee, though I had swore
Each man is loath to die, both far and near,
That hath not learned for to die before.
*Spelling and some words modernized from Middle
English

DEATH TO THE PHYSICIAN
Master of physique, which on your urine
So look and gaze and stare against the sun,
For all your craft and study of medicine,
All pratique and science that ye summon,
Your life's course so thus far is run.
Again my might your craft may not endure,
For all the gold that ye thereby have won:
Good leech° is he that he himself can cure.

DEATH TO THE MINSTREL
Oh thou minstrel, that can so pipe and play
Unto folks for to do pleasance
By the right hand anon I shall thee stay,
With these other to go upon my dance.
There's no escape nor avoidance,
On no side to contrary my sentence,
For in music by craft and accordance
Who master is shall show his science.

THE MINSTREL ANSWERS
This new dance is to me so strange,
Wonder diverse and passingly contrary;
The dreadful footing doth so often change,
And the measures so ofttimes vary,
Which now to me is nothing necessary
If it were so I might be still
But many a man, if I shall not tarry,
Oft danceth, though against his will.

°Doctor

EXPERIENCING THE POEM

Without analyzing, interpreting, or even considering metaphoric language or meanings, reread "Ars
Poetica" (page 8) and see what immediate impact it
has on you. Do you still find it fresh? Does it seem
even richer now?

CHAPTER 3
THE POEM AS
A METAPHOR: X/Y

You may have noticed that some poems not only contain metaphoric language but also seem to have a central metaphoric idea that is worked out over the entire poem. We looked at several such poems in Chapter 1, including "A Patch of Old Snow," "The Pearl," "The Song Wants to Be Light," and "At the Outskirts of the World." In "A Patch of Old Snow," for example, the main metaphor is a patch of old snow (X) is (like) a blown-away newspaper (Y). We might call this the CENTRAL METAPHORIC RELATIONSHIP. A secondary or *local metaphor*, dirt on the snow = newsprint, is connected to this. Similarly, in Jonson's "Houre-glasse," the central metaphor is the lovers (X) compared to ashes in the glass (Y). This is supported by the local metaphor of the lover, who is (like) a "flie in a flame," as well as by images of ashes, cinders, atoms, etc.

Clearly, delineating the central metaphor does not explicate the poem because it is precisely the details surrounding and amplifying the central relationship which bring it to life. But the central metaphoric relationship is the direction, the focus of interest and poetic action. It shapes the poem. Think, for instance, of "The Rape of the Lock," where the basic relationship involves juxtaposing London high society (X) with the world of the epic (Y). In the process of working this out, literally hundreds of images, local metaphors, puns, paradoxes, etc., are developed, all connecting with the central metaphor and heightening its impact. You might even say that the various elements (distinct and evocative in themselves) are "spun like a web" around this center.

In this chapter we'll look at central metaphors which are X/Y relationships extended throughout a poem. This sort of relationship might work ironically (as with Whitman's "When I Heard the Learn'd Astronomer": the astronomer's theories [X] versus the reality of the universe [Y]), paradoxically (as in "On Nothing"), or even in punning ("Subject: Object: Sentence"). In any case, the poems here have both X and Y terms that are stated or obvious, and the focus is on how the relationship is worked out. Generally, the discussions and considerations in this and the following chapters will touch on only major points. You can investigate detailed aspects of tone and levels of meaning yourself.

The central metaphoric relationship is stated in the title of this sixteenth-century poem. The distraught lover (X) is (like) a ship on a stormy sea (Y). The poem itself elaborates this comparison in remarkable detail.*

Sir Thomas Wyatt

THE LOVER COMPARETH HIS STATE TO A SHIP IN PERILOUS STORM TOSSED ON THE SEA

My galley charged with forgetfulness
Through sharp seas in winter nights doth pass
'Tween Rock and Rock; and eke° my enemy, alas,
That is my lord, steereth with cruelness.
And every oar a thought in readiness,
As though that death were light in such a case;
An endless wind doth tear the sail apace
Of forced sighs and trusty fearfulness.
A rain of tears, a cloud of dark disdain,
Have done the wearied cords great hinderance;
Wreathed with error and eke with ignorance.
The stars be hid that led me to this pain.
Drown'd is reason that should me consort,
And I remain, despairing of the port.

*This piece is a famous example of *conceit.*
°Also

Considerations

1. Why is the poet's galley "charged with forget-fulness"? What does "charged" imply here?
2. What do the sharp seas and winter nights suggest to you in terms of the lover's state? Is each an *X* referring to some *Y* or *Y*'s? What do the rocks suggest? The oars?
3. Who or what might the enemy be? Is the enemy also the Lord?
4. How do you explain the near paradox (ambiguity) in the line "As though that death were light in such a case"?
5. Consider the "endless wind" and "sail." Could they be *X*'s with unstated *Y*'s too? If so, what possible things could they refer to? What about the "wearied cords" in terms of the lover's state?
6. What kind of "error" could be involved in this state? What "ignorance"? What are the "stars" that led the lover to his "pain"? What is the port the narrator despairs of?
7. Could the lover be referring to his love for God too? Could you read this poem consistently as a religious poem?
8. Can you really give specific answers to the above questions without limiting the poem? Can you experience and understand this piece without knowing what these things mean?

Notice Wyatt's striking use of local metaphors, all related to the central metaphor: the lover's state is (like) a ship on a stormy sea. Given this central comparison, every detail takes on metaphoric possibilities: the galley of forgetfulness; the oars (like) thoughts in readiness; the sea, rocks, wind, sails—every item brings new vision and focus. Are the rocks the lovers' quarrels? Desires? How is every oar a thought in readiness? Readiness for what—to move the galley further into these stormy metaphoric seas? The simple central comparison mysteriously fills out with connotation and nuance.

Interestingly, we are given *no* information about the love relationship, who the poet's lover is, or why he is in this "state." But we sense the reason for it out of our own experience of love. Can you feel how we seem to *know*, for example, what "ignorance," "cruelness," and "fearfulness" he is talking about here?

Technical Notes

This piece is a PETRARCHAN SONNET written in iambic pentameter.

We have discussed how a poem can spin a complex web of association and meaning using metaphoric language. In Marvell's "On a Drop of Dew," though the central metaphoric idea is relatively simple (a drop of dew = the soul) the relationship is worked out in vivid detail, linking idea and image to make one of the richest, most intricate short poems in the language.

Andrew Marvell

ON A DROP OF DEW

See how the orient dew,
Shed from the bosom of the morn
Into the blowing roses,
Yet careless of its mansion new,
For the clear region where 'twas born,
Round in its self incloses;
And in its little globe's extent,
Frames as it can its native element.
How it the purple flower does slight,
Scarce touching where it lies,
But gazing back upon the skies,
Shines with a mournful light,
Like its own tear,
Because so long divided from the sphere.
Restless it rolls and unsecure,
Trembling lest it grow impure:
Till the warm sun pity its pain,
And to the skies exhale it back again.
So the soul, that drop, that ray
Of the clear fountain of Eternal Day,
Could it within the human flower be seen,
Rememb'ring still its former height,
Shuns the sweet leaves and blossoms green;
And, recollecting its own light,
Does, in its pure and circling thoughts, express
The greater heaven in an heaven less.
In how coy a figure wound,
Every way it turns away:
So the world excluding round,
Yet receiving in the Day.
Dark beneath, but bright above:
Here disdaining, there in love.
How loose and easy hence to go:
How girt and ready to ascend.
Moving but on a point below,
It all about does upward bend.
Such did the manna's sacred dew distill;
White, and entire, though congealed and chill.
Congealed on earth: but does, dissolving, run
Into the glories of th' Almighty Sun.

Considerations

If we paraphrased the drop-of-dew argument, we might write: "God and the soul are of one nature, though separated; therefore, the soul longs to return to God." But in metaphor this argument is transformed: The soul and its longing seem "real," palpable, irrefutable, or at least we have no desire to refute it. Could even an atheist fail to be affected, to react to this extremely sensual image? And if he could reject the argument, or what he might take for argument, that would still leave the substance of the poem to be experienced.

The accompanying diagram is an attempt to illustrate the remarkable interaction of terms in

this poem. There are probably dozens of alternatives to this diagram, and it is far from complete, but it may help you visualize how we get so many meanings out of a poem, why poems seem so rich. Here we can see how virtually every detail in Marvell's piece extends the basic metaphoric relation (drop of dew = soul) and combines with other terms to create a web of meaning. It is not surprising that a poem like this stays unique and insightful reading after reading. On each approach to the piece we come in on a different strand, and so our view of the whole looks different.

In the diagram only two of the terms ("self" and

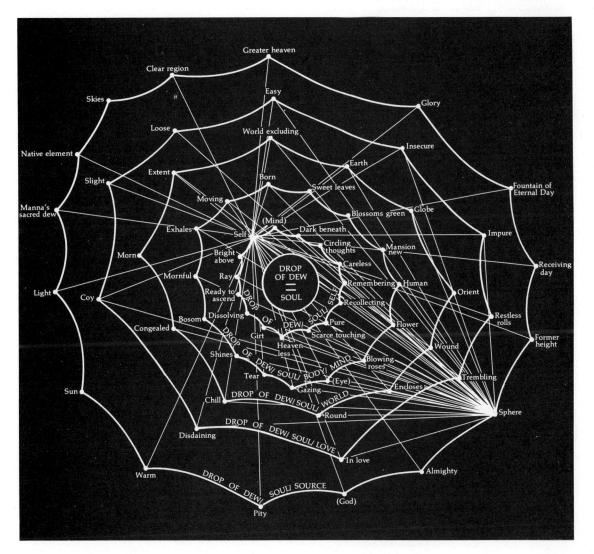

"sphere") have been connected up with others to which they relate. The terms in parentheses, like "mind," are ideas unstated but clearly implied by poetic context. As you see, the diagram is extremely dense with just two terms. Can you imagine what it would look like if all the terms were interconnected to reflect the comparison, contrast, identity, and association in the poem? No logical presentation tied to its premises could develop this range of meaning.

1. Consider how the central metaphor (soul = drop of dew) relates to the other details in the poem. What is associated, contrasted, compared, or identified with the drop of dew? What are the possible implications of these associations (for example, the image of the dewdrop as "Dark beneath, but bright above" or as "careless")?

2. The term "God" is never used in this poem. There is no bearded old man, flights of angels, or clouds here. What kind of picture do we have of where the soul comes from and where it goes?

3. What is the difference between the *sense* of the soul that you get from Marvell's poem and the *idea* of the soul you might get from theology?

Technical Notes

This poem interweaves lines of five distinct meters. Marvell has indicated them by indenting his left-hand margin. Starting with the lines beginning at the margin, these meters are (1) iambic pentameter, (2) iambic tetrameter, (3) TROCHAIC tetrameter, (4) iambic trimeter, and (5) iambic dimeter ("Like its own tear").

Compare the effect of "On a Drop of Dew" with that of the next poem, written in about the same period. Which do you think is more effective?

Sir John Davies

OF THE SOUL OF MAN AND THE IMMORTALITY THEREOF

O Light! (which mak'st the light, which mak'st the day;
Which sett'st the eye without, and mind within)
Lighten my spirit with one clear heavenly ray!
Which not to view itself doth first begin.

For her true form how can my spark discern?
Which, dim by nature, art did never clear;
When the great wits, of whom all skill we learn,
Are ignorant both what she is and where!
. . . .
Thou! that hast fashioned twice this soul of ours,
So that she is by double title Thine!
Thou only knowest her nature and her powers;
Her subtle form Thou only canst define!

To judge herself, she must herself transcend;
As greater circles comprehend the less:
But she wants power her own powers to extend;
As fettered men cannot their strength express.

But thou bright morning Star! Thou, rising Sun!
Which, in these later times, has brought to light
Those mysteries that, since the world begun,
Lay hid in darkness and eternal night!

Thou, like the sun, dost with indifferent ray
Into the palace and the cottage shine,
And showest the soul, both to the clerk and lay,
By the clear lamp of thy oracle divine!

This lamp, through all the regions of my brain,
Where my soul sits, doth spread such beams of grace,
As now, methinks, I do distinguish plain
Each subtle line of her immortal face!

Considerations

Davies's poem aims to inspire, and he certainly
chose an inspiring subject—but his result inspires
a certain drowsiness. There's nothing like the
brightness and excitement we found in Marvell's
piece. Not that Davies's poem is particularly
"bad"—the point is that Marvell's metaphor is
immediate, untheoretical, and independent of
argument or systems of belief. Instead of statements, opinions, hopes, and ideas, Marvell presents the drop of dew, and the complex web spun
around his gleaming globe has infinitely more
power and reality than Davies's assertions and
heartfelt piety.

1. Compare the tone of "On a Drop of Dew" with
   the tone of this poem. What is the difference?
   Can you account for it?
2. Consider Davies's use of local metaphor. Are
   Marvell's local metaphors more effective?
   What difference does Marvell's use of a central
   relationship make?
3. Do you think a poem's "truth" depends on
   whether you agree or disagree with its point of
   view?

*Whitman's "When I Heard the Learn'd Astronomer"
dropped traditional meter and rhyme. This poem has
gone a step further. Not even the way the lines are
printed on the page tells you it is poetry. However,
the obvious metaphoric relationships locate the piece
within poetic tradition.*

Karl Shapiro

THE DIRTY WORD

The dirty word hops in the cage of the mind
like the Pondicherry vulture, stomping with
its heavy left claw on the sweet meat of the
brain and tearing it with its vicious beak,
ripping and chopping the flesh. Terrified, the
small boy bears the big bird of the dirty word
into the house, and grunting, puffing, carries
it up the stairs to his own room in the skull.
Bits of black feather cling to his clothes and
his hair as he locks the staring creature in the
dark closet.

All day the small boy returns to the closet
to examine and feed the bird, to caress and
kick the bird, that now snaps and flaps its
wings savagely whenever the door is opened.
How the boy trembles and delights at the
sight of the white excrement of the bird! How
the bird leaps and rushes against the walls of
the skull, trying to escape from the zoo of the
vocabulary! How wildly snaps the sweet meat
of the brain in its rage.

And the bird outlives the man, being freed
at the man's death-funeral by a word from the
rabbi.

But I one morning went upstairs and
opened the door and entered the closet and
found in the cage of my mind the great bird
dead. Softly I wept it and softly removed it
and softly buried the body of the bird in the
hollyhock garden of the house I lived in
twenty years before. And out of the worn
black feathers of the wing have I made pens
to write these elegies, for I have outlived the
bird, and I have murdered it in my early
manhood.

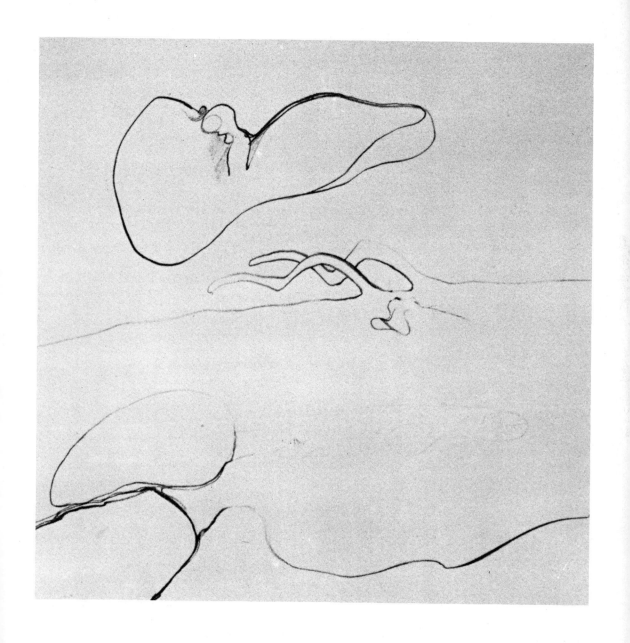

Considerations

1. What are the *X* and *Y* terms of the poem's central metaphor?
2. Can you find any secondary or local metaphors in the poem? What are they? How do they relate to the central metaphoric relationship?
3. Even though the point this poem is making seems fairly clear, can you see where the poet's use of metaphor adds dimension, a sort of unknown and unknowable quality to the idea?
4. Do you think the ending of this poem limits it in any way?

What is the central metaphoric relationship in this poem by a famous nineteenth-century French poet?

Paul Verlaine

CLAIR DE LUNE

(Light of the Moon)

Your soul is the chosen landscape
Where charmed troubadors go,
Playing their lutes and dancing;
Beneath fantastic masks half-sad.

Singing in a minor key
Enchanted tales of love and pleasure,
Of happiness they can never quite believe,
Their song is dissolving in the light of the moon.

Pale light of the moon, so sad and lovely,
Makes birds dream in the trees,
And fountains sob with ecstasy,
Slender and wishful among statues of stone.

Translation from French by John Briggs

Considerations

Consider the details of Verlaine's landscape of the soul. What are some of the possibilities for the meaning (*Y* levels) in each of these details?

1. Who or what are the "charmed troubadors"?
2. Why are they "half-sad"?
3. Why are they singing in "a minor key" of "Enchanted tales of love and pleasure"?
4. Why is their song "dissolving in the light of the moon"?

5. What is the light of the moon metaphorically? Reality? Fantasy?
6. What are some of the implications of the last two lines?
7. The illustrator of this poem has chosen to treat the piece abstractly. Can you see any connection between the artist's vision and Verlaine's?

Here, as in Wyatt's poem, the complete metaphoric relationship is given in the title. But instead of the usual metaphor comparing an abstraction *(time or the lover's state) to something* concrete *(a "wingèd chariot" or a ship on a stormy sea), here an* abstraction *is compared to an* abstraction. *See whether you can tell how the poet makes this difficult central comparison work.*

W. H. Auden

LAW LIKE LOVE

[1]
Law, say the gardeners, is the sun,
Law is the one
All gardeners obey
To-morrow, yesterday, to-day.

[2]
Law is the wisdom of the old,
The impotent grandfathers shrilly scold;
The grandchildren put out a treble tongue,
Law is the senses of the young.

[3]
Law, says the priest with a priestly look,
Expounding to an unpriestly people,
Law is the words in my priestly book,
Law is my pulpit and my steeple.

[4]
Law, says the judge as he looks down his nose,
Speaking clearly and most severely,
Law is as I've told you before,
Law is as you know I suppose,
Law is but let me explain it once more,
Law is The Law.

[5]
Yet law-abiding scholars write:
Law is neither wrong nor right,
Law is only crimes
Punished by places and by times,
Law is the clothes men wear
Anytime, anywhere,
Law is Good morning and Good night.

[6]
Others say, Law is our Fate;
Others say, Law is our State;
Others say, others say
Law is no more
Law has gone away.

[7]
And always the loud angry crowd
Very angry and very loud
Law is We,
And always the soft idiot softly Me.

[8]
If we, dear, know we know no more
Than they about the law,
If I no more than you

Know what we should and should not do
Except that all agree
Gladly or miserably
That the law is
And that all know this,
If therefore thinking it absurd
To identify Law with some other word,
Unlike so many men
I cannot say Law is again,
No more than they can we suppress
The universal wish to guess
Or slip out of our own position
Into an unconcerned condition.
Although I can at least confine
Your vanity and mine
To stating timidly
A timid similarity,
We shall boast anyway:
Like love I say.

[9]
Like love we don't know where or why
Like love we can't compel or fly
Like love we often weep
Like love we seldom keep.

Considerations

Here Auden, like most poets before him, explores the issue of love. But after several centuries of literary convention the traditional metaphors for love (metaphors usually made up of *natural* or *literary-natural* images like flowers, clouds, stars, and shepherds) have been pretty much worn out. In any case, writing in the age of science and the "death" of God, twentieth-century poets tend not to express romance in Marlowe's way; their tone is closer to Donne's or Marvell's: unsentimental, ironical, "logical." In fact, in this poem, when Auden talks about love, his voice almost suggests the sociologist—taking account of all points of view, looking at the question with an analytic, investigative eye. His (and our) metaphoric "leap," however, leaves all this intellectual machinery behind.

By itself, the comparison of law to love is interesting but pale. In fact law, like a pair of compasses

or a technological discussion, seems a surprisingly dry and unpoetic thing to compare to love. But again, we find that the secondary relationships give force to the primary, or central, relationship.

First notice that although the central comparison is *abstraction* with *abstraction*, the poem does not lack concrete references: The "sun," "shrilly scold," the "priestly look," "clothes men wear," "soft idiot," etc.

Second, having asserted that law is like love, Auden casts the entire poem (except for the last stanza) in terms of the law (X), which is not, in fact, the main subject. So there is a vision of law which simultaneously is a vision of his subject, love (Y). Since the unlike factor in this comparison is great, the author gains considerable distance on his subject. Recall how Marvell did this with a drop of dew. Here the distance gives the tone a touch of cynicism, as well as amplifying the poetic tension.

A simple way to follow how Auden works around his central metaphor is to examine the effect of local metaphor and image. A minute drama is enacted in each of the first seven stanzas, with characters speaking as priests, judges, children, and so on.

In the first stanza, instead of saying something like "law equals eternal natural processes," the poet presents gardeners who talk about the sun. Can you grasp how this metaphoric image reaches beyond the statement underlying it (law equals eternal natural law)?

Similarly, in stanza two, instead of "law equals experience" (whether of age or of the senses), grandfathers and children present a little enactment of the age-old conflict between generations. How does this reach past the more abstract statement underlying it? Can you connect with this?

In the third stanza law equals symbols; in the fourth, law equals itself; and stanza five offers us law as various customs, the product of social history.

In stanza six what the previous stanzas have been implying is focused: law equals whatever our opinion about the world is. Then stanza seven draws a kind of conclusion: law equals the ego, the self, self-interest, the "I." But, again, the dramatization—the crowd, the idiot—is clearly richer than the statement that law equals ego, the self, etc.

In stanza eight, there is a sudden change of voice; after the caustic irony of the first half, a "dear" is being addressed, a reminder (in case we had forgotten) that the main term of the central metaphor is love. Perhaps we just now realize that this is in fact a love poem. The key line, in the eighth stanza, might be: "That the law is." On one level, law (or love) *exists*, but all efforts to define *what* it is are futile or, worse, involve us in the opinionated foolishness of the little characters the poem mocks. So this "universal wish to guess" what law/love *is* leads to "an unconcerned condition," perhaps imagining we "know," having our petty opinions, avoiding the essentially unknowable dimensions of it.

Within this frame of reference, how do you understand the final stanza? This is one approach: The law/love relationship plays on our assumptions because we assume that law is sound, fixed, understood, all worked out. Metaphoric tension reveals a mysterious dimension to law by exposing how the concept is entangled with conceit, egotism, and prejudice. The truth of law and love, we sense here, is something other than this human confusion which binds and conceals it.

1. Most of the first seven stanzas involve the use of irony in the descriptions of the characters (the grandfathers, the priest, the scholars, etc.). What is the irony in each case, and how does it affect the overall tone of the poem?
2. In stanza five, what is the irony in the "law-abiding scholars'" position? What new angle does the poet add with "Law is Good morning and Good night"? How do we use these terms ordinarily?
3. Consider the tone change in stanza eight. What factors account for this change?
4. What kinds of insight does this poem spark in you? Can you come up with angles of interpretation different from the one above?

Technical Notes

This poem is written in accentual meter, predominately four stresses to a line. It is a modern adaptation of the rhythm used in traditional nursery rhymes. (See also Blake's "Auguries of Innocence," page 28.)

What is the central metaphoric relationship in this poem? Do you see anything particularly unusual about it?

Francesca Petrarca (Petrarch)

THE WHITENED, SPRUNG OLD MAN . . .

The whitened, sprung old man carries the pain
That has become himself and leaves his home
And bent in silence walks the bitter road
Leaving his family with their helpless love
And bears his last living days on the road to Rome;
With weak and delicate steps he goes
Alone with time and the hurt of a long life,
His will bent, strong but shaky as his stick.

In Rome he dreams of the image of God
And longs to see below what waits above;
Even the dead and clumsy picture of heaven
Quickens him more than all the breathing earth.

This is how I look for you my love:
Seeing in all other lovers the imitation of you.

  Translation from Italian by Richard Monaco

Considerations

The old man dreaming of God (*X*) is compared to the lover dreaming of his love (*Y*). The metaphor is striking for several reasons: (1) Fourteenth- and fifteenth-century poets often used love for a woman to illustrate love for God, but here the traditional comparison is reversed; (2) there is a contrast between an old man and young lovers; and (3) most of the poem elaborates the image of the old man—the *Y* term appears only at the very end, in effect causing us to re-react to the poem and relate the earlier details to lovers.

This last effect is very strong. How *is* the old man's journey to Rome like a lover's yearning? The "bitter road," the "will bent, strong but shaky," "alone with time"—these certainly fit with the lovers' "state," but what happens when we try to superimpose the lover and his longing on the whole vivid picture of the old man? Is there some eerie vision of young love as old age, of fleshly desire as celestial longing? Do you somehow *feel* the two are the same?

1. Consider the local metaphor: will = stick. How is this metaphor connected to the central metaphoric relationship? For example, how do the words "strong" and "shaky" relate to the lover? Is there a sexual connotation too?
2. The image of the "bitter road" is actually a covert local metaphor. What are its terms?
3. Taking the "road to Rome" is an expression symbolically equivalent to traveling toward your ultimate objective or goal. ("All roads lead to Rome.") How does the symbolic road to Rome relate to the central metaphor here?

What other associations are there to Rome? Are there any religious associations?

4. Would the poem be as effective without the last two lines? Would the old man's journey still have metaphoric meaning?
5. Consider any of the other details of this poem in terms of the central metaphor.

Technical Notes

In the original Italian this poem is a sonnet, rhyming *a b b a a b b a c d e c d e*. This version of the sonnet was picked up by English RENAISSANCE poets (Wyatt among them), who popularized the form in our language.

The central metaphoric relationship of this poem might be stated as: the lover's emotional state (X) is (like) a businessman in financial trouble (Y). Here the central metaphor is not stated outright, as in the previous poems; still, it is clear enough.

Sir Philip Sidney

WITH WHAT SHARP
CHECKS . . .

With what sharp checks I in myself am shent,°
When into Reason's audit I do go:
And by just counts myself a bankrupt know
Of all those goods, which heav'n to me hath lent:
Unable quite to pay even Nature's rent,
Which unto it by birthright I do owe:
And, which is worse, no good excuse can show,
But that my wealth I have most idly spent.
My youth doth waste, my knowledge brings forth toys,
My wit doth strive those passions to defend,
Which for reward spoil it with vain annoys.
I see my course to lose myself doth bend:
    I see and yet no greater sorrow take,
    Than that I lose no more for Stella's sake.

°Punished

Considerations

Consider the possible levels of meaning in the details supporting Sidney's central metaphor here.

1. What is "Reasons's audit"?
2. What are the "goods" which heaven has "lent" the narrator?
3. What is "Nature's rent"? (Note the possible pun.)
4. Why does knowledge bring forth "toys"?
5. In what ways could the narrator "lose" himself? What is the AMBIGUITY in the line "Than that I lose no more for Stella's sake"?

Somewhat like the Petrarch poem, this one contains two entirely different situations juxtaposed to make up the central metaphoric relationship.

Richard Wilbur

THE WRITER

In her room at the top of the house
Where light breaks, and the windows are tossed with linden, [shade tree]
My daughter is writing a story.

I pause in the stairwell, hearing
From her shut door a commotion of typewriter-keys
Like a chain hauled over a gunwale. [upper edge of ship's side]

Young as she is, the stuff
Of her life is a great cargo, and some of it heavy:
I wish her a lucky passage.

But now it is she who pauses,
As if to reject my thought and its easy figure. [metaphor]
A stillness greatens, in which

The whole house seems to be thinking,
And then she is at it again with a bunched clamor
Of strokes, and again is silent.

I remember the dazed starling [bird]
Which was trapped in that very room, two years ago;
How we stole in, lifted a sash

And retreated, not to affright it;
And how for a helpless hour, through the crack of the door,
We watched the sleek, wild, dark

[rainbow colors]
And iridescent creature
Batter against the brilliance, drop like a glove
To the hard floor, or the desk-top,

And wait then, humped and bloody,
For the wits to try it again; and how our spirits
Rose when, suddenly sure,

It lifted off from a chair-back,
Beating a smooth course for the right window
And clearing the sill of the world.

It is always a matter, my darling,
Of life or death, as I had forgotten. I wish
What I wished you before, but harder.

Considerations

1. What are the terms of the central metaphor in this poem?
2. Consider the local metaphors in the first five stanzas. How do they relate to the central metaphoric idea, particularly the details of "passage"?
3. What does Wilbur's choice of a starling add to the implications of the poem?
4. What kinds of things might the bird itself mean in terms of the poem?

The first five stanzas present the situation in detail:

The narrator's daughter is writing a story (X). The next five stanzas shift to the description of the starling (Y). The final stanza overtly ties the two together. Notice Wilbur's effective use of parallel details: the daughter clattering on the typewriter juxtaposed to the starling clashing against the window.

Technical Notes

The poem is written in accentual meter. Each stanza is composed of two three-stress lines with one five-stress line in the middle.

Can you see any similarity in approach between this Wyatt poem and the Wilbur piece we just read? Consider it in detail.

Sir Thomas Wyatt

THE LOVER SHOWETH HOW HE IS FORSAKEN OF SUCH AS HE SOMETIME ENJOYED

They flee from me that sometime did me seek
With naked foot stalking in my chamber.
I have seen them gentle tame and meek
That now are wild and do not remember
That sometime they put themselves in danger
To take bread at my hand; and now they range
Basely seeking with a continual change.

Thanked by fortune, it hath been otherwise
Twenty times better; but once in special,
In thine array after a pleasant guise
When her loose gown from her shoulders did fall,
And she caught me in her armes long and small;
Therewith all sweetly did me kiss,
And softly said, "Dear heart, how like you this?"

It was no dream: I lay broad waking.
But all is turned thorough my gentleness
Into a strange fashion of forsaking;
And I have leave to go of her goodness,
And she also to use new fangledness.
But since that I so kindly am served,
I would fain know what she hath deserved.

In this piece the cause of grief is probed metaphorically. Can you see the stated central metaphoric relationship?

Gerard Manley Hopkins

SPRING AND FALL:

To a Young Child

Márgarét, are you gríeving
Over Goldengrove unleaving?
Leáves líke the things of man, you
With your fresh thoughts care for, can you?
Ah! ás the heart grows older
It will come to such sights colder
By and by, nor spare a sigh
Though worlds of wanwood leafmeal lie;
And yet you wíll weep and know why.
Now no matter, child, the name:
Sórrow's spríngs áre the same.
Nor mouth had, no nor mind, expressed
What heart heard of, ghost guessed:
It ís the blight man was born for,
It is Margaret you mourn for.

Considerations

1. What makes the word "blight" particularly appropriate in the second-to-last line?
2. In what ways does the last line relate to the rest of the poem?
3. What is the tone of the poem? How do you account for it?
4. Notice how Hopkins, in his eccentric style, compresses images. The bright, fall-leaved trees become "Goldengrove"; the pale, shattered autumn leaves become "wanwood leafmeal." Do you perceive metaphoric action here? It might be interesting to compare Hop-

kins with various Anglo-saxon poets in this respect. See "The Seafarer" (page 284) and also the definition of KENNINGS in the Glossary.

Technical Notes

Hopkins wrote poems in what he called SPRUNG RHYTHM. The accented syllables are an attempt to control our reading of the poem. The rhyming is in couplets, with one exception.

The next two poems have the same X terms and similar Y terms, but the poets' choice of details (secondary relations) makes the pieces quite different in tone and sense. Notice that Taylor extends his initial comparison in a manner reminiscent of Marvell's "On a Drop of Dew."

As you read consider:

1. *How does each poet use the details of the spider and the spider web to further meaning?*
2. *What abstractions does each poet associate with the spider?*
3. *Do the different abstractions associated with the spider account for part of the difference in tone?*

Edward Taylor

UPON A SPIDER CATCHING A FLY

Thou sorrow, venom elf:
  Is this thy play,
To spin a web out of thyself
  To catch a fly?
    For why?

I saw a pettish[1] wasp
  Fall foul therein,
Whom yet thy whorl-pins[2] did not clasp
  Lest he should fling
    His sting.

But as afraid, remote
  Didst stand hereat
And with thy little fingers stroke
 - And gently tap
    His back.

Thus gently him didst treat
  Lest he should pet,
And in a froppish,[3] waspish heat
  Should greatly fret
    Thy net.

Whereas the silly fly,
  Caught by its leg
Thou by the throat tookst hastily
  And hind the head
    Bite dead.

This goes to pot, that not
  Nature doth call.
Strive not above what strength hath got
  Lest in the brawl
    Thou fall.

This fray seems thus to us.
  Hell's spider gets
His entrails spun to whip-cords thus,
  And wove to nets
    And sets.

To tangle Adam's race
  In's strategems
To their destructions, spoiled, made base
  By venom things,
    Damned sins.

But mighty, gracious Lord
  Communicate
Thy grace to break the cord, afford
  Us glory's gate
    And state.

We'll nightingale sing like
  When perched on high
In glory's cage, thy glory, bright,
  And thankfully,
    For joy.

[1]Peevish
[2]The flywheel on a spinning wheel; indicates the spider's legs here
[3]Fretful

Walt Whitman

A NOISELESS PATIENT SPIDER

A noiseless patient spider,
I mark'd where on a little promontory it stood isolated,
Mark'd how to explore the vacant vast surrounding,
It launch'd forth filament, filament, filament, out of itself,
Ever unreeling them, ever tirelessly speeding them.

And you O my soul where you stand,
Surrounded, detached, in measureless oceans of space,
Ceaselessly musing, venturing, throwing, seeking the spheres to connect
   them,
Till the bridge you will need be form'd, till the ductile anchor hold,
Till the gossamer thread you fling catch somewhere, O my soul.

Compare the next three poems in terms of:

1. The central metaphor
2. The elaboration in detail of the central metaphor
3. Tone—differences and similarities

Marianne Moore

THE MIND IS AN ENCHANTING THING

is an enchanted thing
    like the glaze on a
katydid-wing
        subdivided by sun
        till the nettings are legion.
Like Gieseking playing Scarlatti;[1]
like the apteryx-awl[2]
    as a beak, or the
kiwi's rain-shawl
        of haired feathers, the mind
        feeling its way as though blind,
walks along with its eyes on the ground.
It has memory's ear
    that can hear without
having to hear.
        Like the gyroscope's fall,
        truly unequivocal
because trued by regnant certainty,

it is a power of
    strong enchantment. It
is like the dove-
        neck animated by
        sun; it is memory's eye;
it's conscientious inconsistency.
It tears off the veil; tears
    the temptation, the
mist the heart wears,
        from its eyes,—if the heart
        has a face; it takes apart
dejection. It's fire in the dove-neck's
iridescence, in the
    inconsistencies
of Scarlatti.
        Unconfusion submits
        its confusion to proof; it's
not a Herod's oath that cannot change.

[1]Seventeenth-century Italian composer
[2]A kiwi—a flightless bird with a long slender beak

Sir Edward Dyer

MY MIND TO ME A KINGDOM IS

My mind to me a kingdom is,
  Such present joys therein I find,
That it excels all other bliss
  That world affords or grows by kind.
Though much I want which most would have,
Yet still my mind forbids to crave.

No princely pomp, no wealthy store,
  No force to win the victory,
No wily wit to salve a sore,
  No shape to feed a loving eye;
To none of these I yield as thrall,
For why my mind doth serve for all.

I see how plenty suffers oft,
  And hasty climbers soon do fall;
I see that those which are aloft
  Mishap doth threaten most of all;
They get with toil, they keep with fear:
Such cares my mind could never bear.

Content I live, this is my stay,
  I seek no more than may suffice;
I press to bear no haughty sway;
  Look, what I lack my mind supplies.
Lo! thus I triumph like a king,
Content with that my mind doth bring.

Some have too much, yet still do crave;
  I little have, and seek no more.
They are but poor, though much they have,
  And I am rich with little store.
They poor, I rich; they beg, I give;
They lack, I leave; they pine, I live.

I laugh not at another's loss;
  I grudge not at another's gain;
No worldly waves my mind can toss;
  My state at one doth still remain.
I fear no foe, I fawn no friend;
I loathe not life, nor dread my end.

Some weigh their pleasure by their lust,
  Their wisdom by their rage of will;
Their treasure is their only trust,
  A cloakèd craft their store of skill:
But all the pleasure that I find
Is to maintain a quiet mind.

My wealth is health and perfect ease,
  My conscience clear my choice defence;
I neither seek by bribes to please,
  Nor by deceit to breed offence.
Thus do I live; thus will I die;
Would all did so as well as I!

Ted Hughes

THE THOUGHT-FOX

I imagine the midnight moment's forest:
Something else is alive
Beside the clock's loneliness
And this blank page where my fingers move.

Through the window I see no star:
Something more near
Though deeper within darkness
Is entering the loneliness:

Cold, delicately as the dark snow,
A fox's nose touches twig, leaf;
Two eyes serve a movement, that now
And again now, and now, and now

Sets neat prints into the snow
Between trees, and warily a lame
Shadow lags by stump and in hollow
Of a body that is bold to come
                    √ courageous
Across clearings, an eye,
A widening deepening greenness,
Brilliantly, concentratedly,
Coming about its own business

Till, with a sudden sharp hot stink of fox
It enters the dark hole of the head.
The window is starless still; the clock ticks,
The page is printed.

LINES OF INQUIRY

As you read each of the following poems, consider:

1. What is the central metaphoric relationship?
2. How do the details (images, local metaphors, symbols, etc.) relate to the central X/Y idea?

John Gay

TO A LADY

On Her Passion for Old China

What ecstasies her bosom fire!
How her eyes languish with desire!
How blest, how happy should I be,
Were that fond glance bestowed on me!
New doubts and fears within me war:
What rival's near? a China jar.
  China's the passion of her soul;
A cup, a plate, a dish, a bowl
Can kindle wishes in her breast,
Inflame with joy, or break her rest.
  Some gems collect; some medals prize,
And view the rust with lovers' eyes;
Some court the stars at midnight hours;
Some dote on Nature's charms in flowers!
But ev'ry beauty I can trace
In Laura's mind, in Laura's face;
My stars are in this brighter sphere,
My lily and my rose is here.
  Philosophers more grave than wise
Hunt science down in butterflies;
Or fondly poring on a spider,
Stretch human contemplation wider;
Fossils give joy to Galen's[1] soul,
He digs for knowledge, like a mole;
In shells so learned, that all agree
No fish that swims knows more than he!
In such pursuits if wisdom lies,
Who, Laura, shall thy taste despise?
  When I some antique jar behold,
Or white, or blue, or specked with gold,
Vessels so pure, and so refined
Appear the types of woman-kind:

[1]Second-century Greek physician

Are they not valued for their beauty,
Too fair, too fine for household duty?
With flowers and gold and azure dyed,
Of ev'ry house the grace and pride?
How white, how polished is their skin,
And valued most when only seen!
She who before was highest prized
Is for a crack or flaw despised;
I grant they're frail, yet they're so rare,
The treasure cannot cost too dear!
But man is made of coarser stuff,
And serves convenience well enough;
He's a strong earthen vessel made,
For drudging, labour, toil and trade;
And when wives lose their other self,
With ease they bear the loss of Delf.[2]

Husbands more covetous than sage
Condemn this China-buying rage;
They count that woman's prudence little,
Who sets her heart on things so brittle.
But are those wise-men's inclinations
Fixed on more strong, more sure foundations?
If all that's frail we must despise,
No human view or scheme is wise.
Are not ambition's hopes as weak?
They swell like bubbles, shine and break.
A courtier's promise is so slight,
'Tis made at noon, and broke at night.
What pleasure's sure? The Miss you keep
Breaks both your fortune and your sleep.
The man who loves a country life,
Breaks all the comforts of his wife;
And if he quit his farm and plough,
His wife in town may break her vow.
Love, Laura, love, while youth is warm,
For each new winter breaks a charm;
And woman's not like China sold,
But cheaper grows in growing old;
Then quickly choose the prudent part,
Or else you break a faithful heart.

[2]A particularly fine type of china

Ovid

THE HOUSE OF RUMOUR

Circle's center: boundary
of earth, ocean, air, a triple world.
Everything everywhere visible from there:
the far, deep, ancient.
Voice resonates in the center's hollow,
as in empty ears. On this summit,
Rumour's house, built with limitless
entrances, a thousand windows.
No doors bar her thresholds.
Open night and day, resounding like
a trumpet, but full of murmurs,
collecting voices, repeating what is heard.
No quiet within, not even partial silence;
no great noise, rather, wordless mouthings:
like remote seawaves or distant thunder
resounding when Jupiter claps
dark clouds together.

Confusion reigns in the hall;
a vulgar crowd comes and goes.
A thousand vague speeches wander about,
mingling with truth in passing.
Jumbled words fly. Some of these
fill ears with empty discourse;
others carry tales. Fictions grow
enormous as each author adds
to what he's heard. Here, every
blind belief, each stupid error,
hollow joy and paralyzing fear,
sudden quarrels and false whispers.
Rumour herself watches what passes for life
on land, at sea, in heaven,
measuring its circumference.

*Translated from Latin
by J. C. Jacobs*

John Berryman

THE BALL POEM

What is the boy now, who has lost his ball,
What, what is he to do? I saw it go
Merrily bouncing, down the street, and then
Merrily over—there it is in the water!
No use to say 'O there are other balls':
An ultimate shaking grief fixes the boy
As he stands rigid, trembling, staring down
All his young days into the harbour where
His ball went. I would not intrude on him,
A dime, another ball, is worthless. Now
He senses first responsibility
In a world of possessions. People will take balls,
Balls will be lost always, little boy,
And no one buys a ball back. Money is external.
He is learning, well behind his desperate eyes,
The epistemology of loss, how to stand up
Knowing what every man must one day know
And most know many days, how to stand up.
And gradually light returns to the street,
A whistle blows, the ball is out of sight,
Soon part of me will explore the deep and dark
Floor of the harbour . . I am everywhere,
I suffer and move, my mind and my heart move
With all that move me, under the water
Or whistling, I am not a little boy.

Charles Baudelaire

THE BLIND

Contemplate them, my soul; they are truly shocking,
Vaguely ridiculous, like mannequins,
Hideously intense as sleepwalkers, staring
One doesn't know where, with vacant, darting eyes.

Their eyes, from which all divine sparkle has gone,
As though trying to look at themselves from afar.
Staring upward to the sky; you never see them bend
Their weary heads in dream.

They traverse a limitless night,
A blackness like cosmic silence. O city!
While around us you sing and laugh, carouse

In ecstasies of atrocious pleasure,
See how I stumble on more dazed than they.
What do they search for in the sky?

Translation from French by John Briggs

Henry Wadsworth Longfellow

SNOW-FLAKES

Out of the bosom of the Air,
   Out of the cloud-folds of her garments shaken,
Over the woodlands brown and bare,
   Over the harvest-fields forsaken,
      Silent, and soft, and slow
      Descends the snow.

Even as our cloudy fancies take
   Suddenly shape in some divine expression,
Even as the troubled heart doth make
   In the white countenance confession,
      The troubled sky reveals
      The grief it feels.

This is the poem of the air,
   Slowly in silent syllables recorded;
This is the secret of despair,
   Long in its cloudy bosom hoarded,
    · Now whispered and revealed
      To wood and field.

Philip Freneau

THE WILD HONEYSUCKLE

Fair flower, that dost so comely grow,
Hid in this silent, dull retreat,
Untouched thy honied blossoms blow,
Unseen thy little branches greet:
   No roving foot shall crush thee here,
   No busy hand provoke a tear.

By Nature's self in white arrayed,
She bade thee shun the vulgar eye,
And planted here the guardian shade,
And sent soft waters murmuring by;
   Thus quietly thy summer goes,
   Thy days declining to repose.

Smit with those charms, that must decay,
I grieve to see your future doom;
They died—nor were those flowers more gay,
The flowers that did in Eden bloom;
   Unpitying frosts, and Autumn's power
   Shall leave no vestige of this flower.

From morning suns and evening dews
At first thy little being came:
If nothing once, you nothing lose,
For when you die you are the same;
   The space between, is but an hour,
   The frail duration of a flower.

Sir John Suckling

'TIS NOW, SINCE I SAT DOWN

'Tis now, since I sat down before
That foolish fort, a heart,
(Time strangely spent!) a year and more,
And still I did my part.

Made my approaches, from her hand
Unto her lip did rise;
And did already understand
The language of her eyes.

Proceeded on with no less art,
My tongue was engineer;
I thought to undermine the heart,
By whispering in the ear.

When this did nothing, I brought down
Great cannon oaths, and shot
A thousand thousand to the town
And still it yielded not.

Then I resolved to starve the place,
By cutting off all kisses,
Praising and gazing on her face,
And all such little blisses.

To draw her out and from her strength,
I drew all batteries in;
And brought myself to lie, at length,
As if no siege had been.

When I had done what man could do,
And thought the place my own,
The enemy lay quiet too,
And smiled at all was done.

I sent to know from whence, and where,
These hopes and this relief?
A spy informed, honor was there,
And did command in chief.

March, march (quoth I); the word straight give,
Let's lose no time, but leave her;
That giant upon air will live,
And hold it out forever.

To such a place our camp remove
As will no siege abide;
I hate a fool that starves her love,
Only to feed her pride.

Algernon Charles Swinburne

STAGE LOVE

When the game began between them for a jest,
He played king and she played queen to match the best;
Laughter soft as tears, and tears that turned to laughter,
These were things she sought for years and sorrowed after.

Pleasure with dry lips, and pain that walks by night;
All the sting and all the stain of long delight;
These were things she knew not of, that knew not of her,
When she played at half a love with half a lover.

Time was chorus, gave them cues to laugh or cry;
They would kill, befool, amuse him, let him die;
Set him webs to weave to-day and break to-morrow,
Till he died for good in play, and rose in sorrow.

What the years mean; how time dies and is not slain;
How love grows and laughs and cries and wanes again;
These were things she came to know, and take their measure,
When the play was played out so for one man's pleasure.

Sir Philip Sidney

LIKE SOME WEAK LORDS

Like some weak lords, neighbor'd by mighty kings,
To keep themselves and their chief cities free,
Do easily yield, that all their coasts may be
Ready to store their camps of needful things:
So Stella's heart finding what power Love brings,
To keep itself in life and liberty,
Doth willing grant, that in the frontiers he
Use all to help his other conquerings:
And thus her heart escapes, but thus her eyes
Serve him with shot, her lips his heralds are;
Her breasts his tents, legs his triumphal car;
Her flesh his food, her skin his armor brave,
   And I, but for because my prosepct lies
   Upon that coast, am giv'n up for a slave.

Jules LaForgue

ROMANCE

Hamlet: To a Nunnery, Go

I have a thousand pale gray seabirds
nesting in the ceilings of my lovely soul.
They fill sad rooms of days with rhythms
like the beat of slender oars of old.

But all flesh they have spattered with their filth;
on the coral and seashells let it fall;
as they fly in circles crazily—and knock themselves
against these upright family walls.

Pale birds, birds so foul and demented,
when my lady-love opens the door,
show her a necklace of these tiny shells.
And while decaying flesh gives off bad odor,

let her say, "O this soul is too powerful for my
little nose. The smell of it makes one feel ill.
But this beautiful necklace—uhmm, shall I take it?"
. . . It'll do her no good, poor girl.

Translation from French

Samuel Daniel

ARE THEY SHADOWS THAT WE SEE?

from *Tethys Festival*

Are they shadowes that we see?
And can shadowes pleasure give?
Pleasures onely shadowes bee
Cast by bodies we conceive,
And are made the thinges we deeme,
In those figures which they seeme.
But these pleasures vanish fast,
Which by shadowes are exprest:
Pleasures are not, if they last,
In their passing, is their best.
Glory is most bright and gay
In a flash, and so away.
Feed apace then greedy eyes
On the wonder you behold.
Take it sudden as it flies
Though you take it not to hold:
When your eyes have done their part,
Thought must length it in the hart.

Dwight Robhs

LOVE AND CELESTIAL MECHANICS
For David and Marlys

I strain in her void as she abhors her vacuum:
Alone in our orbits, linking up again
In worldless distances where no breath breathes,
Where even lovers know no up or down,
We keep preserved in insulated systems
(Here in a bounded but infinite bed)
With life support a measure of what's dying.

Sealed up like astronauts within,
Peering out through screens and tinted ports
With flashing half-truths on our instruments:
Electric groping of thoughts or hands
Over flesh or the unending stillness
And vast simplicity of space or love.

Above the world and still bound to it
By the affinities of moving bodies,
Newtonian in passion we spin on . . .
God help us, at times we go outside,
Float loose from communications nets;
Spacefish hung in the free fall of the heart,
Weightless together in the narrow bed;

Sail motionless where clocks are stilled
Where no thought ticks, no body beats,
No measured whirring from the nightstand,
Nothing to mark or count. Exposed
Without direction between worlds,
Exhaled, without a word for yesterday

Or air for talk; full as empty sky
With all there is and in our hush
No artifice of lover, tangent,
Angle, attitude of flight . . .
A lifetime of momentum pulls us down
To earth, to merciless gravity again,
Flopping wingless on a dull bed.

We strain to rise but don't lift off.
The serious flesh is fallen.
My back hurts and you're travel-sore.
Reseal the openings, secure the systems;
We gasp for breath, we're back inside,
God help us, we remember everything.

Thomas Campion

FOLLOWE THY FAIRE SUNNE, UNHAPPY SHADOWE

Followe thy faire sunne, unhappy shadowe,
Though thou be blacke as night,
And she made all of light,
Yet follow thy faire sun, unhappie shadowe.

Follow her whose light thy light depriveth,
Though here thou liv'st disgrac't,
And she in heaven is plac't,
Yet follow her whose light the world reviveth.

Follow those pure beames whose beautie burneth,
That so have scorched thee,
As thou still blacke must bee,
Til her kind beames thy black to brightnes turneth.

Follow her while yet her glorie shineth:
There comes a luckles night,
That will dim all her light;
And this the black unhappie shade devineth.

Follow still since so thy fates ordained;
The Sunne must have his shade,
Till both at once doe fade,
The Sun still proud, the shadow still disdained.

Robert Frost

THE SILKEN TENT

She is as in a field a silken tent
At midday when a sunny summer breeze
Has dried the dew and all its ropes relent,
So that in guys it gently sways at ease,
And its supporting central cedar pole,
That is its pinnacle to heavenward
And signifies the sureness of the soul,
Seems to owe naught to any single cord,
But strictly held by none, is loosely bound
By countless silken ties of love and thought
To everything on earth the compass round,
And only by one's going slightly taut
In the capriciousness of summer air
Is of the slightest bondage made aware.

George Gordon, Lord Byron

SHE WALKS IN BEAUTY

She walks in beauty, like the night
  Of cloudless climes and starry skies;
And all that's best of dark and bright
  Meet in her aspect and her eyes:
Thus mellow'd to that tender light
  Which heaven to gaudy day denies.

One shade the more, one ray the less,
  Had half impair'd the nameless grace
Which waves in every raven tress,
  Or softly lightens o'er her face;
Where thoughts serenely sweet express
  How pure, how dear, their dwelling-place.

And on that cheek, and o'er that brow,
  So soft, so calm, yet eloquent,
The smiles that win, the tints that glow,
  But tell of days in goodness spent,
A mind at peace with all below,
  A heart whose love is innocent!

Lluellyn

COELIA IN LOVE

I felt my heart, and found a flame,
That for relief and shelter came;
I entertain'd the treacherous guest,
And gave it welcome to my breast—
Poor Coelia! whither wilt thou go?
To cool in streams, or freeze in snow?
Or gentle zephyrus intreat
To chill thy flames, and fan thy heat?
Perhaps a taper's fading beams
May die in air, or quench in streams;
But love is a mysterious fire,
Nor can in air or ice expire:
Nor will this phoenix be suppressed
But with the ruin of its nest.

William Shakespeare

SHALL I COMPARE THEE . . .

Shall I compare thee to a summer's day?
Thou art more lovely and more temperate: → mild; self-restrained
Rough winds do shake the darling buds of May,
And summer's lease hath all too short a date:
Sometime too hot the eye of heaven shines, → sun
And often is his gold complexion dimmed; (cloudy skies)
And every fair from fair sometime declines, → summer declines Seasons change
By chance, or nature's changing course untrimmed; → when nothing good can stay w/help
But thy eternal summer shall not fade, [BEAUTY]
Nor lose possession of that fair thou owest, → to own or to be undebt
Nor shall Death brag thou wander'st in his shade, → to nature for beauty
When in eternal lines to time thou growest; → Death's shadow
    So long as men can breathe, or eyes can see,
    So long lives this, and this gives life to thee.

(margin: 3RD QUATRAIN → Change in Point of View)

Rubén Darío

THE SEASHELL

For Antonio Machado

Along this shore I found a golden shell,
heavy and precious from the sea.
Europa had held it in her goddess hands
as she plunged across the billows on the celestial bull.

I brought to my lips that sonorous shell
and raised in it the echo of the sea's long call—
brought it to my ear and heard the azure deeps
whispering of strange and secret treasure.

And stung by salt spray, felt the bitter winds
that had swelled in the sails of the vessel Argo
when heaven urged on Jason° in his dream.

And I heard surf crashing on an unknown shore,
and the rise and the surge of a mysterious wind.
(The shell has the shape of a heart.)

> *Translation from Spanish by John Briggs*

°An allusion to the story of Jason and the Argonauts'
quest for the Golden Fleece

William Drummond

THIS WORLD A HUNTING IS

This world a hunting is,
The prey poor man; the Nimrod° fierce is death;
His speedy greyhounds are
Lust, sickness, envy, care,
Strife, that ne'er falls amiss,
With all these ills that haunt us while we've breath;
Now, if by chance we fly
Of these the eager chase,
Old age, with stealing pace,
Casts on his nets, and then we panting die.

°An expert hunter, great-grandson of Noah

Henry David Thoreau

I AM A PARCEL OF VAIN
STRIVINGS TIED

I am a parcel of vain strivings tied
    By a chance bond together,
  Dangling this way and that, their links
      Were made so loose and wide,
            Methinks,
        For milder weather.
A bunch of violets without their roots,
    And sorrel intermixed,
  Encircled by a wisp of straw
      Once coiled about their shoots,
            The law
        By which I'm fixed.
A nosegay which Time clutched from out
    Those fair Elysian fields,
  With weeds and broken stems, in haste,
      Doth make the rabble rout
            That waste
        The day he yields.
And here I bloom for a short hour unseen,
    Drinking my juices up,
  With no root in the land
      To keep my branches green,
            But stand
        In a bare cup.
Some tender buds were left upon my stem
    In mimicry of life,
  But ah! the children will not know,
      Till time has withered them,
            The woe
        With which they're rife.
But now I see I was not plucked for naught,
    And after in life's vase
  Of glass set while I might survive,
      But by a kind hand brought
            Alive
        To a strange place.
That stock thus thinned will soon redeem its hours,
    And by another year,
  Such as God knows, with freer air,
      More fruits and fairer flowers
            Will bear,
        While I droop here.

David Galler

A DREAM

I stood, nonplussed, in a forest of towering trees,
All greatest oaks, whose crowns, unstirred by breeze,
Were black in the pale light they let down in.
Gray earth bore not a blade nor print; no din
Of birds fell from the high branches. The wide-
trunked trees stepped forth from gloom on either side
As I began to walk. Already I knew
I'd meet no one; that there was no way through.

This is my life, I thought, wherever I wait
Is center of this wood; it is too late
To leave. With that, I struck the nearest tree.
A gong roared from its depths. "To comfort thee,"
A small voice said, "this is an unreal wood—
For such as give up sooner than they should."

Thomas Gray

ODE ON THE DEATH OF A FAVOURITE CAT, DROWNED IN A TUB OF GOLD FISHES

'Twas on a lofty vase's side,
Where China's gayest art had dy'd
　The azure flowers, that blow;
Demurest of the tabby kind,
The pensive Selima[1] reclin'd,
　Gazed on the lake below.

Her conscious tail her joy declar'd;
The fair round face, the snowy beard,
　The velvet of her paws,
Her coat, that with the tortoise vies,
Her ears of jet, and emerald eyes,
　She saw; and purr'd applause.

Still had she gaz'd; but 'midst the tide
Two angel forms were seen to glide,
　The Genii of the stream:
Their scaly armour's Tyrian[2] hue
Thro' richest purple to the view
　Betray'd a golden gleam.

The hapless Nymph with wonder saw:
A whisker first and then a claw,
　With many an ardent wish,

She stretch'd in vain to reach the prize.
What female heart can gold despise?
　What Cat's averse to fish?

Presumptuous Maid! with looks intent
Again she stretch'd, again she bent,
　Nor knew the gulf between.
(Malignant Fate sat by, and smil'd)
The slipp'ry verge her feet beguil'd,
　She tumbled headlong in.

Eight times emerging from the flood
She mew'd to ev'ry watry God,
　Some speedy aid to send.
No Dolphin came, no Nereid[3] stirr'd:
Nor cruel *Tom*, nor *Susan* heard.
　A Fav'rite has no friend!

From hence, ye Beauties, undeceiv'd,
Know, one false step is ne'er retriev'd,
　And be with caution bold.
Not all that tempts your wand'ring eyes
And heedless hearts, is lawful prize;
　Nor all, that glisters, gold.

[1] A fashionable name for a pet cat

[2] Crimson-purple

[3] Sea nymph

Ezra Pound

THE WHITE STAG

I ha' seen them 'mid the clouds on the heather.
Lo! they pause not for love nor for sorrow,
Yet their eyes are as the eyes of a maid to her lover,
When the white hart breaks his cover
And the white wind breaks the morn.
　"'Tis the white stag, Fame, we're a-hunting,
　Bid the world's hounds come to horn!"

Edmund Spenser

AFTER AT SEA

After at Sea a tall Ship did appear,
Made all of Heben and white Ivory,
The sails of Gold, of Silk the tackle were:
Mild was the wind, calm seemed the sea to be:
The clear Sky there did show full bright and fair.
With rich treasures this gay ship freighted was.
But sudden storm did so turmoil the air,
And tumbled up the sea, that she, alas,
Struck on a rock that under water lay.
O great misfortune, O great grief, I say,
Thus in one moment to see lost and drowned
So great riches, as like can not be found.

William Oldys

THE FLY

An Anacreontic

Busy, curious, thirsty fly,
Gently drink, and drink as I;
Freely welcome to my cup,
Could'st thou sip, and sip it up;
Make the most of life you may,
Life is short and wears away.

Just alike, both mine and thine,
Hasten quick to their decline;
Thine's a summer, mine's no more,
Though repeated to threescore;
Threescore summers when they're gone,
Will appear as short as one.

Jorge Luis Borges

CHESS

I
In their serious corner, the players
move the gradual pieces. The board
detains them until dawn in its hard
compass: the hatred of two colors.

In the game, the forms give off a severe
magic: Homeric castle, gay
knight, warlike queen, king solitary,
oblique bishop, and pawns at war.

Finally, when the players have gone in,
and when time has eventually consumed them,
surely the rites then will not be done.

In the east, this war has taken fire.
Today, the whole earth is its provenance.
Like that other, this game is for ever.

II
Tenuous king, slant bishop, bitter queen,
straightforward castle and the crafty pawn—
over the checkered black and white terrain
they seek out and enjoin their armed campaign.

They do not realize the dominant
hand of the player rules their destiny.
They do not know an adamantine fate
governs their choices and controls their journey.

The player, too, is captive of caprice
(the sentence is Omar's)° on another ground
crisscrossed with black nights and white days.
God moves the player, he, in turn, the piece.
But what god beyond God begins the round
of dust and time and dream and agonies?

Translation from Spanish by Alastair Reid

°A reference to "Rubáiyát of Omar Khayyám" (Chapter 1)

EXPERIENCING THE POEM

Without analyzing, interpreting, or considering the metaphors, reread "Ode on Melancholy" (page 9). Don't try to remember what was said about it. Just reread to experience. What effect does the poem have on you this time?

CHAPTER 4
THE POEM AS
A METAPHOR: *X/Y*'S

Instead of a *single* central metaphoric *relationship* (as in a drop of dew[X] = the soul [Y]), each poem here has what we might call a METAPHORIC SUBJECT (X) which relates to *several* Y's—whether images, local metaphors, or ideas. Actually, we saw this type of poem in the first two chapters. Remember that in MacLeish's "Ars Poetica," the X term ("a poem") was identified, compared, contrasted, and associated with various specific items ("mute as a globed fruit," the feel of "old medallions to the thumb," the moon climbing through the trees), presenting a rich image and impression of poetic dynamics. Dorn's "Knowledge of Silence" (Chapter 2) is compared ans associated with a museum, marble the "sculpting mind," etc., producing a comparable effect.

So like the X/Y relationship just dealt with, the principle here is simple, though the result can be very complicated: the metaphoric subject (X) is related to various Y's in the poem. In the process, the X term gathers potency and weight. To judge the effectiveness of this technique, let's look at some examples. Once more, detailed interpretation is left to you.

*Even a casual reading of this poem would probably reveal that it is much more
than a vivid description of a bullfight. The bull and the fight are metaphorically
exploring profound and complex territory.*

W. S. Merwin

TORO

Black, black, the sheen of his back and shoulders
Blazing, his brawn and wide forehead plunging
On, on into wrath, hooves detonating the dust
Under his rushing darkness, the green and white
Streamers fixed in the hump of his anger rattling
And snapping behind like slaver from a mad mouth, and
The high-shaken lances of his tossing horns seeking
Bodies for shock, his wrath like a ghost seeking
Bodies to sink in, to house in, destruction to be wrought,
Out of the starving dark, daring headlong
The one-way doors of day, he hurls himself now
Into the orange light, and lunging down
Like judgment erupting or a dark planet he crashes
Across the spread glare and becomes the raging centre
Of these flickering faces ranged in rings, who thirst
For his darkness, who stare like blains
In the sun-blaze. They thought it was they
Who for their thirst's sake, and that their black fear might be
Loosed and defeated in the familiar light, conceived
A darkness and set him there. But all black
Is the abyss brooding, and he brings into the day
The one dark, that was there before the world was. Low
In his own shadow deep as a mountain he waited
Till they said, "Now we are all together
And seem brave in the light, let the challenging shadow
Show itself among us; now, that we may shame it,
Let there be dark." And he heard the first day
Of Creation banging on the barrier, and, ravenous,
His red eyes saw the light. And, look: he became
The black sun and burst among them, and the sun has horns
As the moon has, whereby all dawns shall be bloody
And all wests ripped with crimson! Bull. And legs,
Spoke-flashing of knees, even thunder of hooves seem as
    nothing
To pillar and propel that bulk and fury. His belly gulping
For breath sucks up and drops like a blast-shaken
Floor; between his flanks censer and tassel
Of generation swing and lurch, and nothing in the profound world
Blares deep as now his maddened bellow. What torment is it

That baits him, that wrings forth this roar: for the men
Performing with bright darts are toys merely,
Masquers playing with emblems, signifying far off
The one faceless pain, momentary puppets
Of the infliction he tolls. The blood and burning
In his eyes are not blindness, but bring the world's rage
To be seen red as it is. And oh do not suppose
Because a thin blade may empty him suddenly
Of fury, and his black become the colour of quiet,
That it means that the known earth is broad world enough
To be his battling-ground. His death, though dedicated,
May end much, but will fulfill nothing; will be adequate
Neither to sate the size and lust of his fury
Nor to gather and bless with acceptable sacrifice
Those faces so small, so faint and far that still
They sit and sway in a world where such things
As danger are. But he, for all fear's reasons
Worshipful, slumps back into fear's secret
And abyss, more terrible, for his rage disdains now
All that they know of pain, and looks like infinite
Gentleness, waiting, forever patient,
Black, with long horns. What trouble is it
That baits them now, since the shape they made of their fear
Is dead? The light is different. And they are alone.

Considerations

First let's list some terms the poet relates to his
central metaphoric subject (the bull) in the opening
lines. The bull (X) is associated with or likened to
(Y):

wrath
rushing darkness
anger
madness
a ghost seeking bodies
a ghost seeking destruction
a product of the "starving dark"
daring
judgment
a dark planet
a raging center
black fear
the abyss brooding
Dark, that was there before the world was

Do you see how the interaction of these terms
resembles the relationships in "On a Drop of
Dew"? By means of numerous associations the
bull (and therefore the bullfight) gathers great
significance.

Note that Merwin uses black and darkness as the
bull's primary associations, playing off the connotations of anger, evil, mystery, and so on.
Compare this with Stevens' use of black in "Thirteen Ways of Looking at a Blackbird" (page 23).

In "Toro" the drama of the bullfight becomes a
drama of meaning. By the end of the poem, even
the bull and audience itself are united in the
"moment of truth" (the bull's death): it is "the
shape they had made of their fear." With this
audience-bull association in mind, go back and
reread the poem and see how this adds a significant new dimension.

If the poet simply listed what his central metaphoric subject "meant," would there be such impact? Instead, we have a description, a story or
picture that is activated metaphorically by stress,
context, and association and so extends past the
literal level (things seen and heard) into *deeper*
meanings. For example, the description of the bull

lunging out of the chutes into the bullring "like judgment erupting or a dark planet" gives both a visual picture and a deeper response, something like "arrows of desire." We can imagine the bull lunging out of the ring, but the relation of this image to judgment we can "see" only with our intuition.

1. Metaphorically, what reasons do you feel there are for holding this bullfight? Consider in particular the audience's relation to the bull.
2. Consider any of the local metaphors or images (such as "and his black become the colour of quiet") and observe its connection with the whole poem. What does it add to the bull's meaning?
3. Can you answer the poet's question about the bull: "What torment is it/That baits him, that wrings forth this roar?"
4. What levels of meaning do the last lines suggest?
5. What do you think the bull and the bullfight come to represent in this poem? Can you see several viable possibilities?

Technical Notes

The poem is written in accentual pentameter (five strong stresses to the line).

In this poem a nineteenth-century Russian employs one of poetry's favorite metaphoric subjects, the natural image, a flower. Look for the Y's that are linked to this X.

Alexander Pushkin

THE FLOWER

A dead, pale flower falls,
forgotten, from a dusty book.
And so by a strange dream
my soul is filled.

When did this flower bloom? And where?
In what lost spring? Was it a familiar
or a stranger's hand which picked it?
Who pressed it in these pages here? And why?

Was it in memory of a tender meeting?
The token of a fatal parting?
Or memento of a lonely walk—in the silence
of the fields, or woody shade?

And is he still living?—And is she?
Together did they find their place?
Or were they lost, like love, like youth—
like this forgotten flower?

Translation from Russian

Considerations

1. What does the poet associate with the flower? What two abstractions are specifically identified with the flower? Are there also unstated abstractions the flower could imply?
2. What do you think the flower comes to mean? How?
3. Why does the narrator ask all these questions of the flower?
4. How would you describe the tone of this poem? Is it sentimental? What effect does the tone have on the meaning? How does the poet keep the poem from being a cliché (like a popular, sentimental song: "He loved her and now she's gone, and all that's left is this flower")?

What is really the central metaphoric subject of this rather outlandishly humorous poem? Is it the girdle?

Edmund Waller

ON A GIRDLE

That which her slender waist confin'd,
Shall now my joyful temples bind:
No monarch but would give his crown,
His arms might do what this has done.

It was my heart's extremest sphere,
The pale which held that lovely deer.
My joy, my grief, my hope, my love,
Did all within this circle move!

A narrow compass! and yet there
Dwelt all that's good, and all that's fair:
Give me but what this riband bound,
Take all the rest the sun goes round.

Considerations

1. How many different circles do you see in the poem?
2. What different things are identified or associated with circles?
3. What is the effect of the poem?
4. What makes this poem funny?

See whether you can tell how this poem works. What is the central metaphoric subject here?

Emily Dickinson

THERE'S A CERTAIN SLANT OF LIGHT

There's a certain slant of light,
On winter afternoons,
That oppresses, like the weight
Of cathedral tunes.

Heavenly hurt it gives us;
We can find no scar,
But internal difference
Where the meanings are.

None may teach it anything,
'Tis the seal, despair,—
An imperial affliction
Sent us of the air.

When it comes, the landscape listens,
Shadows hold their breath;
When it goes, 'tis like the distance
On the look of death.

Considerations

Several local metaphors are associated with the "slant of light," the central *X* term, which is (like) several *Y*'s: oppression "like the weight of cathedral tunes," a "heavenly hurt," an "internal difference where the meanings are," a "seal," "despair," an "imperial affliction," something which makes landscape listen and "shadows hold their breath," and "the distance on the look of death."

Also consider the fact that the subject is light. Light has connotations of wisdom, God, reason, life, etc., and the poet plays off these. Moreover, we are dealing with a "slant" of light, and therefore an "angle" of wisdom, God, life, etc. What is it? Could we ever say for sure? For instance, why do the images and local metaphors paradoxically relate this *light* to experience usually associated with *darkness* despair, affliction, death? How is this paradox resolved in the last two lines? Do you agree that the question of what the slant of light means is probably less important than our intuitive experience of the highly charged area of interplay between light and darkness "where the meanings are"?

1. Consider each of the local metaphors and images. How do they extend the meaning of the slant of light?
2. Is there a paradox in the phrase "heavenly hurt"? What are the levels of meaning here?
3. Consider the lines "When it comes, the landscape listens" and "When it goes, 'tis like the distance." These are the two longest lines in the poem. Do their length and sound bear any relation to their meaning? Is it possible to separate their length or sound from their meaning? What would have been the effect on the entire poem if the poet had written as the last line, "When it goes, 'tis like the look of death"?
4. What do you feel the slant of light means in the poem—or can you say? Could it be read consistently as meaning love? Insight? The poem itself?

This poem is among the most quoted in English literary history and one of the most elusive. Its central metaphoric subject is obvious.

John Keats

ODE ON A GRECIAN URN

Thou still unravish'd bride of quietness,
   Thou foster-child of silence and slow time,
Sylvan historian, who canst thus express
   A flowery tale more sweetly than our rhyme:
What leaf-fring'd legend haunts about thy shape
   Of deities or mortals, or of both,
     In Tempe[1] or the dales of Arcady?[2]
   What men or gods are these? What maidens loth?
What mad pursuit? What struggle to escape?
   What pipes and timbrels? What wild ecstasy?

Heard melodies are sweet, but those unheard
   Are sweeter; therefore, ye soft pipes, play on;
Not to the sensual ear, but, more endear'd,
   Pipe to the spirit ditties of no tone:
Fair youth, beneath the trees, thou canst not leave
   Thy song, nor ever can those trees be bare;
     Bold Lover, never, never canst thou kiss,
Though winning near the goal—yet, do not grieve;
   She cannot fade, though thou hast not thy bliss,
     For ever wilt thou love, and she be fair!

Ah, happy, happy boughs! that cannot shed
   Your leaves, nor ever bid the Spring adieu;
And, happy melodist, unwearièd,
   For ever piping songs for ever new;

[1] A valley sacred to the Greek god Apollo
[2] A Greek pastoral district

More happy love! more happy, happy love!
  For ever warm and still to be enjoy'd,
    For ever panting, and for ever young;
All breathing human passion far above,
  That leaves a heart high-sorrowful and cloy'd,
    A burning forehead, and a parching tongue.

Who are these coming to the sacrifice?
  To what green altar, O mysterious priest,
Lead'st thou that heifer lowing at the skies,
  And all her silken flanks with garlands drest?
What little town by river or sea shore,
  Or mountain-built with peaceful citadel,
    Is emptied of this folk, this pious morn?
And, little town, thy streets for evermore
  Will silent be; and not a soul to tell
    Why thou art desolate, can e'er return.

O Attic shape! Fair attitude! with brede[3]
  Of marble men and maidens overwrought,
With forest branches and the trodden weed;
  Thou, silent form, dost tease us out of thought
As doth eternity: Cold Pastoral!
  When old age shall this generation waste,
    Thou shalt remain, in midst of other woe
Than ours, a friend to man, to whom thou say'st,
  "Beauty is truth, truth beauty,"—that is all
    Ye know on earth, and all ye need to know.

[3]Braid or embroidery, doubtless a pun

Considerations

Critics have been puzzled by the phrase "Beauty is truth, truth beauty." If you take it for itself, outside the poem's context, and think of it as having some general meaning, it seems a tautology, like saying "A rose is a rose." Can we take this statement outside the poem? Is this just a vague, abstract, and unpoetic "idea"?

The central metaphoric subject (X) of the poem is the urn. The narrator associates it with various terms which not only describe the urn but also shape its meaning. For example, it is a "bride of quietness, a "Sylvan historian," a "fair attitude" (note the pun: attitude as a feeling about something and attitude as physical posture), a "Cold

Pastoral," and a "friend to man," among other things. In addition, it expresses "a flowery tale," pipes "not to the sensual ear" but to "the spirit ditties of no tone," and teases "us out of thought as doth eternity."

Now, how does our statement about truth and beauty relate to all this and the urn? By the time we reach this statement, it is clearly possible to associate the urn with beauty. So on the metaphoric level we have: the urn (X) is (like) truth (Y). There is a recognizable metaphor. Everything we know about the urn, all the complex meaning gathered through the four previous stanzas, is compressed into one line. What seems abstract is actually identified with a concrete image. If beauty is (like) the urn and if the urn pipes to the spirit and teases "us out of thought as doth eternity," then on one level is the concept that beauty* takes us *beyond* thought to an intuition of *truth*, and this truth is (like) eternity— timeless, free from birth and death, "for ever piping songs for ever new." So in the truth/beauty metaphor Keats is expressing the effect of poetry itself. We should not mistake it for some vague or general conclusion separable from the poem.

And this is but one aspect of the piece. Consider, as another way of getting into it, the contrast between the hot life depicted on the urn (*X*) and the cold pastoral—the "brede of marble men and maidens" (*Y*). What do we discover in this juxtaposition of art to life? How does it relate to the truth/beauty equation? The poem explores these and other profound territories not by logically playing to our "sensual" ear but by "piping," so to speak, metaphor to the spirit.

1. Consider the terms Keats uses to describe the urn ("unravished bride of quietness," "Sylvan historian," etc.). What does each add to the total meaning of the urn?
2. In what way is the scene depicted on the urn ironic? What levels of meaning does this irony add?

*Which here cannot be logically defined apart from the metaphoric context

3. What does the progress of Keats's description (from the first stanza to the last) tell you about the meaning of the urn? The psychology of the narrator? How does his mood change? What is the significance of his describing scenes *not* on the urn?
4. Consider whether the progress of the description of the urn mirrors in some way the cloying passion of life which the urn figures are said to have escaped.
5. Why is the urn a "Cold Pastoral"? How does this phrase affect you, coming where it does? How does it relate to the truth/beauty metaphor?
6. Who is the "Ye" in the last line?
7. It's obvious how thought can be said to come and go, live and die. Is it possible, then, to *think* about a state untouched by living and dying? Why must we be teased "out of thought"? Can the logic of experience come to any conclusions here? How is Keats suggesting that the metaphoric experience of beauty/ truth ceases when conclusions about beauty/ truth are drawn?

Technical Notes

The poem is an ode in basic iambic meter, the stanzas rhyming *a b a b c d e c d e*.

In a Greek myth, Queen Philomela sent her husband Tereus to bring her sister, Procne, for a visit. As soon as Tereus saw Procne, he desired her. His desires became desperate, and on the return voyage he carried her off. When Procne rejected him, he raped her, cut out her tongue, and returned home to Philomela with the lie that Procne had died during the voyage. Procne, however, wove the story of her miseries into a tapestry which she sent to Philomela, who rescued her. Then together they slew Procne's and Tereus's son and served him to his father as a stew. As a result of these pleasantries the gods pursued the trio and transformed Tereus into a hawk, Procne into a sparrow, and Philomela into a nightingale destined forever to sing and lament the tragedy.

This myth of the nightingale's origin fascinated poets for centuries, and the bird became a symbol of sorrow, grief, betrayal, immortality, and passion. In this piece, the nineteenth-century poet Matthew Arnold has structured this symbol as a metaphoric subject.

Matthew Arnold

PHILOMELA

Hark! ah, the nightingale—
The tawny-throated!
Hark, from that moonlit cedar what a burst!
What triumph! hark!—what pain!

O wanderer from a Grecian shore,
Still, after many years, in distant lands,
Still nourishing in thy bewilder'd brain
That wild, unquench'd, deep-sunken, old-world pain—
Say, will it never heal?
And can this fragrant lawn
With its cool trees, and night,
And the sweet, tranquil Thames,
And moonshine, and the dew,
To thy rack'd heart and brain
Afford no balm?
Dost thou to-night behold,
Here, through the moonlight on this English grass,
The unfriendly palace in the Thracian wild?
Dost thou again peruse
With hot cheeks, and sear'd eyes
The too clear web, and thy dumb sister's shame?
Dost thou once more assay
Thy flight, and feel come over thee,
Poor fugitive, the feathery change
Once more, and once more seem to make resound
With love and hate, triumph and agony,
Lone Daulis, and the high Cephissian vale?°
Listen, Eugenia—
How thick the bursts come crowding through the leaves!
Again—thou hearest?
Eternal passion!
Eternal pain!

°Locale in which the story of Philomela is said to have
taken place

Considerations

1. What does Arnold associate with the nightingale?
2. The nightingale is a symbol of sorrow, grief, immortality, etc. How does Arnold make this symbol metaphoric? That is, how does he go beyond the defined *idea* of the nightingale to make the bird mean something complex and indefinable?

3. Consider the tone in which the narrator addresses the nightingale. How does this contribute to the poem's levels of meaning?
4. How do the details of landscape add to the significance of the nightingale? Is there any comparison of landscapes here? For instance, how is the "Thracian wild" associated with "English grass"?
5. How is landscape related to time?

As you read the following poem, consider:
1. *What is the central metaphoric subject?*
2. *What does the poet identify with the central subject?*
3. *How does this metaphoric identification add to the subject's meaning?*

Christopher Collins

SEEPAGE ON A JANUARY NIGHT

For Jean Colleran

I
I feel the waters everywhere seeping into my country
At midnight after the thousand stale blue rooms are finished
And the highway cleared   Only   now and then a truck
Storms by   It is violently gone. The sound of marsh-rushes again.
The meanings everywhere of the waters of the three-days-rain,
   returning.

While I wait for the bus back to New York while I stand under
   a lowrunning sky,
Lit up from below like smoke by the cold wattage of the city
Twenty miles across the bay, the swampgrass along the highway
   is being pushed
Down by the shoving gusts—the cattails, the winter trancing reeds—
And now with the wind stopped they heave back and have become
   intensely motionless

II
I know this land, these eighty or so square yards of asphalt,
This depot (deserted now, with twenty buses, back
   from the commuter runs,
Stabled in hunched sleep back against the big willows).
I know this land: it was a pond and the rain that fell
In the hills to the south—Chapel Hill, Beacon Hill, Red Oaks—

Seeped down through the loam and the pebbly subsoil, down
To the small rushing dark streams that, though sunless, give
   life to the world,
And some of them used to sluice into a marsh pond where
   sumacs and willows
Sucked the wet. And frogs lived there spring and summer
   and in the winter
It was all iced over and once a twelve-year-old boy drowned in it.

III
I feel the waters everywhere seeping through my life
Into the land no longer mine, into the years encased beneath my feet,
Under this asphalt, under this foot of gravel, these several yards
   of fill,

Rock, concrete, incinerated garbage, bulldozed fields
And the trenched faces, that need to be forgotten, of children
and animals.

Under all this the dark streams seek their deep joining.
I can feel them everywhere in the night. They are unlamenting.
They are unromantic. They are mud.
They wait for the roothairs of the marsh grass, the frogs' sloughed ova
And, finding nothing, continue strong and ultimate,
To subvert in continuous victory these deathly pavements.

IV
Tonight I understand. Beneath a country frozen for war,
Beneath the frozen daily ritual of the defeat of people
Beneath the ledgers of lifetimes audited by the surveyor's transit,
Another freedom works. It was always there. The only final defeat
Is to stand in the depot night of America and not to hear it,

Not to feel through our lives the waters seeping below
the frost line,
Crumbling the guarded surfaces   breaking out.
Guerrilleros hardly to be dreaded, hardly to be cheered, they are
now and always
Loosing the jammed strata into dateless insurrection,
The budburst, the chalice of chaos forever hoisted to the sun.

Considerations

Almost every gesture and detail here gains significance in relation to the metaphoric subject (*X*): "the waters . . . seeping." For instance, in stanza two the marsh pond where the boy drowned is mentioned. The detail of the drowning suggests something sinister about the waters. Consider "the small rushing dark streams that, though sunless, give life to the world." What are these streams metaphorically? Cosmic forces? Emotions? Insights? Mystery? Later on (in stanza three) these dark streams "seek their deep joining." The "seeping" (and meaning) expands progressively through association with death, civilization (as "rock, concrete, incinerated garbage"), war, etc.

1. What is the relation between the trappings of civilization and the waters?
2. Consider the local metaphors and images (for example, "a lowrunning sky,/Lit up from below like smoke," "deathly pavements," "depot night"). How do they relate to the central idea?
3. What relation does the last line bear to the central idea of the poem?
4. What does Collins's illustration tell you about what he had in mind in this poem?

Compare this poem with Merrill's "Laboratory Poem" (page 62). What is the central subject in the Robhs piece? Is this also the central subject of Merrill's poem? How are the two different?

Dwight Robhs

SLICE OF LIFE

For Judy

1) each pair will share one frog apiece(lovers
touch hands at the dissecting tray: the tools
sharp, cool to the hand are oddly familiar)
2) turn to the ventral side

3) cut down from chin to groin (expose what beats,
bleeds, feels and fills; trace what delicate webs
shuddered with life—stopped—lovers risk unknitting)
4) when most vital substance is removed or when
(in short, when the heart is out of something
the tangle that's left is dead to the touch)
by dead is meant (this wonderful design
no longer works—fingers touch as if
untying—light, outside and in, includes them)
5) next notice the heart, expose it by lifting

aside (whatever conceals it: intimate
discovery gleams in feral light, almost
suggests the probe that skews the symmetry
of life's woven ease) 6) peel the nerves from flesh;
these stringy radial extensions (once told
cold from heat from pain) 7) cut

the cord below the medulla (striking
how, careful and gentle,

they pull the dead apart and call it
understanding life: a tangle of ends
fingers distinguish with some urgency)
8) turn to the dorsal side 9) now bend the skull
to the chest until you hear a snap,
then part the head from trunk—chip bone with care
or else the brain will smear (their fine fingers
untie the delicate knots of being:
call this understanding another's mind:
this head, in one sense, holds no secrets:
this kind of learning can be killing)
observe (it is all here)

sketch, make notes, measure, probe in detail
(this bloody lesson sprawls in the tray
naked in a way that lovers are not:
a fear persists for all their science;
the scalpels of knowledge feel familiar to hands
that discovered another's nakedness,
loosened and undressed the self, and knew
fear in carnal wisdom)

10) write a report (his hand in her webs
of hair weaves golden glints
as fingers ripple shine—electric light
hones the scalpel's edge with fire, she winces at
the light, perhaps at more: all myths of love
start with the fear of finding out too much:
Lamian terrors wake

at intimate moments—the stripped frog marks
off one extreme, lovers
the other, between them both the numbered
text explains what it can—
demanding lovers pull the live apart
understanding death.

Considerations

1. What are some of the possible meanings that death takes on in this poem? For example, does death have to do with a dissective way of living or looking at the world?

2. What is the tone of the numbered text? What kind of a contrast do you detect between the pure lyrical passages and the lines with numbers? How is this connected to the central subject?

3. Look at some of the images. For instance, why have the "delicate webs *shuddered* with life"? How do the images relate to the central subject?

4. How do the abstract statements, such as "a fear persists for all their science," relate to the central subject?

Here are three more poems on the nightingale.

1. *What kinds of associations does each poet make to this literary-natural image (symbol)?*
2. *How are the poems different? How are they similar?*
3. *In particular, what are the similarities and differences in tone?*

William Drummond

TO THE NIGHTINGALE

Dear chorister, who from those shadows sends,
Before that blushing morn dare show her light,
Such sad lamenting strains, that night attends
(Become all ear), stars stay to hear thy plight;
If one, whose grief even reach of thought transcends,
Who never, not in a dream, did taste delight,
May thee importune, who like case pretends,
And seems to joy in woe, in woe's despite;
Tell me (so may thou fortune milder try,
And long, long sing!) for what thou thus complains,
Since winter's gone, and sun in dappled sky
Enamoured smiles on woods and flowery plains?
The bird, as if my questions did he move,
With trembling wings sigh'd forth, I love, I love.

Mark Akenside

THE NIGHTINGALE

To-night retired, the queen of heaven
  With young Endymion[1] stays;
And now to Hesper it is given
Awhile to rule the vacant sky,
Till she shall to her lamp supply
  A stream of brighter rays.

Propitious send thy golden ray,
  Thou purest light above!
Let no false flame seduce to stray
Where gulf or steep lie hid for harm;
But lead where music's healing charm
  May soothe afflicted love.

To them, by many a grateful song
  In happier seasons vow'd,
These lawns, Olympia's[2] haunts, belong:
Oft by yon silver stream we walk'd,
Or fix'd, while Philomela talk'd,
  Beneath yon copses stood.

Nor seldom, where the beechen boughs
  That roofless tower invade,
We came, while her enchanting Muse
The radiant moon above us held:
Till, by a clamorous owl compell'd
  She fled the solemn shade.

But hark! I hear her liquid tone!
  Now Hesper[3] guide my feet!
Down the red marl with moss o'ergrown,
Through yon wild thicket next the plain,
Whose hawthorns choke the winding lane
  Which leads to her retreat.

See the green space: on either hand
  Enlarged it spreads around:
See, in the midst she takes her stand,
Where one old oak his awful shade
Extends o'er half the level mead,
  Enclosed in woods profound.

Hark! how through many a melting note

[1] A beautiful youth, associated with moon
[2] Where the Greek Olympian games were held
[3] Venus

She now prolongs her lays:
How sweetly down the void they float!
The breeze their magic path attends;
The stars shine out; the forest bends;
  The wakeful heifers graze.

Whoe'er thou art whom chance may bring
  To this sequester'd spot,
If then the plaintive Siren sing,
Oh softly tread beneath her bower
And think of Heaven's disposing power,
  Of man's uncertain lot.

Oh think, o'er all this moral stage
  What mournful scenes arise:
What ruin waits on kingly rage;
How often virtue dwells with woe;
How many griefs from knowledge flow;
  How swiftly pleasure flies!

Oh sacred bird! let me at eve,
  Thus wandering all alone,
Thy tender counsel oft receive,
Bear witness to thy pensive airs,
And pity Nature's common cares,
  Till I forget my own.

John Keats

ODE TO A NIGHTINGALE

My heart aches, and a drowsy numbness pains
  My sense, as though of hemlock I had drunk,
Or emptied some some dull opiate to the drains
  One minute past, and Lethe-wards had sunk:
'Tis not through envy of thy happy lot,
  But being too happy in thy happiness,—
    That thou, light-wingèd Dryad of the trees,
      In some melodious plot
  Of beechen green, and shadows numberless,
    Singest of summer in full-throated ease.

O, for a draught of vintage! that hath been
  Cool'd a long age in the deep-delvèd earth,
Tasting of Flora and the country green,
  Dance, and Provençal song, and sunburnt mirth!
O for a beaker full of the warm South,
  Full of the true, the blushful Hippocrene,°
    With beaded bubbles winking at the brim,
      And purple-stainèd mouth;
  That I might drink, and leave the world unseen,
    And with thee fade away into the forest dim:

Fade far away, dissolve, and quite forget
  What thou among the leaves hast never known,
The weariness, the fever, and the fret
  Here, where men sit and hear each other groan;
Where palsy shakes a few, sad, last grey hairs,
  Where youth grows pale, and spectre-thin, and dies;
    Where but to think is to be full of sorrow
      And leaden-eyed despairs,
  Where Beauty cannot keep her lustrous eyes,
    Or new Love pine at them beyond to-morrow.

Away! away! for I will fly to thee,
  Not charioted by Bacchus and his pards,
But on the viewless wings of Poesy,
  Though the dull brain perplexes and retards:
Already with thee! tender is the night,
  And haply the Queen-Moon is on her throne,
    Cluster'd around by all her starry Fays;
      But here there is no light,
  Save what from heaven is with the breezes blown
    Through verdurous glooms and winding mossy ways.

I cannot see what flowers are at my feet,
  Nor what soft incense hangs upon the boughs,
But, in embalmèd darkness, guess each sweet
  Wherewith the seasonable month endows
The grass, the thicket, and the fruit-tree wild;
  White hawthorn, and the pastoral eglantine;
    Fast fading violets cover'd up in leaves;
        And mid-May's eldest child,
  The coming musk-rose, full of dewy wine,
    The murmurous haunt of flies on summer eves.

Darkling I listen; and, for many a time
  I have been half in love with easeful Death,
Call'd him soft names in many a musèd rhyme,
  To take into the air my quiet breath;
Now more than ever seems it rich to die,
  To cease upon the midnight with no pain,
    While thou art pouring forth thy soul abroad
        In such an ecstasy!
  Still wouldst thou sing, and I have ears in vain—
    To thy high requiem become a sod.

Thou wast not born for death, immortal Bird!
  No hungry generations tread thee down;
The voice I hear this passing night was heard
  In ancient days by emperor and clown:
Perhaps the self-same song that found a path
  Through the sad heart of Ruth, when, sick for home,
    She stood in tears amid the alien corn;
        The same that oft-times hath
  Charm'd magic casements, opening on the foam
    Of perilous seas, in faery lands forlorn.

Forlorn! the very word is like a bell
  To toll me back from thee to my sole self!
Adieu! the fancy cannot cheat so well
  As she is fam'd to do, deceiving elf.
Adieu! adieu! thy plaintive anthem fades
  Past the near meadows, over the still stream,
    Up the hillside; and now 'tis buried deep
        In the next valley-glades:
  Was it a vision, or a waking dream?
    Fled is that music:—Do I wake or sleep?

°Greek: a spring associated with poetic inspiration

In the following poems find the central metaphoric subject and consider:

1. What things are related to this subject?
2. What meaning does the subject gain in the course of the poem?

Louis Phillips

A METAPHOR CARRIED ALMOST TO EXCESS

Let grief be as bone
& mend as bone,
Fibers intertwining
As we once intertwined.

What is often broken
Often heals,
& sometimes stronger
At the join & feels

Solid as if it carries
Greater weight,
Growing firm
At the tissues' bite

In the jagged vertebrae's
Links & heals.
Who would know
A sorrow lest he feels

It to the bone,
Stiff grief
& marrow
Of this life,

In constant rending.
Let grief be as bone
That we grow strong
In our mending. . . .

Geoffrey Chaucer

THE COMPLAINT OF CHAUCER TO HIS EMPTY PURSE

To you, my purse and to none other wight[1]
Complain I, for ye be my lady dear!
I am so sorry, now that ye be light;
For certain, but ye make heavy cheer,
Me were as leif[2] be laid up-on my bier;
For which unto your mercy thus I cry:
Beeth heavy again, or else must I die!

Now voucheth safe[3] this day, or it be night,
That I of you the blissful sun may hear,
Or see your color like the sun bright,
That of yellowness had never peer.
Ye be my life, ye be mine hearts steer,[4]
Queen of comfort and of good company:
Beeth heavy again, or else must I die!

Now purse, that be to me my life's light,
And savior, as down in this world here,
Out of this town help me through your might,
Since that ye will not be my treasure;
For I am shaved as near as any frere.[5]
But yet, I pray unto your courtesy:
Beeth heavy again, or else might I die!

L'ENVOY DE CHAUCER
O conquerer of Brute Albion![6]
Which that by line and free election
Be verily kind, this song to you I send;
And ye, that might all our harm amend,
Have mind upon my supplication!

[1]Creature
[2]As soon
[3]Grant
[4]Guide
[5]Monks (frères) had their heads shaved, in other words. The narrator is so poor that he is cutting it close.
[6]England

Richard Eberhart

ON A SQUIRREL CROSSING
THE ROAD IN AUTUMN,
IN NEW ENGLAND

It is what he does not know,
Crossing the road under the elm trees,
About the mechanism of my car,
About the Commonwealth of Massachusetts,
About Mozart, India, Arcturus,

That wins my praise. I engage
At once in whirling squirrel-praise.

He obeys the orders of nature
Without knowing them.
It is what he does not know
That makes him beautiful.
Such a knot of little purposeful nature!

I who can see him as he cannot see himself
Repose in the ignorance that is his blessing.

It is what man does not know of God
Composes the visible poem of the world.
              . . . . Just missed him!

John Skleton

UPON A DEAD MAN'S HEAD

From Pithy, Pleasaunt, and Profitable
Works of Maister Skelton

Skelton Laureate, upon a dead man's head that
was sent to him from an honorable gentlewoman
for a token, devised this ghostly meditation in
English, covenable in sentence, commendable,
lamentable, lacrimable, profitable for the soul.

Your ugly token
My mind hath broken
from worldly lust,
For I have discuss'd
We are but dust
And die we must.
    It is general
To be mortal:
I have well espi'd
No man may him hide
From Death hollow-eyed
With sinews widered,[1]
With bones shidered,[2]
With his worm-eaten maw,

[1]Whithered
[2]Splintered

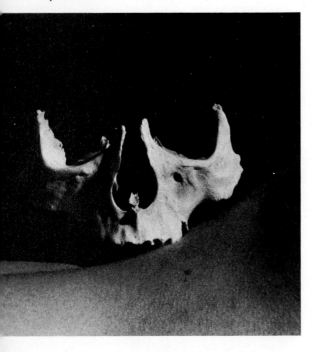

And his ghastly jaw
Gasping aside,
Naked of hide,
Neither flesh nor fell.
    Then by my counsel
Look that ye spell
Well this gospel,
For whereso we dwell
Death will us quell
And with us mell.
    For all our pamper'd paunches
There may no fraunchis[3]
Nor worldly bliss
Redeem us from this:
Our days be dated
To be checkmated
With drawttis[4] of Death,
Stopping our breath;
Our eyen sinking,
Our bodies stinking,
Our gums grinning,
Our souls brinning.
To whom, then, shall we sue
For to have rescue
But to sweet Jesu
On us then for to rue?
    O goodly Child
Of Mary mild,
Then be our shild,
That we be not exil'd
To the dyne dale
Of bottomless bale,
Nor to the lake
Of fiends black.
    But grant us grace
To see Thy face,
And to purchase
Thine heavenly place,
And thy palace
Full of solace
Above the sky
That is so high,
Eternally
To behold and see
The Trinity.
    Amen,
    Mirres vous y.[5]

[3]Exemptions granted
[4]Draughts
[5]Old French for "consider this"

Abraham Cowley

DRINKING

The thirsty earth soaks up the rain,
And drinks, and gapes for drink again.
The plants suck in the earth, and are
With constant drinking fresh and fair.
The sea itself, which one would think
Should have but little need of drink,
Drinks ten thousand rivers up,
So filled that they o'erflow the cup.
The busy sun—and one would guess
By's drunken, fiery face no less—
Drinks up the sea, and when he's done,
The moon and stars drink up the sun.
They drink and dance by their own light;
They drink and revel all the night.
Nothing in nature's sober found,
But an eternal health goes round.
Fill up the bowl, then, fill it high,
Fill all the glasses there, for why
Should every creature drink but I?
Why, man of morals, tell me why?

J. C. Jacobs

THE RECLUSE

She sits embroidering them,
those spots of mind
where darkness kinks.
Her privacy, a quiet room
to pace in now the going's done.
Sewing empty flowers,
their outlines blooming,
threaded shaky as her pulse,
she senses how the outside evening deepens,
when the hour women weep arrives, departs.
She adjusts her lamp and fixes tea;
she'd eaten early. A warm sip
and she sighs out over silence.
Her eyes lightly close
on wallpaper ovals,
like the hoops of years,
vacant, trimmed with roses.
She circles round the rim of pain,
loops a stitch, mechanical,
and circles round again.

John Donne

THE WILL

Before I sigh my last gaspe, let me breath,
Great love, some Legacies; Here I bequeath
Mine eyes to *Argus*,[1] if mine eyes can see,
If they be blinde, then Love, I give them thee;
My tongue to Fame; to'Embassadours mine eares;
   To women or the sea, my teares.
Thou, Love, hast taught mee heretofore
By making mee serve her who'had twenty more,
That I should give to none, but such, as had too much before.

My constancie I to the planets give;
My truth to them, who at the Court doe live;
Mine ingenuity and opennesse,
To Jesuites; to Buffones my pensivenesse;
My silence to'any, who abroad hath beene;
   My mony to a Capuchin.[2]
Thou Love taught'st me, by appointing mee

[1] A legendary creature with a thousand eyes
[2] Monks who took strenuous vows of poverty

To love there, where no love receiv'd can be,
Onely to give to such as have an incapacitie.

My faith I give to Roman Catholiques;
All my good works unto the Schismaticks[3]
Of Amsterdam: my best civility
And Courtship, to an Universitie;
My modesty I give to souldiers bare;
    My patience let gamesters share.
Thou Love taughtst mee, by making mee
  Love her that holds my love disparity,
Onely to give to those that count my gifts indignity.

I give my reputation to those
Which were my friends; Mine industrie to foes;
To Schoolemen I bequeath my doubtfulnesse;
My sicknesse to Physitians, or excesse;
To Nature, all that I in Ryme have writ;
    And to my company my wit.
Thou Love, by making mee adore
  Her, who begot this love in mee before,
Taughtst me to make, as though I gave, when I did but restore.

To him for whom the passing bell next tolls,
I give my physick bookes; my writen rowles
Of Morall counsels, I to Bedlam give;
My brazen medals, unto them which live
In want of bread; To them which passe among
    All forrainers, mine English tongue.
Thou, Love, by making mee love one
  Who thinkes her friendship a fit portion
For yonger lovers, dost my gifts thus disproportion.

Therefore I'll give no more; But I'll undoe
The world by dying; because love dies too.
Then all your beauties will be no more worth
Than gold in Mines, where none doth draw it forth;
And all your graces no more use shall have
    Than a Sun dyall in a grave.
Thou Love taughtst mee, by making mee
  Love her, who doth neglect both mee and thee,
To'invent, and practise this one way, to'annihilate all three.

[3]Those who sought to divide the Church

Thomas Nashe

SUMMER'S FAREWELL

*From Summer's Last Will and Testament (lines
1969 to 2029)*

This is the last stroke my tongue's clock must strike,
My last will, which I will that you performe.
My crowne I have disposed already of.
Item, I give my withered flowers and herbes,
Unto dead corpses, for to decke them with.
My shady walkes to great mens servitors,
Who in their masters shadowes walke secure.
My pleasant open air, and fragrant smels,
To Croyden and the grounds abutting round.
My heate and warmth to toyling labourers,
My long dayes to bondmen, and prisoners,
My shortest nights to young marrièd soules,
My drought and thirst to drunkards quenchlesse throates;
My fruites to *Autumne*, my adopted heire,
My murmuring springs, musicians of sweete sleepe,
To murmuring malcontents, whose well tun'd cares,
Channel'd in a sweete falling quaterzaine,
Do lull their eares asleepe, listning themselves.
And finally,—O words, now clense your course!—
Unto *Eliza* that most sacred Dame,
Whom none but Saints and Angels ought to name;
All my faire dayes remaining, I bequeath
To waite upon her till she be returnd.
Autumne, I charge thee, when that I am dead,
Be prest and serviceable at her beck,
Present her with thy goodliest ripened fruites;
Unclothe no Arbors where she ever sate,
Touch not a tree, thou thinkst she may passe by.
And *Winter*, with thy wrythen frostie face,
Smoothe up thy visage, when thou lookst on her,
Thou never lookst on such bright majestie:
A charmed circle draw about her court,
Wherein warme dayes may dance, and no cold comes.
On seas let winds make warre, not vexe her rest,
Quiet inclose her bed, thought flye her brest.
Ah, gracious Queene, though *Summer* pine away,
Yet let thy flourishing stand at a stay!
First droupe this universals aged frame,
E're any malady thy strength should tame:
Heaven raise up pillers to uphold thy hand,
Peace may have still his temple in thy land.
Loe, I have said! this is the totall summe.
Autumne and *Winter*, on your faithfulnesse
For the performance I do firmely builde.

Farewell, my friends, *Summer* bids you farewell,
Archers, and bowlers, all my followers,
Adieu, and dwell with desolation;
Silence must be your masters mansion:
Now marching thus, discend I to the feends.
Weepe heavens, mourne earth, here *Summer* ends.

Here the Satyres and Wood-nimphes carry him out,
Singing as he came in.

Sylvia Plath

MIRROR

I am silver and exact, I have no preconceptions.
Whatever I see I swallow immediately
Just as it is, unmisted by love or dislike.
I am not cruel, only truthful—
The eye of a little god, four-cornered.
Most of the time, I meditate on the opposite wall.
It is pink, with speckles. I have looked at it so long
I think it is a part of my heart. But it flickers.
Faces and darkness separate us over and over.

Now I am a lake. A woman bends over me,
Searching my reaches for what she really is.
Then she turns to those liars, the candles or the moon.
I see her back, and reflect it faithfully.
She rewards me with tears and an agitation of hands.
I am important to her. She comes and goes.
Each morning it is her face that replaces the darkness.
In me she has drowned a young girl, and in me an old woman
Rises toward her day after day, like a terrible fish.

Thomas Traherne

SHADOWS IN THE WATER

In unexperienc'd Infancy
Many a sweet Mistake doth ly:
Mistake, tho false, intending tru;
A *Seeming* somwhat more than *View*;
 That doth instruct the Mind
 In Things that ly behind,
And many Secrets to us show
Which afterwards we com to know.

Thus did I by the Water's brink
Another World beneath me think;
And while the lofty spacious Skies
Reversed there abus'd mine Eys,
 I fancy'd other Feet
 Came mine to touch or meet;
As by som Puddle I did play
Another World within it lay.

Beneath the Water Peeple drown'd,
Yet with another Hev'n crown'd,
In spacious Regions seem'd to go
As freely moving to and fro:
 In bright and open Space
 I saw their very face;
Eys, Hands, and Feet they had like mine;
Another Sun did with them shine.

'Twas strange that Peeple there should walk,
And yet I could not hear them talk:
That throu a little watry Chink,
Which one dry Ox or Horse might drink,
 We other Worlds should see,
 Yet not admitted be;
And other Confines there behold
Of Light and Darkness, Heat and Cold.

I call'd them oft, but call'd in vain;
No Speeches we could entertain:
Yet did I there expect to find
Som other World, to pleas my Mind.
 I plainly saw by these
 A new *Antipodes*,
Whom, tho they were so plainly seen,
A Film kept off that stood between.

By walking Men's reversed Feet
I chanc'd another World to meet;
Tho it did not to View exceed
A Phantasm, 'tis a World indeed,
 Where Skies beneath us shine,
 And Earth by Art divine
Another face presents below,
Where Peeple's feet against Ours go.

Within the Regions of the Air,
Compass'd about with Hev'ns fair,
Great Tracts of Land there may be found
Enricht with Fields and fertil Ground;
 Where many num'rous Hosts,
 In those far distant Coasts,
For other great and glorious Ends,
Inhabit, my yet unknown Friends.

O ye that stand upon the Brink,
Whom I so near me, throu the Chink,
With Wonder see: What Faces there,
Whose Feet, whose Bodies, do ye wear?
 I my Companions see
 In You, another Me.
They seemed Others, but are We;
Our second Selvs those Shadows be.

Look how far off those lower Skies
Extend themselves! scarce with mine Eys
I can them reach. O ye my Friends,
What *Secret* borders on those Ends?
 Are lofty Hevens hurl'd
 'Bout your inferior World?
Are ye the Representatives
Of other Peopl's distant Lives?

Of all the Play-mates which I knew
That here I do the Image view
In other Selvs; what can it mean?
But that below the purling Stream
 Som unknown Joys there be
 Laid up in Store for me;
To which I shall, when that thin Skin
Is broken, be admitted in.

William Wordsworth

SHE WAS A PHANTOM
OF DELIGHT

She was a Phantom of delight
When first she gleamed upon my sight;
A lovely Apparition, sent
To be a moment's ornament;
Her eyes as stars of Twilight fair;
Like Twilight's, too, her dusky hair;
But all things else about her drawn
From May-time and the cheerful Dawn;
A dancing Shape, an Image gay,
To haunt, to startle, and way-lay.

I saw her upon nearer view,
A Spirit, yet a Woman too!
Her household motions light and free,
And steps of virgin-liberty;
A countenance in which did meet

Sweet records, promises as sweet;
A Creature not too bright or good
For human nature's daily food;
For transient sorrows, simple wiles,
Praise, blame, love, kisses, tears, and smiles.

And now I see with eye serene
The very pulse of the machine;
A Being breathing thoughtful breath,
A Traveller between life and death;
The reason firm, the temperate will,
Endurance, foresight, strength, and skill;
A perfect Woman, nobly planned,
To warn, to comfort, and command;
And yet a Spirit still, and bright
With something of angelic light.

Karen Swenson

HECUBA°

Hecuba I want to know,
behind that mask
taut and intransigent as the glaze on my best china,
what grimace did you make
when Hector at Achilles' heel flopped like a fish
over the old dishcloth heaps of other dead men.

The flies
rose and settled
rose and settled
play parachutes disturbed by chariot wheels.

Did you think how luxuriant
the grass would be next year
rooting around Troy's wall?
Or of wars and whores and how
old men pimp the prostitute of death
to watch the young men lay her?

°The Queen of Troy

Some women wear their dead
as generals their medals,
a decoration of their own bravery.
They were able to bear this death.

Did you put a black handkerchief around his picture
and send the maid out
for the wax smugness of a lily?
More than two thousand years later,
two thousand years of the aphorism of graves and grass
(neither eggbeaters nor philosophy change anything)

I have a son,
a minnow in time's mouth. Hecuba,
behind old Homer's blind mask,
I want to know.

Sir Richard Fanshawe

A ROSE

After Góngora

Blown in the Morning, thou shalt fade ere Noon:
What boots a Life which in such hast forsakes thee?
Th'art wondrous frolic being to die so soon:
And passing proud a little colour makes thee.
If thee thy brittle beauty so deceives,
Know then the thing that swells thee is thy bane;
For the same beauty doth in bloody leaves
The sentence of thy early death contain.
Some Clown's coarse Lungs will poison thy sweet flow'r,
If by the careless Plough thou shalt be torn:
And many Herods lie in wait each hour
To murder thee as soon as thou are born,
   Nay, force thy Bud to blow; their Tyrant breath
   Anticipating Life, to hasten death.

John Donne

A JEAT RING SENT

Thou art not so black, as my heart,
Nor halfe so brittle, as her heart, thou art;
What would'st thou say? shall both our properties by thee bee spoke,
Nothing more endlesse, nothing sooner broke?

Marriage rings are not of this stuffe;
Oh, why should ought lesse precious, or lesse tough
Figure our loves? Except in thy name thou have bid it say,
I'am cheap, and nought but fashion, fling me'away.

Yet stay with mee since thou art come,
Circle this fingers top, which did'st her thombe.
Be justly proud, and gladly safe, that thou dost dwell with me,
She that, Oh, broke her faith, would soon breake thee.

Howard Nemerov

I ONLY AM ESCAPED ALONE TO TELL THEE°

I tell you that I see her still
At the dark entrance of the hall.
One gas lamp burning near her shoulder
Shone also from her other side
Where hung the long inaccurate glass
Whose pictures were as troubled water.
An immense shadow had its hand
Between us on the floor, and seemed
To hump the knuckles nervously,
A giant crab readying to walk,
Or a blanket moving in its sleep.

You will remember, with a smile
Instructed by movies to reminisce,
How strict her corsets must have been,
How the huge arrangements of her hair
Would certainly betray the least
Impassionate displacement there.

It was no rig for dallying,
And maybe only marriage could
Derange that queenly scaffolding—
As when a great ship, coming home,
Coasts in the harbor, dropping sail
And loosing all the tackle that had laced
Her in the long lanes . . .
                                        I know
We need not draw this figure out
But all that whalebone came from whales
And all the whales lived in the sea,
In calm beneath the troubled glass,
Until the needle drew their blood.

I see her standing in the hall,
Where the mirror's lashed to blood and foam,
And the black flukes of agony
Beat at the air till the light blows out.

°Closing words from Melville's *Moby Dick*

Percy Bysshe Shelley

ODE TO THE WEST WIND

I
O wild West Wind, thou breath of Autumn's being,
Thou, from whose unseen presence the leaves dead
Are driven, like ghosts from an enchanter fleeing,

Yellow, and black, and pale, and hectic red,
Pestilence-stricken multitudes: O thou,
Who chariotest to their dark wintry bed

The wingèd seeds, where they life cold and low,
Each like a corpse within its grave, until
Thine azure sister of the Spring shall blow

Her clarion o'er the dreaming earth, and fill
(Driving sweet buds like flocks to feed in air)
With living hues and odours plain and hill:

Wild Spirit, which art moving everywhere;
Destroyer and preserver; hear, oh, hear!

II

Thou on whose stream, mid the steep sky's commotion,
Loose clouds like earth's decaying leaves are shed,
Shook from the tangled boughs of Heaven and Ocean,

Angels of rain and lightning: there are spread
On the blue surface of thine aëry surge,
Like the bright hair uplifted from the head

Of some fierce Maenad,° even from the dim verge
Of the horizon to the zenith's height,
The locks of the approaching storm. Thou dirge

Of the dying year, to which this closing night
Will be the dome of a vast sepulchre,
Vaulted with all thy congregated might

Of vapours, from whose solid atmosphere
Black rain, and fire, and hail will burst: oh, hear!

III

Thou who didst waken from his summer dreams
The blue Mediterranean, where he lay,
Lulled by the coil of his crystàlline streams,

Beside a pumice isle in Baiae's bay,
And saw in sleep old palaces and towers
Quivering within the wave's intenser day,

All overgrown with azure moss and flowers
So sweet, the sense faints picturing them! Thou
For whose path the Atlantic's level powers

Cleave themselves into chasms, while far below
The sea-blooms and the oozy woods which wear
The sapless foliage of the ocean, know

Thy voice, and suddenly grow gray with fear,
And tremble and despoil themselves: oh, hear!

IV

If I were a dead leaf thou mightest bear;
If I were a swift cloud to fly with thee;
A wave to pant beneath thy power, and share

The impulse of thy strength, only less free
Than thou, O uncontrollable! If even
I were as in my boyhood, and could be

°Legendary worshipers of Dionysus, noted for their wild
ecstasies

The comrade of thy wanderings over Heaven,
As then, when to outstrip thy skiey speed
Scarce seemed a vision; I would ne'er have striven

As thus with thee in prayer in my sore need.
Oh, lift me as a wave, a leaf, a cloud!
I fall upon the thorns of life! I bleed!

A heavy weight of hours has chained and bowed
One too like thee: tameless, and swift, and proud.

V
Make me thy lyre, even as the forest is:
What if my leaves are falling like its own!
The tumult of thy mighty harmonies

Will take from both a deep, autumnal tone,
Sweet though in sadness. Be thou, Spirit fierce,
My spirit! Be thou me, impetuous one!

Drive my dead thoughts over the universe
Like withered leaves to quicken a new birth!
And, by the incantation of this verse,

Scatter, as from an unextinguished hearth
Ashes and sparks, my words among mankind!
Be through my lips to unawakened earth

The trumpet of a prophecy! O, Wind,
If Winter comes, can Spring be far behind?

EXPERIENCING THE POEM

Reread Andrew Marvell's "To His Coy Mistress"
(page 16) and see what *immediate* impact it has
now.

CHAPTER 5
THE POEM AS A
METAPHOR: *X/?*

The poems in this chapter have one characteristic in common: The central subject (or situation) described by each is obviously meant to be taken metaphorically (that is, as an *X*), though the subject is not explicitly compared to anything. In order to get an idea of how this works, let's look at the Frost poem we referred to before.

Robert Frost

THE ROAD NOT TAKEN

Two roads diverged in a yellow wood,
And sorry I could not travel both
And be one traveler, long I stood
And looked down one as far as I could.
To where it bent in the undergrowth;

Then took the other, as just as fair,
And having perhaps the better claim,
Because it was grassy and wanted wear;
Though as for that, the passing there
Had worn them really about the same,

And both that morning equally lay
In leaves no step had trodden black.
Oh, I kept the first for another day!
Yet knowing how way leads on to way,
I doubted if I should ever come back.

I shall be telling this with a sigh
Somewhere ages and ages hence:
Two roads diverged in a wood, and I—
I took the one less traveled by,
And that has made all the difference.

Reading this poem literally (as many have), we might conclude, as one student did, that "it's about a man who comes to a place where there are two roads; he can't decide which one to take, and so he takes the one that looks less used and he's glad." That is basically the story, the "plot." But if you don't see past that and go deeper, you stop short of the real experience. This issue is basic to a common misapprehension of poetry, that is, the idea that poetry is mainly a pretty description or a fancy way of expressing everyday adventures.

A superficial reading of the Frost piece leaves a superficial impression, just a pleasant description of the poet's feelings while taking a morning walk. This is a problem because it's easy to let Frost's simple diction beguile you into thinking he writes simple poems. Some imitators call him a nature poet who captures our open-air moods. But Frost's surface simplicity belies a subtle, sophisticated treatment of metaphor. "The Road Not Taken" turns out to be a complicated ironic statement.

Notice that there are none of the local metaphors or striking images we usually see in poetry. One reason for this is that Frost *structures the entire situation to be metaphoric*, to constitute an X referring to some unstated Y or Y's.

But how can we identify metaphor shorn of the usual poetic language? The poet does not provide the sort of direct statements or relationships we've been getting used to. He does not say "the road of time" or "two roads like life." Instead, we are given just a seemingly literal picture of a man choosing between two roads while taking a walk.

One way to grasp the metaphor is to "feel" what the tone stresses, to perceive how the narrator puts weight on the situation. Lines like "I took the one less traveled by,/And that has made all the difference" tend to reveal the metaphoric intentions; once you are alert to this, it's quite easy to see. Anyone who wants to take this poem as mere mood and description still has to relate the last stanza to the body of the poem, and the great weight of these lines is absurd if the rest of the piece is seen only on a literal level: why has a choice between two roads made "*all* the difference"? To what? What level connects with "ages and ages hence"? So metaphoric action takes place as soon as you become sensitive to the contrast between the clearly far-reaching conclusions of the last lines and the "simple" presentation of the opening stanzas.

The narrator's situation implies at least two abstract subjects (Y's). One we might call "decision making," and the other "human limitation"; that is, the narrator choosing between the roads discovers that he is limited, that he can take only one of them. This concrete situation allows Frost to explore these abstractions without ever seeming abstract. We cannot really take his remarks as advice or cracker-barrel philosophy, as if someone said, "You can never tell when you make a decision what's going to happen" or "You know, every time you make a decision you have to leave something behind." Yet, in a sense these statements are contained in the lines "And looked down one as far as I could" and "Yet knowing how way leads on to way/I doubted if I should ever come back." These lines do not present philosophy, but description; so, as we have seen in other cases, in poetic context we *experience* certain philosophic implications, and the experience is very different from merely hearing about an idea.

In addition, the central metaphor permits many of the details of the concrete situation to become X's with unstated Y's. Consider, in this light, some questions about various images and statements in the poem:

1. Look at the images such as the "yellow wood," "leaves," "trodden black," and "undergrowth." What are some of the Y's you could connect with each of these images in terms of decision making and human limitation?
2. The lines "Though as for that, the passing there/Had worn them really about the same" are descriptive. Are they also metaphoric? How? Of what?
3. How does the title, "The Road Not Taken," add to the meaning of the poem?
4. Could the line "And that has made all the difference" be ironic? If so, how?

In examining the "undergrowth" detail, for example, do you encounter Y levels here? Without trying to specify them, can you feel, as a kind of effect of the context, the connotations of this image? If you do, it becomes clear that in understanding the central or primary metaphoric subject (in this case, the choice between roads), we become alert to all the implications of images, local metaphors, and statements.

Interestingly, the germinal idea behind Frost's poem is a cliché. "Being on the right road," "going down the road to salvation (or destruction)," "the fork in the road of life," and "the paths of life" are all standard versions of Frost's central metaphor. An insight becomes a cliché because at first we see some truth in it; then overuse deadens the impact. We specify a conclusion about what is meant, and insight is over; it stops stimulating new responses. Frost puts new life and depth into the cliché by presenting two specific roads. The secret here is that you experience the image of the roads first, and *then* the meanings, and that the meanings remain *unstated*. The reverse order would be hard to take—for example, "I've reached a fork in the road of life in a yellow wood, and sorry. . . ."

In each of the following poems it's obvious (but not actually stated) that we are meant to take the entire poem as an X in relation to some Y or Y's. Usually there is a concrete subject or situation, like choosing between two roads, and we're implicitly asked to discover the abstraction or abstractions it evokes. We have already seen at least one poem of this type—Blake's "The Sick Rose" (page 70). It is certain that the rose relates to something (is meant metaphorically), though we are not openly told what. Can you find other poems of this type in earlier chapters?

Bear in mind that although we have been dividing poems into categories (X/Y, X/Y's, $X/$?), this is only for the purpose of getting into them. In fact, many pieces presented in one chapter could be discussed in another. Poems do not fit neatly into intellectual niches. For example, "Ode on a Grecian Urn" might be treated as a poem of X/Y form if we took the tack that the urn is (like) beauty and truth and related everything else in the piece around that central metaphor. "The Ball Poem" (page 149) might be an $X/$? since we are never really shown what the ball is compared to. But the idea is not to spend time trying to define or categorize poems, but just to use the categories as a way of approaching given pieces. In the end, to experience poetry in a complete way, we must totally discard all the fragmentary and often distracting techniques we used to make a beginning. Once you have learned to swim, you no longer think about how to kick your legs or move your arms.

The wild swans in this delicate poem obviously have great meaning, and much of the effect of the piece depends on that meaning remaining unstated and mysterious.

A. What abstractions do you see as Y levels for the swans (X)?
B. What relation does the narrator's age have to the significance of the swans?
C. How are the details of the description metaphoric?

William Butler Yeats

THE WILD SWANS AT COOLE

The trees are in their autumn beauty,
The woodland paths are dry,
Under the October twilight the water
Mirrors a still sky;
Upon the brimming water among the stones
Are nine-and-fifty swans.

The nineteenth autumn has come upon me
Since I first made my count;
I saw, before I had well finished,
All suddenly mount
And scatter wheeling in great broken rings
Upon their clamorous wings.

I have looked upon those brilliant creatures,
And now my heart is sore.
All's changed since I, hearing at twilight,
The first time on this shore,
The bell-beat of their wings above my head,
Trod with a lighter tread.

Unwearied still, lover by lover,
They paddle in the cold
Companionable streams or climb the air;
Their hearts have not grown old;
Passion or conquest, wander where they will,
Attend upon them still.

But now they drift on the still water,
Mysterious, beautiful;
Among what rushes will they build,
By what lake's edge or pool
Delight men's eyes when I awake some day
To find they have flown away?

Considerations

Like the poems in the last chapter, this poem's metaphoric subject (swans) associates with specific Y's (passion and conquest, for example), but the real significance of the birds remains unstated. What are the swans? Life? Youth? Art? Perfection? The soul? Each detail in the poem seems to add to their mystery and meaning.

In the first lines the swans float over water mirroring a "still sky" (sky=heaven?). Do the trees, paths, stones, and twilight here seem to have metaphoric potentiality? How about autumn itself?

Later, the swans "suddenly mount/And scatter wheeling in great broken rings/Upon their clamorous wings." Their action suggests some great significance: why "clamorous wings," for example? What are they clamoring for? Could this refer to just the sound alone? The narrator says that when this happened, nineteen years earlier, he had been trying to count the swans when they flew away. Were they some portent, some omen he misread then but now seems dimly to grasp? A portent of what? Was the act of counting a hopeless attempt to bring a rational order to bear on what cannot be measured? Notice how we are forced to keep asking (without ever answering the question): *What are these swans?*

In the third stanza they are "brilliant creatures" exciting awareness of some change (apparently for the worse) that has taken place since the narrator first heard the "bell-beat of wings." Can we know whether it is an internal or external change? Can you see how the swans as lovers are somehow being subtly compared with human lovers and love? Why are the streams "cold/Companionable"?

In the end, when the swans have flown, we're left with unanswered questions. The swans remain mysterious, unknown. In trying to relate to them and all the implications of their coming and going, their very being, the narrator has an indefinable yet profound experience. This may hold for us as well, but can it be talked about? Since metaphoric insight can only be evoked, never stated, the experience is somehow very private, isn't it? We can reason, discuss, and analyze, right to the threshold of poetic awareness, but once across it we come upon this mysterious silence that Yeats has gathered into the image of the swans.

1. In lines three and four of the last stanza, do you find that the natural images are metaphoric in the way Frost's roads are? How about other natural images throughout the piece?
2. The swans might represent (among other things) some permanent, natural perfection, some ideal form, that the speaker can keep in sight only for a time because they come and go beyond his control. Does that feeling touch your own life?
3. Why does the speaker say, "when I *awake* someday"? Does he simply mean that some morning they will be gone? Is this a literal sleep? *Now*, he says, the experience is with him; *someday* it will end. But what will he awaken to? Some realization? Or has he been asleep all along? Can we ever really come to a conclusion about this?

Technical Notes

The poem's stanzas are SESTETS of *a a b b c c* rhyme. Iambic and anapestic feet predominate.

In this piece by Wyatt, unlike "The Lover Compareth His State . . ." poem we looked at in the last chapter, the poet does not tell us what the Y term is. As you read, try to see how many things the deer in this piece might signify.

Sir Thomas Wyatt

WHOSO LIST TO HUNT

Whoso list[1] to hunt, I know where is an hind,[2]
But as for me, *helas*! I may no more.
The vain travail hath wearied me so sore,
I am of them that furthest come behind.
Yet may I, by no means, my wearied mind
Draw from the deer; but as she fleeth afore
Fainting I follow. I leave off therefore,
Since in a net I seek to hold the wind.
Who list her hunt, I put him out of doubt,
As well as I, may spend his time in vain;
And graven with diamonds in letters plain
There is written, her fair neck round about,
Noli me tangere,[3] for Caesar's I am,
And wild for to hold, though I seem tame.

[1]Wishes, desires
[2]A doe
[3]Latin for "Do not touch me!"

Considerations

Your list of *Y* terms could include money, fame, success, a girl friend, a boy friend, good luck, youth, happiness, life, etc. Any of these would make sense in terms of the poem. Many feel that because the poet was alleged to have had an affair with the Queen of England, the doe stands for this particular woman. But you can't prove that just by referring to the piece.

However, what if the poet had told us that the deer was something specific, the Queen or money, for example? Would the poem be as effective? You can see that equating chasing the deer to chasing money, for example, would reduce the piece to an aphorism: "Money is easy to chase but hard to catch," an opinion we might even argue over.

The reference to Caesar in the second-to-last line is an allusion to the point in the New Testament where Christ, when asked about paying taxes, responds: "Render therefore unto Caesar the things which are Caesar's; and unto God the things that are God's." In other words, Caesar's things are the things of this world, while God's are beyond it. So, on one level, chasing the deer is (like) chasing after the things of this world. But even this formulation misses something. Why?

Because the deer's meaning is unstated, mysterious, the poem engages us beyond the level of idea and opinion. This is because we understand what it is to pursue things we want and can't have but continue to pursue. We don't simply identify this with some specific area of life (love, money, or whatever), but we seem to understand it in a profounder sense. Without the deer's mysterious quality, would such an understanding be possible?

1. How is the local metaphor "since in a net I seek to hold the wind" related to the central metaphoric subject?
2. Could "Caesar" be a reference to some specific king or prince of Wyatt's era? How would the poem read then?
3. Consider Wyatt's delicate use of detail: "Fainting I follow," "my wearied mind draw from the deer," and the last line. What sort of impression do you get from the tone of the narrator's pursuit of the deer?

Technical Notes

This is a variation of a Petrarchan sonnet. Iambic meter predominates.

The Kraken is the Scandinavian version of the sea dragon. What is Tennyson's Kraken? What are some of the possible abstractions you could associate with it?

Alfred, Lord Tennyson

THE KRAKEN

Below the thunders of the upper deep;
Far, far beneath in the abysmal sea,
His ancient, dreamless, uninvaded sleep
The Kraken sleepeth: faintest sunlights flee
About his shadowy sides: above him swell
Huge sponges of millennial growth and height;
And far away into the sickly light,
From many a wondrous grot and secret cell
Unnumber'd and enormous polypi
Winnow with giant arms the slumbering green.
There hath he lain for ages and will lie
Battening° upon huge seaworms in his sleep,
Until the latter fire shall heat the deep;
Then once by man and angels to be seen,
In roaring he shall rise and on the surface die.

°Feeding gluttonously and growing fat

As the title of this poem indicates, X is a road, but quite a different one from Robert Frost's. As you read this unusual contemporary piece, try to see how the poet gets his road to become intensely meaningful. Here again, as in the Yeats poem, although specific things are associated with the subject, its essential significance remains unstated.

Richard Hugo

BLONDE ROAD

This road dips and climbs but never bends.
The line it finally is, strings far beyond
My sight, still the color of useless dirt.
Trees are a hundred greens in varying light
As sky breaks black on silver over and in
The sea. Not one home or car. No shacks
Abandoned to the storms. On one side,
Miles of high grass; on the other, weather
And the sea reflecting tons of a wild day.

The wind is from Malay. Tigers in the wind
Make lovers claw each other orange. Blonde
Dirt rises to recite the lies of summer
Before the wind goes north and cats rip
White holes in the sky. Fields are grim
And the birds along this road are always stone.

I planned to cheat the road with laughter.
Build a home no storm could crack
And sing my Fridays over centuries of water—
Once more, have me back, my awkward weather—
But the land is not for sale. Centuries
Are strung; a blonde road north and south
And no one will improve it with macadam.

The road is greased by wind. Sun has turned
The blonde dirt brown, the brown grass
Black and dark ideas of the ocean
Silver. Each month rolls along the road
With an hour's effort. Now the lovers
Can't recall each other or identify
That roar: the northern pain of tigers

I know that just a word I'll never have
Could make the brown road blonde again
And send the stone birds climbing to their names.

Considerations

1. What does the poet associate with the road and the landscape surrounding it? How are these things metaphoric? Is there any consistent quality to what is associated with the road?
2. How does "I planned to cheat the road with laughter" add to the meaning of the road?
3. What is the relation of time (centuries, months) to the road?
4. If the poet had said "golden" road instead of "blonde" road, would the poem be easier to interpret? Why?
5. Can you see any tension between the blonde road (X) and homes, cars, and macadam (Y)? What is it? How does this tension relate to the "tigers" and "tons of a wild day"?
6. Why doesn't the narrator have the word that will "make the brown road blonde again"? Does this statement suggest that the road is ultimately an X with an unstated Y? Is the road suggesting time's passage, age, fate, etc.?

On the first reading, this may seem a difficult poem. Giving a logical interpretation would be a problem, but experiencing the piece involves simply perceiving that the road has hidden meaning, metaphoric implication, and so all the details (images, ideas, etc.) reflect and develop this meaning. The metaphoric tension tells us something. For example, look at the line (from stanza three) "And sing my Fridays over centuries of water." Notice how the word "Fridays" (like "leaven" in the Christ parable, Chapter 1) obviously means more than just a day of the week. It's much more effective than if the poet said, "And I sing my happiness over centuries of water." Fridays are the end of the workweek and therefore represent pleasure, relief, etc. And how is water like centuries? In effect, the poem acts as a metaphoric puzzle, and as we try to solve it (perhaps asking ourselves: What is this road?), while we may get no specific answer, we make discoveries.

*In this peculiarly mystifying poem the central metaphoric subject (yachts) leads
us to find another principal metaphoric subject of almost equal weight. Can you
find this second subject?*

William Carlos Williams

THE YACHTS

[1]
contend in a sea which the land partly encloses
shielding them from the too heavy blows
of an ungoverned ocean which when it chooses

[2]
tortures the biggest hulls, the best man knows
to pit against its beatings, and sinks them pitilessly.
Mothlike in mists, scintillant in the minute

[3]
brilliance of cloudless days, with broad bellying sails
they glide to the wind tossing green water
from their sharp prows while over them the crew crawls

[4]
ant like, solicitously grooming them, releasing,
making fast as they turn, lean far over and having
caught the wind again, side by side, head for the mark.

[5]
In a well guarded arena of open water surrounded by
lesser and greater craft which, sycophant, lumbering
and flittering follow them, they appear youthful, rare

[6]
as the light of a happy eye, live with the grace
of all that in the mind is feckless, free and
naturally to be desired. Now the sea which holds them

[7]
is moody, lapping their glossy sides, as if feeling
for some slightest flaw but fails completely.
Today no race. Then the wind comes again. The yachts

[8]
move, jockeying for a start, the signal is set and they
are off. Now the waves strike at them but they are too
well made, they slip through, though they take in canvas.

[9]
Arms with hands grasping seek to clutch at the prows.
Bodies thrown recklessly in the way are cut aside.
It is a sea of faces about them in agony, in despair

[10]
until the horror of the race dawns staggering the mind,
the whole sea become an entanglement of watery bodies
lost to the world bearing what they cannot hold. Broken,

[11]
beaten, desolate, reaching from the dead to be taken up
they cry out, failing, failing! their cries rising
in waves still as the skillful yachts pass over.

Considerations

1. What qualities are associated with the yachts?
2. What happens to the sea in stanza nine? What new relationship is established?
3. What qualities are associated with the sea? How is the "ungoverned ocean" related to the "sea which the land partly encloses"? Are these metaphoric X's? For what?
4. What is the relationship between the yachts and the sea at the end of the poem?

We feel that the situation is metaphoric, that the dramatic little yacht race refers to other things.

In stanzas three through six, the yachts personify sleek, skillful, clever people. In stanza seven the description of the sea as "moody," "feeling for some slightest flaw" in the boats, introduces a sinister tone. The ominous feeling in the first two stanzas may suggest that the sea will ultimately master these delicate craft. Stanza eight supports this idea. But suddenly in the ninth stanza the sea itself is mastered. The surreal personification in which waves become the hands and arms of drowning people shifts our focus from the yachts to the sea they "pass over."

So we find ourselves (as in previous poems) with more questions than answers about what the yachts and the sea are expressing. These questions are not imposed on the poem (to promote some specific point of view) but, rather, arise naturally out of it.

The Stevens piece was written first. Cassegrain uses a basically similar central subject and even some similar phrasing derived from the original, but the result is quite different. Why?

Wallace Stevens

OF MERE BEING

The palm at the end of the mind,
Beyond the last thought, rises
In the bronze distance,

A gold-feathered bird
Sings in the palm, without human meaning,
Without human feeling, a foreign song.

You know then that it is not the reason
That makes us happy or unhappy.
The bird sings. Its feathers shine.

The palm stands on the edge of space.
The wind moves slowly in the branches.
The bird's fire-fangled feathers dangle down.

William Cassegrain

OF MERE BEING

A Variation for Wallace Stevens

In the fog at the end of the mind,
Beyond the last thought,
a gaunt tree rises
(in the pale distance)

The tree is stark,
—and in its branches, black with rain,
appears a bird: a
quick bird,
frail
and not exotic.

The tree stands at the edge of space;
the fog clings palely to its branches.
The body of the bird
flicks;
its head jerks up . . .
The eye is furious.

Considerations

1. How are the central subjects in the poems the same? How are they different?
2. How is the tone of each affected by the choice of details?
3. How has Cassegrain altered the tone of the Stevens piece? What aspects of tone has he maintained?
4. What different sense do you get from each of the birds?
5. What levels of meaning do you get from each poem?

Long after the event, one of the three wise men who journeyed to the place of Christ's birth here recalls his long trek from the East and meditates upon the meaning of that experience.

T. S. Eliot

JOURNEY OF THE MAGI

'A cold coming we had of it,
Just the worst time of the year
For a journey, and such a long journey:
The ways deep and the weather sharp,
The very dead of winter.'
And the camels galled, sore-footed, refractory,
Lying down in the melting snow.
There were times we regretted
The summer palaces on slopes, the terraces,
And the silken girls bringing sherbet.
Then the camel men cursing and grumbling
And running away, and wanting their liquor and women,
And the night-fires going out, and the lack of shelters.
And the cities hostile and the towns unfriendly
And the villages dirty and charging high prices:
A hard time we had of it.
At the end we preferred to travel all night,
Sleeping in snatches,
With the voices singing in our ears, saying
That this was all folly.

Then at dawn we came down to a temperate valley,
Wet, below the snow line, smelling of vegetation;
With a running stream and a water-mill beating the darkness,
And three trees on the low sky,
And an old white horse galloped away in the meadow.
Then we came to a tavern with vine-leaves over the lintel,
Six hands at an open door dicing for pieces of silver,
And feet kicking the empty wine-skins.
But there was no information, and so we continued
And arrived at evening, not a moment too soon
Finding the place; it was (you may say) satisfactory.
All this was a long time ago, I remember,
And I would do it again, but set down
This set down
This: were we led all that way for
Birth or Death? There was a Birth, certainly,
We had evidence and no doubt. I had seen birth and death,
But had thought they were different; this Birth was
Hard and bitter agony for us, like Death, our death.
We returned to our places, these Kingdoms,
But no longer at ease here, in the old dispensation,
With an alien people clutching their gods.
I should be glad of another death.

Considerations

1. What is the central metaphoric subject here?
2. This poem is about the journey of the wise men to see Christ. Can you see any allusions to, and symbols for, the *death* of Christ?
3. What kinds of comparisons, contrasts, and identifications does the narrator make between birth and death?

4. Is this only a description of the journey of the Magi, or could the poem be about other kinds of journeying? If so, how?
5. What do details like "the snow line," "a water-mill beating the darkness," "three trees on the low sky," etc., suggest?

[handwritten annotations: "heart of life", "line of unjoyence", "crosses"]

In each of the next three poems a predatory jungle cat is forged into an image of powerful but unspecified meaning.

1. *Without trying to define what the animal implies in each case, can you say what sense you get from it? What do the details of description add to the central subject in each poem?*
2. *How are the three cats similar? How are they different?*
3. *Is there a similarity in tone among these poems?*
4. *Are there similarities in the poets' development of the metaphoric subject (the progress of images, local metaphors, and ideas from the beginning of the poem to the end)? How are the concluding lines similar? How are they different?*

William Blake

THE TIGER

Tiger! Tiger! burning bright
In the forests of the night,
What immortal hand or eye
Could frame thy fearful symmetry?

In what distant deeps or skies
Burnt the fire of thine eyes?
On what wings dare he aspire?
What the hand dare seize the fire?

And what shoulder, and what art,
Could twist the sinews of thy heart?
And when thy heart began to beat,
What dread hand? and what dread feet?

What the hammer? what the chain?
In what furnace was thy brain?
What the anvil? what dread grasp
Dare its deadly terrors clasp?

When the stars threw down their spears,
And water'd heaven with their tears,
Did he smile his work to see?
Did he who made the Lamb make thee?

Tiger! Tiger! burning bright
In the forests of the night,
What immortal hand or eye,
Dare frame thy fearful symmetry?

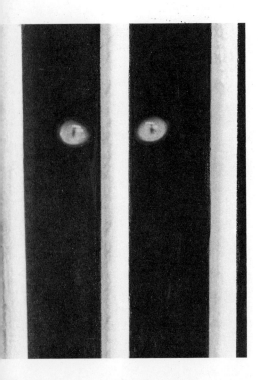

Rainer Maria Rilke

THE PANTHER

Jardin des Plantes, Paris

His sight from always pacing past the bars
has grown so weary it sees only blurs.
For him the only things that are are bars
and behind a thousand bars no universe.

The soft pad of that supple powerful stride,
that turns in a little ring, is like a dance
of strength about some central point inside,
where, stupefied, a massive will stands.

At times the curtains of his eyes part
soundlessly—. Then will an image enter,
pass through the tensed limbs' stillness,
aim for the heart, and die once it has
reached the center.

Translation from German by Christopher Collins

Ted Hughes

THE JAGUAR

The apes yawn and adore their fleas in the sun.
The parrots shriek as if they were on fire, or strut
Like cheap tarts to attract the stroller with the nut.
Fatigued with indolence, tiger and lion

Lie still as the sun. The boa-constrictor's coil
Is a fossil. Cage after cage seems empty, or
Stinks of sleepers from the breathing straw.
It might be painted on a nursery wall.

But who runs like the rest past these arrives
At a cage where the crowd stands, stares, mesmerized,
As a child at a dream, at a jaguar hurrying enraged
Through prison darkness after the drills of his eyes

On a short fierce fuse. Not in boredom—
The eye satisfied to be blind in fire,
By the bang of blood in the brain deaf the ear—
He spins from the bars, but there's no cage to him

More than to the visionary his cell:
His stride is wildernesses of freedom:
The world rolls under the long thrust of his heel
Over the cage floor the horizons come.

LINES OF INQUIRY

Read the following poems, considering in each case:

1. *What is the central metaphoric subject?*
2. *How do the details in the poem suggest the central metaphor's meaning?*
3. *How do the details become meaningful in relation to the central subject?*

John Keats

LA BELLE DAME SANS MERCI

O what can ail thee, knight-at-arms,
 Alone and palely loitering?
The sedge has wither'd from the lake,
 And no birds sing.

O what can ail thee, knight-at-arms,
 So haggard and so woe-begone?
The squirrel's granary is full,
 And the harvest's done.

I see a lilly on thy brow
 With anguish moist and fever dew
And on thy cheeks a fading rose
 Fast withereth too.

I met a lady in the meads,
 Full beautiful—a faery's child,
Her hair was long, her foot was light,
 And her eyes were wild.

I made a garland for her head,
 And bracelets too, and fragrant zone;
She look'd at me as she did love,
 And made sweet moan.

I set her on my pacing steed,
 And nothing else saw all day long,
For sidelong would she bend, and sing
 A faery's song.

She found me roots·of relish sweet,
 And honey wild, and manna dew,
And sure in language strange she said,
 "I love thee true."

She took me to her elfin grot,
 And there she wept, and sigh'd full sore,
And there I shut her wild wild eyes
 With kisses four.

And there she lullèd me asleep
 And there I dream'd—Ah! woe betide!
The latest dream I ever dream'd
 On the cold hill side.

I saw pale kings, and princes too,
 Pale warriors, death-pale were they all;
They cried—"La belle Dame sans Merci
 Hath thee in thrall!"

I saw their starved lips in the gloam
 With horrid warning gapèd wide,
And I awoke and found me here
 On the cold hill's side.

And this is why I sojourn here
 Alone and palely loitering,
Though the sedge is wither'd from the lake,
 And no birds sing.

William Cassegrain

LUCID PRODIGY IN SNOW

For Joe LaRocca

The winter buries things.
The world is shapeless in a generality
of snow.
I hike across
a strangely frozen landscape (to feel
alone) . . .
The icebound lake lies absolute and
still;
air seems airless; far-off trees
look stark . . .

Across the cold and abstract land I tramp
—to find—above a buried stream—
a pool of ice,
where wind has blown
a fragment's clearness . . .
(view another world)

Around me evening settles
dim and cold.
Long winds stir.
Flakes across the silent desolation
swirl

So I retreat.
Across the darkened snowland go—And
know a secret fear that bends me homeward:

know the wind that blows such cosmic snow
has blown through all dark space

William Blake

THE CRYSTAL CABINET

The Maiden caught me in the Wild,
Where I was dancing merrily;
She put me into her Cabinet,
And Lock'd me up with a golden Key.

This Cabinet is form'd of Gold
And Pearl and Crystal shining bright,
And within it opens into a World
And a little lovely Moony Night.

Another England there I saw,
Another London with its Tower,
Another Thames and other Hills,
And another pleasant Surrey Bower,

Another Maiden like herself,
Translucent, lovely, shining clear,
Threefold each in the other clos'd,—
O what a pleasant trembling fear!

O what a smile! a threefold smile
Fill'd me that like a flame I burn'd;
I bent to kiss the lovely Maid,
And found a Threefold Kiss return'd.

I strove to seize the inmost Form
With ardor fierce and hands of flame,
But burst the Crystal Cabinet,
And like a Weeping Babe became—

A weeping Babe upon the wild,
And Weeping Woman pale reclin'd,
And in the outward air again
I fill'd with woes the passing Wind.

William Stanley Braithwaite

THE WAY

He could not tell the way he came,
  Because his chart was lost:
Yet all his way was paved with flame
  From the bourne he crossed.

He did not know the way to go,
  Because he had no map:
He followed where the winds blow—
  And the April sap.

He never knew upon his brow
  The secret that he bore,—
And laughs away the mystery now
  The dark's at his door.

Edgar Allan Poe

ELDORADO°

  Gaily bedight,
  A gallant knight,
In sunshine and in shadow,
  Had journeyed long,
  Singing a song,
In search of Eldorado.

  But he grew old—
  This knight so bold—
And o'er his heart a shadow
  Fell as he found
  No spot of ground
That looked like Eldorado.

  And, as his strength
  Failed him at length,
He met a pilgrim shadow—
  "Shadow," said he,
  "Where can it be—
This land of Eldorado?"

  "Over the Mountains
  Of the Moon,
Down the Valley of the Shadow,
  Ride, boldly ride,"
  The shade replied,—
"If you seek for Eldorado!"

°The legendary eternal city of gold

Herman Melville

THE BERG

A Dream

I saw a ship of martial build
(Her standards set, her brave apparel on)
Directed as by madness mere
Against a stolid iceberg steer,
Nor budge it, though the infatuate ship went down.
The impact made huge ice-cubes fall
Sullen, in tons that crashed the deck;
But that one avalanche was all—
No other movement save the foundering wreck.

Along the spurs of ridges pale,
Not any slenderest shaft and frail,
A prism over glass-green gorges lone,
Toppled; nor lace of traceries fine,
Nor pendant drops in grot or mine
Were jarred, when the stunned ship went down.
Nor sole the gulls in cloud that wheeled
Circling one snow-flanked peak afar,

But nearer fowl the floes that skimmed
And crystal beaches, felt no jar.
No thrill transmitted stirred the lock
Of jack-straw needle-ice at base;
Towers undermined by waves—the block
Atilt impending—kept their place.
Seals, dozing sleek on sliddery ledges
Slipt never, when by loftier edges
Through very inertia overthrown,
The impetuous ship in bafflement went down.

Hard Berg (methought), so cold, so vast,
With mortal damps self-overcast;
Exhaling still thy dankish breath—
Adrift dissolving, bound for death;
Though lumpish thou, a lumbering one—
A lumbering lubbard, loitering slow,
Impingers rue thee and go down,
Sounding thy precipice below,
Nor stir the slimy slug that sprawls
Along thy dead indifference of walls.

Bertold Brecht

THE PLUM-TREE

There in the yard a plum-tree grows.
You won't believe me, I suppose.
  It's ringed by a tiny fence
  For fear of accidents.
The little guy can grow no more.
Of course, he'd like to grow up more.
  Don't worry, anyone—
  There's just too little sun.

Because he never bore a plum
This plum-tree prompts your disbelief.
  But this *is* a plum-tree: anyone
  Can tell it by its leaf.

Translation from German by Christopher Collins

Philip Larkin

AN ARUNDEL TOMB

Side by side, their faces blurred,
The earl and countess lie in stone
Their proper habits vaguely shown
As jointed armour, stiffened pleat,
And that faint hint of the absurd—
The little dogs under their feet.

Such plainness of the pre-baroque
Hardly involves the eye, until
It meets his left-hand gauntlet, still
Clasped empty in the other; and
One sees, with a sharp tender shock,
His hand withdrawn, holding her hand.

They would not think to lie so long.
Such faithfulness in effigy
Was just a detail friends would see:
A sculptor's sweet commissioned grace
Thrown off in helping to prolong
The Latin names around the base.

They would not guess how early in
Their supine stationary voyage
The air would change to soundless damage,
Turn the old tenantry away;
How soon succeeding eyes begin
To look, not read. Rigidly they

Persisted, linked, through lengths and breadths
Of time. Snow fell, undated. Light
Each summer thronged the glass. A bright
Litter of birdcalls strewed the same
Bone-riddled ground. And up the paths
The endless altered people came,

Washing at their identity.
Now, helpless in the hollow of
An unarmorial age, a trough
Of smoke in slow suspended skeins
Above their scrap of history,
Only their attitude remains.

Time has transfigured them into
Untruth. The stone fidelity
They hardly meant has come to be
Their final blazon, and to prove
Our almost-instinct almost true:
What will survive of us is love.

Walt Whitman

TO A LOCOMOTIVE IN WINTER

Thee for my recitative,
Thee in the driving storm even as now, the snow, the
    winter-day declining,
Thee in thy panoply, thy measur'd dual throbbing and
    thy beat convulsive,
Thy black cylindric body, golden brass and silvery steel,
Thy ponderous side-bars, parallel and connecting rods,
    gyrating, shuttling at thy sides,
Thy metrical, now swelling pant and roar, now tapering
    in the distance,
Thy great protruding head-light fix'd in front,
Thy long, pale, floating vapor-pennants, tinged with
    delicate purple,
The dense and murky clouds out-belching from thy
    smoke-stack,
Thy knitted frame, thy springs and valves, the trem-
    ulous twinkle of thy wheels,
Thy train of cars behind, obedient, merrily following,
Through gale or calm, now swift, now slack, yet steadily
    careering;
Type of the modern—emblem of motion and power—
    pulse of the continent,
For once come serve the Muse and merge in verse, even
    as here I see thee,
With storm and buffeting gusts of wind and falling
    snow,
By day thy warning ringing bell to sound its notes,
By night thy silent signal lamps to swing.

Richard Hugo

IN STAFFORD COUNTRY

No hills. Raw wind unchecked, brings word
Of death from Texas. No shade. Sun bruises
The oats gold. With homes exposed
No wonder people love. Farms absorb
The quiet of the snow, and birds
Are black and nameless miles away.

Without a shield of hills, a barricade
Of elms, one resorts to magic, hiding
The joker well behind the gesturing hand.
Childish wars continue in our minds.
Paint is the gray it was in Carthage.

Where land is flat, words are far apart.
Each word is seen, coming from far off,
A calm storm, almost familiar, across
The plain. The word floats by, alive
Homes are empty and the love goes on
As the odor of grain jumps in the wind.

Paul Valéry

LOST WINE

One day I cast into the ocean
(though I no longer know beneath what skies)
a dram of precious wine,
like an offer to Nothing.

Liquor, who willed your loss?
Did I obey some god?
Or was it a fear of the heart,
that spilling the wine, I thought of blood?

A blue transparency resumed
after the smoky touch of rose;
and the sea was once more pure.

Lost was the wine! Drunk were the waves! . . .
Then I saw bounding in the sparkling air
the figures of mysterious forms.

Translation from French by John Briggs

Galway Kinnell

TO CHRIST OUR LORD

The legs of the elk punctured the snow's crust
And wolves floated lightfooted on the land
Hunting Christmas elk living and frozen.
Indoors snow melted in a basin and a woman basted
A bird spread over coals by its wings and head.

Snow had sealed the windows; candles lit
The Christmas meal. The special grace chilled
The cooked bird, being long-winded and the room cold.
During the words a boy thought, is it fitting
To eat this creature killed on the wing?

For he had shot it himself, climbing out
Alone on snowshoes in the Christmas dawn,
The fallen snow swirling and the snowfall gone,
Heard its throat scream as the rifle shouted,
Watched it drop, and fished from the snow the dead.

He had not wanted to shoot. The sound
Of wings beating into the hushed morning
Had stirred his love, and the things
In his gloves froze, and he wondered,
Even famishing, could he fire? Then he fired.

Now the grace praised his wicked act. At its end
The bird on the plate
Stared at his stricken appetite.
There had been nothing to do but surrender,
To kill and to eat; he ate as he had killed, with wonder.

At night on snowshoes on the drifting field
He wondered again, for whom had love stirred?
The stars glittered on the snow and nothing answered.
Then the Swan spread her wings, cross of the cold north,
The pattern and mirror of the acts of earth.

This poem humorously tells the story of a hunt by an expedition of outlandish people for an imaginary animal. Besides entertaining us, the poem suggests that this hunt can be taken in other ways too. Can you sense other levels here?

Charles L. Dodgson
(Lewis Carroll)

THE HUNTING OF THE SNARK

FIT THE FIRST

The Landing

"Just the place for a Snark!" the Bellman cried,
    As he landed his crew with care;
Supporting each man on the top of the tide
    By a finger entwined in his hair.

"Just the place for a Snark! I have said it twice:
    That alone should encourage the crew.
Just the place for a Snark! I have said it thrice:
    What I tell you three times is true."

The crew was complete: it included a Boots—
    A marker of Bonnets and Hoods—
A Barrister, brought to arrange their disputes—
    And a Broker, to value their goods.

A Billiard-marker, whose skill was immense,
    Might perhaps have won more than his share—
But a Banker, engaged at enormous expense,
    Had the whole of their cash in his care.

There was also a Beaver, that placed on the deck,
    Or would sit making lace in the bow:
And had often (the Bellman said) saved them from wreck,
    Though none of the sailors knew how.

There was one who was famed for the number of things
    He forgot when he entered the ship:
His umbrella, his watch, all his jewels and rings,
    And the clothes he had bought for the trip.

He had forty-two boxes, all carefully packed,
    With his name painted clearly on each:
But, since he omitted to mention the fact,
    They were all left behind on the beach.

The loss of his clothes hardly mattered, because
   He had seven coats on when he came,
With three pair of boots—but the worst of it was,
   He had wholly forgotten his name.

He would answer to "Hi!" or to any loud cry,
   Such as "Fry me!" or "Fritter my wig!"
To "What-you-may-call-um!" or "What-was-his-name!"
   But especially "Thing-um-a-jig!"

While, for those who preferred a more forcible word,
   He had different names from these:
His intimate friends called him "Candle-ends,"
   And his enemies "Toasted-cheese."

"His form is ungainly—his intellect small—"
   (So the Bellman would often remark)
"But his courage is perfect! And that, after all,
   Is the thing that one needs with a Snark."

He would joke with hyænas, returning their stare
   With an impudent wag of the head:
And he once went a walk, paw-in-paw, with a bear,
   "Just to keep up its spirits," he said.

He came as a Baker: but owned, when too late—
    And it drove the poor Bellman half-mad—
He could only bake Bride-cake—for which, I may state,
    No materials were to be had.

The last of the crew needs especial remark,
    Though he looked an incredible dunce:
He had just one idea—but, that one being "Snark,"
    The good Bellman engaged him at once.

He came as a Butcher: but gravely declared,
    When the ship had been sailing a week,
He could only kill Beavers. The Bellman looked scared,
    And was almost too frightened to speak:

But at length he explained, in a tremulous tone,
    There was only one Beaver on board;
And that was a tame one he had of his own,
    Whose death would be deeply deplored.

The Beaver, who happened to hear the remark,
    Protested, with tears in its eyes,
That not even the rapture of hunting the Snark
    Could atone for that dismal surprise!

It strongly advised that the Butcher should be
    Conveyed in a separate ship:
But the Bellman declared that would never agree
    With the plans he had made for the trip:

Navigation was always a difficult art,
    Though with only one ship and one bell:
And he feared he must really decline, for his part,
    Undertaking another as well.

The Beaver's best course was, no doubt, to procure
    A second-hand dagger-proof coat—
So the Baker advised it—and next, to insure
    Its life in some Office of note:

This the Banker suggested, and offered for hire
    (On moderate terms), or for sale,
Two excellent Policies, one Against Fire,
    And one Against Damage From Hail.

Yet still, ever after that sorrowful day,
    Whenever the Butcher was by,
The Beaver kept looking the opposite way,
    And appeared unaccountably shy.

FIT THE SECOND

The Bellman's Speech

The Bellman himself they all praised to the skies—
    Such a carriage, such ease and such grace!
Such solemnity, too! One could see he was wise,
    The moment one looked in his face!

He had brought a large map representing the sea,
    Without the least vestige of land:
And the crew were much pleased when they found it to be
    A map they could all understand.

"What's the good of Mercator's North Poles and Equators,
    Tropics, Zones, and Meridian Lines?"
So the Bellman would cry: and the crew would reply
    "They are merely conventional signs!

"Other maps are such shapes, with their islands and capes!
    But we've got our brave Captain to thank"
(So the crew would protest) "that he's bought *us* the best—
    A perfect and absolute blank!"

This was charming, no doubt: but they shortly found out
    That the Captain they trusted so well
Had only one notion for crossing the ocean,
    And that was to tingle his bell.

He was thoughtful and grave—but the orders he gave
    Were enough to bewilder a crew.
When he cried "Steer to starboard, but keep her head larboard!"
    What on earth was the helmsman to do?

Then the bowsprit got mixed with the rudder sometimes:
    A thing, as the Bellman remarked,
That frequently happens in tropical climes,
    When a vessel is, so to speak, "snarked."

But the principal failing occurred in the sailing,
    And the Bellman, perplexed and distressed,
Said he *had* hoped, at least, when the wind blew due East,
    That the ship would *not* travel due West!

But the danger was past—they had landed at last,
    With their boxes, portmanteaus, and bags:
Yet at first sight the crew were not pleased with the view,
    Which consisted of chasms and crags.

The Bellman perceived that their spirits were low,
    And repeated in musical tone

Some jokes he had kept for a season of woe—
  But the crew would do nothing but groan.

He served out some grog with a liberal hand,
  And bade them sit down on the beach:
And they could not but own that their Captain looked grand,
  As he stood and delivered his speech.

"Friends, Romans, and countrymen, lend me your ears!"
  (They were all of them fond of quotations:
So they drank to his health, and they gave him three cheers,
  While he served out additional rations).

"We have sailed many months, we have sailed many weeks,
  (Four weeks to the month you may mark),
But never as yet ('tis your Captain who speaks)
  Have we caught the least glimpse of a Snark!

"We have sailed many weeks, we have sailed many days,
  (Seven days to the week I allow),
But a Snark, on the which we might lovingly gaze,
  We have never beheld till now!

"Come, listen, my men, while I tell you again
  The five unmistakable marks
By which you may know, wheresoever you go,
  The warranted genuine Snarks.

"Let us take them in order. The first is the taste,
  Which is meagre and hollow, but crisp:
Like a coat that is rather too tight in the waist,
  With a flavour of Will-o'-the-Wisp.

"Its habit of getting up late you'll agree
  That it carries too far, when I say
That it frequently breakfasts at five-o'clock tea,
  And dines on the following day.

"The third is its slowness in taking a jest.
  Should you happen to venture on one,
It will sigh like a thing that is deeply distressed:
  And it always looks grave at a pun.

"The fourth is its fondness for bathing-machines,
  Which it constantly carries about,
And believes that they add to the beauty of scenes—
  A sentiment open to doubt.

"The fifth is ambition. It next will be right
  To describe each particular batch:

Distinguishing those that have feathers, and bite,
 From those that have whiskers, and scratch.

"For, although common Snarks do no manner of harm,
 Yet I feel it my duty to say
Some are Boojums—" The Bellman broke off in alarm,
 For the Baker had fainted away.

FIT THE THIRD

The Baker's Tale

They roused him with muffins—they roused him with ice—
 They roused him with mustard and cress—
They roused him with jam and judicious advice—
 They set him conundrums to guess.

When at length he sat up and was able to speak,
 His sad story he offered to tell;
And the Bellman cried "Silence! Not even a shriek!"
 And excitedly tingled his bell.

There was silence supreme! Not a shriek, not a scream,
 Scarcely even a howl or a groan,
As the man they called "Ho!" told his story of woe
 In an antediluvian tone.

"My father and mother were honest, though poor—"
 "Skip all that!" cried the Bellman in haste.
"If it once becomes dark, there's no chance of a Snark—
 We have hardly a minute to waste!"

"I skip forty years," said the Baker, in tears,
 "And proceed without further remark
To the day when you took me aboard of your ship
 To help you in hunting the Snark.

"A dear uncle of mine (after whom I was named)
 Remarked, when I bade him farewell—"
"Oh, skip your dear uncle!" the Bellman exclaimed,
 As he angrily tingled his bell.

"He remarked to me then," said that mildest of men,
 "'If your Snark be a Snark, that is right:
Fetch it home by all means—you may serve it with greens,
 And it's handy for striking a light.

"You may seek it with thimbles—and seek it with care,
 You may hunt it with forks and hope;
You may threaten its life with a railway-share;
 You may charm it with smiles and soap—'"

("That's exactly the method," the Bellman bold
  In a hasty parenthesis cried,
"That's exactly the way I have always been told
  That the capture of Snarks should be tried!")

"'But oh, beamish nephew, beware of the day,
  If your Snark be a Boojum! For then
You will softly and suddenly vanish away,
  And never be met with again!'

"It is this, it is this that oppresses my soul,
  When I think of my uncle's last words:
And my heart is like nothing so much as a bowl
  Brimming over with quivering curds!

"'It is this, it is this—' We have had that before!"
  The Bellman indignantly said.
And the Baker replied "Let me say it once more.
  It is this, it is this that I dread!

"I engage with the Snark—every night after dark—
  In a dreamy delirious fight:
I serve it with greens in those shadowy scenes,
  And I use it for striking a light:

"But if ever I meet with a Boojum, that day,
  In a moment (of this I am sure),
I shall softly and suddenly vanish away—
  And the notion I cannot endure!"

FIT THE FOURTH

The Hunting

The Bellman looked uffish, and wrinkled his brow.
  "If only you'd spoken before!
It's excessively awkward to mention it now,
  With the Snark, so to speak, at the door!

"We should all of us grieve, as you well may believe,
  If you never were met with again—
But surely, my man, when the voyage began,
  You might have suggested it then?

"It's excessively awkward to mention it now—
  As I think I've already remarked."
And the man they called "Hi!" replied, with a sigh,
  "I informed you the day we embarked.

"You may charge me with murder—or want of sense—
  (We are all of us weak at times):
But the slightest approach to a false pretence
  Was never among my crimes!

"I said it in Hebrew—I said it in Dutch—
  I said it in German and Greek:
But I wholly forgot (and it vexes me much)
  That English is what you speak!"

"'Tis a pitiful tale," said the Bellman, whose face
  Had grown longer at every word:
"But, now that you've stated the whole of your case,
  More debate would be simply absurd.

"The rest of my speech" (he exclaimed to his men)
  "You shall hear when I've leisure to speak it.
But the Snark is at hand, let me tell you again!
  'Tis your glorious duty to seek it!

"To seek it with thimbles, to seek it with care;
  To pursue it with forks and hope;
To threaten its life with a railway-share;
  To charm it with smiles and soap!

"For the Snark's a peculiar creature, that won't
  Be caught in a commonplace way.
Do all that you know, and try all that you don't:
  Not a chance must be wasted to-day!

"For England expects—I forbear to proceed:
  'Tis a maxim tremendous, but trite:

And you'd best be unpacking the things that you need
   To rig yourselves out for the fight."

Then the Banker endorsed a blank cheque (which he crossed),
   And changed his loose silver for notes.
The Baker with care combed his whiskers and hair.
   And shook the dust out of his coats.

The Boots and the Broker were sharpening a spade—
   Each working the grindstone in turn:
But the Beaver went on making lace, and displayed
   No interest in the concern:

Though the Barrister tried to appeal to its pride,
   And vainly proceeded to cite
A number of cases, in which making laces
   Had been proved an infringement of right.

The maker of Bonnets ferociously planned
   A novel arrangement of bows:
While the Billiard-marker with quivering hand
   Was chalking the tip of his nose.

But the Butcher turned nervous, and dressed himself fine,
   With yellow kid gloves and a ruff—
Said he felt it exactly like going to dine,
   Which the Bellman declared was all "stuff."

"Introduce me, now there's a good fellow," he said,
   "If we happen to meet it together!"
And the Bellman, sagaciously nodding his head,
   Said, "That must depend on the weather."

The Beaver went simply galumphing about,
   At seeing the Butcher so shy:
And even the Baker, though stupid and stout,
   Made an effort to wink with one eye.

"Be a man!" cried the Bellman in wrath, as he heard
   The Butcher beginning to sob.
"Should we meet with Jubjub, that desperate bird,
   We shall need all our strength for the job!"

FIT THE FIFTH

The Beaver's Lesson

They sought it with thimbles, they sought it with care;
   They pursued it with forks and hope;
They threatened its life with a railway-share;
   They charmed it with smiles and soap.

Then the Butcher contrived an ingenious plan
    For making a separate sally;
And had fixed on a spot unfrequented by man,
    A dismal and desolate valley.

But the very same plan to the Beaver occurred:
    It had chosen the very same place:
Yet neither betrayed, by a sign or a word,
    The disgust that appeared in his face.

Each thought he was thinking of nothing but "Snark"
    And the glorious work of the day;
And each tried to pretend that he did not remark
    That the other was going that way.

But the valley grew narrow and narrower still,
    And the evening got darker and colder,
Till (merely from nervousness, not from good will)
    They marched along shoulder to shoulder.

Then a scream, shrill and high, rent the shuddering sky,
    And they knew that some danger was near:
The Beaver turned pale to the tip of its tail,
    And even the Butcher felt queer.

He thought of his childhood, left far far behind—
    That blissful and innocent state—
The sound so exactly recalled to his mind
    A pencil that squeaks on a slate!

"'Tis the voice of the Jubjub!" he suddenly cried.
    (This man, that they used to call "Dunce.")
"As the Bellman would tell you," he added with pride,
    "I have uttered that sentiment once.

"'Tis the note of the Jubjub! Keep count, I entreat.
    You will find I have told it you twice.
'Tis the song of the Jubjub! The proof is complete.
    If only I've stated it thrice."

The Beaver had counted with scrupulous care,
    Attending to every word:
But it fairly lost heart, and outgrabe in despair,
    When the third repetition occurred.

It felt that, in spite of all possible pains,
    It had somehow contrived to lose count,
And the only thing now was to rack its poor brains
    By reckoning up the amount.

"Two added to one—if that could but be done,"
  It said, "with one's fingers and thumbs!"
Recollecting with tears how, in earlier years,
  It had taken no pains with its sums.

"The thing can be done," said the Butcher, "I think
  The things must be done, I am sure.
The thing shall be done! Bring me paper and ink,
  The best there is time to procure."

The Beaver brought paper, portfolio, pens,
  And ink in unfailing supplies:
While strange creepy creatures came out of their dens,
  And watched them with wondering eyes.

So engrossed was the Butcher, he heeded them not
  As he wrote with a pen in each hand,
And explained all the while in a popular style
  Which the Beaver could well understand.

"Taking Three as the subject to reason about—
  A convenient number to state—
We add Seven, and Ten, and then multiply out
  By One Thousand diminished by Eight.

"The result we proceed to divide, as you see,
  By Nine Hundred and Ninety and Two:
Then subtract Seventeen, and the answer must be
  Exactly and perfectly true.

"The method employed I would gladly explain,
  While I have it so clear in my head,
If I had but the time and you had but the brain—
  But much yet remains to be said.

"In one moment I've seen what has hitherto been
  Enveloped in absolute mystery,
And without extra charge I will give you at large
  A Lesson in Natural History."

In his genial way he proceeded to say
  (Forgetting all laws of propriety,
And that giving instruction, without introduction,
  Would have caused quite a thrill in Society),

"As to temper the Jubjub's a desperate bird,
  Since it lives in perpetual passion:
Its taste in costume is entirely absurd—
  It is ages ahead of the fashion:

"But it knows any friend it has met once before:
  It never will look at a bribe:
And in charity-meetings it stands at the door,
  And collects—though it does not subscribe.

"Its flavour when cooked is more exquisite far
  Than mutton, or oysters, or eggs:
(Some think it keeps best in an ivory jar,
  And some, in mahogany kegs:)

"You boil it in sawdust: you salt it in glue:
  You condense it with locusts and tape:
Still keeping one principal object in view—
  To preserve its symmetrical shape."

The Butcher would gladly have talked till next day,
  But he felt that the Lesson must end,
And he wept with delight in attempting to say
  He considered the Beaver his friend.

While the Beaver confessed, with affectionate looks
  More eloquent even than tears,
It had learned in ten minutes far more than all books
  Would have taught it in seventy years.

They returned hand-in-hand, and the Bellman, unmanned
  (For a moment) with noble emotion,
Said "This amply repays all the wearisome days
  We have spent on the billowy ocean!"

Such friends, as the Beaver and Butcher became,
  Have seldom if ever been known;
In winter or summer, 'twas always the same—
  You could never meet either alone.

And when quarrels arose—as one frequently finds
  Quarrels will, spite of every endeavour—
The song of the Jubjub recurred to their minds,
  And cemented their friendship for ever!

FIT THE SIXTH

The Barrister's Dream

They sought it with thimbles, they sought it with care;
  They pursued it with forks and hope;
They threatened its life with a railway-share;
  They charmed it with smiles and soap.

But the Barrister, weary of proving in vain
  That the Beaver's lace-making was wrong,
Fell asleep, and in dreams saw the creature quite plain
  That his fancy had dwelt on so long.

He dreamed that he stood in a shadowy Court,
  Where the Snark, with a glass in its eye,
Dressed in gown, bands, and wig, was defending a pig
  On the charge of deserting its sty.

The Witnesses proved, without error or flaw,
  That the sty was deserted when found:
And the Judge kept explaining the state of the law
  In a soft under-current of sound.

The indictment had never been clearly expressed,
  And it seemed that the Snark had begun,
And had spoken three hours, before any one guessed
  What the pig was supposed to have done.

The Jury had each formed a different view
  (Long before the indictment was read),
And they all spoke at once, so that none of them knew
  One word that the others had said.

"You must know—" said the Judge: but the Snark explained "Fudge!
  That statute is obsolete quite!

Let me tell you, my friends, the whole question depends
    On an ancient manorial right.

"In the matter of Treason the pig would appear
    To have aided, but scarcely abetted:
While the charge of Insolvency fails, it is clear,
    If you grant the plea 'never indebted.'

"The fact of Desertion I will not dispute:
    But its guilt, as I trust, is removed
(So far as relates to the costs of this suit)
    By the Alibi which has been proved.

"My poor client's fate now depends on your votes."
    Here the speaker sat down in his place,
And directed the Judge to refer to his notes
    And briefly to sum up the case.

But the Judge said he never had summed up before;
    So the Snark undertook it instead,
And summed it so well that it came to far more
    Than the Witnesses ever had said!

When the verdict was called for, the Jury declined,
    As the word was so puzzling to spell;
But they ventured to hope that the Snark wouldn't mind
    Undertaking that duty as well.

So the Snark found the verdict, although, as it owned,
    It was spent with the toils of the day:
When it said the word "GUILTY!" the Jury all groaned,
    And some of them fainted away.

Then the Snark pronounced sentence, the Judge being quite
    Too nervous to utter a word:
When it rose to its feet, there was silence like night,
    And the fall of a pin might be heard.

"Transportation for life" was the sentence it gave,
    "And *then* to be fined forty pound."
The Jury all cheered, though the Judge said he feared
    That the phrase was not legally sound.

But their wild exultation was suddenly checked
    When the jailer informed them, with tears,
Such a sentence would have not the slightest effect,
    As the pig had been dead for some years.

The Judge left the Court, looking deeply disgusted:
    But the Snark, though a little aghast,
As the lawyer to whom the defence was intrusted,
    Went bellowing on to the last.

Thus the Barrister dreamed, while the bellowing seemed
   To grow every moment more clear:
Till he woke to the knell of a furious bell,
   Which the Bellman rang close at his ear.

FIT THE SEVENTH

The Banker's Fate

They sought it with thimbles, they sought it with care;
   They pursued it with forks and hope;
They threatened its life with a railway-share;
   They charmed it with smiles and soap.

And the Banker, inspired with a courage so new
   It was matter for general remark,
Rushed madly ahead and was lost to their view
   In his zeal to discover the Snark.

But while he was seeking with thimbles and care,
   A Bandersnatch swiftly drew nigh
And grabbed at the Banker, who shrieked in despair,
   For he knew it was useless to fly.

He offered large discount—he offered a cheque
   (Drawn "to bearer") for seven-pounds-ten:
But the Bandersnatch merely extended its neck
   And grabbed at the Banker again.

Without rest or pause—while those frumious jaws
    Went savagely snapping around—
He skipped and he hopped, and he floundered and flopped,
    Till fainting he fell to the ground.

The Bandersnatch fled as the others appeared
    Led on by that fear-stricken yell:
And the Bellman remarked "It is just as I feared!"
    And solemnly tolled on his bell.

He was black in the face, and they scarcely could trace
    The least likeness to what he had been:
While so great was his fright that his waistcoat turned white—
    A wonderful thing to be seen!

To the horror of all who were present that day,
    He uprose in full evening dress,
And with senseless grimaces endeavoured to say
    What his tongue could no longer express.

Down he sank in a chair—ran his hands through his hair—
  And chanted in mimsiest tones
Words whose utter inanity proved his insanity,
  While he rattled a couple of bones.

"Leave him here to his fate—it is getting so late!"
  The Bellman exclaimed in a fright.
"We have lost half the day. Any further delay,
  And we sha'n't catch a Snark before night!"

FIT THE EIGHTH

The Vanishing

They sought it with thimbles, they sought it with care;
  They pursued it with forks and hope;
They threatened its life with a railway-share;
  They charmed it with smiles and soap.

They shuddered to think that the chase might fail,
  And the Beaver, excited at last,
Went bounding along on the tip of its tail,
  For the daylight was nearly past.

"There is Thingumbob shouting!" the Bellman said.
  "He is shouting like mad, only hark!
He is waving his hands, he is wagging his head,
  He has certainly found a Snark!"

They gazed in delight, while the Butcher exclaimed
  "He was always a desperate wag!"
They beheld him—their Baker—their hero unnamed—
  On the top of a neighbouring crag,

Erect and sublime, for one moment of time,
  In the next, that wild figure they saw
(As if stung by a spasm) plunge into a chasm,
  While they waited and listened in awe.

"It's a Snark!" was the sound that first came to their ears,
  And seemed almost too good to be true.
Then followed a torrent of laughter and cheers:
  Then the ominous words "It's a Boo—"

Then, silence. Some fancied they heard in the air
  A weary and wandering sigh
That sounded like "—jum!" but the others declare
  It was only a breeze that went by.

They hunted till darkness came on, but they found
    Not a button, or feather, or mark,
By which they could tell that they stood on the ground
    Where the Baker had met with the Snark.

In the midst of the word he was trying to say,
    In the midst of his laughter and glee,
He had softly and suddenly vanished away—
    For the Snark *was* a Boojum, you see.

EXPERIENCING THE POEM

Reread Wallace Stevens' "Thirteen Ways of Looking at a Blackbird" (page 23). Do you have any
different insights about this poem now?

CHAPTER 6
PROPAGANDA, ARGUMENT, & DESCRIPTION IN POETRY

In this chapter we'll concentrate on two interesting aspects of poetry: (1) poets promoting points of view or causes, making arguments (subtle or obvious), then using logic or rhetoric; and (2) poets (often the same ones) describing objects and events without appearing to present more than an image. In both cases the metaphoric activity may seem to be suppressed or only to serve the poet's point of view. But can poetry really be limited in this way? We have seen that without metaphoric action, a poem is a dead thing, and most of the pieces in this chapter will strike you as very much alive. Actually, as we'll discover, there is no contradiction, but finding out why there isn't one takes alertness and extreme sensitivity to tone.

We've seen that poems cannot be reduced to simple, "logical" statements, but what do we do when the poet seems to want only (or mainly) to convince us of something? For example:

John Donne

CONFINED LOVE

Some man unworthy to be possessor
Of old or new love, himself being false or weak,
Thought his pain and shame would be less,
If on womankind he might his anger wreak,
And thence a law did grow,
One might but one man know;
But are other creatures so?

Are sun, moon, or stars by law forbidden,
To smile where they list, or lend away their light?
Are birds divorced, or are they chidden
If they leave their mate and lie abroad a-night?
Beasts do no jointures lose
Though they new lovers choose,
But we are made worse than those.

Who e'r rigg'd fair ships to lie in harbors,
And not to seek new lands, or not to deal with all?
Or built fair houses, set trees and arbors,
Only to lock up, or else to let them fall?
Good is not good unless
A thousand it possess,
But doth waste with greediness.

Since logic serves its premise (usually a theory or opinion), opinion is really the issue here, not the logical presentation. Opinion is a matter of conditioning: If we are taught (from our early years) certain principles, ethics, moral codes, and ways of looking at the world, then most of us take these things we have heard over and over for granted; they become part of our environment, and we forget that they may not be truths but habits. Even many so-called facts turn out to be opinion—scientific facts which have to be revised as new information becomes available, political facts that shift continually, and so on. In other words, we structure our lives, we define our very selves, on sets of *opinions* (our own and other people's) about what we like and dislike, what's good and bad, what's real and unreal, what's logical and illogical. We have observed that effective poems go deeper than these essentially mechanical reactions to life, that metaphor can free the mind (even if only for a moment) from the closed circle of opinion.

Donne, in the poem above, has done something we all do in conversations, speeches, essays, and textbook writing: He has taken one point of view and set it against another in order to demonstrate that what *he* thinks is "logical." In the poem, at least, it's amusing.

The first lines amount to an idle thought in the vein of: "I'd like to find the one who started all this!" Donne then presents this as a premise: If you believe it, then the rest will follow. Notice that there is no metaphoric activity at all in stanza one—just the open presentation of a point of view.

In stanzas two and three we have metaphors and personifications. Look closely at them. To undercut traditional Western moral attitudes toward marriage and monogamy, the poet sets a contrary opinion and illustrates it with local images and metaphors. Considered as an *idea*, his is clearly no better than the one he opposes. If you agree with him, you like it; if you don't, you don't. You may think your reasons for agreeing or disagreeing are profound, but that's *your* opinion. So the "argument" in a poem is of little consequence. The poet may be serious or not (which you might get from the tone), but what of it? Nevertheless, are there deeper, "opinionless" insights here, despite the propaganda? Surely something happens to the way we see ourselves and our mating habits as a result of human love and rituals (X) being contrasted with the ways of animals (Y). Obviously, this comparison is *not* an opinion, despite the fact that Donne arranges it to serve (or seem to serve) his purposes. Try going into the poem from this angle. Look at the last three lines. What is being said about love apart from (even if including) sexuality? Are the metaphors really limited by the "logic" of the argument?

A number of poems in this chapter involve propaganda in poetry. They seem to promote a slant on life by means of rhetoric (strong, expressive, or hypnotic phrases and literary devices), a form of logic, emotional appeals, or, more frequently, rhetorical description. We'll try to see whether the experience of poetry spills over the boundaries of a poet's intellectual intentions. Other poems here might seem to be just descriptions of moments of intense emotion or beauty, descriptions of the narrator's *feelings* (point of view) about something, or stories with vivid scenes.

Naturally, there is no hard-and-fast division between poems in this chapter and those in previous ones. If you look back at "Ode on a Grecian Urn," you will discover that Keats used arguments; Frost's "The Road Not Taken" is mainly descriptive. But here we'll examine poems where the metaphoric relationships are more fragmented or are harder to see, either because they are obscured by the argument or because they are worked into a picture or story.

Bear in mind that if a statement works poetically, it will reach beyond mere description and transcend opinion. Metaphoric action is action in living, new relationship and cannot be achieved by simply stringing out dead images and putting "like" between them. The action of poetry cannot be expressed mechanically or through some system or other, and no system "proves" a poem poetic; we have to be able to experience it ourselves to find this out.

As you read this piece, you will observe that the poet is insisting on a certain point of view and is slanting his rhetorical description of life to that end. Unlike the Donne poem given at the beginning of the chapter, Ginsberg's does not openly present an argument.

Allen Ginsberg

DEATH ON ALL FRONTS

"The Planet Is Finished"

A new moon looks down on our sick sweet planet
Orion's chased the Immovable Bear halfway across the sky
from winter to winter. I wake, earlier in bed, fly corpses
cover gas lit sheets, my head aches, left temple
brain fibre throbbing for Death I Created on all Fronts.
Poisoned rats in the Chickenhouse and myriad lice
Sprayed with white arsenics filtering to the brook, City
      Cockroaches
stomped on Country kitchen floors. No babies for me.
Cut earth boys & girl hordes by half & breathe free
say Revolutionary expert Computers:
Half the blue globe's germ population's more than enough,
keep the cloudy lung from stinking pneumonia.
I called in Exterminator Who soaked the Wall floor
with bed-bug death-oil. Who'll soak my brain with death-oil
I wake before dawn, dreading my wooden possessions,
my gnostic books, my loud mouth, old loves silent, charms
turned to image money, my body sexless fat, Father dying,
Earth Cities poisoned at war, my art hopeless—
Mind fragmented—and still abstract—Pain in
left temple living death—

Sept. 26, 1969

Considerations

The force of this piece is rhetorical: it is emotionally intense, in places almost an outcry, hammering its points over and over without pretending to be logical. The speaker says, in effect: "This is me, I'm important, I feel this, I'm suffering, look at this!" There is a tone of violent sincerity. In fact, doesn't the very intensity of the piece tend to obscure the opinions underlying it? Donne pretends to argue us into taking his viewpoint, but here we are being pulled toward *identifying* ourselves with the author's voice. Let's write a counter poem:

LIFE EVERYWHERE!
The earth is reborn!

The full moon smiles on our vital world;
Aries has swayed across the sky,
Spring after spring. I get up early
Body light, head clear, my forehead
Tingling for life around me, everywhere.
The chickens gurgle and flap, the morning
Insects buzz, the country stirs.
My children wake, I feel the love in things
Today, lover and children waking
  like the sun
All around the world.

I'm up before dawn anticipating
The rich air, my seeing, touching again,
My body part of the hush of life
And holiness of taking breath again,
Mind feeling the wholeness alive,
About to live.

One man says he is depressed; the other says he's happy. One says the world is dreadful—too many people in it, bad air, ecology gone to hell—and the other feels things couldn't be nicer. Now, opinions about experience, which we can hear on television, read in the papers, and so on, obviously don't trigger the shock of poetry in us. Never mind which piece we happen to prefer reading (*our* opinion); rather, consider whether insisting on suffering or claiming to be in ecstasy makes something true. Poems are not important or unimportant because of their points of view or subject matter. To like or dislike a poem for its ideas is no indication of the quality of its poetry. For example, noticing that we are poisoning our air isn't an *insight*. So where does the poet take us? Is there a deeper level?

The piece is essentially built on metaphoric associations: rats and cockroaches (*X*) with babies and "boys & girl hordes" (*Y*); bedbugs (*X*) with the mind (*Y*); and then insects (implicitly) with all mankind. As a result of these interrelations, is there a surprise, a discovery about the self or the world?

1. How does the use of technological and nonliterary images affect the tone (for example, "death-oil")?
2. In the last lines the poet lists reasons why he is so unhappy. Could you paraphrase this without losing the impact?

Yamanoue Okura

ON THE INSECURITY
OF HUMAN LIFE

We are adrift in this world.
The days, months, years slip past
Like a rapid stream that draws us to oblivion,
Swirled in our private eddies and pain.
Girls, wrists braceleted in exotic stones,
Join hands and dance away their youth.
Time is their dance.
And soon their smooth black hair
Is white as the breaking waves,
And on their tender faces
Cruel age has appeared.

Boys play and take up swords
And hunting bows,
And ride fast horses in pride.
But can their world for a moment remain? . . .
He opens the door,
Where a girl sleeps,
Makes his way in the darkness to her side.
Her arm on the pillow.
Touches the cold stones of her bracelet.
How soon he will be old
and neglected . . .
All this change we resent—
But it is useless.
Bitterly, we long to be the rock,
Enduring and secure
against the tides.
But a man in the river of time
Is in the current and must flow with it, inevitably,
Toward the sea . . .

Rendition from Japanese

Considerations

In common with the Ginsberg piece, this poem is telling us that things are dark. The tone is not cheerful. Like Ginsberg, Okura selects his images and shapes his material to support his views. He does not try to "prove" that man's lot is hopeless; he simply describes and focuses on the process of decay and death. The essential difference (other than the obvious ones of style and period) seems to be that the contemporary piece is an openly subjective interior monologue, whereas this poem strikes us as somehow *objective* in treatment. If we tried to write a counterpoem here, how would it be done? Ginsberg presented "ugly" images so we could respond with "pretty" images. Here, since the facts of human mutability (whether pretty or ugly) are beyond dispute, the only change we could make would be in mood: "I love the awareness that I'm dying moment to moment; I'm delighted to be passing away from this world," or some such.

The poem culminates in a pair of metaphors that go beyond the attitude of despair or depression into a final mood of *reflection*. And there is something hinted at here which goes deeper than our egocentric fears and doubts. There is a sense of the cosmic. In a way, the poet puts an end to his own despairing tone; not that he becomes joyful, of course, but there is a mood of reflection which is insight, which is simply "seeing," which is metaphoric, which is poetic action. This cannot be countered because the opposite of it is dullness, *un*reflection. So the poem has obviously extended past any limited personal viewpoint toward what we call "truth": not what we think or believe, but what we seem to *know*.

1. This poem contains many descriptive passages. What is their prime function?
2. The three lines that open the second section are a description. Do you think the poet really means just to talk about boys playing? Do they constitute an *X* as well? If so, what are the *Y* levels? What other descriptive passages in the poem operate in this way?
3. How do the last lines relate to the rest of the poem?

Like the Okura piece, this one begins in description and moves toward the insights of a reflective mood. Can you spot the underlying point of view (opinion) here? Does this opinion transcend itself in the poem? If so, how?

Matthew Arnold

DOVER BEACH

The sea is calm to-night.
The tide is full, the moon lies fair
Upon the straits;—on the French coast, the light
Gleams, and is gone; the cliffs of England stand,
Glimmering and vast, out in the tranquil bay.
Come to the window, sweet is the night-air!
Only, from the lone line of spray
Where the sea meets the moon-blanch'd sand,
Listen! you hear the grating roar
Of pebbles which the waves draw back, and fling,
At their return, up the high strand,°
Begin, and cease, and then again begin,
With tremulous cadence slow, and bring
The eternal note of sadness in.
Sophocles long ago
Heard it on the Ægæan, and it brought
Into his mind the turbid ebb and flow
Of human misery; we
Find also in the sound a thought,
Hearing it by this distant northern sea.

The Sea of Faith
Was once, too, at the full, and round earth's shore
Lay like the folds of a bright girdle furl'd.
But now I only hear
Its melancholy, long, withdrawing roar,
Retreating to the breath
Of the night-wind down the vast edges drear
And naked shingles of the world.

Ah, love, let us be true
To one another! for the world, which seems
To lie before us like a land of dreams,
So various, so beautiful, so new,
Hath really neither joy, nor love, nor light,
Nor certitude, nor peace, nor help for pain;
And we are here as on a darkling plain
Swept with confused alarms of struggle and flight,
Where ignorant armies clash by night.

°Shore

Considerations

1. The sea (X) the poet describes in stanza one is compared to the "Sea of Faith" (Y). Are the other things in the poem described and *then* compared in open metaphor this way?
2. Do metaphors develop by *context* in the first section of the poem? That is, do individual images like "pebbles" in the first stanza take on metaphoric significance? How? If pebble is X, what is the Y or Y's it is being associated with?
3. Are those images (in the first section) metaphoric for you until you have read "eternal note of sadness" or "Sea of Faith," for example?

Reading this poem twice might be a good idea. It seems to be one sustained image, doesn't it?

Arthur Rimbaud

LE DORMEUR DU VAL

(The Sleeper in the Valley)

The lush, green landscape is breached by a silver river,
Which glides through a tangled meadow,
Glinting in the sunlight beneath lordly crags,
Filling the little valley with the scintillance of afternoon.

A young soldier, open-mouthed, without his hat,
Rests his head in the cool blue grass,
Sleeps, sprawled palely in this herbal bed,
Where sunlight spills through shifting clouds.

His feet stretched out in flowers, he sleeps,
Uncertainty in his smile, like a child who is ill.
Nature cradles him warmly; he is cold.

The fragrances of afternoon do not awaken him.
Hand on his chest, in sunlight, he sleeps tranquilly.
His right side is breached by two red holes.

Translation from French by John Briggs

Considerations

1. Is this poem metaphoric? If so, how?
2. Do you think the poem is actually making a very subtle argument against war?

The metaphors in the third stanza intensify the description, but there is really no *overt* metaphoric action and no apparent central metaphoric relation or unstated metaphor (as in "The Road Not Taken"). Can you see what this piece has in common with Whitman's "When I Heard the Learn'd Astronomer"? A scene is painted with smells and sights; the landscape is almost tangible. Then, like the astronomer piece, the poem becomes violently poetic at the end. The contrast, the raw irony, ignites the metaphor. Remove the last line, and you have the image of a pleasant afternoon and a sketch of a sleeping, if somewhat ambiguous, man. Add the line, and you may be surprised into insight.

Technical Notes

The poem in the original French is a sonnet.

This poem also seems to be pure description, but the tone of the description makes the piece more than just a portrait of the narrator's "last duchess."

Robert Browning

MY LAST DUCHESS

Ferrara

That's my last Duchess painted on the wall,
Looking as if she were alive. I call
That piece a wonder, now: Frà Pandolf's hands
Worked busily a day, and there she stands.
Will't please you sit and look at her? I said
"Frà Pandolf" by design, for never read
Strangers like you that pictured countenance,
The depth and passion of its earnest glance,
But to myself they turned (since none puts by
The curtain I have drawn for you, but I)
And seemed as they would ask me, if they durst,
How such a glance came there; so, not the first
Are you to turn and ask thus. Sir, 'twas not
Her husband's presence only, called that spot
Of joy into the Duchess' cheek: perhaps
Frà Pandolf chanced to say "Her mantle laps
Over my Lady's wrist too much," or "Paint
Must never hope to reproduce the faint
Half-flush that dies along her throat": such stuff
Was courtesy, she thought, and cause enough
For calling up that spot of joy. She had
A heart—how shall I say?—too soon made glad,
Too easily impressed; she liked whate'er
She looked on, and her looks went everywhere.

Sir, 'twas all one! My favour at her breast,
The dropping of the daylight in the West,
The bough of cherries some officious fool
Broke in the orchard for her, the white mule
She rode with round the terrace—all and each
Would draw from her alike the approving speech,
Or blush, at least. She thanked men,—good! but thanked
Somehow—I know not how—as if she ranked
My gift of a nine-hundred-years-old name
With anybody's gift. Who'd stoop to blame
This sort of trifling? Even had you skill
In speech—(which I have not)—to make your will
Quite clear to such an one, and say "Just this
Or that in you disgusts me; here you miss,
Or there exceed the mark"—and if she let
Herself be lessoned so, nor plainly set
Her wits to yours, forsooth, and made excuse,
—E'en then would be some stooping, and I choose
Never to stoop. Oh, Sir, she smiled, no doubt
Whene'er I passed her; but who passed without
Much the same smile? This grew; I gave commands;
Then all smiles stopped together. There she stands
As if alive. Will't please you rise? We'll meet
The company below, then. I repeat,
The Count your master's known munificence
Is ample warrant that no just pretence
Of mine for dowry will be disallowed;
Though his fair daughter's self, as I avowed
At starting, is my object. Nay, we'll go
Together down, Sir! Notice Neptune, tho',
Taming a sea-horse, thought a rarity,
Which Claus of Innsbruck cast in bronze for me!

Considerations

Critics call this type of poem a DRAMATIC MONO-LOGUE; i.e., the narrator is talking to someone we don't hear from but who is obviously there. The poem seems to be all description. Is it metaphoric? Consider:

A. What sort of woman is revealed by the narrator's description?
B. What is revealed about the narrator's relationship to his late wife?

The satiric tone is crucial to perceiving the overall point of view, the poet's opinion, here: The duke is talking about his last wife to an agent of the count (father of his future wife), and through his description he reveals himself as self-important, haughty, unfeeling. It is implied that his former duchess was quite the reverse: modest, democratic, sensitive, full of spirit and freedom. There is a feeling that what the duke could not do to her in life (restrain her) he did after death by framing her portrait, finally stilling, fixing her, possessing her as an object of art. This obviously touches on the profound question of controlling another person and its effects.

Consider the rich levels of metaphoric irony here: The duke (often himself ironic) talks about the duchess, and yet the tone of the poem subtly (and ironically) shows him up without a single external comment (it is all his voice), so that his criticisms of his wife actually work as praise.

1. Do you see a subtle hint that the duke thought his wife unfaithful in the lines "not/Her husband's presence only, called that spot/Of joy" and "Frà Pandolf's hands/Worked busily a day, and there she stands." "Frà" means "brother." Is this perhaps an ironic word choice?
2. Some readers have felt that the duke actually killed his wife. Can you find any evidence to support that view? Could he have killed her, but not literally?
3. Why do you think "as if . . . alive" is said twice?
4. The duke tells the silent listener, *first,* that he is certain he will get a dowry because the count is known to be generous; *then* he adds that of course the daughter herself is his real object. What does this suggest about the duke?
5. Why does the duke keep the painting covered so that no one but himself can look at it? What does this tell us about his relationship to the last duchess?
6. Everything is set up here so that we hear nothing but the duke's point of view. How does the poem transcend his opinions? Most important, how does it transcend even the poet's obvious satiric attitude? Look at the last two lines in particular. On one level the duke is referring to another of his possessions. But how does this relate to the duchess on other levels? What is the significance of the fact that it is a sea horse?
7. Compare the last lines here with the "twist" ending of the Rimbaud poem. Have they some effects in common?

Technical Notes

The poem is in heroic couplets without regular adherence to END-STOPPED lines.

Compare this poem with the last. Again, as in the two previous ones, both a point of view and description are being put forward, but underneath is a complex metaphor. Can you see it?

W. H. Auden

MUSÉE DES BEAUX ARTS

About suffering they were never wrong,
The Old Masters: how well they understood
Its human position; how it takes place
While someone else is eating or opening a window or just walking dully along;
How, when the aged are reverently, passionately waiting
For the miraculous birth, there always must be
Children who did not specially want it to happen, skating
On a pond at the edge of the wood:
They never forgot
That even the dreadful martyrdom must run its course
Anyhow in a corner, some untidy spot
Where the dogs go on with their doggy life and the torturer's horse
Scratches its innocent behind on a tree.

In Brueghel's *Icarus*, for instance: how everything turns away
Quite leisurely from the disaster; the ploughman may
Have heard the splash, the forsaken cry,
But for him it was not an important failure; the sun shone
As it had to on the white legs disappearing into the green
Water; and the expensive delicate ship that must have seen
Something amazing, a boy falling out of the sky,
Had somewhere to get to and sailed calmly on.

Considerations

1. What is the opinion, the point of view being expressed?
2. How do the descriptions of the paintings and the statements about suffering associate with one another and work as metaphor?
3. The second stanza describes the accompanying painting. How does the description of *Icarus* unite the poem and produce powerful metaphoric insight? You might want to consider the story of Icarus to answer this question, as well as the local images "forsaken cry," "expensive delicate ship," etc. What dimensions do all these add to the idea of suffering?

If you didn't know that the poet is referring to famous battles, would this poem make much sense? The particularization here is quite different from that in most of the pieces we have been examining.

Carl Sandburg

GRASS

Pile the bodies high at Austerlitz and Waterloo.
Shovel them under and let me work—
          I am the grass; I cover all.

And pile them high at Gettysburg
And pile them high at Ypres and Verdun.
Shovel them under and let me work.
Two years, ten years, and passengers ask the conductor:
          What place is this?
          Where are we now?

          I am the grass.
          Let me work.

Considerations

Note that the juxtaposition of grass (X) with various bloody battlefields (Y) is really what keeps this from becoming a simple prose statement.

1. Can you see the structure of the implied arguments here? What is the poet for and against, etc.?

2. What are the levels of meaning in the line "Let me work"?

Technical Notes

The poem is in free verse.

Does this poem involve (like the Okura and Arnold poems) a reflective mood? Or is it (like the Browning poem) ironic description? Is this piece metaphoric at all?

Alexander Blok

THE NIGHT, A STREET

The night, a street, a pharmacy, a lamp,
a light cast, dead and meaningless.
Even if you live for another quarter century,
it will be like this.
There is no way out.
You will die. And it will begin again.
Everything will be repeated, as before:
The night, cold ripples on the dark canal,
the pharmacy, the street,
the lamp.

Translation from Russian

Considerations

You might say that on the surface, this piece is *all* statement (opinion) and description. There is no argument or intense rhetoric. The speaker says, "This is how life is. Period."

But can you see an implicit metaphor where the street, pharmacy, lamp—the whole landscape—are (like) a prison of some kind, a sort of cosmic treadmill where you go round and round without getting anywhere?

As before, it makes no difference whether we agree or disagree with the statements: maybe things *will* change; maybe we could see meaning in the light; maybe "it" will be nothing at all like this again. The point is that the speaker's whole "dead" vision acts as an X to contrast Y, the living world which we conceive of as changing and meaningful. Through this contrast we may grasp something of deadness, narrowness, repeating patterns imposed on our life or underlying it. Thus we may suddenly confront our familiar world with new (perhaps frightened) awareness.

1. How is the statement "Everything will be repeated" reinforced by the very structure of the poem?
2. What is the effect of the added image at the end of the poem, "cold ripples on the dark canal"?
3. "Night" is a loaded word. Is it being used as an X here? What are the possible Y's?
4. What do you think this poem means? Can we ever say for sure?

Basically, the following two poems are not making arguments or promoting points of view with their descriptions. About all they are "selling" is mood. We will be looking to see how they extend past their moods into metaphoric discovery.

John Keats

TO AUTUMN

Season of mists and mellow fruitfulness,
  Close bosom-friend of the maturing sun;
Conspiring with him how to load and bless
  With fruit the vines that round the thatch-eaves run;
To bend with apples the moss'd cottage trees,
  And fill all fruit with ripeness to the core;
    To swell the gourd, and plump the hazel shells
  With a sweet kernel; to set budding more,
And still more, later flowers for the bees,
Until they think warm days will never cease,
    For Summer has o'er-brimmed their clammy cells.

Who hath not seen thee oft amid thy store?
  Sometimes whoever seeks abroad may find
Thee sitting careless on a granary floor,
  Thy hair soft-lifted by the winnowing wind;
Or on a half-reap'd furrow sound asleep,
  Drows'd with the fume of poppies, while thy hook
    Spares the next swath and all its twinèd flowers:
And sometimes like a gleaner thou dost keep
  Steady thy laden head across a brook;
  Or by a cider-press, with patient look,
    Thou watchest the last oozings hours by hours.

Where are the songs of Spring? Aye, where are they?
  Think not of them, thou hast thy music too,—
While barrèd clouds bloom the soft-dying day,
  And touch the stubble-plains with rosy hue;
Then in a wailful choir the small gnats mourn
  Among the river sallows, borne aloft
    Or sinking as the light wind lives or dies;
And full-grown lambs loud bleat from hilly bourn;
  Hedge-crickets sing; and now with treble soft
The red-breast whistles from a garden-croft;
  And gathering swallows twitter in the skies.

Dwight Robhs

TO AUTUMN

Countless sparrows riot in the trees,
The air stirs dryly and the landscape stiffens,
Thinned woods fill with shadow and I feel
The tears of another century rise
And stop—And I know why they wept
Or said they wept: it takes you as the wind
Unwinds a shape in the dark leaves, sparrows
Stutter in the sky . . .

You want to cry:
"These sensations dim and drum in me,
The bones of life now show beneath the skin
And shadows like the footfalls of centuries
Stalk through the woods and stalk across my lawn . . ."

You know it was all real: priapic
Shelley wasted with abstract love, and Keats
Ached his gleaming, shadowed head and saw
The mournful body of the season move
Like mist across the fields of all his days . . .

The sparrows wheel and gust through crinkly air
And scatter; darkness fills the woods in
As gleaming silence fills me—The fluent
Raptures of old grief are stuttered now . . .
You see the form of Autumn stir and stride
And tangle through the shadows with her scythe
And hear it sweep and whisper like the wind
That starts and gusts through the stunned leaves.

Considerations

Keats's poem (which obviously came first) lushly describes autumn scenes and heaps natural image upon natural image until we think he'll "never cease." There are several metaphoric levels here: *First,* the opening stanza, with many images of ripeness and fullness, sets up a *contrast* with the last half of the second stanza, where *over*ripeness is about to be cut into by the winter edge of autumn. So possibly autumn is an *X* for a very traditional *Y*: human life, labor, approaching death. Expressions like "maturing sun" reinforce this idea. *Second,* the *personification* of autumn certainly (as in Keats's "Ode on Melancholy") sets up a basic comparison between human characteristics and the ways of nature. Where autumn is "conspiring" with the sun or where "small gnats mourn," human behavior is being grafted onto, or interpreted into, nature.

But the unique thing here is that the *mood* of the piece seems to overwhelm our usual associations. Despite the metaphoric relations, description dominates to the end, and what we are most taken with is the richness and intensity of image. So, *third,* on a deeper level, this poem presents an experience of autumn and compares this *essence,* this life, this intensity of beauty in itself (*X*) to the fact (*Y*) that it is passing, dying moment to moment—in short, beauty (*X*) is contrasted to (*Y*) *time* (remember that time's symbol is the scythe), a sense of eternal *now* against eternal passing away. The piece is really not a description of a scene; rather, it is an experience of mood, and more than mood. All these images are used to evoke a state that is indescribable. Isn't this the action of metaphor?

The second piece, while complete in itself, uses the Keats poem as a frame of reference. Robhs has played off the tone, keying his conception to the scythe, the sense of winter and death. One of the subjects of his poem is Keats's life and times and philosophy of poetry. Autumn personified and season as a metaphor for human life appear explicitly when "The bones of life now show beneath the skin." It's useful to see the vast difference in mood, despite the fact that the second piece is consciously related to the first. They both reflect similar feelings and perceptions, but in the second poem description is much more openly metaphoric.

1. In Robhs's poem, the speaker is saying that *romantic* poetry (critics consider Keats a romantic poet) is a moment of nostalgia for him. What is he implicitly contrasting this romantic feeling with?
2. Why does Robhs's speaker say, "Or said they wept"? What does this reveal about his attitude toward Keats?
3. How deeply do the two moods contrast? Which poem seems to have greater "distance" from the subject matter? How does this affect the tone?
4. Consider how both poems slant their moods by choice of image and diction: birds "riot" in one and "twitter" in the other, for instance.
5. Is the cider press (in the Keats poem) a metaphor? For what?
6. What other metaphoric aspects do you see in these pieces?

Technical Notes

The Keats poem is in iambic pentameter. The Robhs poem uses iambic feet with more variation and a pentameter background.

How do these poems play on mood? How are they metaphoric?

William Blake

NEVER SEEK TO TELL
THY LOVE

Never seek to tell thy love
Love that never told can be;
For the gentle wind does move
Silently, invisibly.

I told my love, I told my love,
I told her all my heart,
Trembling, cold, in ghastly fears—
Ah, she doth depart.

Soon as she was gone from me
A traveller came by
Silently, invisibly—
O, was no deny.

Considerations

This poem is a LYRIC; it sounds like a song. You
might say that the first two lines are imperative
opinion, and the next two a statement-description
of wind. Notice that the first two are an *X,* the
second two their *Y.* Love is implicitly compared
to the "gentle wind," and a causal, relation between them is suggested.

Notice the pattern: (1) Don't tell / the wind
is silent, etc.; (2) I told / she left me; (3)
she was gone / the invisible traveler came. In
the first and third cases Blake makes an *X/Y* by
disjunction, by leaving out any logical-looking
connections.

1. Wind (*X*) is (like) traveler (*Y*). Blake describes
   the traveler and the wind. Do you have a sense
   of what they refer to?
2. Does the description of the traveler actually
   describe anything at all? Is it completely metaphoric?

William Butler Yeats
LONG-LEGGED FLY

That civilisation may not sink,
Its great battle lost,
Quiet the dog, tether the pony
To a distant post;
Our master Caesar is in the tent
Where the maps are spread,
His eyes fixed upon nothing,
A hand under his head.
Like a long-legged fly upon the stream
His mind moves upon silence.

That the topless towers be burnt
And men recall that face,
Move most gently if move you must
In this lonely place.
She thinks, part woman, three parts a child,
That nobody looks; her feet
Practise a tinker shuffle
Picked up on a street.
Like a long-legged fly upon the stream
Her mind moves upon silence.

That girls at puberty may find
The first Adam in their thought,
Shut the door of the Pope's chapel,
Keep those children out.
There on that scaffolding reclines
Michael Angelo.
With no more sound than the mice make
His hand moves to and fro.
Like a long-legged fly upon the stream
His mind moves upon silence.

Considerations

1. Each stanza is built around a core of description. After each stanza there is an enigmatic open metaphor in italics. How is this REFRAIN related to the description in the stanzas?
2. Are the two elements (refrain and stanza) in an *X/Y* relationship? What can you say about it?
3. Try reading the piece and leaving out the refrain. What happens to the impact and meaning? Is there any metaphoric action now?
4. What are the levels of meaning here?

Meng Chiao

SADNESS OF THE GORGES

Looking up from the gorges the sky winds
   like a thread;
Down the steep slope cords of water twist.
Sunlight on a tilt sprays the rims; by night
The moon spreads ghostlight like silver dew.
The bases vibrate to unceasing waves.
Centuries of shadow frozen in the depths
Stunned by a needle of light . . . another . . .
These long rays tilt past noon down
   into darkness . . .
At the most deadly twists white water raves
Like the drool of brute and naked appetite.
Treeroots stitch and knot through
   crumbled coffins,
And dangle the unstrung skeletons upright
As if they were just setting out in life . . .
The bony branches bare and white with frost
Tune the wind to clear and distant notes
That grieve harmoniously everywhere.

The guts of the exile shrivel, boil and burn
In the water and fire of his life;
Life spun out like the finest thread . . .
The rising road is bordered by the hand rope
Frail hands clutch at.
When he offers his silver tears to the spirits
   of the stream
Those ghosts gather, shimmer there . . .

Rendition from Chinese by Richard Monaco

Considerations

1. When you finish the poem, consider whether
   you would call the first four lines pure description setting the scene, or do you feel there has
   been metaphoric "action" created by the context? If so, what specifically is this action?
2. Are the individual images (description) in the
   poem metaphoric? What kinds of things do
   they aim at?

The next piece is a NARRATIVE POEM: *it tells a story. How does it express its*
metaphoric levels?

Alfred, Lord Tennyson

THE LADY OF SHALOTT

PART I

On either side of the river lie
Long fields of barley and of rye,
That clothe the wold and meet the sky;
And thro' the field the road runs by
    To many-tower'd Camelot;
And up and down the people go,
Gazing where the lilies blow
Round an island there below,
    The island of Shalott.

Willows whiten, aspens quiver,
Little breezes dusk and shiver
Thro' the wave that runs forever
By the island in the river
    Flowing down to Camelot.
Four grey walls, and four grey towers,
Overlook a space of flowers,
And the silent isle imbowers
    The Lady of Shalott.

By the margin, willow-veil'd,
Slide the heavy barges trail'd
By slow horses; and unhail'd
The shallop'[1] flitteth silken-sail'd
    Skimming down to Camelot:
But who hath seen her wave her hand?
Or at the casement seen her stand?
Or is she known in all the land,
    The Lady of Shalott?

Only reapers, reaping early
In among the bearded barley,
Hear a song that echoes cheerly
From the river winding clearly,
    Down to tower'd Camelot:
And by the moon the reaper weary,
Piling sheaves in uplands airy,
Listening, whispers, "'Tis the fairy
    Lady of Shalott."

[1] A small, light boat

PART II

There she weaves by night and day
A magic web with colours gay.
She has heard a whisper say,
A curse is on her if she stay
    To look down to Camelot.
She knows not what the curse may be,
And so she weaveth steadily,
And little other care hath she,
    The Lady of Shalott.

And moving thro' a mirror clear
That hangs before her all the year,
Shadows of the world appear.
There she sees the highway near
    Winding down to Camelot:
There the river eddy whirls,
And there the surly village-churls,[2]
And the red cloaks of market girls,
    Pass onward from Shalott.

Sometimes a troop of damsels glad,
An abbot on an ambling pad,
Sometimes a curly shepherd-lad,
Or long-hair'd page in crimson clad,
    Goes by to tower'd Camelot;
And sometimes thro' the mirror blue
The knights come riding two and two;
She hath no loyal knight and true,
    The Lady of Shalott.

But in her web she still delights
To weave the mirror's magic sights,
For often thro' the silent nights
A funeral, with plumes and lights
    And music, went to Camelot:
Or when the moon was overhead,
Came two young lovers lately wed;
"I am half sick of shadows," said
    The Lady of Shalott.

[2] Medieval peasant

PART III

A bow-shot from her bower-eaves,
He rode between the barley-sheaves,
The sun came dazzling thro' the leaves,
And flamed upon the brazen greaves[3]
   Of bold Sir Lancelot.
A red-cross knight forever kneel'd
To a lady in his shield,
That sparkled on the yellow field,
   Beside remote Shalott.

The gemmy bridle glitter'd free,
Like to some branch of stars we see
Hung in the golden Galaxy.
The bridle bells rang merrily
  As he rode down to Camelot:
And from his blazon'd baldric[4] slung
A mighty silver bugle hung,
And as he rode his armour rung,
   Beside remote Shalott.

All in the blue unclouded weather
Thick-jewell'd shone the saddle-leather,
The helmet and the helmet-feather
Burn'd like one burning flame together,
  As he rode down to Camelot.
As often thro' the purple night,
Below the starry clusters bright,
Some bearded meteor trailing light,
   Moves over still Shalott.

His broad clear brow in sunlight glow'd;
On burnish'd hooves his war-horse strode;
From underneath his helmet flow'd
His coal-black curls as on he rode,
  As he rode down to Camelot.
From the bank and from the river
He flash'd into the crystal mirror,
"Tirra lirra," by the river
   Sang Sir Lancelot.

She left the web, she left the loom,
She made three paces thro' the room,
She saw the water-lilly bloom,
She saw the helmet and the plume,
  She look'd down to Camelot.
Out flew the web and floated wide;
The mirror crack'd from side to side;
"The curse is come upon me," cried
   The Lady of Shalott.

[3]Part of a knight's armour
[4]Belt supporting a sword

PART IV

In the stormy east-wind straining,
The pale yellow woods were waning,
The broad stream in his banks complaining,
Heavily the low sky raining,
   Over tower'd Camelot;
Down she came and found a boat
Beneath a willow left afloat,
And round about the prow she wrote
   The Lady of Shalott.

And down the river's dim expanse
Like some bold seer in a trance,
Seeing all his own mischance—
With a glassy countenance
   Did she look to Camelot.
And at the closing of the day
She loosed the chain, and down she lay;
The broad stream bore her far away,
   The Lady of Shalott.

Lying, robed in snowy white,
That loosely flew to left and right—
The leaves upon her falling light—
Thro' the noises of the night
   She floated down to Camelot:
And as the boat-head wound along
The willowy hills and fields among,
They heard her singing her last song,
   The Lady of Shalott.

Heard a carol, mournful, holy,
Chanted loudly, chanted lowly,
Till her blood was frozen slowly,
And her eyes were darken'd wholly,
   Turn'd to tower'd Camelot.
For ere she reach'd upon the tide
The first house by the water-side,
Singing in her song she died,
   The Lady of Shalott.

Under tower and balcony,
By garden-wall and gallery,
A gleaming shape she floated by,
Dead-pale between the houses high,
   Silent into Camelot.
Out upon the wharfs they came,
Knight and burgher, lord and dame,
And round the prow they read her name,
   The Lady of Shalott.

Who is this? and what is here?
And in the lighted palace near
Died the sound of royal cheer;
And they cross'd themselves for fear,
    All the knights at Camelot:
But Lancelot mused a little space;
He said, "She has a lovely face;
God in his mercy lend her grace,
    The Lady of Shalott."

Considerations

1. How do local metaphors add to the intensity? Do they add *levels* to the story?
2. Consider the story as description: is it, in itself, acting metaphorically? Is the story an *X* for which you can discover possible *Y*'s?

LINES OF INQUIRY

The following poems can be looked at in the same general way as the preceding ones. You ought to be able to get into them fairly easily.

1. *Can you find a propaganda element?*
2. *Does the poet get beyond his or her ideas or description by initiating metaphoric action (not all of them necessarily do)? Is there a sense of discovery in each piece? If so, what is it? If not, why not?*

Jonathan Swift

A DESCRIPTION OF A CITY SHOWER

Careful observers may foretell the hour
(By sure prognostics) when to dread a shower.
While rain depends, the pensive cat gives o'er
Her frolics, and pursues her tail no more.
Returning home at night, you'll find the sink
Strike your offended sense with double stink.
If you be wise, then go not far to dine;
You'll spend in coach-hire more than save in wine.
A coming shower your shooting corns presage;
Old aches throb, your hollow tooth will rage.
Saunt'ring in coffee-house is Dulman seen;
He damns the climate, and complains of spleen.
    Meanwhile the South, rising with dabbled wings,
A sable cloud athwart the welkin° flings,
That swilled more liquor than it could contain,
And, like a drunkard, gives it up again.
Brisk Susan whips her linen from the rope,
While the first drizzling shower is borne aslope:
Such is that sprinkling which some careless quean
Flirts on you from her mop, but not so clean.
You fly, invoke the gods; then turning, stop
To rail; she, singing, still whirls on her mop.
°The Sky

Nor yet the dust had shunned th'unequal strife,
But, aided by the wind, fought still for life,
And wafted with its foe by violent gust,
'Twas doubtful which was rain, and which was dust.
Ah! where must needy poet seek for aid,
When dust and rain at once his coat invade?
Sole coat, where dust cemented by the rain
Erects the nap, and leaves a cloudy stain.
  Now in contiguous drops the flood comes down,
Threat'ning with deluge this *devoted* town.
To shops in crowds the daggled females fly,
Pretend to cheapen goods, but nothing buy.
The Templar spruce, while every spout's abroach,
Stays till 'tis fair, yet seems to call a coach.
The tucked-up sempstress walks with hasty strides,
While streams run down her oiled umbrella's sides.
Here various kinds, by various fortunes led,
Commence acquaintance underneath a shed.
Triumphant Tories and desponding Whigs
Forget their feuds, and join to save their wigs.
Boxed in a chair the beau impatient sits,
While spouts run clatt'ring o'er the roof by fits;
And ever and anon with frightful din
The leather sounds; he trembles from within.
So when Troy chairmen bore the wooden steed,
Pregnant with Greeks impatient to be freed
(Those bully Greeks, who, as the moderns do,

Instead of paying chairmen, run them through),
Laocoön struck the outside with his spear,
And each imprisoned hero quaked for fear.
   Now from all parts the swelling kennels flow,
And bear their trophies with them as they go.
Filths of all hues and odors seem to tell
What streets they sailed from, by their sight and smell.
They, as each torrent drives, with rapid force
From Smithfield or St. Pulchre's shape their course,
And in huge confluent joined at Snow-Hill ridge,
Fall from the conduit prone to Holborn Bridge.
Sweepings from butchers' stalls, dung, guts, and blood,
Drowned puppies, stinking sprats, all drenched in mud,
Dead cats and turnip-tops come tumbling down the flood.

Horace

ODE IV

Rigid winter relaxes into the sweet flux of spring and the west wind:
there are techniques to ease dry hulls down into water;
the sheep forgets its shed, the farmer his fire;
hoarfrost melts on what were white frozen fields.

Under bare moonlight Venus at her most Venusian leads song and dance,
and, joined almost bodily with nymphs, chaste graces
excite the earth with rhythmic steps while Vulcan,
urgent, ignites the violent workshops of the Cyclopes.

Let's weave green myrtle into our hair, scenting it, or
a flower born of thawing earth;
let's sacrifice in thicketshade to Pan's desire
for a ewelamb or kid.

Death, passionless, stamps out the ashes of
poor man's hut, king's palace. Darling Sestius,
the brief sum of life won't let us add up hopes for long.
Soon true night's rumoured darkness will reduce you

to the Plutonian realm outside earth and heaven where you cannot
throw die to sit at the head of the table and visually caress
gentle Lycidas. Now boys feel a glowing ache
for him and soon even maidens will be aroused.

   · *Translation from Latin by J. C. Jacobs*

David Wagoner

STAYING ALIVE

Staying alive in the woods is a matter of calming down
At first and deciding whether to wait for rescue,
Trusting to others,
Or simply to start walking and walking in one direction
Till you come out—or something happens to stop you.
By far the safer choice
Is to settle down where you are, and try to make a living
Off the land, camping near water, away from shadows.
Eat no white berries;
Spit out all bitterness. Shooting at anything
Means hiking further and further every day
To hunt survivors;
It may be best to learn what you have to learn without a gun,
Not killing but watching birds and animals go
In and out of shelter
At will. Following their example, build for a whole season:
Facing across the wind in your lean-to,
You may feel wilder,
But nothing, not even you, will have to stay in hiding.
If you have no matches, a stick and a fire-bow
Will keep you warmer,
Or the crystal of your watch, filled with water, held up to the sun
Will do the same in time. In case of snow
Drifting toward winter,
Don't try to stay awake through the night, afraid of freezing—
The bottom of your mind knows all about zero;
It will turn you over
And shake you till you waken. If you have trouble sleeping
Even in the best of weather, jumping to follow
With eyes strained to their corners
The unidentifiable noises of the night and feeling
Bears and packs of wolves nuzzling your elbow,
Remember the trappers
Who treated them indifferently and were left alone.
If you hurt yourself, no one will comfort you
Or take your temperature,
So stumbling, wading, and climbing are as dangerous as flying.
But if you decide, at last, you must break through
In spite of all danger,
Think of yourself by time and not by distance, counting
Wherever you're going by how long it takes you;
No other measure
Will bring you safe to nightfall. Follow no streams: they run
Under the ground or fall into wilder country.
Remember the stars
And moss when your mind runs into circles. If it should rain
Or the fog should roll the horizon in around you,

Hold still for hours
Or days if you must, or weeks, for seeing is believing
In the wilderness. And if you find a pathway,
Wheel-rut, or fence-wire,
Retrace it left or right: someone knew where he was going
Once upon a time, and you can follow
Hopefully, somewhere,
Just in case. There may even come, on some uncanny evening,
A time when you're warm and dry, well fed, not thirsty,
Uninjured, without fear,
When nothing, either good or bad, is happening.
This is called staying alive. It's temporary.
What occurs after
Is doubtful. You must always be ready for something to come bursting
Through the far edge of a clearing, running toward you,
Grinning from ear to ear
And hoarse with welcome. Or something crossing and hovering
Overhead, as light as air, like a break in the sky,
Wondering what you are.
Here you are face to face with the problem of recognition.
Having no time to make smoke, too much to say,
You should have a mirror
With a tiny hole in the back for better aiming, for reflecting
Whatever disaster you can think of, to show
The way you suffer.
These body signals have universal meaning: If you are lying
Flat on your back with arms outstretched behind you,
You say you require
Emergency treatment; if you are standing erect and holding
Arms horizontal, you mean you are not ready;
If you hold them over
Your head, you want to be picked up. Three of anything
Is a sign of distress. Afterward, if you see
No ropes, no ladders,
No maps or messages falling, no searchlights or trails blazing,
Then, chances are, you should be prepared to burrow
Deep for a deep winter.

Horace

TO THE LAWYER, TORQUATUS

the snow has disbanded / the grass is coming back in the fields,
in the trees the loosed leaves

the land renews the forever mutable / the streams having crested
glide along their old banks
the spirits of the sacred forest / graces and nymphs / are out
careless and naked and dancing

no immortal yearnings for you / warns the year and the hour that
comes by to collect your day
cold the springwind mildens it / spring the summer tramples it
down / doomed from the start
apple fall unloads his harvests / and all too soon
is the winter back deadstill

a few swift moons repair one damaged cycle / but we
when our fall arrives and we
unto father aeneas and rich tullus and ancus[1] are gathered
are fistfuls of dust and shadow
and who of us knows that the gods intend to credit one day
/ tomorrow / to his account
tomorrow all that you will have given out of love will scatter
from the griping clutches of your heirs

when night falls final / and upon you / minos[2] judger of souls
pronounces stately sentence
then no / torquatus / your family connections / no not your wit
no nor all your rightthinking
will ever reinstate you / after all diana[3] does not
from the dark below loose
her hippolytus for all his heroic chastity
nor theseus[4] have the strength
to snap the manacles / of lethean sleep / that bind
his loved pirithöos

      Translation from Latin by Christopher Collins

[1]Considered patron fathers of ancient Rome
[2]Ancient king of Crete, mythic
[3]Greek myth: Diana fell in love with Hippolytus who
rejected her. She had him destroyed by Neptune
(Poseidon).
[4]Greek myth: Theseus and Pirithöos were bound to a
rock in Hades. Hercules rescued Theseus but Pirithöos
remained forever in death.

Helen Chasin

THINKING ABOUT PARADISE

Imagine
Gauguin up and going that way: *au 'voir*
and he's gone out into the South Seas
sunset, your best daydreams' bastard's *bon voyage*:
bad, leaving
the wife, the little ones like that
and those nine-to-fiving five days a week
for a living, for weekends
and for what?
            You imagine a sun
that ripens his days and brown women
under it whose hot blood
swells their breasts like melons, their lips
push out and pout for his love-bites, their
eyelids heavy, half-drawn over dark bedroom eyes
and the skirts like pieces of bedspread, batiks
that unwrap like a curl of kumquat easier than
crooking a finger *come here*, barefoot
to begin with those women
fall to him like fruit, ah sweet
and that's all, no making something of it
after and they feed him too and give him
a place to live, their system of trade's
that simple. What is it to him
when the mailboat fails or shows up?
There's a whole ocean out there, it ends
tropical blue at his island. You imagine
the man living your wildest hope
of sin: heat, jungle gin, the lush
flowers, skin, a few words, painting only when he wants

that land of delight you have him in: it's pure Gauguin
and the sea a clear, deep
sky blue there's no other use for
for him, he'll never ever sail out over it again.

Walther Von Der Vogelweide

UNDER DER LINDEN

Under the tree in shadow and sunlight
We made our bed.
You could see
Where we picked flowers and grass.
In the forest
Where the nightingale sang.

I went to the meadow and he was there,
My lover, and he said:
"Noble Lady!" And I
Have the echo of joy
Still in my mind.
Did he kiss me?
Still in my mind,
And see the sweet bruise of my mouth.

His tender hands had shaped a bed
Of flowers and shaped
More than those; whoever
passes there
Will see
My imprint in crushed roses.

If any knew where he lay—
God forbid it!—
Ah the tender shame!
Let the two of us know what was done,
And the singing, secret bird.

Rendition from German

James Dickey

CHERRYLOG ROAD

Off Highway 106
At Cherrylog Road I entered
The '34 Ford without wheels,
Smothered in kudzu,
With a seat pulled out to run
Corn whiskey down from the hills,

And then from the other side
Crept into an Essex
With a rumble seat of red leather
And then out again, aboard
A blue Chevrolet, releasing
The rust from its other color,

Reared up on three building blocks.
None had the same body heat;
I changed with them inward, toward
The weedy heart of the junkyard,
For I knew that Doris Holbrook
Would escape from her father at noon

And would come from the farm
To seek parts owned by the sun
Among the abandoned chassis,
Sitting in each in turn
As I did, leaning forward
As in a wild stock-car race

In the parking lot of the dead.
Time after time, I climbed in
And out the other side, like
An envoy or movie star
Met at the station by crickets.
A radiator cap raised its head,

Become a real toad or a kingsnake
As I neared the hub of the yard,
Passing through many states,
Many lives, to reach
Some grandmother's long Pierce-Arrow
Sending platters of blindness forth

From its nickel hubcaps
And spilling its tender upholstery
On sleepy roaches,
The glass panel in between
Lady and colored driver
Not all the way broken out,

The back-seat phone
Still on its hook.
I got in as though to exclaim,
"Let us go to the orphan asylum,
John; I have some old toys
For children who say their prayers."

I popped with sweat as I thought
I heard Doris Holbrook scrape
Like a mouse in the southern-state sun
That was eating the paint in blisters
From a hundred car tops and hoods.
She was tapping like code,

Loosening the screws,
Carrying off headlights,
Sparkplugs, bumpers,
Cracked mirrors and gear-knobs,
Getting ready, already,
To go back with something to show

Other than her lips' new trembling
I would hold to me soon, soon,
Where I sat in the ripped back seat
Talking over the interphone,
Praying for Doris Holbrook
To come from her father's farm

And to get back there
With no trace of me on her face
To be seen by her red-haired father
Who would change, in the squalling barn,
Her back's pale skin with a strop,
Then lay for me

In a bootlegger's roasting car
With a string-triggered 12-gauge shotgun
To blast the breath from the air.

Not cut by the jagged windshields,
Through the acres of wrecks she came
With a wrench in her hand,

Through dust where the blacksnake dies
Of boredom, and the beetle knows
The compost has no more life.
Someone outside would have seen
The oldest car's door inexplicably
Close from within:

I held her and held her and held her,
Convoyed at terrific speed
By the stalled, dreaming traffic around us,
So the blacksnake, stiff
With inaction, curved back
Into life, and hunted the mouse

With deadly overexcitement,
The beetles reclaimed their field
As we clung, glued together,
With the hooks of the seat springs
Working through to catch us red-handed
Amidst the gray, breathless batting

That burst from the seat at our backs.
We left by separate doors
Into the changed, other bodies
Of cars, she down Cherrylog Road
And I to my motorcycle
Parked like the soul of the junkyard

Restored, a bicycle fleshed
With power, and tore off
Up Highway 106, continually
Drunk on the wind in my mouth,
Wringing the handlebar for speed,
Wild to be wreckage forever.

Anonymous
WESTERN WIND

Western wind, when will thou blow,
The small rain down can rain?
Christ, if my love were in my arms
And I in my bed again!

Amaru
SHE DIDN'T TURN

She didn't turn from him
or criticize.
She didn't lock him out,
or drive him off.

She simply looked at him,
who had just been her lover,
as at any other man.

Rendition from Sanskrit

Bharthari
PAWNS, KNIGHTS, BISHOPS

Pawns, knights, bishops, rooks and queens
all go down, the wild
and complex board is simplified;
sudden after hours of building up.
Time and the goddess death play together.
We lose whoever wins.

Rendition from Sanskrit

Anonymous
NOW SPRINGS THE SPRAY

Now the spray is springing
And all for love I am so sick
That I may do no sleeping.

The other day as I was riding,
O my playing's ring,
I saw a little maid there being
And she began to sing:
"The clot him cling!
To him I love I bring
Woe for his living."

Soon as I heard that merry beat
there I rode.
I found her in a garden sweet
Among the trees she showed.
In joyous mode
I soon asked: "Merry maid why do you
Sing as you do?"

Then answered that maiden sweet
With words few:
"My lover did me entreat
To love true:
But he changes anew.
If I may he shall this rue
By this day."

Translation from Middle English

A. E. Housman

THIS TIME OF YEAR

This time of year a twelvemonth past,
  When Fred and I would meet,
We needs must jangle, till at last
  We fought and I was beat.

So then the summer fields about,
  Till rainy days began,
Rose Harland on her Sundays out
  Walked with the better man.

The better man she walks with still,
  Though now 'tis not with Fred:
A lad that lives and has his will
  Is worth a dozen dead.

Fred keeps the house all kinds of weather,
  And clay's the house he keeps;
When Rose and I walk out together
  Stock-still lies Fred and sleeps.

William Cartwright

NO PLATONIQUE LOVE

Tell me no more of Minds embracing Minds,
  And hearts exchang'd for hearts;
That Spirits Spirits meet, as Winds do winds,
  And mix their subt'lest parts;
That two unbodi'd Essences may kiss,
And then like Angels, twist and feel one Bliss.

I was that silly thing that once was wrought
  To Practise this thin Love;
I climb'd from Sex to Soul, from Soul to Thought;
  But thinking there to move,
Headlong I rowl'd from Thought to Soul, and then
From Soul I lighted at the Sex agen.

As some strict down-look'd Men pretend to fast,
  Who yet in Closets Eat;
So Lovers who profess they Spirits taste,
  Feed yet on grosser meat;
I know they boast they Soules to Soules Convey,
Howe'r they meet, the Body is the Way.

Come, I will undeceive thee, they that tread
  Those vain Aëriall waies,
Are like young Heyrs and Alchymists misled
  To waste their Wealth and Daies,
For searching thus to be for ever Rich,
They only find a Med'cine for the Itch.

This poem is traditionally attributed to Virgil. If he was indeed its author, he probably wrote it while in his early twenties (circa 37 B.C.). This English translation retains the original metrical form, the elegiac couplet.

Virgil

THE WAITRESS

Hair bound back in a Greek-looking headband, the Syrian waitress,
    castanets over her head, wriggles an excellent hip.
Funny-drunk, she does her act in the smoky casino,
    letting the ribboned flutes joggle and splay at her elbow:
"Why were you walking the earth, worn down in the dust of the summer,
    when you could just as well sink down on a drinker's divan?
Here there are casks and glasses, flutes and citherns and roses,
    also a garden in back, trellised and shady and cool.
Listen—the very essential sound of Arcadian grottos.
    Hear it? the pastoral pipe played by a genuine hind!
So ? you drink no wine ? The clear water chimes in the brook and
    recently one cask leaked: flat wine is also for sale.
Wreathes we provide inwoven with tiny saffrony violets,
    chaplets of roses, as well, yellow ones plaited with red;
Look, here are lilies in baskets, plucked from virginal freshets,
    flowers the sea-girl[1] fetched floating to Naples to die.
Cheeses small and oval are hung up to dry in rush packets,
    and when the autumn comes: plums are served, smoother than wax;
Blackberries dark as gore and grapes in thick dangling clusters;
    hung by its thongy stem, cucumber green as the sea;
Chestnut and sweetly ripening, sweetly ruddying apple;
    wheat-clean Ceres and Love, linked with the loud Lord of Wine.
Out in the garden you see the figure of watchman Priapus[2]
    flaunting his club from his crotch (neither too fearsome nor firm).
You out there, traveler, come in. That tired little donkey is sweaty.
    Give him a rest. Don't you know donkeys are pets of the gods?
Now all the thickets crack with the constant call of the locusts.
    Even the lizard lies, hiding in cool noonday shade.
Were you as wise, you would douse yourself with a summery goblet,
    or with a series of drinks brimming in crystalline cups.
Eia ! come on, you're worn out, lie down in the vine-leafy shade and
    fit to your heavy head roses wound round in a crown.
Beautifully take to your lips the mouth of a tender young girl and
    Oh let him die who looks grave—righteous and prudent and prim!
Why reserve for your funeral all of those sweet-smelling blossoms?
    Wreathes for your headstone you'll have: what about wreathes for your head?
Place your orders and place your bets! Why question the future?
    Death left a short note for you: 'Live' says the message, 'I come.'"

Translation from Latin by Christopher Collins

---

[1]Parthenope, a sea divinity and one of the Sirens. Having been ignored by Odysseus, she threw herself into the sea. Her body floated to the shore upon which Naples was later built.

[2]A fertility god whose rustic statue was adorned with a long detachable phallus—a handy club used by householders to scare off trespassers.

Thomas, Lord Vaux

THE AGED LOVER RENOUNCETH LOVE

I loathe that I did love,
  In youth that I thought sweet,
As time requires for my behove,
  Methinks they are not meet.

My lusts they do me leave,
  My fancies all be fled,
And tract of time begins to weave
  Grey hairs upon my head.

For age with stealing steps
  Hath clawed me with his crutch,
And lusty life away she leaps
  As there had been none such.

My Muse doth not delight
  Me as she did before;
My hand and pen are not in plight,
  As they have been of yore.

For reason me denies
  This youthly idle rhyme;
And day by day to me she cries,
  "Leave off these toys in time."

The wrinkles in my brow,
  The furrows in my face,
Say, limping age will lodge him now
  Where youth must give him place.

The harbinger of death,
  To me I see him ride,
The cough, the cold, the gasping breath
  Doth bid me to provide

A pickaxe and a spade,
  And eke a shrouding sheet,
A house of clay for to be made
  For such a guest most meet.

Methinks I hear the clark
  That knolls the careful knell,
And bids me leave my woeful wark,
  Ere nature me compel.

My keepers knit the knot
  That youth did laugh to scorn,
Of me that clean shall be forgot
  As I had not been born.

Thus must I youth give up,
  Whose badge I long did wear;
To them I yield the wanton cup
  That better may it bear.

Lo, here the bared skull,
  By whose bald sign I know
That stooping age away shall pull
  Which youthful years did sow.

For beauty with her band
  These crooked cares hath wrought,
And shipped me into the land
  From whence I first was brought.

And ye that bide behind,
  Have ye none other trust:
As ye of clay were cast by kind,
  So shall ye waste to dust.

Oliver Goldsmith

ELEGY ON MADAM BLAIZE

Good people all, with one accord,
  Lament for Madam Blaize;
Who never wanted a good word—
  From those who spoke her praise.

The needy seldom passed her door,
  And always found her kind;
She freely lent to all the poor—
  Who left a pledge behind.

She strove the neighbourhood to please,
  With manners wondrous winning;
She never followed wicked ways—
  Unless when she was sinning.

At church, in silks and satins new,
  With hoop of monstrous size,
She never slumbered in her pew—
  But when she shut her eyes.

Her love was sought, I do aver,
  By twenty beaux, or more;
The king himself has followed her—
  When she has walked before.

But now, her wealth and finery fled,
  Her hangers-on cut short all,
Her doctors found, when she was dead—
  Her last disorder mortal.

Let us lament, in sorrow sore,
  For Kent Street well may say,
That, had she lived a twelvemonth more—
  She had not died to-day.

Sappho

HE EQUALS AN ENCHANTED GOD

He equals an enchanted god
seated facing you, stunned,
submits to your sweet tones,
inviting smile. Stunned too,
the heart in my breast.
I watch, swallow my voice,
my tongue breaks; narrow flames
encase me like a second skin.
Blind, deaf but for a drumming,
running sweat, I tremble
paler than dry, autumn grass.
I know death and suffer its emptiness.

Translation from Greek by J. C. Jacobs

Pindar

OLYMPIAN XI

For Agesidamos of Western Lokroi, Winner in the Boys' Boxing

Winds come to men when needed most
or heaven's waters, refreshing as
the dewy bloom of children.
If anyone does his best, let
sweet praise begin to be sung,
an oath loyal to those virtuous deeds,
an unenvied accolade, dedicated
to Olympian victors. This,
my words strive to tend; God
in his wisdom nourishes man's understanding.
Know now, child of Archestratus,
Agesidamos, because of your boxing
I shall sing music to put the
finishing touches on your crown
of golden olive, honoring
the race of Western Lokrians.
Rejoice with them! I promise,
by the Muses, you'll not find
an army that puts strangers to flight,
though to have flowered in wisdom
takes a warrior. Red fox and
roaring lions differ in nature.

Translation from Greek by J. C. Jacobs

Robert Bridges
LONDON SNOW

When men were all asleep the snow came flying,
In large white flakes falling on the city brown,
Stealthily and perpetually settling and loosely lying,
   Hushing the latest traffic of the drowsy town;
Deadening, muffling, stifling its murmurs failing;
Lazily and incessantly floating down and down:
   Silently sifting and veiling road, roof and railing;
Hiding difference, making unevenness even,
Into angles and crevices softly drifting and sailing.
   All night it fell, and when full inches seven
It lay in the depth of its uncompacted lightness,
The clouds blew off from a high and frosty heaven;
   And all woke earlier for the unaccustomed brightness
Of the winter dawning, the strange unheavenly glare:
The eye marvelled—marvelled at the dazzling whiteness;
   The ear hearkened to the stillness of the solemn air;
No sound of wheel rumbling nor of foot falling,
And the busy morning cries came thin and spare.
   Then boys I heard, as they went to school, calling,
They gathered up the crystal manna to freeze

Their tongues with tasting, their hands with snowballing;
   Or rioted in a drift, plunging up to the knees;
Or peering up from under the white-mossed wonder,
"O look at the trees!" they cried, "O look at the trees!"
   With lessened load a few carts creak and blunder,
Following along the white deserted way,
A country company long dispersed asunder:
   When now already the sun, in pale display
Standing by Paul's high dome, spread forth below
His sparkling beams, and awoke the stir of the day.
   For now doors open, and war is waged with the snow;
And trains of sombre men, past tale of number,
Tread long brown paths, as towards their toil they go:
   But even for them awhile no cares encumber
Their minds diverted; the daily word is unspoken,
The daily thoughts of labour and sorrow slumber
At the sight of the beauty that greets them, for the
     charm they have broken.

Francisco de Quevedo

IN THIS WHITE, BLINDING DAY

In this white, blinding day, if only I could
open my eyes to that Ultimate Shadow,
loosen my soul from the flames of its desires,
I would be so sweetly free.

But this human abyss before me. Not on that
other side may I leave Memory burning.
For the soul must be purified by flight
through the cold iron heights of the Law.

Soul for whom all God is prison,
veins which must fuel the fire,
marrow which must be gloriously consumed.

This body I will leave behind, but not its care;
ashes it will be, but the ashes of feeling;
dust it must be—but the dust of love.

               Rendition from Spanish

William Cowper

LIGHT SHINING OUT
OF DARKNESS

God moves in a mysterious way,
　His wonders to perform;
He plants His footsteps in the sea,
　And rides upon the storm.

Deep in unfathomable mines
　Of never failing skill,
He treasures up His bright designs,
　And works His sovereign will.

Ye fearful saints fresh courage take,
　The clouds ye so much dread
Are big with mercy, and shall break
　In blessings on your head.

Judge not the Lord by feeble sense,
　But trust Him for His grace;
Behind a frowning providence,
　He hides a smiling face.

His purposes will ripen fast,
　Unfolding ev'ry hour;
The bud may have a bitter taste,
　But sweet will be the flow'r.

Blind unbelief is sure to err,
　And scan His work in vain;
God is His own interpreter,
　And He will make it plain.

Saint John of the Cross

SONG OF THE SOUL IN
INTIMATE UNION WITH
GOD'S LOVE

Oh living flame of love,
That sweetly sears my
Soul in its deepest center!
Since you're no longer shy,
End it now, if you desire.
Rend my priest's robe with our encounter!

Oh tender wound!
Pain like a gift.
Oh gentle hand! Oh delicate touch!
To know eternity
And pay all fleshly debts!
Killing me, this death is life.

Oh fiery lamp
Whose resplendence sounds
The depths of the caverns of sense
Which were so dark and blind.
With what strange beauty heat and flame
You join to your beloved.

What soft and loving
Thoughts absorb my heart,
Remembering that, when secretly alone,
You called me—recalling your sweet breath
Of good and glorious completeness.
How delicately you made me fall in love!

Translation from Spanish

E. E. Cummings

BUFFALO BILL'S

Buffalo Bill's
defunct
　　　who used to
　　　ride a watersmooth-silver
　　　　　　　　　　　stallion
and break onetwothreefourfive pigeonsjustlikethat
　　　　　　　　　　　　　　Jesus

he was a handsome man
　　　　　　　and what i want to know is
how do you like your blueeyed boy
Mister Death

John Donne

HOLY SONNET IX

If poysonous mineralls, and if that tree,
Whose fruit threw death on else immortall us,
If lecherous goats, if serpents envious
Cannot be damn'd; Alas; why should I bee?
Why should intent or reason, borne in mee,
Make sinnes, else equall, in mee more heinous?
And mercy being easie, and glorious
To God; in his sterne wrath, why threatens hee?
But who am I, that dare dispute with thee
O God? Oh! of thine onely worthy blood,
And my teares, make a heavenly Lethean flood,
And drowne in it my sinnes blacke memorie;
    That thou remember them, some claime as debt,
    I thinke it mercy, if thou wilt forget.

Lord Herbert of Cherbury

TO HIS WATCH, WHEN HE
COULD NOT SLEEP

Uncessant Minutes, whil'st you move you tell
The time that tells our life, which though it run
Never so fast or farr, you'r new begun
Short steps shall overtake; for though life well

May scrape his own Account, it shall not yours,
You are Death's Auditors, that both divide
And summ what ere that life inspir'd endures
Past a beginning, and through you we bide

The doom of Fate, whose unrecall'd Decree
You date, bring, execute; making what's new
Ill and good, old, for as we die in you,
You die in Time, Time in Eternity.

Christian Morgenstern

THE LOCAL AUTHORITIES

Korf receives a questionnaire,
An angry note from the police
Which asks: Who are you? How? And where?

Your past addresses, if you please.
Married? Yes? If not, why not?
Place of birth? Baptismal fees?

Do the authorities allot,
Assign, or otherwise permit . . .?
And what religion have you got?

Should these answers fail to fit,
The above is subject to arrest.
Signatures: Borowsky, Schmitt.
Korf then gets it off his chest,
In brief: "Dear Sirs: This certifies
Officially that the above addressed,

Otherwise human, merchandise
Has checked himself at his own expense
And does respectfully apprize

The precinct that, in the proper sense
And spirit of the cited Act,
He is non-existent, thus . . . and hence. . . .

Etcetera . . . and to be exact . . .
Must here regretfully aquaint
The local authorities with that fact.

Yrs. Korf." The missive duly sent
The clerk in charge who reads the tract
Is plunged into deep bewilderment.

Translation from German by Christopher Collins

Douglas Worth

BOURGOGNE

We saw too many Christs—his death became
part of the landscape, like the hanging-tree
pictured in every tenth-grade history—
a heritage, no one of us to blame.

Prague broke as we left Autun; Daley's men
butchered our stay in Paris, hounding us
till all that lifting harmony of glass
and stone at Sainte Chapelle had seemed undone.

Back in New York, *The Times* feels heavy, day
skids by on squealing rubber—as we'd feared
things were not changed by nights when stars appeared
so close our hands might have brushed them away,
or noons of sunlight where we lay and fed
each other's honied mouths with wine and bread.

Anonymous

THE SEAFARER

What I know, I shall launch in this stave[1]—
  Truth, from tired days.
The trailing hours, toilsome and grave,
  When the heart says:—
"All ships are keeps of care, islands of fear,
In the heavy bright water!"
                    But night hid the clear
When we knocked past the cliffs—
Strait was the watch of old
Which found me at the stern in the pining cold,
My feet chained down with ice.—But burning care
Boiled round my heart.—And hunger often files
Its way in flesh.—
          O, when a man finds fair
Fortune on the isles,
He has then no thought for these rime-cold
Sliding seas of winter where I spend
This exile and tract of life! —Dead is my friend.
Icicles hang around me.—Hail is flung in the air!—
  Only the crawling of the wave
  I heard, and the ice-bound surges die.
Sometimes the swan would be so brave
  As, in her lonely way, to cry.

[1]Poem

I made gay thoughts out of gannet's notes,
    I held the puffin-bird could smile:
The sea-mew was singing instead of the throats
    In the mead-hall, that beat up a ballad erewhile.
Storms struck the stone-cliffs as the tern
    With her dewy feathers screamed above.
Over and over answered the erne
    With icy wings—
            No friend, no shelter of love
For the want in my heart!—
        So the burgher in lust
Who lives within great walls, engrossing joy,
    Happy and high with wine—drinks and does not trust
    This talk of sailing—
            While I live, weary!

It darkens. From the North
The curling snow steals forth.
The frost is on the land.
A smallish warning band
Of hailstones falls in chain—
The coldest kind of grain!
And the thought knocks my heart
To tempt those deep streams!

Often in the day
My wish tells me the way
Over the sport of the waves
To far lands!

O no man is proud yet in the earth,
   So gifted of heaven, so young or so hale,
So loved by his God, or so sure of his worth
   That he does not fear danger setting to sail!
He wonders how heaven will treat him.
   He hasn't the pleasure in gold
Nor the heart for a harp, nor the joy in a wife—

All the pastimes of earth are grown old—
He can think about only the rolling and strife
Of big waves beating the hold—
So his heart is fed with longing who wends to the blue and the cold!

The boughs take blossom, towns are gay,
The meadows green, and Spring's in train:
All these things urge me on my way
To seek the lonely floods again.
O vainly does the cuckoo sing
(The keeper of the gate of Spring)
Who pines my ear with her boding tone!

(A thing to happier men unknown
What exiles feel, who tempt strange ways
With danger!)
                As my mind turns back the days,
It leaves the breast, the locker-up of woes,
To cross the whale's wet country—yearns and goes
Where men live happy—comes once more to me
Dropping and sad—till the slow bird of the sea
That wheels alone; and presses me from rest,
Chides my ship on, to cross a new sea-crest!

The bliss of heaven is warm as a breath,
But this dead life is cold to my clay.
What Life thinks weal[2] is brushed away
Greedily, after a glance, by Death!

Ere a man die, three things suffice
To bring him to despair:—
Age or disease or feud efface
His keen life out of the air!

The firmest track a man may leave
Is in the thought of his land:
Then let him bring the Devil to grieve

²Health, well being

By the dear works of his hand,
That the children of men make a tale of him
And he hold heaven fast!

But such deeds are fled, Caesar is dead,
Kings look best in the past.
Lordship is nothing to the old days
When men lived in loyal fame.
The flower is fallen, this is the stubble,
Weak men walk in a world of trouble,
What was noble runs lame!

The deeds that were glory halt out of our ways
Like each man in our province called Earth who grows old:
When age creeps upon him and powders his head;
the hoar-pate mourns that his friend is dead,
A son of the great—ready of the mould!

See then, the body, when the life is ta'en,
May not taste sweetness, may not sense a sore,
Or raise a hand, or reason with its brain!
And though a man should place a thing of worth
Early beside his brother in the grave,
It climbs not with that soul, but rots in earth . . .

Fear towards God is great, 'twas he who framed
The strong roots of the world, and the plains for men,
The leaning sky. A fool who fears not is shamed,
Death comes in a moment and nooses him again.
But the humble man whose belief is sure
God will help to endure.

EXPERIENCING THE POEM

Reread for its immediate effect Robert Lowell's
"Myopia: A Night" (page 34).

CHAPTER 7
DENSE, SUBTLE, &
COMPLEX POETRY

Many of the poems we'll treat in this chapter will seem the reverse of those in the last, where we had to discover the metaphor in apparently artless description and expository argument. Here the elements of scene, time, place, and logic will frequently seem lost in a storm of metaphors, abstract images, symbols, and allusions. In the following poems things may get very complex, but there is nothing essentially new. In previous chapters we have seen basic techniques; here the techniques are pushed to extremes. It's really just a question of being alert to what we know because the experience of poetry is no different here from what it has been elsewhere: it's a matter of following the poet's particular strategy as he presents that experience.

First we have to penetrate the abstractions—the dense, perhaps confusing, and ambiguous images. Collections of words that don't mean anything, don't get at anything, certainly aren't poetic. Unless we can *find* the *X/Y*, we might only be able to say, "That was a strange sentence," or something to that effect. People sometimes claim to like a certain poem but, when pressed, admit that they have no idea what it's about, except they think "the images are interesting." Unless the poet is trying to make poetic relationships, to understand something, he is babbling like anyone else who makes no sense. As we hope you've seen throughout this book, poets are not madmen exempted from having to be coherent, but rather the reverse: When one leaves (even for the space of a single poem) the safety of his habits and daily "logic," he has to be especially keen and alert, and his intellect has to function smoothly right up to where intuition, insight, truth, or whatever we call it takes over. Without discoverable order there is no metaphoric action and, as a result, there is no poetry. So working with the subtleties and complexities of technique is the real problem here, not meaning. An insight, after all, isn't "hard" or "easy"; it simply *is*. Once the technique is grasped, insight can manifest.

The complex, far-reaching imagery in this contemporary love poem is structured partly by a central metaphoric relationship along the lines of: the speaker's love (X) is (like) the world, the universe (Y).

Stanley Kunitz

THE SCIENCE OF THE NIGHT

I touch you in the night, whose gift was you,
My careless sprawler,
And I touch you cold, unstirring, star-bemused,
That are become the land of your self-strangeness.
What long seduction of the bone has led you
Down the imploring roads I cannot take
Into the arms of ghosts I never knew,
Leaving my manhood on a rumpled field
To guard you where you lie so deep
In absent-mindedness,
Caught in the calcium snows of sleep?

And even should I track you to your birth
Through all the cities of your mortal trial,
As in my jealous thought I try to do,
You would escape me—from the brink of earth
Take off to where the lawless auroras run,

You with your wild and metaphysic heart.
My touch is on you, who are light-years gone.
We are not souls but systems, and we move
In clouds of our unknowing
                              like great nebulae.
Our very motives swirl and have their start
With father lion and with mother crab.
Dreamer, my own lost rib,
Whose planetary dust is blowing
Past archipelagoes of myth and light,

What far Magellans are you mistress of
To whom you speed the pleasure of your art?
As through a glass that magnifies my loss
I see the lines of your spectrum shifting red,
The universe expanding, thinning out,
Our worlds flying, oh flying, fast apart.

From hooded powers and from abstract flight
I summon you, your person and your pride.
Fall to me now from outer space,
Still fastened desperately to my side;
Through gulfs of streaming air
Bring me the mornings of the milky ways
Down to my threshold in your drowsy eyes;
And by the virtue of your honeyed word
Restore the liquid language of the moon,
That in gold mines of secrecy you delve.
Awake!
          My whirling hands stay at the noon,
Each cell within my body holds a heart
And all my hearts in unison strike twelve.

Considerations

The scene: The speaker is in bed beside his lover, reflecting on the gulfs between people. The poem TROPES (elaborates) on this. Overall, the central relationship is worked out straightforwardly, but certain metaphoric twists and turns are especially dense and subtle.

First, notice that the "you" of lines three and four is identified with "the land of your self-strangeness." This makes "you" an X term compared to the Y's "land" and "self-strangeness." So the speaker's lover is like an isolated world, "star-bemused." Another identification is also suggested: land (the earth, the world) with the heavens (stars). (This central relationship will be amplified in stanza two.) The rest of stanza one is clear enough metaphorically, though dense with connotations. Consider what the lines beginning "What long seduction of the bone" might mean. Among other things, is the bone identified as the body? Is the poet suggesting that the body essentially isolates us from one another? How does this connect with "the calcium snows of sleep"? Note that calcium is an interesting case of natural, nonliterary imagery. What is the effect on tone of this and technological expressions like "spectrum shifting red" later on?

In stanza two the speaker considers tracking his lover through the "land" (which is herself, her "self-strangeness"), but he sees she would escape him "from the brink of earth," where she becomes identified with the vast, intergalactic universe. Covertly, inner space is identified with outer, and the central relationship of lover as world/universe continues to unfold. With "metaphysic" the poet makes a direct reference to Donne and the metaphysical poets of the seventeenth century, and from here on he superimposes aspects of their metaphoric techniques onto his poem.

"We are not souls but systems" in the comparison to "great nebulae" expresses the mysterious motions and complexities of human personality and motive, and "systems," applied to stars, becomes a pun on human systems of thought, habit, behavior, etc. So star systems (X) are associated with human systems (Y). "Father lion" and "mother crab" refer, among other things, to the astrological signs Leo (the lion) and Cancer (the crab). Astrologers say that Leo is ruled by the sun (which gives life to the soul as well as to our solar system) and that Cancer is ruled by the moon (which shapes form and personality).

"My own lost rib" is an allusion obviously comparing the speaker's lover with Eve, who was formed from Adam's rib. In the next line, what is the lover's "planetary dust" like? Can you untangle this complex metaphor? Scientists have speculated that suns and world systems are formed from interstellar dust and, conversely, that this substance is the remains of novas, exploded stars. What are the "archipelagoes of myth and light"? Are her imaginations, mysteries, understandings, and dreams all possible Y terms here? The very swirlings of her "dust" are identified with "art." Why? Do you see any irony in identifying her with dust?

In the next lines the poet compares his vision of her to looking through a telescope ("that magnifies my loss"), revealing, once more, how far she is from him and how beautiful: he sees "the lines of [her] spectrum shifting red." If you recall, in the Donne "Valediction," we noticed a similar "impossible" distance between the associated terms. Astronomers say that the most distant stars are moving the fastest and therefore their light (seen through a spectroscope) shifts toward the red end of the visible spectrum. So the poet is saying that his lover is moving far away from him. What else do you get from "red"? In terms of the next two lines, what other levels work here?

In stanza four the narrator calls her back, again playing on the paradox that she is infinitely far away and yet right beside him. He sees the whole universe of her, and in her, and the resulting metaphoric tension has enormous suggestive power.

1. In stanza four how might "language of the moon" relate to "gold mines of secrecy"? Gold is the color of the sun. Is there a connection? What else?
2. How are the images in the last stanza connected to those in the previous stanzas?
3. On one level, the last two lines are a way for the narrator to say he loves his lover with his entire being. How does the metaphor tie clocks in with the poem as a whole?

Technical Notes

Most of the lines are iambic pentameter, linked—often distantly—by exact and slant rhyme.

*Here is another modern love poem. Again, technological and nonliterary images
are stressed. Try to get into this piece by keeping track of the local metaphors
that relate to the woman as the central metaphoric subject (an X with many Y's).*

Theodore Roethke

I KNEW A WOMAN

I knew a woman, lovely in her bones,
When small birds sighed, she would sigh back at them;
Ah, when she moved, she moved more ways than one:
The shapes a bright container can contain!
Of her choice virtues only gods should speak,
Or English poets who grew up on Greek
(I'd have them sing in chorus, cheek to cheek).

How well her wishes went! She stroked my chin,
She taught me Turn, and Counter-turn, and Stand;
She taught me Touch, that undulant white skin;
I nibbled meekly from her proffered hand;
She was the sickle; I, poor I, the rake,
Coming behind her for her pretty sake
(But what prodigious mowing we did make).

Loves like a gander, and adores a goose:
Her full lips pursed, the errant note to seize;
She played it quick, she played it light and loose;
My eyes, they dazzled at her flowing knees;
Her several parts could keep a pure repose,
Or one hip quiver with a mobile nose
(She moved in circles, and those circles moved).

Let seed be grass, and grass turn into hay:
I'm martyr to a motion not my own;
What's freedom for? To know eternity.
I swear she cast a shadow white as stone.
But who would count eternity in days?
These old bones live to learn her wanton ways:
(I measure time by how a body sways).

Considerations

1. Notice how a statement like "she's beautiful to the core" is pale and unmetaphoric beside "lovely in her bones." Compare the next line with its paraphrase: "she's very sensitive and seems a part of nature or in tune with it." What implications do the metaphors add in these lines? For example, we may paraphrase and say, "she's bright and has many forms." How does saying that she (X) is (like) a bright container (Y) extend the levels of meaning even just for the adjective "bright"?

2. In stanza two the narrator represents himself as a kind of house pet the woman is training; then the open metaphor (sickle and rake) concludes the section. What kinds of associations does the last line in this stanza touch off in you? What are the implications of mowing?

3. At the end of stanza three, what do you get out of "she moved in circles, and those circles moved"? We have run into the implications of circles before in Stevens' blackbird poem (page 23) and Donne's "A Valediction: Forbidding Mourning" (page 80).

4. In stanza four the narrator reflects on how her circles have enclosed him: "I'm martyr to a motion not my own." The next line suggests ideas about man being free to discover the eternal nature of his universe. In the stone metaphor, the speaker now considers something about the woman, his love for her, its metaphoric *deeper* meaning, its connection with eternity. As in the Kunitz poem, but from a different angle, the woman is beyond time and the mundane world. The poet reveals clearly that she herself is a metaphor for something else, an X with unstated Y's. With these considerations in mind, what do you make of the last three lines?

5. Do you detect any irony in this piece? If so, what effect does it have?

6. Consider any of the images or metaphors in relation to the poem as a whole.

Unlike the two previous poems, which seem complex at first glance, this one seems simple. But as we have seen in other examples of his poetry ("A Patch of Old Snow" and "The Road Not Taken"), Frost is often straightforward on the surface but extremely subtle underneath. When people say Frost wrote "nature poetry," they see only that he favored natural images that seem pure description, overlooking the fact that these images function as terms of dense, implicit, or covert metaphors. Here, as in "The Road Not Taken," we have a central subject, the oven bird (X). Y levels are implicit.

Robert Frost

THE OVEN BIRD

There is a singer everyone has heard,
Loud, a mid-summer and a mid-wood bird,
Who makes the solid tree trunks sound again.
He says that leaves are old and that for flowers
Mid-summer is to spring as one to ten.
He says the early petal-fall is past,
When pear and cherry bloom went down in showers
On sunny days a moment overcast;
And comes that other fall we name the fall.
He says the highway dust is over all.
The bird would cease and be as other birds
But that he knows in singing not to sing.
The question that he frames in all but words
Is what to make of a diminished thing.

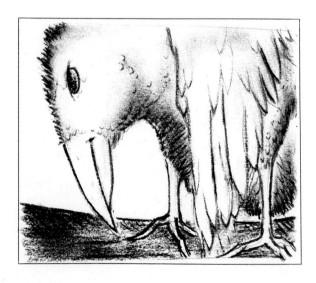

Considerations

1. Compare this poem with Keats's "To Autumn" in the last chapter. If the oven bird is a metaphoric subject here (*X*), does one of the unstated *Y*'s have something to do with becoming aware of time, the end of fullness, etc.? What are other *Y*'s?
2. Very often poets (like Frost) who write seemingly artless, descriptive poems use the pun as a way of setting up their *X/Y* relationships, letting us know these relationships exist. In the line beginning "And comes that other fall," can you see a pun? What relationships does it suggest?
3. The lines beginning "The bird would cease" present a little paradox: The oven bird is special; in singing, he doesn't sing. And the question that he frames is in "all but words." Could one level of this poem suggest intuition, insight? Could the bird reflect the poet himself trying to see the truth, trying to understand?
4. Why does the narrator say that everyone has heard the song of this bird?
5. Consider the three lines beginning "He says the early petal-fall." Could the poem on some levels be referring to the "ages (or seasons) of man"? Might these lines refer to being very young, when pain is keen and there is special vulnerability?
6. How does the last line relate to the rest of the poem? Consider the individual images in the poem. What levels do you find? How do they relate to the central subject?

Technical Notes

The poem is an irregularly rhymed sonnet with an OCTAVE and a sestet. The first eight lines set the stage, and the last six draw conclusions. The final two lines of the sestet appear as a separate unit of thought.

In this poem there is no scene or story, as in the previous three pieces. The framework of the piece (in the sense that scene and story are frameworks) is a structure of ideas about philosophy and religion. Concepts are personified and given concrete terms, and as you can see immediately, the poem extends far beyond its ideas. Images become metaphorically rich with meanings. It is worthwhile to read the poem rather slowly, letting the compact associations work on you.

Andrew Marvell

A DIALOGUE BETWEEN THE SOUL AND BODY

SOUL
O who shall, from this dungeon, raise
A soul enslaved so many ways?
With bolts of bones, that fettered stands
In feet; and manacled in hands:
Here blinded with an eye; and there
Deaf with the drumming of an ear:
A soul hung up, as 'twere, in chains
Of nerves, and arteries, and veins:
Tortured, besides each other part,
In a vain head, and double heart.

BODY
O who shall me deliver whole,
From bonds of this tyrannic soul?
Which stretched upright, impales me so,
That mine own precipice I go;
And warms and moves this needless frame
(A fever could but do the same);
And, wanting where its spite to try,
Has made me live to let me die:
A body that could never rest,
Since this ill spirit it possest.

SOUL

What magic could me thus confine
Within another's grief to pine?
Where whatsoever it complain,
I feel, that cannot feel, the pain.
And all my care itself employs,
That to preserve, which me destroys:
Constrained not only to endure
Diseases, but, what's worse, the cure:
And ready oft the port to gain,
Am shipwrecked into health again.

BODY

But physic yet could never reach
The maladies thou me dost teach:
Whom first the cramp of hope does tear;
And then the palsy shakes of fear:
The pestilence of love does heat;
Or hatred's hidden ulcer eat:
Joy's cheerful madness does perplex;
Or sorrow's other madness vex:
Which knowledge forces me to know;
And memory will not forgo.
What but a soul could have the wit
To build me up for sin so fit?
So architects do square and hew,
Green trees that in the forest grew.

Considerations

The metaphors here are dense, and so it might help if we untied a few of the "knotty" places. Step by step, let's look over this dialogue.

First, bones, which are *within* the flesh, are identified as "bolts." We think of bolts and bars around the *outside* of something, a prison or jail. Great metaphoric tension results from this minor paradox. At this stage, you should be able to grasp these metaphors fairly quickly, though the last two lines of the first stanza might puzzle you briefly. First, untangle the diction: Besides the body being a torture (for the soul) in every gross respect, the "vain head" (a reference, perhaps, to foolish, useless, or egotistical thinking, dreams, ideals, etc.) makes things worse. Unscrambled, we can say: "The soul is tortured by being *within* a 'vain head.'" In "double heart" there may be a specific philosophic reference to Plato, but what can we get directly from this image? Double-dealing? Deceiving? Dualistic feelings?

The next stanza takes up the body's point of view. Why is the soul "stretched upright"? This is a dense metaphor. On one level, the soul points upward, heavenward, is "upright" in every sense of the word. The body, being animalistic, wants to crawl. Since man "stretched" up by the soul is compelled to move upright, unlike the animals he alone is in danger of falling. Falling is an implied term of "precipice," suggesting the fall of man, falling low. The soul's effect is then compared to a fever, and the rest is obvious. In lines one and two of the third stanza there is a minor case of complex diction (the soul is the body's grief); in lines four, six, and seven there are several (sometimes humorous) paradoxes.

The last four lines of the final stanza are worth extra care. In effect, the soul (*X*) is blamed for making sin possible and so is compared to architects (*Y*). As well as standing for the soul, might architects also refer to something else? Can you see what it might be?

1. Does the final couplet really seem intended to win the body's argument? Does squaring and hewing suggest, perhaps, a valid and necessary purpose? Why does the poet say "green trees"? What does green suggest in this context? Why is the soul said to be the cause of sin here?
2. In the last four lines of stanza three, why is the "cure" so troublesome to the soul? What does the "port" refer to?
3. Consider the extent to which this poem goes beyond its structure of ideas. Does it convey a sense of truth to you even though you might disagree or find irrelevant its specific ideas of sin? Can you account for this? How do the metaphors go beyond the notion of sin?

Technical Notes

The poem is written in iambic tetrameter. The rhyme scheme is *a a b b c c*, etc.

As in the Marvell poem, it is partly the old-fashioned diction that gives this piece a difficult look.

Sir Philip Sidney

WHEN FAR-SPENT NIGHT

When far-spent night persuades each mortal eye,
To whom nor art nor nature granted light,
To lay his then mark-wanting shafts of sight,
Clos'd with their quivers, in sleep's armory;
With windows ope then most my mind doth lie,
Viewing the shape of darkness and delight,
Takes in that sad hue which the inward night
Of his maz'd powers keeps perfect harmony;
But when birds charm, and that sweet air which is
Morn's messenger, with rose enamel'd skies,
Calls each wight[1] to salute the flower of bliss,
In tomb of lids then buried are mine eyes,
    Forc'd by their lord, who is asham'd to find
    Such light in sense, with such a darken'd mind.

[1]creature.

Considerations

In stanza one, "mark-wanting" means arrows lacking a mark or target. Eyes are compared to these arrows, and they are stored in "sleep's armory."

In stanza two, "With windows ope" (the mind is covertly compared to a house), the narrator takes in dreams ("the shape of darkness"), the sad color and harmony of "inward night," the order of the "maz'd" (tangled, confused) dreams and visions. He is saying that in sleep, the pattern of dreaming moves in its own order, independent of consciousness.

In stanza three the narrator calls the sun "the flower of bliss." "Inward night" implies, among other things, a relationship between night and darkness as *ignorance*, ignorance of truth. The sun then suggests Y's referring to "enlightenment", heaven—and the whole poem gains a new unified level of metaphoric connections. Compare this with the Marvell piece we just went through. Look at "In tomb of lids." The body is again being represented as prisonlike. The flesh itself is cutting off the direct sight of the rising sun (God, truth, bliss, love, etc.,—recall "Almighty Sun" in "On a Drop of Dew"). But the flesh is "forc'd by their lord."

On *one* level, "Such light in sense" could be interpreted to mean that the senses (eyes) perceive the sunlight and waken to it—that the senses are illuminated—but that the mind remains dark to the reality *behind* this light.

1. Why is "their lord" ashamed?
2. Is sleep here being identified with death? Is the morn hinting at resurrection? Can you work out a death and resurrection scheme here?
3. Does the poem have a strong effect even in a direct way without reference to the subtle levels of meaning we touched on above?
4. What are the ironies in this piece?

Technical Notes

The poem is a sonnet with an octave, sestet and couplet. The rhyme scheme is *a b b a a b b a c d c d e e.*

In this poem we have a dramatic human situation expressed in a metaphoric scene. Notice how the elements of the physical picture of a beach are tied to abstractions.

J. C. Jacobs

WHAT EXISTS

A tidal wave of thought breaks,
rolls in foaming sequences.
Weary mind exhausted on the shore,
lid flipped partway open
admits an astral breeze.

Sharp, pointed, diamond-shaped,
senses glint like faces in the dark,
rocks and stars tumbling me together.
I'm getting there, I say, repeat
until the words lie flat on the pale beach.

Dunes catapult time
through dark, glittering grasses
along the ridge of hill,
inundating memories clung to in the vast night
under the white pebble of a moon.

Considerations

Thought is (like) a wave; onshore, the narrator is *out* of water (thought). What are the "lid" and the "astral breeze"? Notice the dead metaphor revived: "lid flipped partway open" suggests a touch of madness (the expression "flipped his lid"). Thought is exhausted, and with the narrator in an unusual mental state, the "astral breeze" blows in. "Astral" suggests stars, but also refers to the spirit, the soul or astral body, and is perhaps the star body, partly representative of the nuances of feeling and emotion. So a spiritual insight, vision, or state of some kind occurred after the speaker was hurled free of thought. But it is only a breeze, not a wind; just a hint.

In stanza two, the senses are sharp but altered and "glint like faces." The speaker is in a chaotic environment. The last four lines in this stanza are densely metaphoric. Can you work out the relationships?

In the last stanza, time is flung, as thoughts were in stanza one. The initial metaphor has been extended and altered. The speaker is drowned and tossed again; even on the "beach" memories (which are thoughts) are being inundated by the "grasses" and time. There is a sense that thought itself is inundating and fragmenting thought. There is no stability for the "weary mind," and the *cosmic scope* of all this is emphasized by the "white pebble of a moon."

1. Consider the phrase "rolls in foaming sequences." What does it suggest?
2. Look at the images of the poem, like "pale beach" and "moon." Are these *X*'s with *Y* levels?
3. How does the "pebble of a moon" relate to the rocks and stars in the second stanza?

Here we have an unusual dramatic contemplation of death. Instead of a scene, as in the last poem, the narrator arranges his metaphors around a sense of something, a mood.

W. S. Merwin

FOR THE ANNIVERSARY OF MY DEATH

Every year without knowing it I have passed the day
When the last fires will wave to me
And the silence will set out
Tireless traveller
Like the beam of a lightless star

Then I will no longer
Find myself in life as in a strange garment
Surprised at the earth
And the love of one woman
And the shamelessness of men
As today writing after three days of rain
Hearing the wren sing and the falling cease
And bowing not knowing to what

Considerations

1. The poem is based on the idea that we can have an anniversary for something that lies in the future. Is this logically possible? On one level, since the date of death is unknown, does this have the effect of making this anniversary (and death) always there?

2. Is silence associated with death in the first stanza? How? Silence is compared to a "tireless traveller" and to the paradoxical "beam of a lightless star." What is the effect of these comparisons?

3. In the second stanza the poet compares his life to a "strange garment." What or who, then, wears this garment, do you think? Is this a modern version of the old soul-body relation we saw in the Marvell dialogue and other poems?

4. At the end of the poem the narrator is struck by a suggestive natural event ("Hearing the wren sing and the falling cease"). Why does he bow "not knowing to what"?

This poem pictures something we have probably all seen. Can you find the metaphoric threads here? They are subtly buried in the description. The hidden metaphoric X's here are qualities rather than objects.

Denise Levertov

MERRITT PARKWAY

        As if it were
forever that they move, that we
    keep moving—

            Under a wan sky where
        as the lights went on a star
                pierced the haze and now
        follows steadily
                            a constant
        above our six lanes
        the dreamlike continuum . . .

And the people—ourselves!
        the humans from inside the
        cars, apparent
        only at gasoline stops
                                unsure,
            eyeing each other

                drink coffee hastily at the
            slot machines and hurry
        back to the cars
            vanish
            into them forever, to
            keep moving—

Houses now and then beyond the
sealed road, the trees / trees, bushes
passing by, passing
        the cars that
            keep moving ahead of

        us, past us, pressing behind us
                                and
                over left, those that come
            toward us shining too brightly
moving relentlessly

            in six lanes, gliding
        north and south, speeding with
        a slurred sound—

Considerations

1. How many things can you discover here that are "sealed" in or isolated in some way? What associations does this suggest?
2. How many things can you find that relate to "continuum," that is, things that go on and on? What are the implications of this?
3. How are the things that are sealed connected with things in continuum?

As we have said, you must grasp a poem's own peculiar "logic" order or to experience it. You have to orient yourself in the work's "environment" before you can go beyond anything and discover metaphoric richness.

Wallace Stevens

THE SENSE OF THE SLEIGHT-OF-HAND MAN

One's grand flights, one's Sunday baths,
One's tootings at the weddings of the soul
Occur as they occur. So bluish clouds
Occurred above the empty house and the leaves
Of the rhododendrons rattled their gold,
As if someone lived there. Such floods of white
Came bursting from the clouds. So the wind
Threw its contorted strength around the sky.

Could you have said the bluejay suddenly
Would swoop to earth? It is a wheel, the rays
Around the sun. The wheel survives the myths.
The fire eye in the clouds survives the gods.
To think of a dove with an eye of grenadine
And pines that are cornets, so it occurs,
And a little island full of geese and stars:
It may be that the ignorant man, alone,
Has any chance to mate his life with life
That is the sensual, pearly spouse, the life
That is fluent in even the wintriest bronze.

Considerations

Let's move carefully through this piece and uncover its structure. First, we quickly see that there is no story here and no argument, as in the Marvell dialogue. The structure is built instead on *concepts* that are animated and given form as vivid, natural images. Although these images may be private symbols, let's suppose there is no way to be sure of this and treat the poem on its immediate metaphoric level.

The poem opens with a comparison: "grand flights" to "Sunday baths" to "tootings at the weddings of the soul." "Grand flights" suggests an exceptional state but is tempered with possible irony. Can you see that? Thus flights of imagination, intuition, vision—or whatever—are linked with the most mundane of activities, and then both of these are linked with a slightly sarcastic statement about some kind of spiritual marriage. What kind of wedding might this be? To "toot" suggests the colloquial "blowing your own horn." The poet says these three things (grand flights, baths, and tootings) "occur as they occur," they are what they are, and happen as they happen. Taken as a unit, these three terms become an X added to "so bluish clouds/Occurred" (Y). So these occurrences are (like) the unpremeditated, natural, somehow inevitable appearance of clouds (a sense of inscrutable cosmic order?).

In lines four to six the leaves are rattling around the empty house. This natural image is associated metaphorically with "as if someone lived there." Why? Leaves move in the wind whether or not someone holds a lease. A subtle irony directs the reader: a human *pretension* (X) that events in the world somehow depend on us observing them happen is set against the fact that the universe goes on all by itself (Y). The house is empty and the occupants may be dead for all we know, but the clouds swell and fill, the flowers move, etc. Nature has taken no notice of human coming and going. Would it be at all consistent with the tone and direction of this piece to imagine that the motions suggest life and someone moving around the grounds? Why "gold" leaves? Look at the images in the last three lines of stanza one. What do they add to the concepts already developed?

So far the poem suggests concepts of transience and the incomprehensible process of reality, which might seem random to our eyes:, Such as the Bluejay "suddenly" swooping to earth. Following this image is a symbol, operating as a metaphor: the wheel. The sun is compared to a wheel, and the shape and function of a wheel set up X/Y: endless turning (as in the expression, the sun "wheels" through the sky); a circle (which has no beginning); the wheel of fortune; samskara, the Hindu wheel of birth and death, being and decay; etc. And "the wheel survives the myths": The pure *fact* of the sun and its motion marking off time and the seasons outlasts all man's stories about it, all human theories and imaginings, perhaps humanity itself. Notice that the irony is unrelenting all through the piece. From the "fire eye" Stevens shifts (and makes an implicit comparison) to the dove's eye. Now one of the poet's imaginative "flights" or "tootings" occurs. Why "pines," "cornets," and the "little island"?

The structure is finally delineated completely in the last four lines: The "ignorant man" (ignorant of what?), without ideas, theories, or imaginings

and living the rhythm of reality without imposing on it, perhaps can "mate his life with life," unite with the actual flux and flow of existence and become one with the fierce sun and occurring clouds. Recall here "weddings of the soul." The "sensual, pearly spouse" intensely personifies a way of living which is finally said, in effect, to flow smoothly and easily in even the coldest moments.

1. What might "bronze" imply here? A work of art?
2. Linking pines with cornets results in a metaphor which connects with "tootings." How? Why do you think the poet wants to make this connection here?
3. Do you think the "ignorant man" is really meant to be considered ignorant? In what sense is he ignorant, then? Is there irony here as well?
4. What levels might the empty house signify?
5. Is the one who thinks of the dove, etc., the "ignorant man," or is he being ironically contrasted with him?
6. The poet, when he imagines cornets, etc., is "tooting" himself. Does Stevens suggest that the poet goes *beyond* imagination in making his metaphors and that he contacts this reality? Then why should the poet be the "ignorant man"? Any new experience of life obviously can be had only *when* it occurs. Could Stevens really be talking about the disparity between the actual experience and what you can *say* about it?
7. Who is the "sleight-of-hand man"? Could it be the poet? How does the poem suggest this? In the title, is "sense" meaning, intelligence, or *perceptions*? All three? How about "sense" as in "sense of humor"?

Technical Notes

The poem is written in free verse; internal and slant rhymes are used.

Again, we have the themes of love and human mortality. What makes the piece seem dense is the poet's tendency to present abstract images and statements— (X) terms—as though they were facts, objects. Compare this with the Kunitz poem. Is the irony sharper here?

W. H. Auden

LULLABY

Lay your sleeping head, my love,
Human on my faithless arm;
Time and fevers burn away
Individual beauty from
Thoughtful children, and the grave
Proves the child ephemeral:
But in my arms till break of day
Let the living creature lie,
Mortal, guilty, but to me
The entirely beautiful.

Soul and body have no bounds:
To lovers as they lie upon
Her tolerant enchanted slope
In their ordinary swoon,
Grave the vision Venus sends
Of supernatural sympathy,
Universal love and hope;
While an abstract insight wakes
Among the glaciers and the rocks
The hermit's sensual ecstasy.

Certainty, fidelity
On the stroke of midnight pass
Like vibrations of a bell,
And fashionable madmen raise
Their pedantic boring cry:
Every farthing of the cost,
All the dreaded cards foretell,
Shall be paid, but from this night
Not a whisper, not a thought,
Not a kiss nor look be lost.

Beauty, midnight, vision dies:
Let the winds of dawn that blow
Softly round your dreaming head
Such a day of sweetness show
Eye and knocking heart may bless,
Find the mortal world enough;
Noons of dryness see you fed
By the involuntary powers,
Nights of insult let you pass
Watched by every human love.

Considerations

1. Notice the abstract images and statements like "fashionable madmen" and "tolerant enchanted slope." Stevens makes images work as concepts. What is Auden doing here?
2. Notice in stanza two the contrast of the lovers, who are *concretely* acting out sensuality and see the "grave" vision, the serious truth of universal love, with the hermit, who is acting out resistance to carnal urges *abstractly* and feels the "sensual ecstasy." What sort of things does this contrast imply??
3. Stanza three brings back the theme of stanza one: Life is ephemeral. No matter what is said or done, it dies out from under us. So *love* is all

we really have. Who might the "fashionable madmen" be? Scholars, scientists, analysts, textbook authors?
4. In stanza two, whose is the "tolerant enchanted slope"? Why are there "glaciers and the rocks"? What do these images implicitly contrast with?
5. In stanza three, what are the "dreaded cards"?
6. In stanza four, take apart the metaphor in "noons of dryness." What are the Y levels? What or who are the "involuntary powers"?
7. How do the last two lines relate to the rest of the poem?

Allusions twisted into shocking, violently juxtaposed images make this poem seem complex.

David Posner

IN DAVID HOCKNEY'S STUDIO

Jean Harlow's nailed in the alcove,
Her belly bursting like the bloated
Flowers that don't make a garden
Five stories above the beach. Shall I jump?
If I land in water, I'll swim awhile.
But it's rock from here to there.
A black cat stands on white steps below us
Licking her whiskers. The hungry portrait of
Mr. Isherwood lies trapped
Between his bowl of fruit and withered books.
Who will write a prayer for Christopher
Like old Soutine with his butcher's eye
Lunging at every passing saint,
Hanging himself every week on his hooks,
Drawing blood from a piece of rotten meat,
Until each maggot turns into a fly.
The snakes are singing around my feet!
Goodnight, David, I'll dance the way you paint.

Considerations

1. The first line makes a complex covert comparison between Jean Harlow (the actress of the thirties who died from uremic poisoning following an abortion, when her mother, out of religious beliefs, refused to call in a doctor) and Christ crucified. She is nailed in an alcove like a crucifix. The poem suggests that a picture or painting of her is nailed there, of course. Perhaps it's painted so that her belly appears to be bursting. What do you get from the comparison of "belly" to "bloated flowers" and the "garden"? Is the last an allusion-symbol?

2. Do you think there is any significance to the fact that the narrator sees a black cat on the steps?

3. The portrait of Christopher Isherwood (a religious writer) is "hungry." Hungry for what? Why is he "trapped/Between his bowl of fruit and withered books"?

4. Soutine was partial to painting hunks of raw meat as well as gross-looking portraits (the poet suggests) that turned men into "meat." Can you get the drift of the metaphor from this? What is the connection to Isherwood?

5. Why are the snakes "singing" around his feet?

6. Do you see a kind of underlying logic to the way the poet makes his associations, relating Harlow to the cat to Isherwood to Soutine to the snakes?

This poem seems to be a kind of musing interior monologue in which statements of mundane facts are mixed with sudden, vivid imaginings. The difficulty is seeing how these are related.

John Berryman

DREAM SONG 176

All that hair flashing over the Atlantic,
Henry's girl's gone. She'll find Paris a sweet place
as many times he did.
She's there now, having left yesterday. I held
her cousin's hand, all innocence, on the climb to the tower.
Her cousin is if possible more beautiful than she is.

All over the world grades are being turned in,
and isn't that a truly gloomy thought.
All over the world.
It's June, God help us, when the sight we fought
clears. One day when I take my sock
off the skin will come with it

and I'll run blood, horrible on the floor
the streaming blood reminds me of my love
Wolves run in & out
take wolves, but terrible enough
I am dreaming of my love's hair & all her front teeth are false
as were my anti-hopes.

Considerations

The hair in the first line stands for the whole girl (see SYNECDOCHE). She has flown to Paris. The first nine lines of the poem contain personal, rather pedestrian comments on life: Henry liked Paris; his girl will like it; the speaker was out with her beautiful cousin; all over the world semesters are ending. Then, "God help us, when the sight we fought clears." Here, implicitly, all the trivial events of life (X) are being compared to sight (Y). As we have seen in many poems, sight suggests such things as knowing, illumination, and realization.

1. In stanza two another mundane image, "When I take my sock off," becomes a metaphor of death (among other things); how is

this put in an X/Y relationship with "my love"?

2. Can you see how the image of wolves is made a covert metaphor? What do these sudden, savage animals of death (and sexuality) suggest? It's very unspecific, but can you feel the violent shift of tone in the poem?

3. Can you unscramble the diction in the last two lines? Is the poet really Henry here? How would that interpretation alter "dreaming of my love's hair"? In these two lines notice the contrast of hair (X) to false teeth (Y)—the illusions of the world versus the ugly truth. Does the "sight" of these things suggest death? Why does the poet say "anti-hopes"? Resistance to hope? Hope *reversed* suggests despair. Would "as were my despairs" work here?

Read this poem over a few times. Try to become aware of the abbreviated references in scene and story, oblique allusions, and compressed and submerged metaphor.

   We have to be careful not to read too much into a poem of this type. We want to work with the levels that are "logically" there, and we need to discover the piece's internal order.

Robert Lowell

THE DEATH OF THE SHERIFF

"Forsitan et Priami Fuerint Quae Fata,
Requiras?"[1]

I

NOLI ME TANGERE[2]

We park and stare. A full sky of the stars
Wheels from the pumpkin setting of the moon
And sparks the windows of the yellow farm
Where the red-flanneled madmen look through bars
At windmills thrashing snowflakes by an arm
Of the Atlantic. Soon
The undertaker who collects antiques
Will let his motor idle at the door
And set his pine-box on the parlor floor.
Our homicidal sheriff howled for weeks;

---

[1]"No doubt you'll have me tell how Priam met his fate?"

[2]Do not touch me.

We kiss. The State had reasons: on the whole,
It is acted out of kindness when it locked
Its servant in this place and had him watched
Until an ordered darkness left his soul
A *tabula rasa*; when the Angel knocked
The sheriff laid his notched
Revolver on the table for the guest.
Night draws us closer in its bearskin wrap
And our loved sightless smother feels the tap
Of the blind stars descending to the west
To lay the Devil in the pit our hands
Are draining like a windmill. Who'll atone
For the unsearchable quicksilver heart
Where spiders stare their eyes out at their own
Spitting and knotted likeness? We must start:
Our aunt, his mother, stands
Singing *O Rock of Ages*, as the light
Wanderers show a man with a white cane
Who comes to take the coffin in his wain,[3]
The thirsty Dipper on the arc of night.

[3]Wagon; also another name for the Big Dipper.

Considerations

Where is the poem set? What is the locale? We
have the outdoors, nighttime, a farm or farm area,
a state institution for the criminally insane ("red-
flannelled madmen"; "the State had reasons . . .
had him watched"; "homicidal sheriff"). If the
poet just presented the facts of the case here as a
story, wouldn't the very impact of the abstract
vision be vitiated?

What is the story, if any? Are there two lovers?
A brother and sister? In any case, one, possibly
both, is cousin to the dead sheriff ("our aunt, his
mother"), have driven up to witness the undertaker's removal of the body. They sit and
watch. They kiss.

The poem takes this experience as a central
metaphoric subject and (1) makes literary, religious, and classical allusions to add dimensions to
it; (2) intensifies everything by surprising turns
and contrasts of local metaphor; and (3) leaves out
literal connections, thereby forcing us immediately
to the metaphoric level.

Without trying to be exhaustive, let's look at
some of the ways the metaphors connect with the
basic "plot." They have parked. "A full sky of the

stars" is a slightly fresher way of saying "a sky full
of stars," which is an obvious cliché. This way
Lowell's line suggests that the sky somehow be-
longs to the stars. The stars are wheeling, moving
against the "pumpkin setting of the moon." The
moon is being compared to a pumpkin. Why? This
suggests autumn for one thing—pumpkins in the
field, the yellowish color of the moon seen in the
northern latitudes around Indian summer. Perhaps
you also feel secondary implications of jack-o'-
lanterns, the grotesque, Halloween, witches, and
darkness. The farm (yellow too) is illuminated,
and the madmen look "At windmills thrashing
snowflakes" near an extension of the ocean. Why
windmills? They might imply flailing aimlessly in
circles as a connection to the madmen and various
general human states of flailing aimlessly in circles
and/or a possible literary reference to Don Quix-
ote, a "madman" himself. Then why "snowflakes"?

The undertaker who "collects antiques" (possible irony) arrives. The couple kisses (in what
sense?), and the speaker reflects. What is the tone
of this reflection? How does he seem to feel about

the "State"? Is "State" metaphoric? A pun? What is the "ordered darkness"? Death? If so, what about death? *Tabula rasa* means a void, a clean slate, and so, doubtless, death has wiped his soul clean. At birth one's mind is said to be a *tabula rasa*. By context the Angel is probably the Angel of Death. Why has the poet introduced this image? The man died—why say that death "knocked" and that the sheriff put his gun on the table? Next, night is compared to a "bearskin wrap," suggesting heaviness and intimacy, and the two are deep in this "loved sightless smother" of close darkness, which may be a version of death too. But what other meanings does this image suggest? This "sightless smother feels the tap." Do the stars now seem to have something to do with the process of time and death? If the "sightless smother" is *not* a state of dying, then the stars "tap" it with time, which is here the mallet of death on one level. Is it that we love our darkness, our blindness to reality? Of course, as often before, there is no hope of a simple answer and no need for one. The windmill image returns (as the stars just did), and we have to deal with "Devil." There are various possible levels: the mythical Devil, the devil in ourselves, sex and the "fall" of man, perhaps the sheriff as a devil. Remember, the windmill thrashes snow but cannot get a grip on anything, and so maybe we are "laying" him in the pit (the grave? our own darkness?) and yet another bit of life is "draining" from us. But is it possible to work *too* hard with these lines?

Next we see that the heart cannot be searched or held (like quicksilver). How about the spiders here? What do they represent? The devil again?

The ego? You can't reduce the line to a statement, obviously. Notice "atone," for instance. The number of possibilities is large. Work through the last lines of this poem yourself.

Like many modern poems, the surface continuity here is broken up. If we couldn't piece together this continuity in some way do you think the poem would work metaphorically?

1. Why do you think the Dipper is "thirsty"? Who is the man with the white cane? Could he be a connection to "the tap of the blind stars" earlier? (Blind people use white canes.) What is the significance of the sheriff's mother singing *O Rock of Ages*?
2. If you know what the Latin title and epigraph mean, does it help you make contact with the poem?
3. Why might the poet have called the stars "light wanderers"? Has another *Y* meaning for them been suggested here? What have the stars been compared to throughout?
4. What have the windmills been associated with?
5. What is the significance of the fact that a sheriff is the subject of this poem?

Technical Notes

All but three of the lines are iambic pentameter. The rhyme scheme is *a b c a c b d e e d.*

You may read this poem, enjoy the images going by, and wonder what the poet is talking about. The poem is extremely dense, strewn with private symbols, and intensely oblique. But there is no technique here that we have not experienced before. Metaphor is pressed against metaphor, and for the piece to work on us effectively, we have to orient ourselves within the poem's structure. Read the work through more than once and try to perceive the "logic," the order.

William Butler Yeats

BYZANTIUM

The unpurged images of day recede;
The Emperor's drunken soldiery are abed;
Night resonance recedes, night-walkers' song
After great cathedral gong;
A starlit or a moonlit dome disdains
All that man is,
All mere complexities,
The fury and the mire of human veins.

Before me floats an image, man or shade,
Shade more than man, more image than a shade;
For Hades' bobbin bound in mummy-cloth
May unwind the winding path;
A mouth that has no moisture and no breath
Breathless mouths may summon;
I hail the superhuman;
I call it death-in-life and life-in-death.

Miracle, bird or golden handiwork,
More miracle than bird or handiwork,
Planted on the star-lit golden bough,
Can like the cocks of Hades crow,
Or, by the moon embittered, scorn aloud
In glory of changeless metal
Common bird or petal
And all complexities of mire or blood.

At midnight on the Emperor's pavement flit
Flames that no faggot feeds, nor steel has lit,
Nor storm disturbs, flames begotten of flame,
Where blood-begotten spirits come
And all complexities of fury leave,
Dying into a dance,
An agony of trance,
An agony of flame that cannot singe a sleeve.

Astraddle on the dolphin's mire and blood,
Spirit after spirit! The smithies break the flood,
The golden smithies of the Emperor!
Marbles of the dancing floor
Break bitter furies of complexity,
Those images that yet
Fresh images beget,
That dolphin-torn, that gong-tormented sea.

Considerations

First, we must consider the title. As mentioned before (page 56), "Byzantium" had special significance for Yeats. Without getting into that, however, the poem itself suggests a kind of fantasy scene: golden towers, exotic works of art, fantastic beings and creatures.

It is night. The "images of day recede," but, "unpurged," they still haunt the scene. Day and night are opposed, and we sense that each has a meaning, although perhaps these meanings never become completely clear; however, we get some idea of them just from everything that is associated with night. Day is obviously not the time when the visions in the poem manifest. Night might have something to do with a visionary consciousness which day tends to blot out. So the images "recede," and night subtleties begin. First, the "Emperor's drunken soldiery" are retired. They are not part of the time of shadows and of less "realistic" perceptions of things. Now we hear the "night-walkers' song." Who are the night-walkers? Perhaps poets as well as anyone else who moves and "sings" in the mysterious "night" of visionary consciousness.

"A starlit or a moonlit dome" is an X term seeking Y's and is contrasted with "all that man is." A dome is an artifact, a kind of work of art, and seems meant to *symbolize* something as well as suggesting levels of purity and beauty. In any case, we certainly can find Y relationships from the context of the comparison to man: man is "merely" complex; his blood is (like) raging mud. Passion is "fury," and "mire" is thick and dull and touches on human impermanence, decay, the very substance of earth. The starlit dome is (like) something pure, calm, lasting in its perfect simplicity, and "disdaining" the limitations of flesh.

In stanza two the speaker, within this night environment, sees an image before him, a man or the shade of a man—not a man of blood and mire, but possibly that which is left when the body (the earthly) falls away. The speaker adds that it is "more image than a shade"—a pure form. (Note how this relates to the dome in stanza one.) So this image is not even necessarily distilled from man (as a shade would be), but somehow was never a part of earth or day.

Already we begin to see that Yeats, in this sense, is working out a familiar structure: the spirit versus flesh contrast we have seen so much of. His structural elaborations happen to be so dense and evocative that the basic contrast is overwhelmed occasionally (at the same time there is constant, tantalizing metaphoric tension and suggestion), but this fundamental structure is always there, providing a track through the complex poetic territory.

Notice how Yeats adds metaphoric life to the allusion, Hades: he speaks of the "bobbin" of Hades, a bobbin that is (like) something characteristic of, or deriving from, Hades—that which winds and unwinds the "mummy-cloth" thread, thus disentangles some entanglement and opens up some (visionary) path. Where might this path go? Can you follow possible Y terms here? All this metaphorically expresses the spiritual deadness in man's physical life, mind, and "day" vision of the world.

The next statement in the stanza may suggest someone in a kind of trance, a breathless yogic state of spiritual perception in which a "breathless mouth" can call up the "image," the thing "superhuman," neither dead nor alive: the eternal vision beyond what lives and dies.

In stanza three, can you see how the "miracle, bird or golden handiwork" is related to the "image" of stanza two and the "dome" of the first stanza? What references or allusions can you associate with the Golden Bough here (see page 57)? This image can crow "like the cocks of Hades" (mystery, death, the classical underworld, reflecting back to the previous stanza) and, when "by the moon embittered," can mock the "complexities of mire and blood," of physical existence. So the body-soul contrast is still being extended and explored.

In the fourth stanza the symbolic hour of midnight arrives. Strange fires burn with paradoxical heatless flames that are self-sustaining, feeding on no substance. Now "blood-begotten [mortal] spirits come" and leave their "complexities of fury" (mortality) behind. In other words, during that trance with "breathless" mouth, the pure, time-free, immortal spirit leaves all the misery and confusion and comes to the heatless, imperishable flame, the visionary fire. What does the "dance" suggest to you here?

In stanza five the dolphin* is a symbol acting metaphorically. It rides the waves of the sea of— what? The flood is obviously a metaphor for something here. If it were a literal sea, the poem would suddenly seem flat and meaningless. Clearly the dolphin's "mire and blood" refers to the physical world again. The spirits ride them through waters that the "golden smithies" *break*. The smiths connect with the creation of the "miracle, bird or golden handiwork" (and the dome). What else might they suggest? They are breaking the furious sea. Waves break, of course, but we associate smiths with pounding on anvils, and so the two meanings are united. Are they freeing men's souls from mire and complexity by smiting the flood? The "marbles of the dancing floor" (where the trance/dance takes place) suggest more handiwork. In stanza four, where we had "Dying into a dance," dance implied harmonious, unified motion and, in context, cosmic harmonies. Now the images (marbles) that are associated with the dance (and so with cosmic simplicity, perfection) are breaking (up) the mortal furies. With the line "Fresh images beget," the images that stream from images, the smiths, the marbles, all are affecting or transforming the bitter "complexity."

Perhaps at the end we experience the sea in association with a vision of all life, the whole motion of worldly existence—all the complex turmoil being torn by the dolphins, their flesh, their

*In a Greek legend, Arion was saved from drowning by a dolphin.

"mire and blood," as the spirits (aspiration, perfection, simplicity?) ride them on and on, the whole unimaginable image shuddering from the spiritual ringing of the gong. (Go back to the "great cathedral gong" in stanza one.)

To repeat, this is *one* way of relating to this piece. No structural examination or explication can explain this poem any more than it can explain or reduce any metaphoric insight into ordinary language. Here we have tried to indicate an expeditionary track through the often bewildering density. We have purposely avoided discussing Yeats's private symbols since any poem first has to be dealt with as it stands. We first have to establish a frame of reference, something the intellect can get a grip on; otherwise, the images are wasted, in a way, and the mind beats its wings in a vacuum. Extraordinary images without familiar connections have no metaphoric impact.

1. Can you provide alternative levels to the ones mentioned above for the major images in this poem: the "image," the bird, dolphins, smiths, etc.?

2. In stanza one, why does the speaker say "unpurged" images? What is implied about these images?

3. What are the levels in "moon embittered" in stanza three? As we have seen in other poems, the moon is often associated with mutability, change. How does this relate here?

4. What are other levels in the "marbles of the dancing floor"? Why do they break the misery of mortality ("bitter furies of complexity")? How are they associated with the images of the bird, the gong, etc?

5. Trace the development and relationships established by any image in the poem. Can you come up with a different track from the one we followed above? What new meanings do you find?

6. Why do you think Yeats is so concerned with image in this poem? Does the word "image" become a metaphor itself?

7. This poem, with all its meaning and insight, comes close to incoherence. Perhaps by considering how this piece finds its order, you may come upon a new understanding of the nature of poetry itself.

8. Compare this poem with "Sailing to Byzantium" (p. 317); pay particular attention to the latter's fourth stanza.

Here is another Yeats poem, not quite as dense as the last. See whether you can get into it yourself.

William Butler Yeats

COOLE PARK AND BALLYLEE

Under my window-ledge the waters race,
Otters below and moor-hens on the top,
Run for a mile undimmed in Heaven's face
Then darkening through 'dark' Raftery's 'cellar' drop,
Run underground, rise in a rocky place
In Coole demesne[1], and there to finish up
Spread to a lake and drop into a hole.
What's water but the generated soul?

Upon the border of that lake's a wood
Now all dry sticks under a wintry sun,
And in a copse of beeches there I stood,
For Nature's pulled her tragic buskin[2] on
And all the rant's a mirror of my mood:
At sudden thunder of the mounting swan
I turned about and looked where branches break
The glittering reaches of the flooded lake.

Another emblem there! That stormy white
But seems a concentration of the sky;
And, like the soul, it sails into the sight
And in the morning's gone, no man knows why;
And is so lovely that it sets to right
What knowledge or its lack had set awry,
So arrogantly pure, a child might think
It can be murdered with a spot of ink.

Sound of a stick upon the floor, a sound
From somebody that toils from chair to chair;
Beloved books that famous hands have bound,
Old marble heads, old pictures everywhere;
Great rooms where travelled men and children found
Content or joy; a last inheritor
Where none has reigned that lacked a name and fame
Or out of folly into folly came.

A spot whereon the founders lived and died
Seemed once more dear than life; ancestral trees,
Or gardens rich in memory glorified
Marriages, alliances and families,
And every bride's ambition satisfied.

[1]Domain
[2]A buskin is a boot symbolizing Greek drama.

Where fashion or mere fantasy decrees
We shift about—all that great glory spent—
Like some poor Arab tribesman and his tent.

We were the last romantics—chose for theme
Traditional sanctity and loveliness;
Whatever's written in what poets name
The book of the people; whatever most can bless
The mind of man or elevate a rhyme;
But all is changed, that high horse riderless,
Though mounted in that saddle Homer rode
Where the swan drifts upon a darkening flood.

Considerations

1. How does the last line in the first stanza transform the description into metaphor?
2. In stanza two another description is made metaphoric by the line "Nature's pulled her tragic buskin on." How does this sudden personification affect you?
3. Since water has already been given "soul" significance, the view of the lake is acting metaphorically. This context makes us think of the swan as being a metaphoric term itself and not just a bird that happens to be in the landscape. At this point can you begin making associations with "swan"?
4. In stanza three the poet uses the same trick and declares the swan to be "another emblem"; that is, it is an *X* in search of *Y*'s. Again we notice Yeats doing what he did in "Byzantium": A bird stands for something supernally pure and unworldly. How does this affect any picture you may have formed of the scene?
5. In stanza four the scene changes totally: The rooms and artifacts invoked suggest various great works—a place of makers, artists, seers. The whole stanza, like the others, becomes an *X*. What sort of *Y*'s turn up?
6. In stanza five all history, individual and general, becomes condensed into a house and grounds. Compare this poetic condensing with, say, someone intellectually trying to sum up all history.
7. In stanza six the only really complex metaphoric action takes place in the last three lines. The poet says that times have changed and that the change does not please him, of course, but there is more. Can you see this? What is the "darkening flood" being identified with? In other words, on what is this "emblem" (metaphor) of perfection afloat?
8. Look at the individual images in the piece in relation to the large-scale metaphoric structures such as the swan or the water as soul.

In light of the previous discussions, try to work with the rest of the poems in this chapter. Delineate the scene that is set or the story (if any). Dig out the basic concepts and follow the metaphors into the structure to uncover the theme—what the piece is basically talking about. Then you can begin to go into it in depth.

William Butler Yeats

SAILING TO BYZANTIUM

I

That is no country for old men. The young
In one another's arms, birds in the trees
—Those dying generations—at their song,
The salmon-falls, the mackerel-crowded seas,
Fish, flesh, or fowl, commend all summer long
Whatever is begotten, born, and dies.
Caught in that sensual music all neglect
Monuments of unageing intellect.

II

An aged man is but a paltry thing,
A tattered coat upon a stick, unless
Soul clap its hands and sing, and louder sing
For every tatter in its mortal dress,
Nor is there singing school but studying
Monuments of its own magnificence;
And therefore I have sailed the seas and come
To the holy city of Byzantium.

III

O sages standing in God's holy fire
As in the gold mosaic of a wall,
Come from the holy fire, pern in a gyre°,
And be the singing-masters of my soul.
Consume my heart away; sick with desire
And fastened to a dying animal
It knows not what it is; and gather me
Into the artifice of eternity.

IV

Once out of nature I shall never take
My bodily form from any natural thing,
But such a form as Grecian goldsmiths make
Of hammered gold and gold enamelling
To keep a drowsy Emperor awake;
Or set upon a golden bough to sing
To lords and ladies of Byzantium
Of what is past, or passing, or to come.

°spin in a spiral

William Butler Yeats

LEDA AND THE SWAN°

A sudden blow: the great wings beating still
Above the staggering girl, her thighs caressed
By the dark webs, her nape caught in his bill,
He holds her helpless breast upon his breast.

How can those terrified vague fingers push
The feathered glory from her loosening thighs?
And how can body, laid in that white rush,
But feel the strange heart beating where it lies?

A shudder in the loins engenders there
The broken wall, the burning roof and tower
And Agamemnon dead.
                                Being so caught up,
So mastered by the brute blood of the air,
Did she put on his knowledge with his power
Before the indifferent beak could let her drop?

°Zeus (in Greek mythology, supreme ruler of gods and
men) transformed himself into a swan in order to rape
Leda, mother of Helen, who was reputed to have been
the cause of the Trojan War. Agamemnon was one of the
Greek leaders, slain by his wife's lover when he returned
home from the war with his mistress.

William Wordsworth

ODE: INTIMATIONS OF IMMORTALITY
FROM RECOLLECTIONS
OF EARLY CHILDHOOD

The Child is father of the Man;
And I could wish my days to be
Bound each to each by natural piety.

There was a time when meadow, grove, and stream,
The earth, and every common sight,
   To me did seem
   Apparelled in celestial light,
The glory and the freshness of a dream.
It is not now as it hath been of yore;—
   Turn wheresoe'er I may,
    By night or day,
The things which I have seen I now can see no more.

Earth fills her lap with pleasures of her own;
Yearnings she hath in her own natural kind,
And, even with something of a Mother's mind,
   And no unworthy aim,
   The homely Nurse doth all she can
To make her Foster-child, her Inmate Man,
   Forget the glories he hath known,
And that imperial palace whence he came.

Behold the Child among his new-born blisses,
A six years' Darling of a pigmy size!
See, where 'mid work of his own hand he lies,
Fretted by sallies of his mother's kisses,
With light upon him from his father's eyes!
See, at his feet, some little plan or chart,
Some fragment from his dream of human life,
Shaped by himself with newly-learned art;
   A wedding or a festival,
   A mourning or a funeral;
    And this hath now his heart,
   And unto this he frames his song:
    Then will he fit his tongue
To dialogues of business, love, or strife;
   But it will not be long
   Ere this be thrown aside,
   And with new joy and pride
The little Actor cons another part;
Filling from time to time his "humorous stage"
With all the Persons, down to palsied Age,
That Life brings with her in her equipage;
   As if his whole vocation
   Were endless imitation.

Thou, whose exterior semblance doth belie
     Thy Soul's immensity;
Thou best Philosopher, who yet dost keep
Thy heritage, thou Eye among the blind,
That, deaf and silent, read'st the eternal deep,
Haunted for ever by the eternal mind,—
     Mighty Prophet! Seer blest!
     On whom those truths do rest,
Which we are toiling all our lives to find,
In darkness lost, the darkness of the grave;
Thou, over whom thy Immortality
Broods like the Day, a Master o'er a Slave,
A Presence which is not to be put by;
Thou little Child, yet glorious in the might
Of heaven-born freedom on thy being's height,
Why with such earnest pains dost thou provoke
The years to bring the inevitable yoke,
Thus blindly with thy blessedness at strife?
Full soon thy Soul shall have her earthly freight,
And custom lie upon thee with a weight,
Heavy as frost, and deep almost as life!

    O joy! that in our embers
    Is something that doth live,
    That nature yet remembers
    What was so fugitive!

The thought of our past years in me doth breed
Perpetual benediction: not indeed
For that which is most worthy to be blest;
Delight and liberty, the simple creed
Of Childhood, whether busy or at rest,
With new-fledged hope still fluttering in his breast:—
      Not for these I raise
      The song of thanks and praise;
    But for those obstinate questionings
    Of sense and outward things,
    Fallings from us, vanishings;
    Blank misgivings of a Creature
Moving about in worlds not realised,
High instincts before which our mortal Nature
Did tremble like a guilty Thing surprised:
    But for those first affections,
    Those shadowy recollections,
   Which, be they what they may,
Are yet the fountain-light of all our day,
Are yet a master-light of all our seeing;
   Uphold us, cherish, and have power to make
Our noisy years seem moments in the being
Of the eternal Silence: truths that wake,
     To perish never:
Which neither listlessness, nor mad endeavour,
    Nor Man nor Boy,
Nor all that is at enmity with joy,
Can utterly abolish or destroy.
    Hence in a season of calm weather
    Though inland far we be,
Our Souls have sight of that immortal sea
    Which brought us hither,
    Can in a moment travel thither,
And see the children sport upon the shore,
And hear the mighty waters rolling evermore.

Then sing, ye Birds, sing, sing a joyous song!
    And let the young Lambs bound
    As to the tabor's sound!
We in thought will join your throng,
    Ye that pipe and ye that play,
    Ye that through your hearts to-day
    Feel the gladness of the May!
What though the radiance which was once so bright
Be now for ever taken from my sight,
    Though nothing can bring back the hour
Of splendour in the grass, of glory in the flower;
    We will grieve not, rather find
    Strength in what remains behind;
    In the primal sympathy

Which having been must ever be;
In the soothing thoughts that spring
Out of human suffering;
In the faith that looks through death,
In years that bring the philosophic mind.

And O, ye Fountains, Meadows, Hills, and Groves,
Forebode not any severing of our loves!
Yet in my heart of hearts I feel your might;
I only have relinquished one delight
To live beneath your more habitual sway.
I love the Brooks which down their channels fret,
Even more than when I tripped lightly as they;
The innocent brightness of a new-born Day
                    Is lovely yet;
The Clouds that gather round the setting sun
Do take a sober colouring from an eye
That hath kept watch o'er man's mortality;
Another race hath been, and other palms are won.
Thanks to the human heart by which we live,
Thanks to its tenderness, its joys, and fears,
To me the meanest flower that blows can give
Thoughts that do often lie too deep for tears.

Rainer Maria Rilke

DIE SONETTE AU ORPHEUS

Only one who has touched the lyre
Among the shadowy dead
Can tremble with and repeat
the unending praise.

Only one who tasted the poppy
Of darkness with the dead
Can sustain
The infinite and gentlest tone.

The image in the pond
may ever dissolve:
Know the image.
Only in the reflected world
Will soft voices endure.

Translation from German

Johann Wolfgang von Goethe

LIED UND GEBILDE

The Greek worried and wrung
Clay[1] into shape
His hands needing the pleasure
And weight of form.

But my delight is to trail
My fingers through the river
With open hands to flow
With all waters . . .[2]

When I have cooled the heat of song
It will sing itself;
When the poet's hand is washed pure
Water will shape itself.

Translation from German by Richard Monaco

[1]Clay is often used as a symbol for mortality, flesh.
[2]Water is often used as a symbol for the spirit.

Samuel Taylor Coleridge

KUBLA KHAN
OR, A VISION IN A DREAM

In Xanadu did Kubla Khan°
A stately pleasure-dome decree:
Where Alph, the sacred river, ran
Through caverns measureless to man
   Down to a sunless sea.
So twice five miles of fertile ground
With walls and towers were girdled round:
And there were gardens bright with sinuous rills,
Where blossomed many an incense-bearing tree;
And here were forests ancient as the hills,
Enfolding sunny spots of greenery.

But oh! that deep romantic chasm which slanted
Down the green hill athwart a cedarn cover!

°Kubla Khan, grandson of the mongol nomad chieftan
Genghis Khan, was the Emperor of China in the thir-
teenth century. He had a huge palace and game preserve
built at Shang-tu (which Coleridge called Xanadu) in
northeastern China.

A savage place! as holy and enchanted
As e'er beneath a waning moon was haunted
By woman wailing for her demon-lover!
And from this chasm, with ceaseless turmoil seething,
As if this earth in fast thick pants were breathing,
A mighty fountain momently was forced:
Amid whose swift half-intermitted burst
Huge fragments vaulted like rebounding hail,
Or chaffy grain beneath the thresher's flail:
And 'mid these dancing rocks at once and ever
It flung up momently the sacred river.
Five miles meandering with a mazy motion
Through wood and dale the sacred river ran,
Then reached the caverns measureless to man,
And sank in tumult to a lifeless ocean:
And 'mid this tumult Kubla heard from far
Ancestral voices prophesying war!
    The shadow of the dome of pleasure
    Floated midway on the waves;
    Where was heard the mingled measure
    From the fountain and the caves.
It was a miracle of rare device,
A sunny pleasure-dome with caves of ice!

    A damsel with a dulcimer
    In a vision once I saw:
    It was an Abyssinian maid,
    And on her dulcimer she played,
    Singing of Mount Abora.
Could I revive within me
Her symphony and song,
To such a deep delight 'twould win me,
That with music loud and long,
I would build that dome in air,
That sunny dome! those caves of ice!
And all who heard should see them there,
And all should cry, Beware! Beware!
His flashing eyes, his floating hair!
Weave a circle round him thrice,
And close your eyes with holy dread,
For he on honey-dew hath fed,
And drunk the milk of Paradise.

David Galler

WORDS FROM A CELL

For John Skelton

I have been neither here
Nor in the world you walk;
Nor known courage nor fear,
Though I have heard you talk.

But I have traveled through
The mists of the cigarette,
Tracking the fine print to
What memories beget.

And I have talked with those
Who never see me now,
Who say what I suppose
And hear what I allow.

And this, this is a world
Like yours, equipped with errors
But ritually unfurled
Each day to tame its terrors.

Like yours, this world will last
Until its dreamer flee
Invention grown too vast
And space too free.

George Herbert

THE PULLEY

When God at first made man,
Having a glass of blessings standing by,
Let us (said He) pour on him all we can.
Let the world's riches, which dispersèd lie,
Contract into a span.

So strength first made a way,
Then beauty flowed, then wisdom,
honour, pleasure.
When almost all was out, God made a stay,
Perceiving that alone of all His treasure
Rest in the bottom lay.

For if I should (said He)
Bestow this jewel also on My creature,
He would adore My gifts instead of Me,
And rest in Nature, not the God of Nature.
So both should losers be.

Yet let him keep the rest,
But keep them with repining restlessness.
Let him be rich and weary, that at least,
If goodness lead him not, yet weariness
May toss him to My breast.

John Donne

THE BROKEN HEART

He is starke mad, who ever sayes,
    That he hath been in love an houre,
Yet not that love so soone decayes,
    But that it can tenne in lesse space devour;
Who will beleeve mee if I sweare
That I have had the plague a yeare?
    Who would not laugh at mee, if I should say,
    I saw a flaske of *powder burne a day*?

Ah, what a trifle is a heart,
    If once into loves hands it come!
All other griefes allow a part
    To other griefes, and aske themselves but some;
They come to us, but us Love draws,
Hee swallows us, and never chawes:
    By him, as by chain'd shot, whole rankes doe dye,
    He is the tyran° Pike, our hearts the Frye.

If 'twere not so, what did become
    Of my heart, when I first saw thee?
I brought a heart into the roome,
    But from the roome, I carried none with mee:
If it had gone to thee, I know
Mine would have taught thine heart to show
    More pitty unto mee: but Love, alas,
    At one first blow did shiver it as glasse.

Yet nothing can to nothing fall,
    Nor any place be empty quite,
Therefore I thinke my breast hath all
    Those peeces still, though they be not unite;
And now as broken glasses show
A hundred lesser faces, so
    My ragges of heart can like, wish, and adore,
    But after one such love, can love no more.

°Tyrant

Anthony Hecht

THE END OF THE WEEKEND

A dying firelight slides along the quirt°
Of the cast-iron cowboy where he leans
Against my father's books. The lariat
Whirls into darkness. My girl, in skin-tight jeans,
Fingers a page of Captain Marryat,
Inviting insolent shadows to her shirt.

We rise together to the second floor.
Outside, across the lake, an endless wind
Whips at the headstones of the dead and wails
In the trees for all who have and have not sinned.
She rubs against me and I feel her nails.
Although we are alone, I lock the door.

The eventual shapes of all our formless prayers,
This dark, this cabin of loose imaginings,
Wind, lake, lip, everything awaits
The slow unloosening of her underthings.
And then the noise. Something is dropped. It grates
Against the attic beams.
                              I climb the stairs,
Armed with a belt.
                              A long magnesium strip
Of moonlight from the dormer cuts a path
Among the shattered skeletons of mice.
A great black presence beats its wings in wrath.
Above the boneyard burn its golden eyes.
Some small grey fur is pulsing in its grip.

°Riding whip with a short handle

Robert Browning

TWO IN THE CAMPAGNA

I wonder do you feel to-day
  As I have felt, since, hand in hand,
We sat down on the grass, to stray
  In spirit better through the land,
This morn of Rome and May?

For me, I touched a thought, I know,
  Has tantalised me many times,
(Like turns of thread the spiders throw
  Mocking across our path) for rhymes
To catch at and let go.

Help me to hold it! First it left
  The yellowing fennel, run to seed
There, branching from the brickwork's cleft,
  Some old tomb's ruin: yonder weed
Took up the floating weft,°

Where one small orange cup amassed
  Five beetles,—blind and green they grope
Among the honey-meal; and last,
  Everywhere on the grassy slope
I traced it. Hold it fast!

The champaign with its endless fleece
  Of feathery grasses everywhere!
Silence and passion, joy and peace,
  An everlasting wash of air—
Rome's ghost since her decease.

Such life there, through such lengths of hours,
  Such miracles performed in play,
Such primal naked forms of flowers,
  Such letting nature have her way
While heaven looks from its towers.

How say you? Let us, O my dove,
  Let us be unashamed of soul,
As earth lies bare to heaven above!
  How is it under our control
To love or not to love?

I would that you were all to me,
  You that are just so much, no more—
Nor yours, nor mine, nor slave nor free!
  Where does the fault lie? what the core
Of the wound, since wound must be?
°Web

I would I could adopt your will,
　　See with your eyes, and set my heart
Beating by yours, and drink my fill
　　At your soul's springs,—your part my part
In life, for good and ill.

No. I yearn upward, touch you close,
　　Then stand away. I kiss your cheek,
Catch your soul's warmth,—I pluck the rose
　　And love it more than tongue can speak—
Then the good minute goes.

Already how am I so far
　　Out of that minute? Must I go
Still like the thistle-ball, no bar,
　　Onward, whenever light winds blow,
Fixed by no friendly star?

Just when I seemed about to learn!
　　Where is the thread now? Off again!
The old trick! Only I discern—
　　Infinite passion, and the pain
Of finite hearts that yearn.

Philip Levine

ROBERT

October. From Simpson's hill
the great moon of stone
frowns in the rain. In the
fields below dark bruises
of spike stiffen into seed.
The cows are shuffling
behind me, back down
to the long chromium sheds
and the painless taking.

I watch an hour pass.
The darkness rises from
the floor of the valley
thickening the air between
branches, between stone
and tree, between my eyes
and what was here.

Now I'm in the dark.
I remember pages torn
from an automotive catalogue,
an ad once fallen from
heaven and hanging in
the city air—"It's never too late . . ."
If I follow my hands
will I feel the winter shake
the almonds into blossom?

Robert Huff

TRADITIONAL RED

Returning after dark, I thought,
The house will have grown small: noises
In the barn I knew, wood and field,
All tree tops visible. My eyes,
I thought, lied then or will lie now;
My ears, even my ears, will tell
Me: small. Then half awake I waited,
Half afraid of the sound light makes
With frost on windowpanes. But night
Birds carried fifteen years away
Like an abandoned nest, put them
To rest somewhere I couldn't see
Without undoing anything,
And when I woke the dawn I saw
Was on the farm as positive as God.

A rooster dipped in sunlight raised
His crown, called to the steaming barn,
Gigantic, red, until my blood
Roared for stupidity, and I
Ran down the path humble with hens
To kneel and stare dumb wonder
At his size. My pride! my pride! O
Jesus, bright dove call! I knelt there
In his thunder, white and small, watched
Him and rose to walk under trees
Whose tops I couldn't see for light,
Dense, golden, moving hosts of leaves
Answering that red cry. And when
I turned I saw the farm house roof
Raking an iron rooster through the sky.

Wallace Stevens

A POSTCARD FROM
THE VOLCANO

Children picking up our bones
Will never know that these were once
As quick as foxes on the hill;

And that in autumn, when the grapes
Made sharp air sharper by their smell
These had a being, breathing frost;

And least will guess that with our bones
We left much more, left what still is
The look of things, left what we felt

At what we saw. The spring clouds blow
Above the shuttered mansion-house,
Beyond our gate and the windy sky

Cries out a literate despair.
We knew for long the mansion's look
And what we said of it became

A part of what it is . . . Children,
Still weaving budded aureoles,
Will speak our speech and never know,

Will say of the mansion that it seems
As if he that lived there left behind
A spirit storming in blank walls,

A dirty house in a gutted world,
A tatter of shadows peaked to white,
Smeared with the gold of the opulent sun.

EXPERIENCING THE POEM

Reread Donne's "A Valediction: Forbidding
Mourning" (page 80) for its immediate effect.

CHAPTER 8
THE POEM ITSELF

How do we tell a good poem from a bad one, the great from the mediocre? Do kinds of metaphor make the difference? Does relative complexity or subtlety of technique make a "better" poem? How can we tell? Or *can* we tell?

It's human to want to evaluate, to judge, to be able to say what's good and what's not—to want to have "good taste." But as you may have realized, there can be no formula for determining what good poetry is because every reader is different and what affects one may leave another cold. If we like the poet's viewpoint or sentiments or find that he is expressing thoughts or feelings we have had ourselves, we may decide his poem is "great" because we identify with it. But someone else may not identify with it, and thus a conflict of taste develops. For example, consider this famous poem by an early-twentieth-century writer, Joyce Kilmer. What do you think of it?

TREES

I think that I shall never see
A poem lovely as a tree.

A tree whose hungry mouth is pressed
Against the earth's sweet flowing breast;

A tree that looks to God all day,
And lifts her leafy arms to pray;

A tree that may in summer wear
A nest of robins in her hair;

Upon whose bosom snow has lain;
Who intimately lives with rain.

Poems are made by fools like me,
But only God can make a tree.

Though many people like it, "Trees" has become a classic example of a "bad" poem. But how do we decide this? Critics, to support their distaste for the piece, point to logical inconsistencies in the metaphors: In stanza two the tree is a babe at the breast; in stanza three its branches are a girl's arms praying; in stanza four the branches are transformed into hair; and in stanza five the tree grows a bosom. Is consistency the key to excellence? Yes, the metaphors in "Trees" are inconsistent, but countless poems that critics consider outstanding also develop "illogical," inconsistent metaphors. Donne's "A Valediction: Forbidding Mourning," for instance, compares the souls of lovers to dying men, beaten gold, and a pair of compasses, and yet the poem is not criticized for this.

The real problem is less obvious; it is a question of seeing that the metaphors are basically presenting opinion, propaganda, and little else. The speaker says, in effect, "I want to prove to you that trees are lovely, and so I'll compare them to things I'm sure you believe are lovely: a girl praying, babies, and bosoms"—all of which reminds us of the politician insisting that he's pure as the American flag. Since most people already feel that trees are lovely, there is no real contrast between the *X* and *Y* terms. The metaphors are dead; they are just description or analogy, as if somebody had asked "What does a tree look like?" and the speaker had answered, "Like a girl lifting her arms to pray," and so on. And straining to make his point, the poet has rendered the images (tree as a mouth, hair full of birds) slightly grotesque. Since we *discover* nothing, we simply have description and opinion *disguised* as metaphor. Though the piece is printed as a poem, its contextual effect is more like that of an advertisement for God, trees, and beauty.

Further, as we have seen, the outlandish, inconsistent metaphors of a Donne or Stevens function within a framework of *tonal* consistency. Their poems are marked by playfulness, irony, and the uncovering of deep levels of meaning. Once you become aware that the tone of "Trees" is deadly serious and lyrical but that the levels are shallow, doesn't the verse seem silly?

As we have frequently observed, if a poem is just a fancy way of telling us what somebody believes, imagines, feels, or wishes were true, then there is no metaphoric experience, no insight. Remember "Ode on Melancholy" (page 9). This poem isn't trying to make us feel depressed or react sentimentally the way a romance, sob story or soap opera might; rather, it focuses on *seeing* melancholy, on providing an insight into it. Understanding the difference here may be very important to discrimination.

Obviously, some of the poems in this text go deeper than others. But how do we tell? Something isn't true just because lots of people (textbook writers, teachers, critics) think so, or false because they don't. Historically, generations of critics and students have often ignored or damned poets that later generations praised, and have praised what later generations found foolish or dull. Possibly this happens because time effaces the ideas, beliefs, and issues once considered important, thus leaving the poem itself. Poems that managed to go beyond the prejudices and issues of the day toward some profound intensity or metaphoric truth have endured, while others, however popular or important they may have seemed at the time, have faded away. This is as true of simple lyrics as it is of monumental epics.

So if there is no formula and no authority—and if even our personal opinions are suspect—what are we to do? First of all (we hope), we are investigating poetry not in order to pass judgment but rather to understand, to learn. We want to discriminate only in order to further our learning. It has been said the best poems can be read repeatedly without going stale. Though our opinions and feelings change over the years, some poems stay new because they obviously have great depth. Trying to develop taste by memorizing the opinions of "authorities" makes us secondhand as human beings and as readers. We don't have to do that when we can develop our own awareness and understanding. If we do, we won't need theories because we can see for ourselves. Only then can we answer the ancient question of why we should read poetry at all, what makes it worth the effort—because the answer lies in our own experience of the insight, awareness, clarity, depth, truth, and freshness that a poem has to offer.

A metaphor cannot work for us unless we first know what the terms mean. "My luve is like a red, red rose," says nothing if we don't know what a rose is. As we've seen, various poems require us to bring varying amounts of connotative and denotative knowledge to them if we expect to move into metaphoric understanding. In some pieces we had to have an idea of what certain illusions referred to. In "Science of the Night," for example, knowing something about astronomy and astrology added depth to the poem. But can we say that "Byzantium" is a better poem than "The Road Not Taken" just because Yeats's technique is more complex or claim that Frost's piece wins out by virtue of being more straightforward? Then what about "Trees"? Notice, however, that regardless of what techniques are used to evoke it, poetic insight is clearly a common denominator here. We can debate stylistics, aesthetics, and all like issues (which have their importance), but either we gain insight or we don't. There's no way to argue it into or out of existence. And isn't a poem's insight something we must *always* find on our own?

In this text we have divided poetry into categories so that the reader could become familiar with metaphoric language; however, *at this point bear in mind that these are imposed categories and should dissolve on contact with an actual poem.* We should not mistake a finger for the thing it is pointing at. Every poem is a unique union of subject matter and metaphoric technique and has (except in rare cases) to be understood as complete in itself, whether it employs local metaphor, central metaphoric relation, metaphoric subject, metaphoric image, argument, irony, paradox, symbol, or whatever. No matter what method is used, the result, as we have seen, stands outside anything we can say about it.

And there is really no system for getting this. If we have missed the poem's flow and magic, any interpretations we could make become empty, conditioned responses, and we simply impose our ideas and desires on the work and learn nothing from it. Since that "state of learning" is what we are actually after, in this chapter there are no categories, and you will have to read each poem here in its own unique terms. In a few cases we'll suggest some strategies for getting into the piece and some things to consider.

You might start to get into this poem by looking at the central metaphoric relationship stated in the first line.

Ezra Pound

PORTRAIT D'UNE FEMME

Your mind and you are our Sargasso Sea,
London has swept about you this score years
And bright ships left you this or that in fee:
Ideas, old gossip, oddments of all things,
Strange spars of knowledge and dimmed wares of price.
Great minds have sought you—lacking someone else.
You have been second always. Tragical?
No. You preferred it to the usual thing:
One dull man, dulling and uxorious,
One average mind—with one thought less, each year.
Oh, you are patient, I have seen you sit
Hours, where something might have floated up.
And now you pay one. Yes, you richly pay.
You are a person of some interest, one comes to you
And takes strange gain away:
Trophies fished up; some curious suggestion;
Fact that leads nowhere; and a tale or two,
Pregnant with mandrakes°, or with something else
That might prove useful and yet never proves,
That never fits a corner or shows use,
Or finds its hour upon the loom of days:
The tarnished, gaudy, wonderful old work;
Idols and ambergris and rare inlays,
These are your riches, your great store; and yet
For all this sea-hoard of deciduous things,
Strange woods half sodden, and new brighter stuff:
In the slow float of differing light and deep,
No! there is nothing! In the whole and all,
Nothing that's quite your own.
                    Yet this is you.

°The mandrake herb was believed to promote conception,
was used as a cathartic or as a narcotic and sleep induce-
ment, and was invested with human attributes.

Try seeing this poem in terms of the subliminal metaphoric relationship between two X's, time and friendship, and Y, financial transactions.

William Shakespeare

WHEN TO THE SESSIONS

When to the sessions of sweet silent thought
I summon up remembrance of things past,
I sigh the lack of many a thing I sought,
And with old woes new wail my dear time's waste:
Then can I drown an eye, unused to flow,
For precious friends hid in death's dateless night,
And weep afresh love's long since cancelled woe,
And moan the expense of many a vanished sight:
Then can I grieve at grievances foregone,
And heavily from woe to woe tell o'er
The sad account of fore-bemoanèd moan,
Which I new pay as if not paid before.
    But if the while I think on thee, dear friend,
    All losses are restored and sorrows end.

In this poem, the situation of the mower and every detail of that situation are metaphoric; some of the metaphors are explicit, others covert.

Andrew Marvell

DAMON THE MOWER

Hark how the Mower Damon sung,
With love of Juliana stung!
While everything did seem to paint
The scene more fit for his complaint:
Like her fair eyes the day was fair;
But scorching like his am'rous care:
Sharp like his scythe his sorrow was,
And withered like his hopes the grass.

"Oh what unusual heats are here,
Which thus our sunburned meadows sear!
The grasshopper its pipe gives o'er;
And hamstringed frogs can dance no more:
But in the brook the green frog wades;
And grasshoppers seek out the shades.
Only the snake, that kept within,
Now glitters in its second skin.

"This heat the sun could never raise,
Nor Dog Star[1] so inflames the days.
It from an higher beauty grow'th,
Which burns the fields and mower both:
Which made the Dog, and makes the sun
Hotter than his own Phaëton.[2]
Not July causeth these extremes,
But Juliana's scorching beams.

"Tell me where I may pass the fires
Of the hot day, or hot desires.
To what cool cave shall I descend,
Or to what gelid fountain bend?
Alas! I look for ease in vain,
When remedies themselves complain:
No moisture but my tears do rest,
Nor cold but in her icy breast.

"How long wilt thou, fair Shepherdess,
Esteem me, and my presents less?
To thee the harmless snake I bring,
Disarmëd of its teeth and sting:
To thee chameleons changing hue,
And oak leaves tipped with honey dew.
Yet thou, ungrateful, hast not sought
Nor what they are, nor who them brought.

"I am the Mower Damon, known
Through all the meadows I have mown.
On me the morn her dew distills
Before her darling daffodils:
And, if at noon my toil me heat,
The sun himself licks off my sweat:
While, going home, the evening sweet
In cowslip-water bathes my feet.

"What though the piping shepherd stock
The plains with an unnumbered flock,
This scythe of mine discovers wide
More ground than all his sheep do hide.
With this the golden fleece[3] I shear
Of all these closes every year.
And though in wool more poor than they,
Yet am I richer far in hay.

"Nor am I so deformed to sight,
If in my scythe I lookëd right;
In which I see my picture done,
As in a crescent moon the sun.
The deathless fairies take me oft
To lead them in their dances soft;
And, when I tune myself to sing,
About me they contract their ring.

[1] Sirius, associates with summer heat
[2] Mythic charioteer of the sun.

[3] Allusion to the legend of Jason's search for the golden fleece

"How happy might I still have mowed,
Had not Love here his thistles sowed!
But now I all the day complain,
Joining my labor to my pain;
And with my scythe cut down the grass,
Yet still my grief is where it was:
But, when the iron blunter grows,
Sighing I whet my scythe and woes."

While thus he threw his elbow round,
Depopulating all the ground,
And, with his whistling scythe, does cut
Each stroke between the earth and root,
The edgèd steel by careless chance
Did into his own ankle glance;
And there among the grass fell down,
By his own scythe, the mower mown.

"Alas!" said he, "these hurts are slight
To those that die by Love's despite.
With shepherd's-purse, and clown's-all-heal,
The blood I staunch, and would I seal.
Only for him no cure is found,
Whom Juliana's eyes do wound.
'Tis death alone that this must do:
For Death, thou art a Mower too."

Considerations

1. Consider the first stanza. How does this set up the central metaphoric situation and prepare us to see all that follows it in metaphoric terms?
2. Consider any image or local metaphor and its implications in terms of the entire piece. For example, in the second-to-last stanza, when Damon throws "his elbow round,/Depopulating all the ground," metaphorically what is he cutting down—in addition to himself, that is? Obviously, several answers are possible.
3. Metaphorically, what is Damon doing when he mows?
4. Is the snake a symbol? How is it being used metaphorically here?
5. What is the relation of death as a mower to Damon as a mower? What is the relation of death to Damon's desire for Juliana?

What makes this description of a walk metaphoric?

Robert Frost

RELUCTANCE

Out through the fields and the woods
   And over the walls I have wended;
I have climbed the hills of view
   And looked at the world, and descended;
I have come by the highway home,
   And lo, it is ended.

The leaves are all dead on the ground,
   Save those that the oak is keeping
To ravel them one by one
   And let them go scraping and creeping
Out over the crusted snow,
   When others are sleeping.

And the dead leaves lie huddled and still,
   No longer blown hither and thither;
The last lone aster is gone;
   The flowers of the witch-hazel wither;
The heart is still aching to seek,
   But the feet question "Whither?"

Ah, when to the heart of man
   Was it ever less than a treason
To go with the drift of things,
   To yield with a grace to reason,
And bow and accept the end
   Of a love or a season?

Considerations

How does each of the details of the narrator's walk relate to the central subject of reluctance? For example, could the leaves "dead on the ground" be memories, beliefs, despairs? What is the poet saying metaphorically when he writes, "I have climbed the hills of view/And looked at the world, and descended"? You can ask similar questions about most of the images in this poem.

George Meredith

MARK WHERE THE PRESSING WIND

Mark where the pressing wind shoots javelin-like
Its skeleton shadow on the broad-backed wave!
Here is a fitting spot to dig Love's grave;
Here where the ponderous breakers plunge and strike,
And dart their hissing tongues high up the sand:
In hearing of the ocean, and in sight
Of those ribbed wind-streaks running into white.
If I the death of Love had deeply planned,
I never could have made it half so sure,
As by the unblest kisses which upbraid
The full-waked sense; or failing that, degrade!
'Tis morning: but no morning can restore
What we have forfeited. I see no sin:
The wrong is mixed. In tragic life, God wot,°
No villain need be! Passions spin the plot:
We are betrayed by what is false within.

°Knows

Considerations

1. Consider Meredith's association to sharp, stark objects or words (javelin, skeletons, dart, etc.). In what ways does this help convey his subject (the death of love)?
2. Why might the scene the poet describes be "a fitting spot to dig Love's grave"?
3. Do you see a pun in the line beginning "'Tis morning"?
4. In the sentence "Passions spin the plot," the term for passions is unstated (passions [X] = ? [Y]). What are some levels of meaning here?

What does the title of this piece mean? Even if you don't understand Latin, you can probably figure out the phrase from the context of the poem. How is the geranium connected to the situation of the narrator?

What do the sailboat and the voyage become in this poem? How is the sailboat related to the poem itself ("this virgin verse")? What is the significance of the greeting at the end?

Louis Phillips

RUS IN URBE

Rus in urbe,
plants in my apartment die,
brown leaves scattered on the rug,
planters turned upon the sill.
I shall not set foot again
in that mountain city
where my wife was raised,
a country girl with city longings. . . . .

Rus in urbe,
a foreign phrase rolls
in a foreign season
where city climates take their toll.
5 floors up, I sweat out
a small drought, one marriage
gone to pot, one pepper plant
gone to seed, one geranium
trampled underfoot. Water
in the tub is not quite a pond,
bears no resemblance to that gorge
near my wife's city
where pines suspend the afternoon
& boulders tempt the climber
from the fall's edge.
Rus in urbe. 5 flights up,
I sweat out my own uprooting.

Stéphane Mallarmé

SALUTE

This froth, this virgin verse
is nothing but a cup
of the foamfar sea,
full of bubbles and mermaids.

We sail, O my various friends,
I on the deck, you at the prow
that crashes through the waves
like stormblasts and winters.

Across these rolling waters
blue drunkenness invades us,
as, braving all dangers,

we make this solitary greeting:
to sea and to sky, we show all
the white care of our sail.

Translation from French by John Briggs

Is the poet just describing a painting, or is the painting a metaphoric subject to get at other things?

Donald Justice

ON A PAINTING BY PATIENT B
OF THE INDEPENDENCE STATE
HOSPITAL FOR THE INSANE

1

These seven houses have learned to face one another,
But not at the expected angles. Those silly brown lumps,
That are probably meant for hills and not other houses,
After ages of being themselves, though naturally slow,
Are learning to be exclusive without offending.
The arches and entrances (down to the right out of sight)
Have mastered the lesson of remaining closed.
And even the skies keep a certain understandable distance,
For these are the houses of the very rich.

2

One sees their children playing with leopards, tamed
At great cost, or perhaps it is only other children,
For none of these objects is anything more than a spot,
And perhaps there are not any children but only leopards
Playing with leopards, and perhaps there are only the spots.
And the little maids from the windows hanging like tongues,
Calling the children in, admiring the leopards,
Are the dashes a child might represent motion by means of,
Or dazzlement possibly, the brilliance of solid-gold houses.

3
The clouds resemble those empty balloons in cartoons
Which approximate silence. These clouds, if clouds they are
(And not the smoke from the seven aspiring chimneys),
The more one studies them the more it appears
They too have expressions. One might almost say
They have their habits, their wrong opinions, that their
Impassivity masks an essentially lovable foolishness,
And they will be given names by those who live under them
Not public like mountains' but private like companions'.

Considerations

1. Consider the poet's use of personification in this piece.
2. What are the metaphoric ironies here? Look at the title, for example.
3. Consider the images—i.e., "children playing with leopards." What abstract meaning does each image suggest?

Petronius Arbiter

DREAMS

Dreams whose fluttering phantoms play with our minds
Are not sent from the dwellings of the gods
Or by aerial deities. We make our own.
When sleep takes our bodies, our minds are free
To sport with their daytime fixations.
The conqueror who wastes quaking kingdoms
And puts the torch to wretched cities conjures
Spears raining on his routed armies, fields
Running blood and the funerals of kings.
Lawyers see their statutes and fearfully
Eye the thronged courtroom. The miser secretes
His gold and discovers buried treasure.
The hunter beats the bush with his dogs.
Mariners snatch their ships from the waves or
Perish and go down with the wreckage.
Harlots write loveletters to their johns and
The adulteress dreams she gives the gift of herself.
Even the hound dreams of tracking the hare.
Night opens our wounds once again.

Translation from Latin by Robert Bongiorno

Considerations

1. Each dream (X) in the "dreams" of this poem is a vivid image of rise and fall, gain and loss, desire and frustration (Y). What is the relation of the last line to the rest of the poem?
2. Do you see any pun or irony in the word "dreams"?

This poem is descriptive. The central metaphoric relation is in the fourth and fifth lines. How is it worked out? What do you get from this poem? Consider the comparison in the last line very carefully, i.e., "mighty heart."

William Wordsworth

COMPOSED UPON WESTMINSTER BRIDGE

September 3, 1802

Earth has not anything to show more fair:
Dull would he be of soul who could pass by
A sight so touching in its majesty:
This City now doth, like a garment, wear
The beauty of the morning; silent, bare,
Ships, towers, domes, theatres, and temples lie
Open unto the fields, and to the sky;
All bright and glittering in the smokeless air.
Never did sun more beautifully steep
In his first splendour, valley, rock, or hill;
Ne'er saw I, never felt, a calm so deep!
The river glideth at his own sweet will:
Dear God! the very houses seem asleep;
And all that mighty heart is lying still!

This poem has a point to make. What is it? Does the poem go beyond its point?

Langston Hughes

AS I GREW OLDER

It was a long time ago.
I have almost forgotten my dream.
But it was there then,
In front of me,
Bright like a sun—
My dream.

And then the wall rose,
Rose slowly,
Slowly,
Between me and my dream.
Rose slowly, slowly,
Dimming,
Hiding,
The light of my dream.
Rose until it touched the sky—
The wall.

Shadow.
I am black.

I lie down in the shadow.
No longer the light of my dream before me,
Above me.
Only the thick wall.
Only the shadow.
My hands!
My dark hands!
Break through the wall!
Find my dream!
Help me to shatter this darkness,
To smash this night,
To break this shadow
Into a thousand lights of sun,
Into a thousand whirling dreams
Of sun!

In this difficult contemporary poem, the central metaphoric subject is time. To what is time related?

John Ashbery

LAST MONTH

No changes of support—only
Patches of gray, here where sunlight fell.
The house seems heavier
Now that they have gone away.
In fact it emptied in record time.
When the flat table used to result
A match recedes, slowly, into the night.
The academy of the future is
Opening its doors and willing
The fruitless sunlight streams into domes
The chairs piled high with books and papers.

The sedate one is this month's skittish one
Confirming the property that,
A timeless value, has changed hands.
And you could have a new automobile
Ping pong set and garage, but the thief
Stole everything like a miracle.
In his book there was a picture of treason only
And in the garden, cries and colors.

Following are two English RENAISSANCE *period translations of a poem by the Italian poet Petrarch. Which do you think is more effective? Why?*

Henry Howard, Earl of Surrey

LOVE THAT DOTH REIGN

Love that doth reign and live within my thought,
And built his seat within my captive breast,
Clad in the arms wherein with me he fought,
Oft in my face he doth his banner rest.
But she that taught me love and suffer pain,
My doubtful hope and eke my hot desire
With shamefast look to shadow and refrain,
Her smiling grace converteth straight to ire,
And coward Love, then, to the heart space
Taketh his flight, where he doth lurk and plain
His purpose lost, and dare not show his face.
For my lord's guilt thus faultless bide I pain;
　Yet from my lord shall not my foot remove:
　Sweet is death that taketh end by love.

Sir Thomas Wyatt

THE LONG LOVE

The long love, that in my thought doth harbor
And in mine heart doth keep his residence,
Into my face presseth with both pretence,
And therein campeth, spreading his banner,
She that learneth to love and suffer,
And wills that my trust and lust's negligence
Be reined by reason, shame, and reverence,
With his hardiness taketh displeasure.
Wherewithall, unto the heart's forest he fleeth,
Leaving his enterprise with pain and cry;
And there him hideth and not appeareth.
What may I do when my master feareth
   But in the field with him to live and die?
   For good is the life ending faithfully.

*In the next poems explore for yourself the various types of metaphoric language
used.*

Matthew Prior

TO A LADY: SHE REFUSING TO CONTINUE A DISPUTE WITH ME, AND LEAVING ME IN THE ARGUMENT

AN ODE

Spare, gen'rous victor, spare the slave,
   Who did unequal war pursue,
That more than triumph he might have,
   In being overcome by you.

In the dispute whate'er I said,
   My heart was by my tongue belied;
And in my looks you might have read
   How much I argued on your side.

You, far from danger as from fear,
   Might have sustained an open fight:
For seldom your opinions err;
   Your eyes are always in the right.

Why, fair one, would you not rely
   On Reason's force with Beauty's joined?
Could I their prevalence deny,
   I must at once be deaf and blind.

Alas! not hoping to subdue,
   I only to the fight aspired;
To keep the beauteous foe in view
   Was all the glory I desired.

But she, howe'er of vict'ry sure,
   Contemns the wreath too long delayed;
And armed with more immediate power,
   Calls cruel silence to her aid.

Deeper to wound, she shuns the fight;
   She drops her arms to gain the field:
Secures her conquest by her flight;
   And triumphs, when she seems to yield.

So when the Parthian° turned his steed,
   And from the hostile camp withdrew;
With cruel skill the backward reed
   He sent; and as he fled, he slew.

°The Parthians developed the technique of having
mounted men, seeming to flee, fire backward with great
accuracy.

Charles Dickens

ODE TO AN EXPIRING FROG

Can I view thee panting, lying
On thy stomach, without sighing;
Can I unmoved see thee dying
        On a log,
        Expiring frog!

Say, have fiends in shape of boys,
With wild halloo, and brutal noise,
Hunted thee from marshy joys,
        With a dog,
        Expiring frog!

Douglas Worth

THE RETURN

Then the Rhine Valley. March. April. Advancing
against the V-2's, while the cherry trees
spattered the hills like shrapnel, on our knees
we came to where bright water bugs were dancing.

For thirty days gauze and string of tags
composed a hero's story—death undone,
my lips could find no meanings when the sun
crept like a Yellow Jacket down the rags
left for my scarecrow limbs . . .

   put out to drowse
long mornings on the valleyside, I grew
simple as leaves, resolving in the blue
each plane's drone to a murmuring of boughs—
home in my yard, a boy climbing with ease
to watch the high white blossoms crawl with bees.

John Webster

ALL THE FLOWERS OF THE SPRING

From The Devil's Law-Case

All the Flowers of the Spring
Meet to perfume our burying:
These have but their growing prime,
And man does flourish but his time.
Survey our progresse from our birth,
We are set, we grow, we turne to earth.
Courts adieu, and all delights,
All bewitching appetites;
Sweetest Breath, and clearest eye,
Like perfumes goe out and dye;
And consequently this is done,
As shadowes wait upon the Sunne.
Vaine the ambition of Kings,
Who seeke by trophies and dead things,
To leave a living name behind,
And weave but nets to catch the wind

Muriel Rukeyser

THE POWER OF SUICIDE

The potflower on the windowsill says to me
In words that are green-edged red leaves :
Flower   flower   flower   flower
Today for the sake of all the dead   Burst into flower.

William Dunbar

LAMENT FOR THE MAKERS

When He Was Sick

I that in health was and gladness,
Am troubled now with great sickness,
And feeble with infirmity;
Timor mortis conturbat me.°

Our pleasure here is all vainglory,
This false world is but transitory,
The flesh is brittle, the fiend is sly;
Timor mortis conturbat me.

°The fear of death appalls me.

The state of man does change and vary,
Now sound, now sick, now blithe, now sorry,
Now dancing merry, now like to die;
Timor mortis conturbat me.

No state on earth here stands secure;
As with the wind waves the wickers,
Waves this world's vanity;
Timor mortis conturbat me.

On to death goes all estates,
Princes, prelates, potentates,
Both rich and poor of all degree;
Timor mortis conturbat me.

He takes the knights in the field,
In armor under helm and shield;
Victor he is in all melee;
Timor mortis conturbat me.

That strong unmerciful king
Takes on the mother's breast sucking
The babe full of benignity;
Timor mortis conturbat me.
. . . .
He spares no lord for his puissance,
Nor clerk for his intelligence;
His awful stroke may no man flee;
Timor mortis conturbat me.

Magicians, and astrologers,
Rhetoricians, logicians, theologers,
No help for them in conclusions sly;
Timor mortis conturbat me.
. . . .
He has piteously devoured
The noble Chaucer, of poetic flower,
The Monk of Berry, and Gower, all three;
Timor mortis conturbat me.
. . . .
Since all my brothers to him have gone,
He will not leave me alone,
Perforce I must his next prey be;
Timor mortis conturbat me.

Since for death there is no remedy,
Best that for death disposed we be,
After we die that live may we;
Timor mortis conturbat me.

Modernized from Middle English

Jean de Sponde

WHO ARE THESE

From Poems on Death

Who are these who make the world their idol
And sprawl at its feet,
Awed by its useless artifice?
Who are these celebrants of idle nonsense?

These gangs of dandies and coquettes
Plying vanities from courtiers,
Fawning for favors and flattering,
Fond of their false masks and *politesse*?

These, who sail out to conquer the world,
In quest of their valuable lives,
Sailing with the rudder of profit or fame,
Winds of fantasy in their rigging.

Sailing the same sea as they,
And trembling to perish, I see that this life
Is a clear, simple beacon
To show me the way to die.

Translation from French

Ralph Waldo Emerson

GRACE

How much, preventing God! how much I owe
To the defenses thou hast round me set:
Example, custom, fear, occasion slow,
These scornéd bondmen were my parapet.
I dare not peep over this parapet
To gauge with glance the roaring gulf below,
The depths of sin to which I had descended,
Had not these me against myself defended.

William Shakespeare

POOR SOUL, THE CENTRE

Poor soul, the centre of my sinful earth,
Thrall to these rebel powers that thee array,
Why dost thou pine within and suffer dearth,
Painting thy outward walls so costly gay?
Why so large cost, having so short a lease,
Dost thou upon thy fading mansion spend?
Shall worms, inheritors of this excess,
Eat up thy charge? Is this thy body's end?
Then, soul, live thou upon thy servant's loss,
And let that pine to aggravate thy store;
Buy terms divine in selling hours of dross;
Within be fed, without be rich no more:
   So shalt thou feed on Death, that feeds on men,
   And Death once dead, there's no more dying then.

Matthew Arnold

GROWING OLD

What is it to grow old?
Is it to lose the glory of the form,
The lustre of the eye?
Is it for beauty to forego her wreath?
—Yes, but not this alone.

Is it to feel our strength—
Not our bloom only, but our strength—decay?
Is it to feel each limb
Grow stiffer, every function less exact,
Each nerve more loosely strung?

Yes, this, and more; but not,
Ah, 'tis not what in youth we dream'd 'twould be!
'Tis not to have our life
Mellow'd and soften'd as with sunset-glow,
A golden day's decline.

'Tis not to see the world
As from a height, with rapt prophetic eyes,
And heart profoundly stirr'd;
And weep, and feel the fulness of the past,
The years that are no more.

It is to spend long days
And not once feel that we were ever young;
It is to add, immured
In the hot prison of the present, month
To month with weary pain.

It is to suffer this,
And feel but half, and feebly, what we feel.
Deep in our hidden heart
Festers the dull remembrance of a change,
But no emotion—none.

It is—last stage of all—
When we are frozen up within, and quite
The phantom of ourselves,
To hear the world applaud the hollow ghost
Which blamed the living man.

George Herbert

EASTER-WINGS

Lord who createdst man in wealth and store,
    Though foolishly he lost the same,
        Decaying more and more,
           Till he became
           Most poore:
           With thee
          O let me rise
        As larks, harmoniously,
    And sing this day thy victories:
Then shall the fall further the flight in me.

    My tender age in sorrow did beginne:
    And still with sicknesses and shame
        Thou didst so punish sinne,
           That I became
           Most thinne.
           With thee
         Let me combine
      And feel this day thy victorie:
    For, if I imp my wing on thine,
Affliction shall advance the flight in me.

Heinrich Heine

MY LIFE IS NEITHER FULL NOR NEAT

My life is neither full nor neat
And this world is so woefully incomplete
That I'm off to visit that worthy man,
The German professor who dared to scan
The cosmic debris and reset the parts
By reason pure and the logical arts,
Who from those fragments redesigned
A world adjusted to man's mind:°
Oh, he stopped up all of the cosmic holes
With his nightcaps and wads of his underclothes.

               Translation from German by
                    Christopher Collins

°Probably Immanuel Kant, author of the *Critique of Pure Reason*

Alfred Dorn

PROGRAM FOR THE COMPUTERIZED

Arrived in a world of equations,
They are classified in their cribs.
Clock hands dictate
When to be washed, fed, laid to sleep.
At school they learn
To become integers without identity—
Mixed fractions daily diminishing
Till they enter the fraternity of zeros.
Drafted, they serve two years as trigger-fingers;
Released, they become buttons on assembly lines.
At length, a number is stamped on every slab.
The mountain lioness still bears her young
In solitude near the sky where blades of sun
Beat naked rock.
The eagle nests on her crag
To hatch fierce brothers of the wind.

John Dryden

A SONG FOR ST. CECILIA'S DAY

November 22, 1687

From Harmony, from heav'nly Harmony
    This universal Frame began;
  When Nature underneath a heap
    Of jarring Atomes lay,
  And cou'd not heave her Head,
The tuneful Voice was heard from high,
    Arise, ye more than dead.
Then cold and hot and moist and dry
  In order to their Stations leap,
    And MUSICK's pow'r obey.
From Harmony, from heavenly Harmony
    This universal Frame began:
    From Harmony to Harmony
Through all the Compass of the Notes it ran,
The Diapason[1] closing full in Man.
What Passion cannot MUSICK raise and quell?
    When *Jubal*[2] struck the corded Shell,
  His listening Brethren stood around,
    And, wond'ring, on their Faces fell
    To worship that Celestial Sound:

[1] A burst of harmonious sound
[2] According to the Bible, Jubal was the originator of musical instruments.

Less than a God they thought there could not dwell
    Within the hollow of the Shell,
    That spoke so sweetly, and so well.
What Passion cannot MUSICK raise and quell?

    The TRUMPETS loud Clangor
      Excites us to Arms
    With shrill Notes of Anger
      And mortal Alarms.
    The double double double beat
      Of the thund'ring DRUM
      Cryes, heark the Foes come;
Charge, Charge, 'tis too late to retreat.

    The soft complaining FLUTE
    In dying Notes discovers
    The Woes of hopeless Lovers,
Whose Dirge is whisper'd by the Warbling LUTE.

    Sharp VIOLINS proclaim
Their jealous Pangs and Desperation,
Fury, frantick Indignation,
Depth of Pains and Height of Passion,
    For the fair, disdainful Dame.

    But oh! what Art can teach
    What human Voice can reach
      The sacred ORGANS Praise?
    Notes inspiring holy Love,
Notes that wing their heavenly Ways
    To mend the Choires above.
Orpheus cou'd lead the savage race,
And Trees unrooted left their Place,
    Sequacious of the Lyre;
But bright CECILIA rais'd the Wonder high'r
When to her Organ vocal Breath was given,
An Angel heard, and straight appear'd
    Mistaking Earth for Heav'n.

GRAND CHORUS
    As from the Pow'r of Sacred Lays
      The Spheres began to move,
    And sung the great Creator's Praise
      To all the bless'd above;

    So, when the last and dreadful Hour
    This crumbling Pageant shall devour,
    The TRUMPET shall be heard on high,
    The dead shall live, the living die,
    And MUSICK shall untune the Sky.

Alexander Pope

BOOK THE FIRST

from *The Dunciad: Book I*

The Mighty Mother, and her Son who brings
The Smithfield Muses[1] to the ear of Kings,
I sing. Say you, her instruments the Great!
Call'd to this work by Dulness, Jove, and Fate;
You by whose care, in vain decry'd and curst,
Still Dunce the second reigns like Dunce the first;
Say how the Goddess bade Britannia sleep,
And pour'd her Spirit o'er the land and deep.
  In eldest time, e'er mortals writ or read,
E'er Pallas issu'd from the Thund'rer's head,[2]
Dulness o'er all possess'd her ancient right,
Daughter of Chaos and eternal Night:
Fate in their dotage this fair Ideot gave,
Gross as her sire, and as her mother grave,
Laborious, heavy, busy, bold, and blind,
She rul'd, in native Anarchy, the mind.
  Still her old Empire to restore she tries,
For, born a Goddess, Dulness never dies.
  O Thou! whatever title please thine ear,
Dean, Drapier, Bickerstaff, or Gulliver![3]
Whether thou chuse Cervantes'[3] serious air,
Or laugh and shake in Rab'lais'[3] easy chair,
Or praise the Court, or magnify Mankind,
Or thy griev'd Country's copper chains unbind;
From thy Boeotia tho' her Pow'r retires,
Mourn not, my SWIFT,[4] at ought our Realm acquires,
Here pleas'd behold her mighty wings out-spread
To hatch a new Saturnian age of Lead.[5]
  Close to those walls where Folly holds her throne,
And laughs to think Monroe[6] would take her down,
Where o'er the gates, by his fam'd father's hand
Great Cibber's[7] brazen, brainless brothers stand;
One Cell there is, conceal'd from vulgar eye,
The Cave of Poverty and Poetry.
Keen, hollow winds howl thro' the bleak recess,
Emblem of Music caus'd by Emptiness.

[1]Smithfield was the low part of town (London).

[2]An allusion to the classical myth according to which
Venus issued from the head of Zeus

[3]Writers of, and characters in, works Pope admired.

[4]Jonathan Swift

[5]As opposed to an age of gold

[6]The physician of a local hospital for the insane

[7]The father of Colly Cibber—the writer Pope is lampoon-
ing

Hence Bards, like Proteus long in vain ty'd down,
Escape in Monsters, and amaze the town.
Hence Miscellanies spring, the weekly boast
Of Curl's chaste press, and Lintot's rubric post:
Hence hymning Tyburn's elegiac lines,
Hence Journals, Medleys, Merc'ries, Magazines.[8]
Sepulchral Lyes, our holy walls to grace,
And New-year Odes,[9] and all the Grub-street race.
    In clouded Majesty here Dulness shone;
Four guardian Virtues, round, support her throne:
Fierce champion Fortitude, that knows no fears
Of hisses, blows, or want, or loss of ears:
Calm Temperance, whose blessings those partake
Who hunger, and who thirst for scribling sake:
Prudence, whose glass presents th' approaching jayl:
Poetic Justice, with her lifted scale,
Where, in nice balance, truth with gold she weighs,
And solid pudding against empty praise.
    Here she beholds the Chaos dark and deep,
Where nameless Somethings in their causes sleep,
'Till genial Jacob, or a warm Third day,
Call forth each mass, a Poem, or a Play:
How hints, like spawn, scarce quick in embryo lie,
How new-born nonsense first is taught to cry,
Maggots half-form'd in rhyme exactly meet,
And learn to crawl upon poetic feet.
Here one poor word an hundred clenches[10] makes,
And ductile dulness new meanders takes;
There motley Images her fancy strike,
Figures ill pair'd, and Similies unlike.
She sees a Mob of Metaphors advance,
Pleas'd with the madness of the mazy dance:
How Tragedy and Comedy embrace;
How Farce and Epic get a jumbled race;
How Time himself stands still at her command,
Realms shift their place, and Ocean turns to land.
Here gay Description Ægypt glads with show'rs,
Or gives to Zembla fruits, to Barca flow'rs;
Glitt'ring with ice here hoary hills are seen,
There painted vallies of eternal green,
In cold December fragrant chaplets blow,
And heavy harvests nod beneath the snow.
    All these, and more, the cloud-compelling Queen
Beholds thro' fogs, that magnify the scene.
She, tinsel'd o'er in robes of varying hues,

[8]Pope's attack on the local publishing industry for its
inferior quality

[9]New Year's odes were written by the poet Laureates,
whom Pope considered representative of dullness.

[10]Puns

With self-applause her wild creation views;
Sees momentary monsters rise and fall,
And with her own fools-colours gilds them all.
　　'Twas on the day, when ★ ★ rich and grave,
Like Cimon, triumph'd both on land and wave:
(Pomps without guilt, of bloodless swords and maces,
Glad chains, warm furs, broad banners, and broad faces)
Now Night descending, the proud scene was o'er,
But liv'd, in Settle's[11] numbers,[12] one day more.
Now May'rs and Shrieves all hush'd and satiate lay,
Yet eat, in dreams, the custard of the day;
While pensive Poets painful vigils keep,
Sleepless themselves, to give their readers sleep.
. . . .
Swearing and supperless the Hero[13] sate,
Blasphem'd his Gods, the Dice, and damn'd his Fate.
Then gnaw'd his pen, then dash'd it on the ground,
Sinking from thought to thought, a vast profound!
Plung'd for his sense, but found no bottom there,
Yet wrote and flounder'd on, in mere despair.
Round him much Embryo, much Abortion lay,
Much future Ode, and abdicated Play;
Nonsense precipitate, like running Lead,
That slip'd thro' Cracks and Zig-zags of the Head;
All that on Folly Frenzy could beget,
Fruits of dull Heat, and Sooterkins[14] of Wit.
Next, o'er his Books his eyes began to roll,
In pleasing memory of all he stole,
How here he sipp'd, how there he plunder'd snug
And suck'd all o'er, like an industrious Bug.
. . . .
How random thoughts now meaning chance to find,
Now leave all memory of sense behind:
How Prologues into Prefaces decay,
And these to Notes are fritter'd quite away:
How Index-learning turns no student pale,
Yet holds the eel of science by the tail:
How, with less reading than makes felons scape,
Less human genius than God gives an ape,
Small thanks to France, and none to Rome or Greece,
A past, vamp'd, future, old, reviv'd, new piece,
'Twixt Plautus, Fletcher, Shakespear, and Corneille,
Can make a Cibber, Tibbald, or Ozell.[15]

[11]Settle was poet to the city of London. Except for "The
Dunciad" his name and works have fallen into oblivion.

[12]Meters; in other words, lines of poetry

[13]Colly Cibber

[14]An imperfect literary composition

[15]Other writers, targets of Pope's satire

The Goddess then, o'er his anointed head,
With mystic words, the sacred Opium shed.
And lo! her bird, (a monster of a fowl,
Something betwixt a Heideggre[16] and owl,)
Perch'd on his crown. 'All hail! and hail again,
My son! the promis'd land expects thy reign.
. . . .
Thou Cibber! thou, his Laurel shalt support,
Folly, my son, has still a Friend at Court. . . .'

[16]An opera-house manager

Percy Bysshe Shelley

TO A SKYLARK

Hail to thee, blithe Spirit!
    Bird thou never wert,
That from Heaven, or near it,
    Pourest thy full heart
In profuse strains of unpremeditated art.

Higher still and higher
    From the earth thou springest
Like a cloud of fire;
    The blue deep thou wingest,
And singing still dost soar, and soaring ever singest.

In the golden lightning
    Of the sunken sun,
O'er which clouds are bright'ning,
    Thou dost float and run;
Like an unbodied joy whose race is just begun.

The pale purple even
    Melts around thy flight;
Like a star of Heaven,
    In the broad daylight
Thou art unseen, but yet I hear thy shrill delight,

Keen as are the arrows
    Of that silver sphere,
Whose intense lamp narrows
    In the white dawn clear
Until we hardly see—we feel that it is there.

All the earth and air
 With thy voice is loud,
As, when night is bare,
 From one lonely cloud
The moon rains out her beams, and Heaven is overflowed.

What thou art we know not;
 What is most like thee?
From rainbow clouds there flow not
 Drops so bright to see
As from thy presence showers a rain of melody.

Like a poet hidden
 In the light of thought,
Singing hymns unbidden,
 Till the world is wrought
To sympathy with hopes and fears it heeded not:

Like a high-born maiden
 In a palace-tower,
Soothing her love-laden
 Soul in secret hour
With music sweet as love, which overflows her bower:

Like a glow-worm golden
 In a dell of dew,
Scattering unbeholden
 Its aëreal hue
Among the flowers and grass, which screen it from the
 view!

Like a rose embowered
 In its own green leaves,
By warm winds deflowered,
 Till the scent it gives
Makes faint with too much sweet those heavy-wingèd
 thieves:

Sound of vernal showers
 On the twinkling grass,
Rain-awakened flowers,
 All that ever was
Joyous, and clear, and fresh, thy music doth surpass:

Teach us, Sprite or Bird,
 What sweet thoughts are thine:
I have never heard
 Praise of love or wine
That painted forth a flood of rapture so divine.

Chorus Hymeneal,°
   Or triumphal chant,
Matched with thine would be all
   But an empty vaunt,
A thing wherein we feel there is some hidden want.

   What objects are the fountains
      Of thy happy strain?
   What fields, or waves, or mountains?
      What shapes of sky or plain?
What love of thine own kind? what ignorance of pain?

   With thy clear keen joyance
      Languor cannot be:
   Shadow of annoyance
      Never came near thee:
Thou lovest—but ne'er knew love's sad satiety.

   Waking or asleep,
      Thou of death must deem
   Things more true and deep
      Than we mortals dream,
Or how could thy notes flow in such a crystal stream?

   We look before and after,
      And pine for what is not:
   Our sincerest laughter
      With some pain is fraught;
Our sweetest songs are those that tell of saddest thought.

   Yet if we could scorn
      Hate, and pride, and fear;
   If we were things born
      Not to shed a tear,
I know not how thy joy we ever should come near.

   Better than all measures
      Of delightful sound,
   Better than all treasures
      That in books are found,
Thy skill to poet were, thou scorner of the ground!

   Teach me half the gladness
      That thy brain must know,
   Such harmonious madness
      From my lips would flow
The world should listen then—as I am listening now.

°marriage song

James Wright

THE JEWEL

There is this cave
In the air behind my body
That nobody is going to touch:
A cloister, a silence
Closing around a blossom of fire.
When I stand upright in the wind,
My bones turn to dark emeralds.

Emily Dickinson

BLOOM IS RESULT

Bloom is result. To meet a flower
And casually glance
Would cause one scarcely to suspect
The minor circumstance

Assisting in the bright affair
So intricately done,
Then offered as a butterfly
To the meridian.

To pack the bud, oppose the worm,
Obtain its right of dew,
Adjust the heat, elude the wind,
Escape the prowling bee,

Great nature not to disappoint
Awaiting her that day—
To be a flower is profound
Responsibility!

Emily Dickinson

THE SOUL SELECTS HER OWN SOCIETY

The soul selects her own society,
Then shuts the door;
On her divine majority
Obtrude no more.

Unmoved, she notes the chariot's pausing
At her low gate;
Unmoved, an emperor is kneeling
Upon her mat.

I've known her from an ample nation
Choose one;
Then close the valves of her attention
Like stone.

John Ford

CAN YOU PAINT A THOUGHT?

From The Broken Heart

Can you paint a thought? or number
Every fancy in a slumber?
Can you count soft minutes roving
From a dyals point by moving?
Can you graspe a sigh? or lastly,
Rob a Virgins honour chastly?
    No, ô no; yet you may
        Sooner doe both that and this,
        This and that, and never misse,
    Then by any praise display
        Beauties beauty, such a glory
        As beyond all Fate, all Story,
            All armes, all arts,
            All loves, all hearts,
        Greater then those, or they,
        Doe, shall, and must obey.

Li Ho

THE LIANG TERRACE

The pool gleams high on the terrace,
Among the stars where the prince of Liang would pause:
Night after night the milky way
Flows through the dark water of heaven;
Before the stairs carved jade dragons lock
Themselves together motionless and dark . . .
And light, green bamboo clashes and trembles
As the breeze flows and starlight gleams
On the dewlit earth like old, old tears . . .

Bells chimed where he drank wine and shot
Arrow after arrow at the sky;
Golden tigers stalked in braid across his furs
and woven blood gushed from woven wounds . . .
All mornings and all evenings he sighed as the tides turned.
And he sewed the sun to the sky and looped the thread
to keep the hours back . . .

Like thickening blood the hibiscus darkened with Autumn;
As spring grew full of time and died the orchids wept . . .
Wandering geese in the island reeds sang spring alive again:
In dark and swampy land the autumn floods whitened . . .

Rendition from Chinese by
Richard Monaco

Guillaume Apollinaire

THE MIRABEAU BRIDGE

Under Mirabeau Bridge flows the Seine
        And all our love
    Must I recall again
Joy always used to come after a pain

      Come the night   strike the hour
      The days go past   I remain

Let's hold hands together and stand face to face
        While there below
    The bridge of our arms pass
Those everlasting looks   those worn down waves

      Come the night   strike the hour
      The days go past   I remain

Our love goes past just as these waters go
        Our love goes past
    Life is so very slow
And what a thing of violence is Hope

      Come the night   strike the hour
      The days go past   I remain

Days pass by and weeks pass in their train
        Neither the past
    Nor old loves come again
Under Mirabeau Bridge flows the Seine

      Come the night   strike the hour
      The days go past   I remain

Translation from French by Christopher Collins

Catullus

NOW SPRING BRINGS BACK

Now Spring brings back her balmy air,
Now Zephyr's playful breezes hush
The fury of equinoctial heaven.
Escape the Phrygian fields Catullus!
Flee the luxurious land of steamy Nicaea
And fly to the bright cities of Asia!
The mind trembles to wander now,
And now my legs feel strong.
Stay well my friends and sweet tourist lovers!
We set out from our distant homes together
And our different ways are bringing us back again.

Translation from Latin by Robert Bongiorno

Richard Hugo

OCEAN ON MONDAY

Here at last is ending
Where gray coordinates with nothing
the horizon wrinkles in the wind.

These will end: shrimp a mile
below, blue shark, sole
Rocks alive as crabs in shifting green.

patent bathers, barnacles, kelp that lies
in wilting whips, jelly-
fish that open lonely as a hand,

space that drives into expanse
boredom banging in your face
the horizon stiff with strain.

Thomas Hardy

THE WALK

You did not walk with me
Of late to the hill-top tree
    By the gated ways
    As in earlier days;
    You were weak and lame,
    So you never came,
And I went alone, and I did not mind,
Not thinking of you as left behind.

    I walked up there to-day
    Just in the former way;
    Surveyed around
    The familiar ground
    By myself again:
    What difference, then?
Only that underlying sense
Of the look of a room on returning thence.

Giacomo Leopardi

XIV
TO THE MOON

(Alla Luna)

O lovely Moon, I remember how, (a year has wound
Down since) I would come to this hilltop, filled with
Anguish, to look upon you: And you hung there
Above the wood, as you do still, illuminating all.
But the tears welling in my eyes made your face
Nebulous and shimmery. Because my life
Was agony . . . is agony, nor has it changed style,
My beloved Moon. Yet, the recollection helps,
As does enumerating the days of my pain.
O how welcome it is in youth, when hope
Is high and the track of memory brief,
To recall things past, though they might be sad
And though the torment might still endure.

        Translation from Italian by
            Robert Bongiorno

Robert Creeley

THE RAIN

All night the sound had
come back again,
and again falls
this quiet, persistent rain.

What am I to myself
that must be remembered,
insisted upon
so often? Is it

that never the ease,
even the hardness,
of rain falling
will have for me

something other than this,
something not so insistent—
am I to be locked in this
final uneasiness.

Love, if you love me,
lie next to me.
Be for me, like rain,
the getting out

of the tiredness, the fatuousness, the semi-
lust of intentional indifference.
Be wet
with a decent happiness.

Sir Philip Sidney

AH, BED!

Ah, bed! the field where joy's peace some do see,
The field where all my thoughts to war be trained,
How is thy grace by my strange fortune stain'd!
How thy lee shores by my sighs stormed be!
With sweet soft shades thou oft invitest me
To steal some rest; but, wretch, I am constrain'd
Spurr'd with love's spur, though gold, and shortly rein'd
With care's hard hand—to turn and toss in thee,
While the black horrors of the silent night
Paint woe's black face so lively to my sight
That tedious leisure makes each wrinkled line.
But when Aurora[1] leads out Phoebus'[2] dance
   Mine eyes then only wink; for spite, perchance,
    That worms should have their sun, and I want mine.

[1]Morning
[2]The sun

Anonymous

CODEX SALAMASIANUS

Tell me what you would do, beautiful Venus,
If your Amor did not repay in kind?
As youth fades, so beauty passes away.
Violets rot after the dew and roses lose their scent.
Lilies scatter whiteness in Spring and wither in a day.
I beg you take these dread examples to your heart
And always give the lover what he has given.
Let every lover in return be loved!

    Translation from Latin by Robert Bongiorno

Dante Gabriel Rosetti

LILITH

For a Picture

Of Adam's first wife, Lilith, it is told
  (The witch he loved before the gift of Eve,)
That, ere the snake's, her sweet tongue could deceive
And her enchanted hair was the first gold.
And still she sits, young while the earth is old,
    And subtly of herself contemplative,
    Draws men to watch the bright net she can weave,
Till heart and body and life are in its hold.

The rose and poppy are her flowers; for where
  Is she not found, O Lilith, whom shed scent
And soft-shed kisses and soft sleep shall snare?
    Los! as that youth's eyes burned at thine, so went
    Thy spell through him, and left his straight neck bent,
And round his heart one strangling golden hair.

Sor Juana Inés de La Cruz

STAY, SHADOW OF
REMOTENESS

Stay, you shadow of my remoteness,
shy substance of my will,
illusion I'm attracted to in joy,
chill prison where I'm bound in pain.

If already to the magnet of your charms
my heart is drawn, obedient as steel,
why pull me on to you,
while trying to escape in scorn?

Your boasting will not prove your tyranny
has triumphed to repel me.
For while you scorn the force this love exerts,

toward which my form's inevitably impelled,
it makes no difference if in substance you have fled,
since in my shadowed thoughts, like iron, you're held.

Translation from Spanish by John Briggs

Aurelian Townshend

A DIALOGUE BETWIXT TIME
AND A PILGRIME

PILGRIME. Aged man, that mowes these fields.
TIME. Pilgrime speak, what is thy will?
PILGRIME. Whose soile is this that such sweet Pasture
    yields?
  Or who are thou whose Foot stand never still?
    Or where am I? TIME. In love.
          PILGRIME. His Lordship lies above.
TIME. Yes and below, and round about
  Where in all sorts of flow'rs are growing
Which as the early Spring puts out,
  Time fals as fast as mowing.
PILGRIME. If thou art Time, these Flow'rs have Lives,
  And then I fear,
Under some Lilly she I love
  May now be growing there.
TIME. And in some Thistle or some spyre of grasse.
My syth thy stalk before hers come may passe.
PILGRIME. Wilt thou provide it may. TIME. No.
      PILGRIME. Alleage the cause.
TIME. Because Time cannot alter but obey Fates laws.
CHORUS. Then happy those whom Fate, that is the
    stronger,
Together twists their threads, and yet draws hers the
    longer.

Hart Crane

LEGENDE

The tossing loneliness of many nights
Rounds off my memory of her.
Like a shell surrendered to evening sands,
Yet called adrift again at every dawn,
She has become a pathos,—
Waif of the tides.

The sand and sea have had their way,
And moons of spring and autumn,—
All, save I.
And even my vision will be erased
As a cameo the waves claim again.

William Brown

THE SIREN'S SONG

IN THE INNER TEMPLE MASK

Steer, hither steer, your winged pines,
All-beaten mariners!
Here lie love's undiscovered mines,
A prey to passengers.
Perfumes far sweeter than the best
Which make the Phoenix'° urn and nest.
Fear not your ships,
Nor any to oppose you, save our lips;
But come on shore,
Where no joy died 'till love hath gotten more.

For swelling waves, our panting breaths,
Where never storms arise,
Exchange; and be a while our guests;
For stars, gaze on our eyes;
The compass love shall hourly ring,
And, as he goes about the ring,
We will not miss
To tell each point he nameth with a kiss.
Then come on shore,
Where no joy dies 'till love hath gotten more.

°The mythical bird of fire, reborn out of its own ashes

Richard Lovelace

TO ALTHEA, FROM PRISON

When Love with unconfinèd wings
  Hovers within my gates;
And my divine Althea brings
  To whisper at the grates:
When I lie tangled in her hair,
  And fettered to her eye;
The birds, that wanton in the air,
  Know no such liberty.

When flowing cups run swiftly round
  With no allaying Thames,
Our careless heads with roses bound,
  Our hearts with loyal flames;
When thirsty grief in wine we steep,
  When healths and draughts go free,
Fishes that tipple in the deep,
  Know no such liberty.

When (like committed linnets) I
  With shriller throat shall sing
The sweetness, mercy, majesty,
  And glories of my King;
When I shall voice aloud, how good
  He is, how great should be;
Enlargèd winds that curl the flood,
  Know no such liberty.

Stone walls do not a prison make,
  Nor iron bars a cage;
Minds innocent and quiet take
  That for an hermitage;
If I have freedom in my Love,
  And in my soul am free;
Angels alone that soar above,
  Enjoy such liberty.

Sir Henry Wotton

YOU MEANER BEAUTIES OF THE NIGHT

You meaner beauties of the night,
   Which poorly satisfy our eyes
More by your number than your light,
   You common people of the skies,
   What are you when the sun doth rise?

Ye violets that first appear,
   By your pure purple mantles known,
Like the proud virgins of the year,
   As if the spring were all your own,
   What are you when the rose is blown?

Ye curious chanters of the wood,
   That warble forth dame nature's lays,
Thinking your passions understood
   By your weak accents, what's your praise
   When Philomel° her voice doth raise?

So, when my mistress' shall be seen
   In sweetness of her looks, and mind;
By virtues first, then choice, a queen,
   Tell me, if she was not design'd
   Th' eclipse and glory of her kind?

°See page 172

Michael Drayton

SINCE THERE'S NO HELPE

Since there's no helpe, Come let us kisse and part,
Nay, I have done: You get no more of Me,
And I am glad, yea glad withall my heart,
That thus so cleanly, I my Selfe can free,
Shake hands for ever, Cancell all our Vowes,
And when We meet at any time againe,
Be it not seene in either of our Browes,
That We one jot of former Love reteyne;
Now at the last gaspe, of Loves latest Breath,
When his Pulse failing, Passion speechlesse lies,
When Faith is kneeling by his bed of Death,
And Innocence is closing up his Eyes,
    Now if thou would'st, when all have given him over,
    From Death to Life, thou might'st him yet recover.

EXPERIENCING THE POEM

Without analyzing, evaluating, or considering metaphoric content, reread any poem in this book
which you particularly liked. Do you still like it?
Did you find something more to like this time?

CHAPTER 9
METAPHOR
AT LARGE

A form of order is imposed on the world (which is various, complex, often frightening, a kaleidoscope of perceptions and responses) by means of language and logic. We make categories: "That's a man," "He's an Englishman," "He's a socialist." Or "This is a desire," "That's a fear," whatever. We say "I believe these things but not those," "I like this and hate that," and so on. In effect, we normally use our words and our logic to define, limit, or break up the continuous flow of experience and to organize it, sort it, come to conclusions. This process involves constructing or interpreting around ourselves a familiar environment—and so breaking up our perceptions and the things perceived, our ideas and feelings, etc., and organizing them according to their similarities, contrasts, causes, and effects. In short, it involves trying to make everything *known*. As we have observed before, often in trying to make everything fit our "knowledge," we say that we are being logical when in fact we are simply promoting a belief—for example, the famous syllogism: all men are mortal, Socrates is a man; therefore, Socrates is mortal. Obviously, though this is logical, you have to agree with the premise. But how can you actually prove it? Maybe a nonmortal man exists somewhere; in fact, many believe that spiritually, we are *all* nonmortal. However, in the syllogism this possibility is excluded, and we accept the statement. Notice that the logical form of the statement does not make it true.

We say we *know* something when we can fit it into our system; if it won't fit, we say it's *un*known, which clearly doesn't mean it's *unreal*. For instance, scientists say they do not fully understand the behavior of subatomic particles; the particles react in a way inconsistent with current logic or theory, and the reason, the logic, for this is *unknown*.

As we have seen, the logic of poetry, metaphor, works another way—in some respects, the opposite way:

1. Poetic metaphor acts to unify experience rather than to fragment it; it joins unlike things (X's and Y's) rather than separating them into categories. Logic tells us that an arrow is one thing, and a desire another. In metaphor the two are united.
2. Metaphor makes use of similarities and contrasts, and sometimes even cause and effect, but never within a systematic framework. Can you see, for example, the difference between the logical contrast, "a pear is not an apple," and Stevens' metaphoric contrast, "pears are not viols, nudes or bottles"? Or think of Blake's "Auguries of Innocence" (page 28): "Each outcry from the hunted Hare/A fibre from the Brain does tear." This metaphor has a cause-and-effect form, but is it really an attempt at logic? The metaphoric relationship between X and Y is not predictable, not the result of theory. It's always unexpected.
3. Poetic metaphor does not aim at making something known, but at

the *experience of the unknown*. Generally we quickly lose interest in the familiar, the known, things fixed in categories, while what is unknown has vitality, spontaneity and demands attention. Notice that in working logically, when we haven't seen something before, we move to identify it with what we know. So the new rapidly and continuously becomes the old. We feel something and instantly say, "What am I feeling—love, fear, desire?" We look for a name, a familiar category which defines and limits the experience. In poetry, however, we discover relationships like "arrows of desire" which aim at something quite different.

Poetic metaphor combines definitions, categories in new ways in order to come at experiences we cannot pin down. Words in their customary usage point at things, feelings, ideas, etc., previously defined, but in metaphor there is no "thing." There is only discovery. And this kind of discovery does not end with a conclusion we can file away in a system and forget *because it exists only while we are looking at it, experiencing it*. There is a process of continual finding out involved, and the moment we say, "This is it, I've got it now, I've explicated this experience," discovery and learning are over. We may have a memory, but a memory is hardly something living and fresh. So no one can say he knows poetry. We write it, talk about it, and react to it, but what is poetic (as any poet will affirm) has to be continually rediscovered. Analytically, the best we can do is, up to a point, comprehend technique.

Since early times, in all parts of the world, poetry has been thought sacred, divine, magical; poets were said to be "inspired" by God, seers who brought back glimpses of the unmeasurable, the timeless, the ultimate reality. Poetry, myth, and spiritual thought have always been closely identified, and metaphor (particularly personification) is one of the primary mythic devices. (I.e., the ancients identified or associated the wind with spirit.) Mythic poetry may have been the first means men used in trying to grasp the unknown. Even God has been considered a kind of poet. According to various religious traditions God spoke the Word (called *Logos* in the west, *vac* in the east) which created the world. Logic, as we have seen, involves using words to categorize objects, ideas, feelings, etc. *Logos* was considered the Word as revelation, intuition, manifestation of the essential, vital creative power, and law of the universe. *Logos* has been conceived to lead to what philosophers call the "being" of things, the force or spirit that underlies them, their essence, and traditionally philosophers—including the twentieth century existentialist, Martin Heidegger—have identified poetry with this "being" because they felt that (like *Logos*) it somehow had the power to go beyond mere words and things to manifest a glimpse of *life* and *truth*. An ancient Chinese philosopher, Chuang Tzu, described the phenomenon of arriving at "being" through words this way:

The fish trap exists because of the fish; once you've gotten the fish, you can forget the trap. The rabbit snare exists because of the rabbit; once you've gotten the rabbit, you can forget the snare. Words exist because of meaning; once you've gotten the meaning, you can forget the words. Where can I find a man who has forgotten words so I can have a word with him?

Religious teachers have frequently used poetry's chief tool to express their sense of the cosmic order. Take, for example, Christ's famous metaphor in Mark 4:30–32:

And he said . . . the kingdom of God . . . is like a grain of mustard seed, which, when it is sown in the earth, is less than all the seeds that be in the earth: but when it is sown, it groweth up, and becometh greater than all the herbs, and shooteth out great branches; so that the fowls of the air may lodge under the shadow of it.

Notice the familiar poetic complexity here, the intensely compact levels of meaning: the paradox of the smallest, most insignificant thing (the seed) being the greatest and most magnificent (heaven); the implication that the seed (soul?) is itself the kingdom of heaven; the suggestion of growth and flowering; the question of free will (Who sows the seed—the individual himself? God? Both?); the suggestion that the object of the sowing and flowering is mercy (the fowls of the air find shelter under it); and more. No logic could restrict this metaphor; no substitution or paraphrase could restate its message. This is not a politician trying to convince us of something or a philosopher illustrating his theory; this is poetic statement taking us beyond the familiar, habit-bound world toward the new and unknown. And this metaphor is still effective after twenty centuries.

The following selections illustrate the poetic use of metaphor by other spiritual teachers.*

First look at a Ch'an Buddhist sage's poem:

THERE IS NOTHING SPECIAL

There is nothing special about what I do every day;
I stay tuned to the truth; I refuse nothing,
I reach for nothing, never agree or argue.
Why do men see different colors?
The blue mountain° is dustless.
Magical powers and miracles
Are like carrying water and bearing a load of wood.

*See also Omar Kháyyám (page 37) and St. John of the Cross (page 281).

°The "blue mountain" is a Ch'an symbol for the absolute reality, the pure nature that does not discriminate, see differences in things or place importance on external phenomena, etc.

From a medieval Sufi (Moslem) poet and sage:

LIGHT

The true lover [of God] finds the light only if, like
the candle, he is his own fuel, consuming himself.

From the sixth-century Hindu sage Shankara:

The ocean of reality is sweet. There are no words to speak of it.
The mind gets no hold upon it. My mind dropped like a hailstone
into God's infinite ocean and melted and joined with Him.

. . . .

I am Reality . . . like space, I cannot be soiled. Like the sun I
reveal all the world to men and yet I am not of the world myself. I
am still as a mountain, boundless as the sea. The sky is not hemmed
in by its clouds neither am I restricted by the body. . . . My outward
shape lives and dies, tastes the sweet and bitter, but my true nature
stays forever. . . . A man is not his shadow. Whatever touches his
shadow does not touch him. This world is the shadow of me. . . .

And this poem by a twentieth-century teacher, Aurobindo:

THE BLUE BIRD

I am the bird of God in His blue;
  Divinely high and clear
I sing the notes of the sweet and the true
  For the gods and the seraph's ear.

I rise like a fire from the mortal's earth
  Into a griefless sky
And drop in the suffering soil of his birth
  Fire-seeds of ecstasy.

My pinions soar beyond Time and Space
  Into unfading Light;
I bring the bliss of the Eternal's face
  And the boon of the Spirit's sight.

I measure the worlds with my ruby eyes;
  I have perched on Wisdom's tree
Thronged with the blossoms of Paradise
  By the streams of Eternity.

Nothing is hid from my burning heart;
   My mind is shoreless and still;
My song is rapture's mystic art,
   My flight immortal will.

Apparently in religious areas (not religion as ritual, dogma, or creed), what has been called "mystical" can be best expressed metaphorically. Men who speak of having direct experience of God, enlightenment, truth, the infinite, or what have you insist that our habits of perception and logic dull us to reality; they claim that the experience of truth (not ideas or opinions) is a totally different state of being from the one we know. J. Krishnamurti expressed this point, saying:

By whatever name it may be called, truth must ever be new, living; but the words "new" and "living" are used only to convey a state that is not static, not dead, not a fixed point within the mind of man. Truth must be discovered anew from moment to moment, it is not an experience that can be repeated; it is a timeless state. . . . Truth is the unknown; it cannot be known; if it is known, it is not truth.

Compare this with what you have experienced of metaphoric action.

Interestingly, many occult systems seem to employ metaphor for the same reason: to break through a conditioned view of life into the unknown (or *not yet* known).

The famous *I Ching* is an example of a metaphoric system designed to trigger awareness. This ancient Chinese book works as follows: A set of poetic statements is arranged so that each is associated with a *line*. A group of six lines forms a "hexagram," which is itself associated with a poetic statement that provides a context for the individual lines. There are sixty-four hexagrams in all. The questioner selects hexagrams and lines from the book by shaking coins or picking up sticks. (This method eliminates conscious choice, and the questioner cannot make a preconditioned selection.) Then he metaphorically interprets the results. There are limited arrangements, and one often gets the same answer for many different questions. (As we have seen questions operate as metaphors in certain poems.) The question itself becomes an *X*, and this directs the comprehension of the answer statement (*Y*). The questioner has to find the connection between them. To give an example, an author learned of a probable delay in the publication date of his book. There was, at the time, some faint hope that the delay could be avoided. The *I Ching* was asked whether the book would go through on time. The response of the device is given below as an instance of this sort of metaphoric interpretation.

HEXAGRAM 12

```
___o___                              __ __
_____          yielding this:      _____
_____                              _____
__ __                                __ __
___x___                              _____
___x___                              _____
```
Stagnation   Joy

The context of the hexagram "Stagnation" indicates the time of autumnal decay when heaven is drawing further away while the earth sinks into the depths. Line 9 in the top place reads: "The standstill comes to an end. First standstill, then good fortune."

A few days later the problem was resolved, and the project went forward. Whether or not you can always discover such direct correspondence between events and your interpretations, experimenting with the *I Ching* is an excellent way to improve your metaphoric eye.

The Tarot cards use a set of symbolic images and function similarly to the *I Ching*. In astrology symbolic referents (planets, degrees, stars, etc.) are assembled by simple calculations into a system unique for each individual event or person to be studied, a kind of personal metaphoric *X* to be understood. In all the above, as with poetry, there are structural elements (in poetry all the constituents of tone, here the hexagram, card spread, astrological chart) and the necessity of going beyond the structure to get at the unknown. The state of mind, the awareness, that grasps the unknown has been called "intuition."

Obviously, to find out whether these methods of inquiry really yield insight, you would have to experiment with them. As with poetry, an opinion (no matter whose) about their validity would be, at best, theoretical.

Poets, mystics, and occultists are by no means the only ones concerned with the state of intuitive awareness; philosophers, scientists, and others are as well. Historically, it seems that those who make new discoveries in any field must break through the prevailing pattern of logic, the familiar description of the world that is considered

**I Ching quotations are from the Wilhelm-Baynes translation published by Princeton University Press.

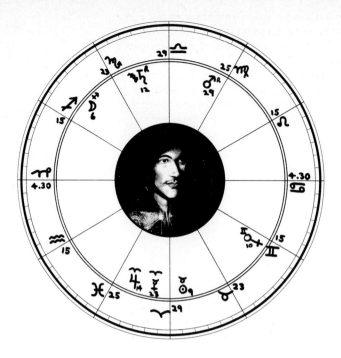

"knowledge" of it. For example, "the earth is flat" was once "knowledge" based on observation. However, certain men sensed that the world was round. "Nature moves toward the sphere as a form," some said. But they could not prove this in any reliable way. Still, they were right, and somehow they broke through the then current logical description. Apparently they jumped intuitively from the known to the unknown. The idea of the internal combustion engine does not follow from a study of the ways of horses, and you do not add together all the previous theories about time and space and come up with Einstein's theory of relativity as a sum. Einstein said himself that the concepts "came" to him.

Poets, mystics, occultists, and discoverers of natural laws often say, in one form or another, that in experiencing the intuitive "leap," they confront the paradox (or seeming paradox) that everything is distinct and individual, and yet everything is one—that all phenomena are unified, or, as the fourth century B.C. Greek philosopher Heraclitus put it: "What is at variance with itself agrees with itself." So from yet another direction we come upon the metaphoric experience: the unity of unlike things.

Thus in a larger sense, metaphor is simply a way of talking about the intuitive state of mind. To paraphrase Chuang Tzu, once you have the experience, you can forget the word. And once you experience poetry deeply, you can forget the textbook.

As we have seen, poetry has many dimensions which give pleasure and excite interest: sound effects, wit, imagination, social comment, philosophy, and so on. But it seems fair to say that the "magic," the enduring and most profound aspect of the art, comes out of metaphor, out of evoking insight. Nearly everyone agrees that technique, however interesting, is never enough; we can see that the moment of intuition, of poetry, is a truth beyond skill, beyond levels of education or culture. Thus the following poems may demonstrate that the poetic utterances of a Bushman can touch us as deeply as the sophisticated or artful complexities of a Goethe or Dante.

Johann Wolfgang von Goethe

GESANG DER GEISTER ÜBER DEN WASSERN

The soul
moves like water:
falls from above,
dissolves, rises,
thickens and falls,
again and again
without end.

Pure water
falls from the peak
where rock is sleek
sprays into cloud
sways and fills
streams smoothly on
within its mists
with slight sounds
moving away
into the valley deeps.

Where rocks
block flow it breaks
foams and spatters
down to the dark.

In lowland meadows
gently becoming
a still lake
it gleams deep and full of stars.

Wind like a lover
flows with and mixes
self with the other
loving in waves.

Human soul
you are water!
Human fate
you are wind!

Rendition from German by Richard Monaco

RE-BIRTH

A PRAYER TO THE NEW MOON
RELATED BY DAI-KWAIN
Young moon, take my face up yonder,
give back to me your face up there,
   take away this pain.

Give me your face, small moon,
that dies, and when you die
living, you return again.
When we see you, and no more we see you
you lie down to sleep and come again.
Give me that I shall be like you
this joy that you possess forever
yonder with you, that living you come back
when we did not see you there.

Once when your child the hare
cried to you, his mother, not to let him die
you told us too that when we died
   we should return again.

        Bushman Prayer; c. after W. H. I. Bleek

Dante Alighieri

PARADISO

At this point in the poem the narrator, Dante, has toured hell, purgatory, and has arrived at the highest level of heaven, at the threshold of directly seeing the divine wisdom face to face. St. Bernard is praying for Dante to be granted this sight.

CANTO XXXIII
"Virgin Mother, daughter of your Son,
Lowest and highest of all beings,
The unmoving end of eternal knowing,
Such a perfection of human form
That the maker let himself be made in it.
Womb of time and love where the flower
Of light and moveless peace unfolded;
Sun forever noon to us,
The living water of hope to men.
Lady, so great and universal
No one has grace where you are not:
His desires drop, wingless, to despair.
Your vast love supports whoever asks,
And many who are mute;
Substance of Mercy, Pity and Light,
The core of sparkling good in every life.
This man, risen from the depths
Of the universal pit to here
Has seen the life of souls from low to high
And begs you for the power of your grace
So that his eyes may fill with final seeing,
And I, who ache to see him see
As much as I ached for my own vision,
Surrender all my praying to you and pray
It is enough for you to scatter
The fogs and clouds of his gross self
And let him fill with the shadowless joy
And his whole being become unending song.
And I pray, Queen, that you
Contain him in your purity forever
After this vision, holding still
The bestial throb and fire of his nature.
Beatrice and the other blest I see
Pray with my prayers!"
The God-illumined, loving eyes
Enfolded the speaker, grateful
For his need and then were turned
To the endless light; incredible
That any eye could receive
Such supernal clarity.
And I, close to the end of all desire,

Ended the violent ardor of final need.
Bernard smiled, gestured upward,
But I was already rapt and bound by sight
To that above and my vision clearing
(Like a stilled pond with the shock of sun)
Into the beam that lights itself alone,
Filled with itself and all else filled with it.
Speech failed forever from that moment
Though time was not and memory blasted
Clean and empty. Like one
Who tries to recover the truth of a dream
And is left with waking uncertainty and hints,
Am I; there is no vision now but vision's absence
And still my heart distills the sweetness of it!
Like a mark in snow dissolved in sunlight,
Like the light leaves fluttering in the Sibylline wind
A stir of truth forever lost.
O light of light beyond the clumsy mind
Straining with narrow thought and dull desire
Allow me it again, free my dead tongue
That I might light a candle of thy truth
In all the vast dark night of time to come
And set a gleam to guide the future lost;
I will try my memory again:
If I had not become the living flame
The shell of tinder that I call myself
Would have been blasted by that incandescense.
There was no self but only truth;
And the vivid goodness of unending end
Met no resistance, I fell into light,
Seeing the sizeless infinite and saw
Bound in one book by love the myriad facts,
The pages blown and scattered everywhere:
Every separateness, every division, every chapter,
Every broken thing and scattered spark
Gathered in a great hush, held,
United in one simple flame.
I think I saw the single form
Of heaven and earth; in telling this
Joy lifts and swells in me . . .
And there is now more darkness in a single moment
Than in 25 centuries since Neptune felt
The shadow of the Argo cross his world.
My mind was fixed and thought was blown away.
And looking itself fanned the fire of sight.
There is nothing more to see after this,
None, once seeing, ever turns away:
The feeble good that smoulders in the world
Is here a flame without a wisp of smoke;
The words, thoughts, passions, kisses, dreams,

What lovers really mean by loving, all
Released from the corpse of form
And tomb of time.
And now I speak in gasps, less capable
Than the child who laps and kisses at the breast.
Not that the living light has many levels
(For eternity is motionless and single)
But I, myself, the I that is and isn't,
Expanded and became a lens for God
The focus changing though the light changed not.
And color that dimmed a thousand suns enclosed me,
Rainbow on rainbow, flame burning flame
And fed by flame alone, O words
Of the dead can never speak of life!
There are no words! O Eternal Light
Living in Thyself, by self sustained,
A love loving love, beginning and end!
The circles beyond measure mere reflection
Of Thy being. I had no
Boundries within what knows no end.
Mind strained to hold and slipped aside
And left me without measure of myself,
Without a center I was everywhere,
And though I could not know I knew;
And what I could not grasp I held;
And as the whole wheel measurelessly spun
So what I was turned too, and moved
Inseperate with the Love that rolls the sun,
Moves all heaven and the endless stars.

Rendition from Italian by Richard Monaco

APPENDIX

NOTES ON PROSODY

by Christopher Collins

Prosody is an activity of the mind not merely distinct from, but positively disruptive to, the writing and reading of poetry. Defined by the dictionary as the "science or study of poetic meters and versification," it is to poetry what the science of theology is to spiritual contemplation or what a clinical study of the human orgasm is to lovemaking. This is not to say it isn't a fascinating subject, that is, for the specialist whose primary interests are not poetic.

How else can we account for the instinctive hostility shown toward prosody by most otherwise open-minded students of poetry and for the frequent contempt showered on it by the poets themselves? Prosodists and writers of poetry texts often argue that students are unwilling to approach the discipline aspects of the craft and that the poets are striking a pose, either of anti-intellectualism or of Masonic secrecy. But the student still says to himself: "When the teacher takes the poem apart and analyzes every detail of structure, he ruins the experience for me." And the poet butts in disconcertingly: "That was a delightful analysis of my open and closed vowels and my falling rhythm. But when I write, I just let it all flow out. I didn't know exactly what I was doing with my sounds." So the student and the poet go off to lunch together, leaving the prosodist holding the bag—a bag crammed with enjambments, anapests, and other curious ingenuities.

Let there be no misunderstanding: The patterns which the prosodist examines are of great importance to the poet. Despite this fact, the practicing poet typically maintains that the science of prosody is irrelevant to his craft. The disagreement apparently hinges on *how* one goes about examining poetic pattern. Ezra Pound stated flatly that "prosody and melody are attained by the listening ear, not by an index of nomenclatures, or by learning that such and such a foot is called a spondee." Perhaps the problem lies here: If verse pattern functions more or less subliminally, providing a background for the poem as a whole, it becomes irrelevant when focused on as a primary factor in itself, when it is brought, so to speak, to the surface. While the fish in the fish store may look like the same fish that swam this

You don't ask an art instructor to give you a recipe for making a Leonardo da Vinci drawing. Hence the extreme boredom caused by the usual professorial documentation or the aspiring thesis on prosody.

Ezra Pound (1934)

TO A SKYLARK

Hail to thee blythe spirit
Bird thou never wert

in heaven or near it,
Pourest thy full heart
in profuse strains of
unpremeditated art.

C. COLLINS

morning into the net, his behavior has markedly changed. If all we knew about the life-style of a flounder was inferred from looking at him glazed-eyed and bedded in shaved ice, we would know very little indeed.

There is a happy ending to the story. Unlike the fish, the poem revives. After a while we forget the prosodic analysis. Suddenly when least expecting it, we encounter the poem as fresh and alive as on the day it was made. The sounds and rhythms—there they are circulating just out of sight below the surface, the whole poem somehow resonating again deep within us. One is relieved, but left wondering why it was ever thought necessary in the first place to scale, trim, gut, and fillet that defenseless poem. There must have been some better way to sensitize ourselves to pattern. Intellectual analysis has evidently too many undesirable side effects. To preserve its life, we must find a way to shield pattern from the destructive rays of analysis.

Then, is there any purpose at all to prosody? For the specialist or the linguist of course, there is a purpose. The reader or writer of poetry, however, has a different need. He must learn to be aware of pattern as it functions. He must live with it in its own shadowy habitat. He must learn to listen out of the corner of his mind. In reading the poetries of the past and of the present, he must attune himself to the various patterns which poets have—from period to period—submerged below the metaphoric surface of the poem.

In the following we will survey the various patterns of English poetry, trace the development of one principal rhythmic base and very briefly consider how twentieth-century poets develop new patterns, as well as modify the old.

> The eagle never lost so much time as when he submitted to learn of the crow.
>
> William Blake (1792)

THE ORIGINS OF ENGLISH METER

The rhythmic pattern underlying English poetry varied as the language developed. The Angles and Saxons, who dominated the Old English period (from about 450 to about 1150), brought with them a language of clearly contrasted stresses: the root element of a noun, verb, or adjective would be pronounced with strong emphasis, while the less important syllables would receive only minor attention. Since poetic rhythm probably always begins as an adaptation of speech rhythm, it is not at all surprising that traditionally poets have made full use of this

> thær mæg níhta gehwǽm‖níth-
> wundor seón
> fýr on flóde.‖No thæs fród léofath
> gúmena béarna‖thæt thone grúnd
> wite.
>
> *From Beowulf* (eighth century)
> A description of Grendel's lair, accents and cæsuras indicated.

feature and have produced a poetry in which only strong stresses, or accents, are counted. (Note here, at the very start of our historical survey, the importance of number *count* in rhythmic structures. This form of counting, or measurement, according to accents is called *accentual meter*.)

While the various Germanic dialects in Britain were coalescing into what became the grandparent of modern English, on the Continent another group of languages was slowly taking shape. These, the Romance languages, developed out of the local vernaculars spoken in the various provinces of the former Roman Empire, namely, in Italy, France, Spain, and Portugal. Unlike Old English, these languages were not strongly stressed. In other words, the degree of contrast between stressed and unstressed syllables in a Romance language was, compared with that in Old English, not significant enough to form the rhythmic base for a native poetry. So, unable to measure by accents, the minstrels and troubadours measured their lines by the number of syllables each line contained. *Syllabic meter*, as this has come to be called, had one distinct advantage—it was beautifully adaptable to music. Without strong stress to worry about, the singer-composer could linger over almost any syllable, raise its melodic pitch, or clip it short. The ease with which words can thus be put to music has given the Romance languages their special lyrical reputation. (Syllabic meter, incidentally, is a very extensively used verse measurement. It is used in such widely diverse poetries as Celtic—Gaelic and Welsh—and Japanese.)

When William marched to the Battle of Hastings in 1066, his army of Frenchified Normans was led forth by the minstrel Taillefer, and so the first outlandish sounds that reached the ears of the blunt, accentual English soldiery were the sounds of syllabic poetry. The lone horseman at the head of the Norman army was singing the ten-syllable lines of the *Song of Roland*. We don't know whether or not these French syllabics charmed this first English audience, but of course we know the English lost the battle and were forced to accept a new ruling class, one which was French in language, cultural allegiances, and political orientation—as well as metric preference. Soon the disenfranchised Englishman who found himself wandering past those newfangled turreted castles began overhearing the strains of Norman French *chansons*, sung poems of marvelously inwoven complexity, rhymed stanzas in a myriad of forms—a whole panoply of structures later known by such names as *ballade*, *villanelle*, *triolet*, and *rime coueé*.

But these social divisions did not last long. The Middle English period (from about 1150 to about 1475) was marked by an

Quant|li|estez|et|la|douce|saisons
fait fuelle et flor et les pres raverdir
et li douz chanz des menuz oisillons
fait as pluisors de joie sovenir . . .

From the early-twelfth-
century "Chansons du
Châtelain de Coucy."

increasing sense of national identity, which was reflected in the gradual coalescence of the Old English and Norman French languages. One effect of this cultural harmonization was the use by poets of a special rhythmic base which could accommodate this new hybrid language.

What they did was perfectly logical: The poets of Chaucer's generation (the latter half of the 1300s) simply superimposed an English system of accents upon a French system of syllables. The result of this union is called, logically enough, *accentual-syllabic meter*. This is the "English meter" which has dominated English poetry for more than five centuries. One simple passage from Chaucer's General Prologue to *The Canterbury Tales* will illustrate this confluence of accents and syllables:

A Knight ther was,‖and that a worthy man,

That,‖fro the tyme that he first began

To riden out,‖he loved chivalrye,

Trouthe and honour,‖fredom and curteisye.

Note first that there are ten syllabic units in each line. These ten units are grouped into two-syllable units known as *feet*. The vertical line (‖) is the traditional "scanning" notation for this division of syllables. Keep in mind that these divisions are there to count sound units only, *not* words, and that the first part of a word may fall into one metric foot, and the second part into the next foot.

So far, we have been examining Chaucer's four-line excerpt as an example of syllabic meter—no matter how we slice them, they are still syllables, ten of them to the line. But now comes the native English contribution, strong accents. Each syllable is accented (ˊ) or unstressed (˘) or is given a sort of intermediate stress called *hovering accent* (ˏ). (Theoretically, the accents could have been arranged very irregularly, but the fact is that in the spoken language, an alternation of accented and unaccented syllables seemed to prevail.)

In addition to syllable count and accent distribution, there is another essential aspect of poetic rhythm which this passage illustrates. That aspect might be called "pacing." The notation ‖ separating the syllables in a line indicates a *caesura*. The caesura (Latin for "cleavage") is the natural pause that occurs at certain points in the flow of language and is usually signaled by some mark of punctuation. Since it may occur *anywhere* in the line, it gives to what might otherwise become a monotonous string of ten syllables an element of surprise and dramatic expressiveness.

Another factor in pacing is the length of pause allowed at the end of each line. In the passage above, the first, third, and fourth lines complete a grammatical unit, are punctuated, and are accordingly called *end-stopped lines*. But when we finish the second line, we make at most only a minimal pause. This line is called a *run-on line*, or an example of *enjambment* (French for "striding over" or "encroachment"). The prime effects of enjambment are to speed up the progression of the verses and expand thought and image development. See Keats's "Ode on Melancholy" (page 9) for examples of these various techniques of pacing.

One final note on scansion: It is only an approximate measurement of rhythmic pattern. There may be several different but perfectly correct ways of distributing accents and inserting pauses in any given line of poetry.

THE TRIUMPH OF IAMBIC PENTAMETER AND WHY NO ONE NEEDS TO UNDERSTAND HOW IT WORKS

This patterned line which Chaucer and others adapted to the requirements of English, the Greek prosodists called *iambic pentameter*. It was called *iambic* because its basic unit was an iamb, that is, a two-syllable foot composed of an unstressed syllable followed by an accented syllable ($\smile\prime$). It was called *pentameter* because it was a measure (meter) of five (penta) units. As we see from the scanned passage above, not all the feet are iambic, and yet all the lines are said to be iambic-pentameter lines. It is a fact that the practiced reader of this type of verse deals subliminally with a musical trio of three simultaneous patterns: the pattern of accents, which may vary dramatically from line to line; the pattern of syllables, which is always ten (with an occasional unstressed syllable tagged on the end); and the pattern of five regular iambs, which he senses as an expectation *even if five regular iambs are not present in the line.*

If all this seems perversely elaborate, be assured that this is precisely the point. The lasting power of iambic pentameter (over 85 percent of all the poetry written in the English language from 1350 to 1900 was written in this pattern) lies in its multilayered subtlety. But why baffle the inquiring reader? Why? Because it's none of his business. No one vulnerable to the beauty of poetic language ever needs to figure out in formal analysis what is happening metrically on the level of rhythmic awareness—no one except the poet, who long ago mastered the basic metric repertoire and who operates now by finely adjusted rhythmic instincts—and except of course the prosodist, that old, indomitable prier into mysteries.

Accent, the chiefe Lord and grave Governour of Numbers.

Samuel Daniel (1602)

[The range of choice in British and American poetry is] strict iambic and loose iambic [and] any length of line up to six feet.

Robert Frost (1946)

As this line developed in the two centuries which separated Chaucer from Shakespeare, one particular intricacy became increasingly important. Prosodists have lavished volumes of admiration on this one fact of English metrics: No decent English poet ever went daDUM daDUM daDUM daDUM daDUM for more than two or three verses without, for example, inserting a *DUMda* daDUM daDUM daDUM daDUM or, if he had the audacity of Milton, a *DUMDUM DUMDUM DUM-DUM* daDUM daDUM. The italicized accent variations from the iambic norm are called *foot substitutions*. Several examples occur in the above-quoted passage from Chaucer.

Besides being at times richly expressive and rhythmically imitative of the meaning of the words, foot substitution serves two more fundamental purposes. When Yeats once remarked that rhythm "hushed the mind with an alluring monotony," he went onto say, "while it holds us waking by variety." Without caesuras and foot substitutions, the metric pattern would become numbingly obvious, so obvious that all we could be conscious of would be the absurdly repeated iambic beat—like staying awake at night just to listen to a dripping faucet. Such regular meter would tend to dull that alertness we need to follow the often intricate and subtle transformation of metaphor. These variations are what lightly jog us awake. The second purpose which foot substitution serves is that of camouflaging the basic metric pattern, that ghostly obbligato of iambs that throbs below the surface of the accents. Just when that repetitive pulse begins to surface in our minds, the poet lets accentual speech rhythm take over as though to say, "Meter? What meter? This is straight English!" But all the while, somewhere within us, that steady beat is sounding, five iambs to a measure.

During the century following Chaucer's death (in 1400), great changes occurred in the language. Thousands of Latin and Greek words began to be imported and naturalized—over the protests of conservative spokesmen who labeled them pseudo-learned or "inkhorn terms." In addition, some of the last vestiges of Old English inflected endings (the short e's which Chaucer still pronounced) were dropped, thus eliminating a whole class of unstressed syllables needed by iambic meter. Fortunately for the continuity of English meter, these two disruptive changes balanced each other out. What the iambic line lost in unstressed e's it more than gained back in unstressed or only slightly stressed prefixes and suffixes attached to words of Latin and Greek origin (for example, pro-, trans-, ad-, -ive, -ic, -ent, -ate, -ive). The following quotation from *Hamlet* illustrates how these two developments in language were adjusted to English meter. The scene takes place on the battlements; as Hamlet awaits his

The essence of verse is regularity, and its ornament is variety.

Samuel Johnson (1781)

father's ghost, he hears drunken shouting coming from his uncle's chambers:

> This heavy-headed revel east and west
> Makes us traduced, and taxed of other nations.
> They clepe us drunkards, and with swinish phrase
> Soil our addition; and indeed it takes
> From our achievements, though performed at height,
> The pith and marrow of our attribute.

Note the classical imports: "traduce" (1535), "phrase" (1530), "addition" (in the sense of "title," 1494), and "attribute" (in the sense of "reputation"), appearing first, according to the *Oxford English Dictionary*, in this speech of Hamlet's (1602). Note also how these "inkhorn terms" associate with such pungent native words as "clepe," "swinish," and "marrow." Note finally all the unpronounced terminal e's, ed's, and es's, which once warranted separate syllable status.

The third great language change which occurred during the fifteenth century has been called the "great vowel shift." This mysterious development resulted in, among other effects, the lengthening of certain vowels and the emergence of the diphthongs i (as in "mile") and ou (as in "house"). This made some classically oriented poets conclude that the proper metric base for English should be the alternation of "long" and "short" syllables, as was the case in Greek and Latin. Classical *quantitative meter*, as this was called, used the "quantity" of syllables (the length of time necessary to pronounce a given syllable), rather than accent, as its organizing principle.

Though these theorists were unsuccessful in quantifying English poetry, they demonstrated one fact: Quantity, like accent, is an essential feature of the language. These lines of Thomas Campion (1567–1620) are undeniably accentual, but it would be a mistake to discount the pattern created by his rich open "long vowels":

> What if a day, or a month, or a year
> Crown thy delights with a thousand sweet contentings?
> Cannot a chance of a night or an hour
> Cross thy desires with many sad tormentings?

or:

> Follow your saint, follow with accents sweet;
> Haste you, sad notes, fall at her flying feet.

We are here at the midpoint of our survey. To sum up: From Old English through Chaucer's Middle English, to the beginnings of modern English in the Elizabethan period, we have

Among all other lessons this should first be learned, that we never affect any strange ynkehorne termes, but so speake as is commonly received. . . . Some seek so far for outlandish Englishe, that they forget altogether their mother's language. And I dare swear this: if some of their mothers were alive, they were not able to tell what they say. . . .

Samuel Daniel (1553)

Samuel Daniel was a good honest man . . . but no poet.

Ben Johnson (1619)

watched English poets work with rhythmic patterns based upon three elements of language—(1) syllable accent (accentual meter), (2) syllable count (syllabic meter), and (3) syllable length (quantitative meter). Poetry was written in each pattern, and with various line lengths, but the iambic-pentameter line, which survived all these variations, proved to be a combination of all three—the accentual-syllabic meter, which Chaucer employed and to which the Elizabethans added the rich vowel music of quantity.

THE GREAT RHYME
CONTROVERSY

If we were asked which aspect of traditional English poetry seems least effective and most contrived to contemporary readers, most of us would probably say "rhyme." Somehow that word has come to suggest all that is "artificial" and old-fashioned in the poetry of the past. It might be worthwhile to find out why we feel this way.

First of all, a rhyme is a type of rhythm. It is a particular sound that recurs perceptibly in a passage of poetry. It may be a recurrence of initial consonants (alliteration), of stressed vowels (assonance), or of final syllables in lines (end rhyme, what we usually mean when we speak of rhyme). Besides these, there are many other minor rhyme formations which, thanks to the prosodists of the past, all bear special names. Those two forms of so-called internal rhyme—alliteration and, to a lesser extent, assonance—performed important functions in Old English poetry. They never deserted English poetry, but it has been end rhyme which, from the time of Chaucer to the beginning of the twentieth century, poets have most heavily relied on. Just as accentual-syllabic meter provided the submerged pattern for the words of the line, end rhyme in its myriad formal arrangements provided patterns for whole lines. It set up a rhythm—similar to meter—of expectation and fulfillment. Its main function was architectonic; that is, it was used to *build* the stanzas (Italian for "rooms") of the poetic edifice. (The stanzas built by rhyme range from the two-line couplet to such intricate feats of poetic engineering as the fourteen-line sonnet.)

However, to the rabid classicist—and every classicist had his rabid moments—rhyme was a barbaric, "gothic" abomination. He maintained that if adaptations had to be tolerated, then only unrhymed iambic pentameter, or blank verse, qualified as an English approximation of the epic line of Homer and Virgil. All rhymed "unclassical" forms of verse were obviously degenerate. Strange as it may seem to us today, much of the literary energies of the seventeenth century were expended defending or attacking rhyme. Ben Jonson vented his humorous, but quite precise,

We can die by it, if not live by love,
  And if unfit for tombs and hearse
Our legend be, it will be fit for verse;
And if no piece of chronicle we prove,
  We'll build in sonnets pretty rooms.

John Donne, 1633

wrath in his poem "A Fit of Rime against Rime" (page 73): "Vulgar [vernacular] languages that want [lack]/Words, and sweetnesse, and be scant/Of true measure,/Tyran[t] Rime hath so abused,/That they long since have refused,/Other ceasure . . . ." "Ceasure" is Jonson's inkhorn anglicization of "caesura," that natural disjuncture within the line which classicists so prized in Homer and Virgil and in the English blank verse of Shakespeare and Marlowe. As Jonson indicates, end rhyme, by emphasizing the last word in the line, tends to reserve the pause for the end of the line, thus minimizing the role of internal caesura. If this seems like a small technical point of contention, consider this other technical point: End rhyme, by increasing the pause at the end of the line, militates against the practice of enjambment, that is, against the unrestricted flow of language, of poetic syntax, of the elaboration of ideas and images. Apparently, emotive connotations of those two political catchwords "liberty" and "license" were very much a part of this great rhyme controversy.

Many poets welcomed end rhyme. The early seventeenth century was an age of unrivaled verbosity and fantastic verbal amusements. Dryden in 1664 wrote of rhyme that it "bounds and circumscribes the fancy. For imagination in a poet is a faculty so wild and lawless, that, like a high-ranging spaniel, it must have clogs tied to it, lest it outrun judgment." Four years later, after he published his classically framed epic, *Paradise Lost*, John Milton felt he had to explain his decision not to use rhyme. His first sentence announces: "The measure is English heroic verse [iambic pentameter] without rhyme. . . ." He goes on to contend that "true musical delight . . . consists only in apt numbers, fit quantity of syllables, and the sense variously drawn out from one verse into another, not in the jingling sound of like endings, a fault avoided by the ancients both in poetry and all good oratory." Of course Milton was Milton and had a great deal of cogent "sense" to draw out variously from one verse into another. But rhyme, and especially the rhymed couplet (the *heroic couplet*), had, as Dryden wryly pointed out, its special justification. Without wishing to do so, William Cowper (1731–1800) often found himself demonstrating the hazards of "English heroic verse without rhyme" (see the example in the margin). Perhaps after just such a bout of verse (somewhat like wrestling a man with an armful of large garden snakes), Cowper confided to a friend, "I do not mean to write blank verse again. Not having the music of rhyme, it requires so close an attention to the pause and the cadence." What Cowper turned to was the well-established heroic couplet, two rhymed iambic-pentameter lines with self-contained syntax and meaning. This cut down on his

And ten low words oft creep in
  one dull line:
While they ring around the same
  unvaried chimes,
With sure returns of still
  expected rhymes.
Where-e'er you find "the cooling
  western breeze,"
In the next line, it "whispers
  through the trees;"
If crystal streams "with pleasing
  murmurs creep,"
The reader's threatened (not in vain)
  with "sleep."

Alexander Pope (1742)

There is a pleasure in poetic pains
Which only poets know. The shifts
  and turns,
Th' expedients and inventions
  multiform,
To which the mind resorts, in chase
  of terms
Though apt, yet coy, and difficult
  to win—
Such joys has he that sings. But ah!
  not such,
Or seldom such, the hearers of his
  song.
Fastidious, or else listless, or
  perhaps
Aware of nothing arduous is a task
They never undertook, they little
  note
His dangers or escapes. . . .

William Cowper (1798)

verbosity, but, as the following couplet suggests, his poetic difficulties were more than merely technical: "The management of tyros of eighteen / Is difficult, their punishment obscene." For examples of considerably more successful heroic couplets, see Pope's "The Rape of the Lock" (page 87).

With the considerable support of Alexander Pope and Samuel Johnson, rhyme became for the eighteenth-century poet the principal element of pattern. In sharp contrast to Milton, Johnson was said to have abhorred "the old manner of continuing sense ungracefully from verse to verse." But here lay a problem. In English the supply of rhymes was limited, a fact which originally made rhyming such a pleasing feat. Still, for how many centuries could breath–death, weep–sleep, life–strife, etc., survive? Rhyme surfaced notably and successfully in the satiric verse of Pope, who did not use it as a subliminal pattern and who consciously raised it to a primary level, *made it in itself an element of wit.* Throughout the eighteenth century the surface of English poetry enjoyed the enrichment of rhyme and formal pattern. But to many of those who came to be called "romantics," this technical brilliance, this conspicuous grace, lacked the resonance of the sixteenth- and seventeenth-century poetry. Such formal restraints on rhythm as the rhymed couplet of Dryden and Pope were closely connected in their minds with restraint on thought and feeling. The "neoclassicists," for their part, associated rhythmic exuberance with all that seemed "unnatural," freakish, and mentally deranged.

The romantic movement is usually regarded as a reaction to this extreme rationalism. In England, poets set out to reclaim subliminal pattern from the poetry of the past: Wordsworth and Coleridge, from medieval balladry; Keats, from medieval and Renaissance romance; Blake, from the cadences of biblical prophecy. As a group, the English romantics, with the exception of Byron, looked upon the period from the death of Milton to the French Revolution (1789) as a time of generally uninspired verse and hoped themselves to restore poetry to the grandeur and vitality they felt it enjoyed in that golden age from 1575 to 1675.

If we consider the rhythmic patterns underlying Victorian poetry from early Tennyson to late Swinburne, we find many experiments and refinements in rhyme, meter, and stanza. The notable exceptions were notably disregarded. The loose but powerful rhythm Blake employed in his prophetical works was thought an oddity. Whitman's rolling Americanese was not sufficiently iambic to justify serious literary attention. Editors carefully edited out Emily Dickinson's slant rhymes. Hopkins's stark accentual meters were prized as mere "prosodic experiments."

```
            —           —
        ⌣       ⌣
    —   —   —
        ⌣   ⌣   ⌣
    —   —   —
        ⌣   ⌣   ⌣
    —           —
        ⌣       ⌣
            —
```

Excerpt from "Fisches Nachtgesang" ("The Fish's Serenade," subtitled "The Deepest of All German Poems")

Christian Morgenstern (1899)

The English critic who said of Miss Emily Dickinson that she might have become a fifth-rate poet "if she had only mastered the rudiments of grammar and gone into metrical training for about fifteen years,"— the rather candid English critic who said this somewhat overstated his case. He had, however, a fairly good case. If Miss Dickinson had undergone the austere curriculum indicated, she would, I am sure, have become an admirable lyric poet of the second magnitude.

Thomas Bailey Aldrich (1892)

TWENTIETH-CENTURY PATTERNS

In the twentieth century, poets loosely adapted accentual-syllabic meter to contemporary speech rhythms—e.g., Frost and Stevens—or reemployed older rhythmic bases: accentual meter, notably by Auden and Spender; syllabic, by Marianne Moore and Dylan Thomas; and quantitative, by Pound and Eliot.

Rhyme, too, was reactivated. Inspired by the rediscovered poetry of Emily Dickinson, poets of the 1920s began to utilize the vast resources of approximate rhyme (e.g., flat-flood, bell-call, numb-home). This subtle technique of sound patterning, usually called *slant rhyme*, furnished the poet a refreshingly wide array of rhyming possibilities. The range of tonal effects was also extensive—from an abrupt dissonance to a richly elusive harmony of sounds. (That popular form, the sonnet, had been consuming the stockpile of available "perfect rhymes" for centuries. An interesting example of a slant-rhyme sonnet is Gwendolyn Brooks's "My dreams, My works, Must Wait till after hell," page 39).

The verse form which made the biggest stir, however, was called *free verse*. "Free verse," as a term, seems to have little descriptive value; as the modern poet Robert Bly has said, "it implies not a technique, but a longing." The term soon was applied to all unrhymed variations of traditional English meter, i.e., accentual-syllabic meter. It was in reality an imitation of French syllabic rhythm together with a type of rhetorical stress more natural to French than to English. Nevertheless it has become perhaps the single most dominant English verse form and most major modern poets have worked with it.

My two rules in writing free verse are that I don't ever scan a line while I am composing it, and that words must fall into lines.

Robert Lowell (1967)

SOME SUGGESTIONS FOR WRITING POEMS

After you have gone through a chapter, consider the suggestions below. Don't be bound by them, but try to use them to help you come upon your own poem.

CHAPTER 1

Think of something that made an impression on you at some time in your life—a natural scene, a human action, or an idea—and write a poem expressing what it was that struck you, using metaphors. Remember that metaphors generally link the *concrete* with the *abstract* in order to reveal new aspects of the poetic subject, so try not to use them merely for descriptive purposes. Concentrate on "seeing" the subject metaphorically.

CHAPTER 2

Take a poem that interests you and derive a new one of your own by altering the tone and redirecting the metaphor(s). For example, look at "Laboratory Poem" (page 62) and "Slice of Life" (page 176); "Of Mere Being" and "Of Mere Being: A Variation for Wallace Stevens" (page 209); and "The Tiger," "The Panther," and "The Jaguar" (pages 211 and 212). Write a poem based on a paradox (see page 74). Write one extending a symbol into metaphor (see page 70).

CHAPTER 3

Establish an explicit central metaphoric relationship—for instance, "The mind is like a fish" or "My love is like a string of beads"—and build a poem around it.

CHAPTER 4

Take some central metaphoric subject, anything you like, and develop a poem that links this subject with various abstractions, ideas, moods, or whatever, as in "Toro" (page 165), "The Flower" (page 167), or "There's a Certain Slant of Light" (page 169).

CHAPTER 5

Try turning some cliché metaphor (such as "the sea of life" or "the wheel of fortune") into a poem. See whether you can evoke a relationship between the cliché and a fresh situation without ever stating your purpose *directly*.

CHAPTER 6

Try a piece based on a basic, an obvious, but not trite perception or fact of life. Study, for example, "On the Insecurity of Human Life" (page 247), which uses the theme "everything is dying," or Auden's "Musée des Beaux Arts," which talks about how we ignore one another's sufferings. Try to express your perception metaphorically so that the truism becomes insight.

CHAPTER 7

Frost's "The Oven Bird" sets up the subject so that we feel it has metaphoric implications. Try to do the same with some other animal or object.

CHAPTER 8

Look at the illustration for Donald Justice's "On a Painting by Patient B of the Independence State Hospital for the Insane" (page 344). Write your own poem describing this or some other picture so that the described images have metaphoric resonance.

abstract—Abstract terms are general terms— "hope," "joy," "love," "time," "beauty," "death." They are idea words. See CONCRETE.

accent—A stressed syllable in a line of poetry. See the discussion of prosody (page 398).

accentual verse meter—Lines measured by a regular pattern of stresses, rather than, for example, a rigid pattern of metric feet. See the discussion of prosody (page 397).

aesthetic distance—Objectivity. The poet presents his subject without the reader's feeling the intrusion of the poet's personality or opinion.

alexandrine—A line of poetry consisting of six IAMBIC feet. The standard line in classical French poetry.

allegory—In order to make a thesis or doctrine interesting, an allegory sets up characters or images to represent concepts, moral qualities, or abstractions on a one-to-one basis. Generally, there is no unlike factor and little or no nuance in an allegory. The character Time in the poem "Time and the Pilgrime" is an allegorical figure. While the poem itself is quite metaphoric, the character Time remains static and one-dimensional.

alliteration—Repetition of the initial or stressed consonants: "The soup bubbling on the back of the stove/The stove starring into the sun" (Philip Levine, page 31). See the discussion of prosody (page 402).

allusion—Literary reference to a person, place, or event. See Chapter 2 (page 53).

ambiguity—The assigning of two or more meanings relevant to a word, phrase, or poem, a characteristic of metaphoric language. In everyday language and expository prose ambiguity is considered a fault and results in a lack of clarity. In poetry, paradoxically, ambiguity often produces clarity and is considered a virtue. See CONNOTATION and METAPHOR.

anapest (anapestic)—A metric foot with two unstressed syllables followed by a stressed syllable (~~/).

antistrophe—See ODE.

apostrophe—The author addressing an absent person, an abstraction, or an inanimate entity. Pope apostrophizes Queen Anne in "The Rape of the Lock": "Here Thou, Great *Anna*! whom three realms obey. . . ."

association (metaphoric)—One kind of metaphoric (*X/Y*) juxtaposition. See JUXTAPOSITION. See Chapter 1 (page 4).

assonance—The repetition of a similar vowel sound, particularly in stressed syllables: "Our blood re*fu*sing to breathe, re*fu*sing to sleep/ Asking the w*ou*nded m*oo*n" (Philip Levine, page 32). See discussion of prosody (page 402).

atmosphere—The mood of a poem: happy, sad, portentious, etc. See TONE.

Augustan Age—Originally, the literary era of the classical poets Virgil, Horace, and Ovid under the Roman Emperor Augustus. Later writers applied the phrase Augustan Age to the first forty-five years of the eighteenth century, the period of Pope and Swift. See NEOCLASSIC PERIOD.

ballad (ballad stanza)—A song which tells a story, for example, "La Belle Dame sans Merci" (page 213). The formal ballad stanza is a quatrain with alternating four- and three-stress lines and *a b c b* rhyme. Many ballads, both formal and informal, employ repeating lines, called *refrains*: "And last year's snows, where are they?" (page 33).

blank verse—Unrhymed lines of iambic pentameter. See the discussion of prosody (page 402).

burlesque—The generic term for literary forms (such as parody, caricature, travesty, satire, and lampoon) in which actions, people, or other literary works are made to seem ridiculous.

caesura—A pause within a line of verse (from "The Rape of the Lock"): "There lay three Garters, half a pair of Gloves." See the discussion of prosody (page 398).

canto—A division of a poem comparable to a chapter in a prose work. See for example the "Paradiso" Canto translated on page 398.

caricature—The exaggeration of a prominent feature of a character or person for the purpose of making him appear ridiculous. In "The Rape of the Lock" Sir Plume is cariactured as a man "With earnest eyes, and round unthinking face."

Caroline period—The period of the reign of Charles I (1625–1649)—the time of the English civil war. Herrick, Suckling, and Lovelace were poets of the period, called *cavalier poets.*

catalexis—The omission of final unaccented syllables in a line of verse.

cavalier poets—See CAROLINE PERIOD.

central metaphoric relationship—A metaphoric *X/Y* relationship worked out over an entire poem, as in Auden's "Law like Love" (page 135). See Chapter 3 (page 126).

central metaphoric subject—A metaphoric *X* associated either with a) various *Y*s in a poem or b) some *unstated Y*s: a) Dickenson's "There's a Certain Slant of Light" and b) Frost's "The Road Not Taken." See Chapter 4 (page 164) and Chapter 5 (page 198).

chiasmus—A reversal in the order of words in two phrases that would otherwise be parallel, for example, Pope's comment on the fate of coquettes: "A *fop* their passion, but their prize a *sot.*"

classical—Usually used in reference to the literature of the Greeks and Romans. Homer, Virgil, Horace, and Petronius Arbiter are called classical poets.

cliché—An expression or idea that was once fresh but has lost its freshness through overuse: "Follow that road through life," for example. A good poet can revive a cliché and give it new meaning, as Frost does in "The Road Not Taken" (page 198).

comparison (metaphoric)—A kind of metaphoric juxtaposition. See JUXTAPOSITION. See Chapter 1 (page 3).

conceit—A metaphor linking two *strikingly* dissimilar things, as where Donne compares compasses to lovers' souls. (see footnote, page 82).

concrete—Concrete terms name specific instances or objects—roses, grapes, a lover waving good-bye, a boat race. See ABSTRACT.

connotation—A meaning that is suggested or implied by a word. For example, the word "owl" might connote death, night, darkness, and mystery, or, alternately, wisdom, in another context. See DENOTATION and Chapter 1 (page 10).

consonance—The repetition of consonants with changes in intervening vowels, for example, love-live, linger-longer.

context—The situation in which a statement or set of statements is made. See Chapter 2 (page 53).

conventional image—An image used frequently in literature.

couplet—Two lines of poetry, usually rhymed: "A poem should be palpable and *mute/*As a globed *fruit.*" See the discussion of prosody (page 404).

criticism—The discussion, analysis, comparison, and evaluation of literary works.

dactyle (dactylic)—A metric foot with a stressed syllable followed by two unstressed syllables ($/\smile\smile$).

dead metaphor—A metaphor that has been so overused it is no longer recognized as a metaphor, for example "the eye of a needle." See Chapter 1 (page 2).

denotation—The definition of a word; the thing it specifically refers to. For example, the word "owl" denotes a species of bird. See CONNOTATION.

diction—The vocabulary (slang, formal, standard, etc.) used in a literary work—the choice of words. See Chapter 2 (page 51).

didactic—The purpose of a didactic work is to teach something: a moral view, a world view, a doctrine. A good didactic poem must have something more, however, otherwise, when the moral or doctrine becomes passé, the poem falls into oblivion. See Chapter 8 (page 334).

dimeter—A line consisting of two metric feet.

dirge—A poem expressing grief over a death. Dirges are usually short and often sung.

distance—See AESTHETIC DISTANCE.

doggerel—A clumsily written verse, usually sing-songy. See "Poetry and Melancholy" (page 12).

dramatic monologue—In a dramatic monologue a single character speaks to one or more people who are not heard in the poem but who are obviously an audience. Robert Browning popularized the dramatic monologue. See "My Last Duchess" (page 251).

dream vision—In this species of poem the narrator says he falls asleep and dreams. *What* he dreams is the material of the poem. This form was particularly popular in the Middle Ages. Dante's "Divine Comedy" is a dream vision. See "Paradiso" (page 389).

ecologue—A poem about shepherds or rural life. See the shepherd poems (page 85).

elegy—A formal poem in lament of a dead person. In the sixteenth and seventeenth centuries, the term "elegy" also meant any poem of serious meditation (such Donne's "A Valediction: Forbidding Mourning," page 80).

elision—A poetic contraction, such as "ne'er" for "never," or "'tween" for "between."

Elizabethan Age—The era of the reign of Queen Elizabeth (1558–1603). It is considered to have been the greatest period of English literature because it was the time of Shakespeare, Marlowe, Jonson, Spenser, and Sidney.

end rhyme—Rhyming words at the end of lines of verse. See also INTERNAL RHYME. Examples of end-rhymed poems are "The Rape of the Lock," "Ars Poetica," and "Ode on Melancholy."

end-stopped line—A line of verse which ends with the completion of a grammatical unit—especially a clause or sentence. See the discussion of prosody (page 399).

enjambment—The continuation, without pause, of a phrase from one line of verse to the next. Also called a *run-on line.* See the discussion of prosody (page 399).

epic—A long poem about an heroic character.

epigram—A short poem, usually with a surprising turn of thought, such as Donne's epigram called "Antiquary": "If in his Studie he hath so much care/To hang all old strange things, let his wife beware."

epithalamion—A poem in celebration of a marriage.

epode—See ode.

exact rhyme—"White" and "night" are an exact rhyme.

falling meter—The *trochee* and the *dactyl* are falling meters.

feminine ending—A line of verse with an extra, unstressed syllable at the end.

figurative language—Metaphoric language. See CONCEIT, HYPERBOLE, IMAGE, IRONY, LITERAL, METAPHOR, METONYMY, OXYMONON, PARADOX, PERSONIFICATION, PUN, SIMILE, TENOR AND VEHICLE, and TROPE.

foot—A unit of alternation of stressed and unstressed syllables in a line of poetry. There are four basic metric feet: *iambic* ($\smile/$), *trochaic* ($/\smile$), *anapestic* ($\smile\smile/$), and *dactylic* ($/\smile\smile$). See the discussion of prosody (page 398).

foreshadowing—An event which occurs later in a piece prefigured by an earlier image or event is said to be foreshadowed. It can be a kind of irony. See Chapter 2 (page 52).

form—A general word that may refer to any or all of the organizational aspects of the poem—meter, rhyme, imagery, metaphor—or to the type (*genre*) of poem.

free verse—Poetry without rhyme or regular meter. See the discussion of prosody (page 405).

genre—A literary form such as an epic, pastoral, or lyric.

haiku—A Japanese poetry form; haikus are poems of seventeen syllables, usually in three lines.

hemistich—A fraction, usually one-half, of a regular line of verse.

heroic couplet—A *couplet* in *iambic pentameter* which forms a complete thought that does not run over into the next lines. Pope's "The Rape of the Lock" (page 87) is written entirely in heroic couplets.

hexameter—A line consisting of six metric feet.

hymn—A song of praise.

hyperbole—A poetic exaggeration, such as Burns's vow to love his lover "'Till all the seas gang dry." Often ironic, as in Marvell's line about his "vegetable love" (page 16). See Chapter 2 (page 52).

iamb (iambic)—A metric foot with an unstressed syllable followed by a stressed syllable. ($\smile/$). See the discussion of prosody (page 399).

identification (metaphoric)—A type of *X/Y* metaphoric juxtaposition. See JUXTAPOSITION. See Chapter 1 (page 10).

image—Description. See Chapter 2 (page 52).

incremental repetition—A *refrain* with a significant change introduced on each repetition.

intentional fallacy—The belief that one can discuss, analyze, or judge a work in terms of what the writer *intended* it to mean is an error of intentional fallacy since it is virtually impossible to know what a writer's intention really was and since, in many cases, he may not have been sure himself.

internal rhyme—The rhyming words are found within a line of verse and at its end. For example, the line, "speaking *clearly* and most *severely*," in Auden's "Law Like Love," employs internal rhyme.

invocation—An address by the poet to some god, gods, or muse for approval of his work or assistance in its composition. For example, Pope humorously invokes as a muse his heroine, Belinda, and friend Caryll in the opening lines of "The Rape of the Lock": "I sing—This Verse to *Caryll*, Muse! is due;/This, ev'n *Belinda* may vouchsafe to view:/Slight is the Subject, but no so the Praise,/If She inspire, and He approve my Lays."

irony—A tension between what a statement means on the surface (*X*) and its real or recognized meaning (*Y*). See Chapter 2 (page 52).

Jacobean Age—The period of the reign of James I (1603–1625), which followed that of Queen Elizabeth. Shakespeare was still active during this period, though Donne, Marvell, Cowley, Jonson, etc., are generally associated with it.

juxtaposition (metaphoric)—Linking two or more unlike terms together in a metaphoric context can be done by comparison association, identification or contrast. See Chapter 1 (page 3 to 4).

kenning—An old English formula metaphor, such as "whale's road" meaning the "sea." Hopkins uses a similar device in "Spring and Fall" (page 142). See also Kennings in "The Seafarer" (page 284).

lampoon—A portrait ridiculing someone in biting language. Colly Cibber is lampooned in "The Dunciad" (page 359).

literal—Adhering to the usual or primary meaning of a word or expression. In a literal statement there are no connotations, no overtones. Literally, for example, an owl is a species of bird. Figuratively, it may suggest any number of other things: death, wisdom, night, etc. See AMBIGUITY, CONNOTATION, DENOTATION, and FIGURATIVE LANGUAGE.

literary convention—An idea, situation or image that has been used repeatedly in literature. See page 86.

literary-natural image—Natural images that have been associated with religion, myth or historical events: the Styx, Mt. Olympus. See Chapter 2 (page 53).

literary-technological image—Images involving technological objects that have been used often in literature: a lyre, a sword, a bow. See Chapter 2 (page 53).

local metaphors—The individual metaphors in a poem as distinguished from the central metaphor governing it.

lyric—See Chapter 6 (page 260).

masculine ending—A line of verse ending with a stressed syllable.

measure—Often used as a synonym for meter or to indicate any system of counting the sound in a line of verse.

metaphor—See Chapter 1 (page 2 to page 6).

metaphysical poets—A group of seventeenth-century poets (including Donne, Marvell, Herbert, and Cowley) said to have written in a "metaphysical style" because of their use of outlandish, extended metaphors; abstruse, logical-sounding arguments; and dramatic diction. See also STYLE.

meter (metric)—The pattern of stressed and unstressed syllables in a line of poetry. See the discussion of prosody (p. 398).

metonymy—A metaphoric relationship in which the name of one thing (*X*) is used for another thing (*Y*) to which it is closely related. Pope's description of the feuding factions at court as "Wigs and "sword knots," in the line "Where Wigs with Wigs, with Sword-knots Sword-knots strive," is an example. A symbol for the thing symbolized.

mock epic—A poem in which trivial events and characters are mocked by being presented as if they were of epic proportions. See "The Rape of the Lock" (page 87).

monometer—A line of verse consisting of one metric foot.

muses—In Greek mythology, the nine goddesses who presided over the arts.

myth—A metaphoric story to explain natural phenomena, such as the myth that when the goddess Proserpine returns from the world of the dead to visit her mother, Ceres, spring arrives.

narrative poem—A poem that has a plot—that tells a story. See "The Lady of Shalott" (page 263).

near rhyme—See SLANT RHYME.

natural image—Involves objects in the world that have connotative depth: the sea, stars, flowers. See Chapter 2 (page 53).

natural, nonliterary image—Involves things generally thought of as prosaic or ugly, unpleasant or lacking in intrinsic depth: fecal matter, fungus. See Chapter 2 (page 54).

neoclassic period—The period of literary activity between the late seventeenth and late eighteenth centuries. Writers of this period generally held classical literature (the literature of the Greeks and Romans) in high esteem. They valued art, polish, and wit in literature and believed that the end of art was to communicate to man in a pleasing, informative fashion: "What oft was thought, but ne'er so well expressed," as Pope put it. Neoclassic poets tended to write in restrictive forms and followed rigid conventions like the *heroic couplet.* See also AUGUSTAN AGE.

objective correlative—A term introduced by the twentieth-century poet T. S. Eliot. He wrote: "The only way of expressing emotion in the form of art is by finding an 'objective correlative'"; in other words, a set of objects, a situation, a chain of events which shall be the formula of that *particular* emotion." In part, it means making the more or less abstract emotion concrete, as Keats does, for example, in "Ode on Melancholy" (page 9).

objective—In so-called objective poems, the poet presents his ideas, images, and metaphors without seeming to become personally involved, that is, without our sensing his voice. See SUBJECTIVE. The distinction between these two terms as applied in criticism is often vague, particularly since, in using them, critics run the risk of the *intentional fallacy.* For example, what seems to be a poet's confession may be more an imagined confession than a real one; that is, what seems to be subjective may really be an objective vehicle for conveying a character or exploring an idea.

occasional poems—Poems written for specific events or on the occasion of deaths, dedications, birthdays, coronations, etc.

octave—See PETRARCHAN SONNET.

ode—A poem in praise of a person, idea, or thing. The classical ode had a rigid form with three parts: a strophe, antistrophe, and epode. Early English poets, however, developed the form such that each ode was allowed to find its own pattern of line lengths, number of lines per stanza, and rhyme scheme.

off-rhyme—See SLANT RHYME.

onomatopoeia—An onomatopoetic word is one formed in imitation of the sound made by, or associated with, what it refers to, for example, "buzz," "crackle," "hiss," and "boom."

ottava rima—Verse in iambic pentameter, rhyming *a b a b a b c c.*

oxymoron—Related to paradox, a combination of contradictory terms, for example, "pleasing pain" and "living death."

paradox—A statement the *seems* self contradictory, as Donne's "death thou shalt die" (page 12). See Chapter 2 (page 53).

parody—A form of burlesque which makes fun of a particular work or style by imitating it grotesquely.

pastoral—See ECOLOGUE.

pentameter—A line of verse consisting of five metric feet.

persona—The speaker in a poem; the mask the poet adopts so that the reader will not assume it is the poet speaking personally.

personification—Ascribing human characteristics (*X*) to nonhuman entities (*Y*). See "Ode on Melancholy" (page 11).

Petrarchan sonnet—A sonnet composed of an octave (eight lines) and a sestet (six lines) and rhyming *a b b a a b b a c d e c d e.*

poetic license—The poet's freedom to depart from ordinary speech patterns (diction), from the logic of everyday reality, or even from conventional poetic forms in order to achieve an effect. In other words, it is difficult to criticize a poet who is illogical or ungrammatical or who does not stick to tradition—as long as he is "effective." Keats's image of pleasure "turning to poison where the bee-mouth sips" (page 9) is an instance of poetic license since, while the image violates reality, it is true to our intuitive perceptions.

point of view—See TONE. Point of view might also include the "I," "he," etc., of a piece. See OBJECTIVE and SUBJECTIVE.

portmanteau word—A made-up word in which two or more meanings are compressed into one term. Lewis Carroll's word "uffish," used to describe the Bellman in "The Hunting of the

Snark," is a portmanteau word, suggesting perhaps "if-ish," "selfish," and maybe even "uppish" (uppity).

private symbol—An image assigned special meanings or connotations by the author. See Chapter 2 (page 56).

prosody—The study of sound pattern, rhyme, meter, verse forms, etc. See the discussion of prosody (page 394).

pun—A play on words of the same or similar sound but different meaning: In "The Oven Bird" (page 296) Frost's use of "fall" as meaning autumn and the fall of man. See Chapter 1 (page 12) and Chapter 2 (page 52).

pyrrhic—A metric foot with two unaccented syllables (˘˘).

quantitative verse (meter)—Verse measurement based on the length of time it takes to pronounce syllables in a line. See the discussion of prosody (page 401).

quatrain—A four-line stanza, perhaps the most common stanza in English poetry.

refrain—See BALLAD.

renaissance—Historically, the period following the Middle Ages. The term is often meant to suggest the rebirth of activity in the arts. The English Renaissance occurred in the sixteenth century and included Wyatt, Surrey, and Sidney among its poets.

restoration period—The period at the end of the English commonwealth (1660) when an English king was returned to the throne. Dryden and the Earl of Rochester were poets of this period. The Augustan age followed, during which time Pope and Swift flourished.

rhetorical figures—The arrangement of words departing from ordinary usage for special effects of sound or sense. See ALLITERATION, ALLUSION, APOSTROPHE, CHIASMUS, INVOCATION, ONOMATOPOEIA, RHETORICAL QUESTION, RHYME, AND ZEUGMA.

rhetorical question—A question asked not for the purpose of receiving a reply, but as a means of emphasis to make a point—for example, "And last year's snows, where are they?" from "Ballad of the Ladies of Old" (page 33).

rhyme—Words with a similar sound, such as "white" and "night," rhyme. See the discussion of prosody (page 402).

rhyme scheme—The pattern of end rhymes. See the discussion of prosody (page 402).

rime-royal—A stanza of iambic pentameter, rhyming *a b a b b c c*.

rising meter—*iambic* and the *anapestic* feet are rising meters.

romantic period—In English poetry, the romantic period is thought of as having begun in 1798, the year of the publication of Wordsworth and Coleridge's *Lyrical Ballads*. The romantics (including Wordsworth, Coleridge, Keats, Byron, and Shelley as major figures) generally favored innovation and individualism in style, as opposed to the traditionalism and classicism of the Augustan age. Emphasis was placed on feeling instead of wit and on natural landscape as opposed to city culture. The period is considered to have ended with the beginning of the Victorian era in the 1830s.

sarcasm—Heavy, obvious irony. See Chapter 2 (page 52).

satire—A work in which the subject is made to look ridiculous; the attitude of a satire is one of contempt or scorn for the object of the satire. Unlike laughter in comedy, laughter in satire is used as a weapon—with a point.

scanning (scansion)—The critical method of noting stressed and unstressed syllables to discern metric patterns. See the discussion of prosody (page 398).

sestet—See PETRATCHAN SONNET.

Shakespearean sonnet—A sonnet composed of three quatrains, and a couplet and rhyming *a b a b c d c d e f e f g g*.

simile—The technical word for a metaphoric comparison employing a term such as "like" or "as" between the *X* and the *Y*. "My luve is like a red, red rose" is a type of metaphor technically called a *simile*.

slant rhyme—Also called OFF-RHYME OR NEAR RHYME. "White" and "night" are an *exact* rhyme. "White" and "wait" are a *slant* rhyme.

sonnet—A famous fourteen-line verse form. See PETRARCHAN SONNET and SHAKESPEAREAN SONNET.

Spenserian stanza—A stanza containing lines of iambic pentamenter and rhyming *a b a b b c b- c c*.

spondee (spondaic)—A metric foot with two stressed syllables (//).

sprung rhythm—A mixed meter with a stressed syllable alone or in combination with two or three unstressed syllables. Sprung rhythm was made popular by Gerard Manley Hopkins (page 142).

stanza—The poetic paragraph. A division of a poem consisting of a group of lines. See the discussion of prosody (page 402).

stock response—A cliché reaction to a work; any reaction based on the reader's habits or opinions rather than a genuine reading and consideration of the piece.

stress—Accented syllable in a line of poetry. See the discussion of prosody (page 397).

strophe—See ODE.

style—The word "style" refers to the characteristic way an author expresses himself. A poet's style may consist in part of his tendency to use certain types of images or metaphors (technological, literary, natural, etc.) or certain combinations of these types. It may consist in part of his tendency to take a certain tone (ironic, serious, confessional, polemical, etc.) in his works or to use formal or colloquial diction. Style may have to do with his tendency to express things simply and matter-of-factly or to stud his works with ornate images and allusions. The term "style" can also refer to the characteristic methods of expression of an era or period of poetry. For example, the tendency of some seventeenth-century poets to use technological conceits (extreme metaphors) is one element of what has been called the *metaphysical* style.

subjective—A subjective poem is one in which the poet seems to be telling of his private thoughts, feelings, and experiences. See OBJECTIVE.

syllabic verse—Verse counted by the number of syllables in a line. See the discussion of prosody (page 397).

symbol—An image with an *assigned* meaning or connotation. See Chapter 2 (pages 55 to 57) and Chapter 7.

synecdoche—A type of metaphor in which a part of something (X) represents the whole of that thing (Y)—for example, "All *hands* were lost when the ship sank." Hands = seamen.

synesthesia—Expressing one sensory experience in terms of another—sight as sound, taste as sight, etc. Keats, in his works, makes extensive use of synesthesia: "Then glut thy sorrow on a morning rose,/Or on the rainbow of the salt sand-wave" (from "Ode on Melancho-

ly"). "Glut," a word associated with *taste*, is applied to objects of *sight*.

tanka—A Japanese poetry form; tankas are poems of thirty-one syllables, usually in five lines.

technological image—Images involving objects fashioned by man. See Chapter 2 (page 53).

tenor and vehicle—Critical words referring to the two terms of a metaphor. The tenor is the main subject of the metaphor (it may be either the X or the Y term); the vehicle is the term used to express it. In "My Luve is like a red, red, rose," "Luve" is the tenor, and "rose" is the vehicle.

tension—This word is used critically in various ways. In its most general application, it signifies the balance of similarities and differences between elements of the poem—the unlike factor. The force that connects the opposing, or unlike, abstract and concrete elements of the piece.

tercet—A three-line stanza, usually having the same rhyme for all three lines.

terza rima—Tercet stanzas linked together by the rhyme scheme *a b a b c b c d c d e d*, etc. Shelley's "Ode to the West Wind" is in terza rimas as is Dante's *Divine Comedy* in the original Italian.

tetrameter—A line of verse consisting of four metric feet.

theme—A term generally used when discussing the abstract concept or idea we think a poem is about. "A Valediction: Forbidding Mourning" could be said to have been written on the theme of parting. The theme of "Ode on a Grecian Urn" might be stated as: "Man dies, but art is eternal." Obviously, there are many ways to state the theme of a work, and disagreement is possible on what the theme really is. Theme is what a poem is "about."

tone—The atmosphere of a piece or the author's attitude toward his subject matter as manifested through the poet's use of metaphors, images, puns, paradoxes, metrical patterns, etc. See Chapter 2, Introduction.

travesty—A type of burlesque or parody that supposedly mocks a heroic or lofty work by treating it in degrading terms.

trimeter—A line of verse consisting of three metric feet.

trochee (trochaic)—A metric foot with a stressed

syllable followed by an unstressed syllable ($/\smile$).

trope—Technically, the class of metaphoric language including conceit, hyperbole, metaphor, metonymy, oxymoron, paradox, personification, pun, simile, and synecdoche. Troping is taking language beyond its literal meaning into the area of connotation and association.

understatement—A type of irony. See Chapter 2 (page 52).

unlike factor—The effect of the *differences* between terms (X and Y) metaphorically related. See Chapter 1 (page 3) and Chapter 2 (page 55).

vers de société—Light verse, generally occasional.

verse—A regular metric line. Synonym for "poetry."

Victorian period—The period from the 1830s to 1901, the reign of Queen Victoria. It followed the ROMANTIC PERIOD. The Victorian era included the poets Arnold, Browning, and Tennyson.

virgule—A line (/) used to indicate the division between one line of poetry and another when written out in a prose paragraph.

voice—Can be used in two ways: (1) to indicate the speaker or narrator of a poem and (2) as a synonym for "tone."

zeugma—The technical word for a single term which relates to two other terms in different ways: "Or *stain* her honor, or her new brocade" (Pope). Somewhat like a pun, a zeugma operates metaphorically. In Pope's line, the abstract significant word "honor" (X) is contrasted to the trivial concrete "brocade" (Y) on the basis of a similarity between them (both can be stained).

INDEX OF TITLES

INDEX OF TITLES

INDEX OF FIRST LINES

INDEX OF FIRST LINES